World Englishes and Culture Wars

Written from a non-Western perspective, this book exposes the inadequacy of oppositions such as *native* vs. *nonnative* Englishes and *English* vs. *New Englishes*. It explains why the label "World Englishes" captures both what the different Englishes share and how they differ from each other. It also criticizes the kinds of power asymmetries that have evolved among the Inner, Outer, and Expanding Circles of English, while showing the extent to which the Outer Circle has enriched their common language and made it suitable for both its heritage and nonheritage users. The narrative is grounded in a wealth of historical knowledge, especially that of the colonization of the Outer Circle. Readers are invited to compare the spread and differentiation of English with those of Latin, which evolved into the Romance languages. This comparison may leave the reader asking: Could English break up into Anglian languages?

BRAJ B. KACHRU spent most of his career at the University of Illinois at Urbana-Champaign, serving also as Head of the Department of Linguistics (1968–1979), Director of the Division of English as an International Language (1985–1991), and Director of the University's Center for Advanced Study (June 1996–January 2000). He became the Jubilee Professor of Liberal Arts and Sciences in 1992 and the Sir Edward Youde Memorial Fund Visiting Professor at Hong Kong University in 1998. He cofounded the International Association of World Englishes and the journal *World Englishes*. He coauthored and coedited more than a dozen books on World Englishes and Kashmiri.

Cambridge Approaches to Language Contact

Founding Editor
SALIKOKO S. MUFWENE, *University of Chicago*

Co-Editor
ANA DEUMERT, *University of Cape Town*

Editorial Board
ROBERT CHAUDENSON, *Université d'Aix-en-Provence*
RAJ MESTHRIE, *University of Cape Town*
LESLEY MILROY, *University of Michigan*
SHANA POPLACK, *University of Ottawa*
MICHAEL SILVERSTEIN, *University of Chicago*

Cambridge Approaches to Language Contact is an interdisciplinary series bringing together work on language contact from a diverse range of research areas. The series focuses on key topics in the study of contact between languages or dialects, including the development of pidgins and creoles, language evolution and change, world Englishes, code-switching and code-mixing, bilingualism and second language acquisition, borrowing, interference and convergence phenomena.

Published titles:
Salikoko Mufwene, *The Ecology of Language Evolution*
Michael Clyne, *Dynamics of Language Contact*
Bernd Heine and Tania Kuteva, *Language Contact and Grammatical Change*
Edgar W. Schneider, *Postcolonial English*
Virginia Yip and Stephen Matthews, *The Bilingual Child*
Bernd Heine and Derek Nurse (eds), *A Linguistic Geography of Africa*
J. Clancy Clements, *The Linguistic Legacy of Spanish and Portuguese*
Umberto Ansaldo, *Contact Languages*
Jan Blommaert, *The Sociolinguistics of Globalization*
Carmen Silva-Corvalán, *Bilingual Language Acquisition*
Lotfi Sayahi, *Diglossia and Language Contact*
Emanuel J. Drechsel, *Language Contact in the Early Colonial Pacific*
Enoch Oladé Aboh, *The Emergence of Hybrid Grammars*
Zhiming Bao, *The Making of Vernacular Singapore English*
Ralph Ludwig, Peter Mühlhäusler and Steve Pagel (eds.), *Linguistic Ecology and Language Contact*
Bridget Drinka, *Language Contact in Europe*
Braj B. Kachru, *World Englishes and Culture Wars*

Further titles planned for the series:
Rakesh Bhatt, *Language Contact and Diaspora*
Gregory D.S. Anderson *Language Extinction*
Ellen Hurst and Rajend Mesthrie (eds.), *Youth Language Varieties in Africa*
Cecile Vigouroux, *Migration, Economy, and Language Practice*

World Englishes and Culture Wars

Braj B. Kachru
University of Illinois, Urbana-Champaign

CAMBRIDGE
UNIVERSITY PRESS

University Printing House, Cambridge CB2 8BS, United Kingdom

Cambridge University Press is part of the University of Cambridge.

It furthers the University's mission by disseminating knowledge in the pursuit of
education, learning, and research at the highest international levels of excellence.

www.cambridge.org
Information on this title: www.cambridge.org/9780521825719

© Braj B. Kachru 2017

This publication is in copyright. Subject to statutory exception
and to the provisions of relevant collective licensing agreements,
no reproduction of any part may take place without the written
permission of Cambridge University Press.

First published 2017

A catalog record for this publication is available from the British Library.

Library of Congress Cataloging-in-Publication Data
Names: Kachru, Braj B., author.
Title: World Englishes and culture wars / Braj Kachru.
Description: Cambridge, United Kingdom : Cambridge University Press, [2016] |
Includes bibliographical references and index.
Identifiers: LCCN 2016032619 | ISBN 9780521825719 (Hardback : alk. paper) |
ISBN 9780521532785 (pbk. : alk. paper)
Subjects: LCSH: English language–Variation–English-speaking countries. |
English language–Variation–Foreign countries. | English language–Social
aspects–English-speaking countries. | Language and culture–English-speaking
countries. | Language and culture–Foreign countries. | Communication,
International. | Intercultural communication. | Sociolinguistics.
Classification: LCC PE2751 .K333 2016 | DDC 427–dc23 LC record available at
https://lccn.loc.gov/2016032619

ISBN 978-0-521–82571-9 Hardback

Cambridge University Press has no responsibility for the persistence or accuracy
of URLs for external or third-party Internet Web sites referred to in this publication
and does not guarantee that any content on such Web sites is, or will remain,
accurate or appropriate.

Contents

Foreword by Salikoko S. Mufwene	*page* ix
Acknowledgments	xvi
Part I World Englishes Today	1
1 The Agony and Ecstasy	3
2 The Second Diaspora	23
3 Culture Wars	45
4 Standards and Codification	66
5 The Power and Politics	85
Part II Context and Creativity	107
6 The Speaking Tree	109
7 Creativity and Literary Canons	121
Part III Past and Prejudice	133
8 Liberation Linguistics	135
9 Sacred Linguistic Cows	151
10 The Paradigms of Marginalization	166
Part IV Ethical Issues and the ELT Empire	183
11 Applying Linguistics	185
12 Leaking Paradigms	206

viii   Table of Contents

Part V   World Englishes and the Classroom   221

13   Mythology in Teaching   223

Part VI   Research Areas and Resources   239

14   Research Resources   241

Select Bibliography   269
Author Index   298
Subject Index   301

Foreword

The Cambridge Approaches to Language Contact (CALC) series was set up to publish outstanding monographs on language contact, especially by authors who approach their specific subject matter from a diachronic or developmental perspective. Our goal is to integrate the ever-growing scholarship on language diversification (including the development of creoles, pidgins, and indigenized varieties of colonial European languages), bilingual language development, code-switching, and language endangerment. We hope to provide a select forum to scholars who contribute insightfully to understanding language evolution from an interdisciplinary perspective. We favor approaches that highlight the role of ecology and draw inspiration both from the authors' own fields of specialization and from related research areas in linguistics or other disciplines. Eclecticism is one of our mottoes, as we endeavor to comprehend the complexity of evolutionary processes associated with contact.

We are proud to add to our list Braj B. Kachru's *World Englishes and Culture Wars*, which sums up, from both a historical and a critical perspective, the scholarship of over the past half-century on the spread of English around the world, its encounters with diverse languages and integration into new cultures, its indigenization and speciation in the process, as well as issues that arise from this particular evolution regarding emergent norms and of course also regarding the ownership of the language. For many people, especially in the Outer Circle, English is now part of their linguascape, and it seems odd that people in the Inner Circle want to keep dictating how this language, now shared by people evolving in different places and producing and practicing diverse cultures, must be spoken and written, and, more specifically, which grammar must be followed. Kachru rightfully compares this differential geographical and demographic expansion of English to that of Latin during the Roman Empire and after the collapse of the latter in the Western Empire.

The comparison highlights both similarities and differences. On the one hand, unlike Latin, English has expanded all over the world in the span of four centuries, since England engaged in the colonial venture in the early

x   Foreword

seventeenth century. However, so far, with the exception of English creoles and pidgins, most of its outgrowths, the new emergent national, regional, and ethnic varieties, are still called English. They are thus considered to be the same language. Is it just a matter of time before they evolve socially into, or are stipulated to be, separate languages? Should we wait until they are no longer mutually intelligible? Is this the (only) reason why we seldom refer to the Romance languages as neo-Latin varieties? Are the new English varieties all mutually intelligible? If so, to what extent?

On the other hand, like that of Latin, the speciation of English is evident and still in process. Whether or not one considers a particular new variety as more divergent than another depends in part on what the *terminus a quo* is: a scholastic variety evolving into a vernacular, as in the case of "indigenized Englishes" of the Outer Circle; a scholastic variety, with (significant) substrate influence, being used as an international lingua franca but without having evolved a national or regional norm yet, as in the Expanding Circle; a vernacular that has simply indigenized in the new ecology of its practice (Mufwene 2009), as in the case of "native Englishes" of the Inner Circle; or a vernacular transmitted naturalistically through a rapid succession of "approximations of approximations" produced by nonheritage speakers in exogenous plantation settings or indigenous trade settings, as in the case of, respectively, creoles and pidgins (Chaudenson 2001, Mufwene 2001).

Kachru does not discuss English creoles and pidgins, whose history may be considered closer to that of the Romance languages (Mufwene 2005, 2008), perhaps because they have typically been disenfranchised in linguistics as not being English anymore, despite the speech continua that, since DeCamp (1971), have been identified in the territories in which they are spoken (e.g., Bickerton 1973, Escure 1981, Rickford 1987, Winford 1988). It is indeed from creolistics, including the study of the origins of African American Vernacular English (AAVE), that sociolinguistics has borrowed the distinction between *basilect*, *mesolect*, and *acrolect*, which Kachru also discusses in passing, under the label of *cline*, in *World Englishes and Culture Wars*. Assuming incorrectly that AAVE had evolved from a Gullah-like creole ancestor, Stewart (1965) invoked this lectal variation to demonstrate the putative decreolization mechanism he needed to prove his position (see discussions in, e.g., Mufwene 2000, 2014, 2015a). The debate remains open on whether English creoles (often reduced, for convenience, to their basilects) are not new nonstandard dialects of English that have been disenfranchised simply because the lexifier was appropriated and restructured primarily by populations of non-European descent (Mufwene 2001). After all, they were lexified by nonstandard varieties of European languages (Chaudenson 2001). At a time when there were already indigenous native speakers of English (albeit a small minority in postcolonial elite families) in

Africa and Asia, the characterization of their Englishes as "nonnative" would not have been too easily accepted if the race of the speakers were not a factor.

I accept an anticipated criticism of some readers, to whom Kachru appears still to assume part of this legacy, as much as he actually fights it in *World Englishes and Culture Wars*. He does not seem to be sure whether Caribbean English varieties fit in the Inner or the Outer Circle. Caribbean Englishes are the only vernaculars that most of their speakers have grown up with, just as North American, Australian, and New Zealand Englishes are for their respective speakers. The fact that they coexist with creoles, in relation to which they have been identified as acrolectal, should not matter. The connection of Caribbean Englishes to the local creole basilects is actually comparable to that of the educated/standard varieties to the most nonstandard varieties; and in both cases a continuum obtains between the acrolectal and basilectal varieties. From an ethnographic perspective, Caribbean Englishes are unlike the "indigenized Englishes" of Africa and Asia, as the majority of speakers of the latter use them only or primarily as lingua francas, regardless of the fact that, as correctly noted by Kachru, the relevant interactions are primarily intranational. And Kachru is also correct in underscoring the fact that this primarily intranational communication, as also in the case of the Inner Circle, shapes the emergence of divergent local/national norms. It is not evident that Caribbean Englishes bear as much influence from African substrate languages as is usually claimed about the corresponding creoles and can also be claimed about indigenized Englishes. So, the race of their speakers set aside, there should be no doubt about the membership of these Englishes in the Inner Circle.

Mutual intelligibility with varieties of the Inner Circle is hard to assess, especially when "native" varieties such as the Cockney in the United Kingdom, the Ocracoke and Newfoundland brogues (in the United States and Canada, respectively), and Australian nonstandard English are introduced into the debate. One is reminded of the greater interest AAVE has aroused among American dialectologists and sociolinguists than, say, Amish English has, because of the presumed putative genetic connection of the former with creoles and certainly with African languages, though the story is undoubtedly much more complex.

Although he often mentions AAVE, regarding its function as a marker of ethnic identity (comparable to using "indigenized Englishes" as identity markers in the belles lettres), not including creoles and pidgins in his discussion enables Kachru to capitalize, without unnecessary conceptual distractions, on why "World Englishes" (WE) is a more adequate term for discussing English globally than various other alternatives are. He wants to capture both continuity and plurality in the spread of English worldwide. He can highlight the unity of a common language and still distinguish between the three "concentric Circles of English" he posited in 1982, which one cannot do with

xii   Foreword

labels such as "New Englishes" and "Indigenized Englishes." The latter terms appear to be mere euphemisms for the old "Non-Native Englishes." In suggesting diversity, the term "World Englishes" also conjures up not only differences among the Englishes of the Inner Circle constructed as national varieties but also a great deal of the intranational variation the varieties exhibit geographically and socially. Thus, the variation between and within "indigenized Englishes" of the Outer Circle need not be constructed as absence of national norms and mere deviations from norms of the Inner Circle, which everybody should be expected to follow, from the point of view of many in both the Inner and the Outer Circles. (See more on norms below.) Other terms Kachru rejects explicitly in this book include "English as an international language" (because it downplays the plurality and diversity of the "English-speaking fellowship"), "English as a lingua franca" (because it overlooks the vernacular functions of English in some parts of the "fellowship"), and "English as a world language" (because it does not factor in the diverse range of functions that the language serves in the different Circles). Yes, Kachru prefers speaking of "fellowship" rather than of "community" in reference to various populations using English around the world, because they are not really united in the same way as in traditional, much smaller and culturally less diverse language or speech communities.

If there are structural and pragmatic changes that account for the divergence of the Outer and Expanding Circles' English varieties from those of the Inner Circle, the latter themselves have likewise evolved too: those of North America, Australia, and New Zealand have diverged from their British counterparts, and the British varieties themselves have also changed since the seventeenth century. This makes it tempting to invoke degrees of divergence, structurally and pragmatically, to justify the distinction between "native" and "nonnative"/"indigenized" Englishes. Whatever yardstick may be used to assess these degrees of divergence, one cannot deny the fact that English has indigenized everywhere outside its birthplace in England (Mufwene 2009). The term "Indigenized Englishes" becomes more obviously a euphemism for "Nonnative Englishes," as "indigenized" is not applied impartially when it is restricted to the Outer and Expanding Circles only. "New Englishes" is not a more adequate alternative, because, from a historical perspective, all the modern varieties are new, and all have been affected by contacts among traditional dialects and with other languages, as in the case of Celtic Englishes in the Inner Circle.

Kachru argues that the opposition between "native" and "nonnative Englishes" (as opposed to the legitimate one between "native" and "nonnative speakers"!) appears to be political, rooted in the colonial ideology of subjugation intended to dictate to the colonized how to behave even linguistically. Only populations of the Inner Circle, whose ancestors colonized populations outside Europe, where speakers of Englishes in the Outer Circle live or

Foreword xiii

originate, claim entitlement to stipulate the norms of English and disavow the divergent adaptations and innovations produced by users in the ecologies of the Outer Circle.

This asymmetrical-relation attitude is of course not accepted by all users of Englishes in the Outer Circle. Thus, Kachru cites authors who either complain against the tyranny of the colonial master or celebrate the domestication and cultural appropriation of the linguistic tool of the former colonizer. *Indigenization* means adapting the otherwise foreign language to serve the communicative needs of the new users in their cultural home (Mufwene 2009). It means that the nonheritage speakers of English are appropriating the colonizer's language as their own and are proud to use it in ways that reflect their cultural identities and their differences from speakers of the Inner Circle. To be sure, as noted above, English has indigenized in every new ecology in which it has been used regularly, in the Inner and Outer Circles alike. The divergence is thus manifold, as every ecology has its historical and cultural peculiarities. Kachru rightly underscores the primacy of intranational communication in the Outer Circle, especially in the postcolonial period, because it, rather than international communication, forges the patterns that the natives produce.

Assuming that evolution is subject to local ecological factors first, it is these ecology-specific communicative dynamics that generate divergence, though there are other reasons that justify the distinction in terms of the three "concentric Circles." These generally have to do with the variation in the specific ways in which English has spread, including whether or not the colonizers intended to assimilate the alloglot populations. Insofar as the Inner and the Outer Circles are concerned, the distinction between settlement and exploitation colonization applies (Mufwene 2001): nonheritage users of English, the colonial auxiliaries, were expected to interface between the colonizers and the masses of the colonized populations but not to benefit as much as the colonizers from the colonial power structure, which the latter wanted to control alone. That was consistent with Thomas Babington Macaulay's 1835 *Minute* articulating how English should be introduced to a segment of the indigenous population in India, to help the British colonial enterprise. That ideology was applied in all British exploitation colonies. The norms to be respected were those stipulated by the metropole; they were enforced by the colonial agents and intended to be spread by their auxiliaries.

Kachru also presents English as a worldwide diasporic phenomenon, which started with the spread of the language in the British Isles, and then to North America, Australia, and New Zealand (the principal other members of the Inner Circle), before spreading everywhere else, first to the Outer Circle (the former exploitation colonies of England or Great Britain) and then to the Expanding Circle. While the status of English has remained that of the dominant vernacular in the Inner Circle, it changed to those of official language and most powerful

xiv   Foreword

lingua franca politically and economically in the Outer Circle, to that of the most important international lingua franca in the Expanding Circle. The color of majority speakers of the diasporic language and the cultures that received it also changed, as the majority speakers in the Outer Circle are non-Europeans, and English is being acculturated in ways that apparently makes it more different from the varieties of the Inner Circle. One can thus see how the issues of power and standards would arise.

However, Kachru also points out that users of English in the Outer Circle now outnumber those in the Inner Circle. Note that they too have contributed to turning English into a true world language and its successful implementation in the Expanding Circle (Mufwene 2015b). Political ideologies have then become intertwined with the "economic power of English as an export commodity." Who controls the form in which English continues to spread in both the Outer and the Expanding Circles? And who controls the industry of teaching English as a foreign language? While natives of the former exploitation colonies could learn English from natives of the Inner Circle, those of the Expanding Circle cannot always afford teachers from the Inner Circle. Natives of the Outer Circle are less expensive and spread different kinds of live models to learners. They are contributing to the divergence of English from those of the Inner Circle, while there is also polarization between primarily the American and British norms. Also, while Australian English has acquired acceptability in Asia (which is evidence that economic power can sell a particular variety), the prevailing ideology is that varieties of the Outer Circle are deviations that at best should be contained for national and/or regional consumption. Thus, the financial benefits from teaching and spreading English in the Expanding Circle are being reaped by the Inner Circle, chiefly by the British Council and similar American institutions that produce the school materials. All members of the English-speaking "fellowship" are not equal, and Kachru shows that the "pluricentric" English-speaking diaspora does not yet share equal authority on the common but diversifying language. Some "centers" wish to keep more control on it than do others.

It is largely regarding norms and standards that the "culture wars" arise, as Kachru compares the "triumphal" spread of English around the world to a multiheaded Hydra in Greek mythology and to the "Speaking Tree" that understands all languages in Indian mythology. In the first case, English can prevail in any form; in the second, it can absorb influences from diverse languages and cultures. It may be this malleability to other cultures and linguistic influences that accounts for the success of its unprecedented spread around the world, although one must not at all ignore the unequaled success of England's colonial enterprise, culminating with the British Empire, which evolved into the British Commonwealth. Next to the emergence of the United States as an economic and military superpower, as well as its rise as a worldwide leader in science and technology, the British Commonwealth crowned, with its geographic and demographic size combined, the importance of English as the foremost world lingua franca.

As a "Speaking Tree," English is used by members of different nations as "a vital weapon for articulating various positions and visions." However, some of these positions and visions are in conflict with each other, for instance, whether English is claimed to be degenerating or to be enriched by innovations in the Outer and Expanding Circles, and whether the significance of the demographic size of English, based on which varieties are considered (un)acceptable, is shrinking or increasing. In short, different members of the English-speaking "fellowship" defend different agendas and self-serving interests; they may be said to have family feuds, even about the best form or kind of English to teach in the classroom, and regarding the best way to write: with or without code-mixing, with or without borrowing from the local indigenous languages, and for what particular kind of readership. The English-speaking "fellowship" is also marked by the tension between "the *nativization* of English" and "the *Englishization* of other world languages," those of "wider communication."

Is English a language of liberation or oppression in the Outer Circle? English enabled the colonized to liberate themselves politically from the colonizers, through those who had been schooled in it. The question is whether this history should be extended to a form of linguistic liberation, with its speakers in the Outer and Expanding Circles accumulating enough authority to innovate outside the censorship of the Inner Circle. Can the Outer Circle, if not also the Expanding Circle, be acknowledged as linguistically independent territories controlling the evolution of English, structurally and pragmatically, outside the control of the Inner Circle? Kachru's argument is that the "English-speaking fellowship" is culturally plural and should be decentralized, with more tolerance for the emergence of national and/or regional norms in the corresponding subfellowships of uses. The "culture war" emerging from this issue opposes "deficit linguistics" (reflecting the views of those advocating central norms, thus the prevalence of those of the Inner Circle) to "liberation linguistics" (reflecting the position of those advocating the "linguistic emancipation" of the Outer and Expanding Circles from the Raj). This reflects the fact that English is evolving in cultural ecologies that are not identical across the world.

As an editor and occasional student of "indigenized Englishes" (in the discriminating tradition), I have been very much enriched by the wealth of information Braj B. Kachru provides in *World Englishes and Culture Wars* and hope the reader will share my satisfaction.

SALIKOKO S. MUFWENE, *University of Chicago*

Acknowledgments

It is by sheer accident, on the occasion of one of my visits to Braj B. Kachru, then both ailing and grieving the death of his wife and collaborator Yamuna Kachru, that I discovered the manuscript of the present book on the coffee table of their living room. Several searches for its electronic copy on their computers and with CUP, with whom a contract had already been signed, yielded nothing. To save the day, Giuseppe Ciaravino, his son-in-law, undertook to scan the 396-page manuscript and then converted it into a Word file, which I could edit. This book would have taken much longer to materialize without Giuseppe's intervention, for which Braj was very grateful and I no less, for the time it saved me. I simply regret that delays on the part of all the rest of us involved in the production of this book prevented Braj from seeing it published before he passed away. I am likewise grateful to Rakesh Mohan Bhatt for helping me figure out the correct forms of the Kashmiri texts distorted by the multiple conversions explained previously, when I no longer had access to original paper version nor, unfortunately, to the author.

Last but not least, I would like to thank Susan Thornton, my copy-editor, and Kalaivani Periassamy, my Project Manager at SPi Global, for reformatting a reconstructed Word file that was posing more formatting challenges than is usually the case, before engaging in an impeccable copy-editing process. I share with the author responsibility for the remaining imperfections, especially regarding the demographic figures.

SALIKOKO S. MUFWENE

Part I

World Englishes Today

1   The Agony and Ecstasy

Introduction

In this chapter the agony and ecstasy discussed are restricted to "Englishes," but this linguistic conflict actually applies to most languages of wider communication (e.g., Chinese, French, Hindi-Urdu, Portuguese, Spanish, Tamil), and to languages of not-so-wide communication (e.g., Dutch, Swedish, Korean, and Serbo-Croatian).[1] All these languages are in varying degrees "pluricentric";[2] they have multilinguistic identities, multiplicity of norms (both endocentric and exocentric), and distinct sociolinguistic histories. However, the pluricentricity of English is overwhelming and unprecedented in linguistic history. It raises a variety of issues of diversification, codification, identity, creativity, cross-cultural intelligibility, and power and ideology.[3] The universalization of English and the power of this language have exacted a price: for some, the implications are agonizing, while for others they are a matter of ecstasy.

In my discussion of these two reactions to the spread and functions of English, I would like to discuss ecstasy over the triumph of English first, and then move to the other part: the agony. But before I do this, my choice of the term *Englishes* calls for an explanation: Why *World Englishes* and not *World English?*[4] This question invariably arises in reaction to my conceptualization of English around the world. The answer to it involves linguistic, attitudinal, ontological, and pragmatic explanations. The term *Englishes* is indicative of distinct identities of the language and literature. *Englishes* symbolizes variation in form and function, use in linguistically and culturally distinct contexts,

---

[1] This chapter highlights a variety of issues concerning the global spread of English, the development of World Englishes, and users' love–hate relationship with the language. I have focused on most of these issues in my teaching and research since the 1960s. This chapter, therefore, draws heavily on my earlier publications and presentations. I have provided extensive references to literature for further details, explanations, and, where necessary, illustrations.

[2] See Kloss (1978 [1952]), specifically pp. 66–67. For a discussion and case studies of pluricentric languages, see Clyne (1992).

[3] See L. Smith and Nelson (1985), L. Smith (1992), B. Kachru (1982b and 1992b, B. Kachru 1985b); regarding power and ideology, see relevant references in B. Kachru (1994d).

[4] For detailed discussion, see B. Kachru (1985b).

4   The Agony and Ecstasy

and a range of varieties in literary creativity. And, above all, the term stresses the *WE-ness* among the users of English, as opposed to *us* vs. *them* (native vs. nonnative). I believe that the traditional concept of *us* vs. *them* used in describing language diffusion does not apply to English in the same way as it does to other languages of wider communication.

It was more than a generation ago, in 1975, that in his presidential address to the English Association in London, George Steiner (1975: 4) referred to the pluricentricity of English, saying that "the linguistic center of English has shifted." Steiner (1975: 5) argued that

this shift of the linguistic center involves far more than statistics. It does look as if the principal energies of the English language, as if its genius for acquisition, for innovation, for metaphoric response, has also moved away from England.

Steiner was not thinking of North America or Australia only, but of East, West, and South Africa; India; Ceylon (now Sri Lanka); and of the U.S. possessions in the Pacific. And during the past two decades this "shift" has become more marked, more institutionalized, and more recognized.

The major characteristics of this unprecedented change in linguistic behavior and the depth and range of the spread are better understood if the English language in diaspora is viewed in several phases. The first phase began closer to home, with initial expansion from England restricted to the British Isles up until the establishment of Great Britain in 1707. The second phase of diaspora takes us to North America (United States and Canada), to Australia, and to New Zealand. This phase entailed movements of English-speaking populations from one part of the globe to another. It is, however, the third phase, the Raj phase, that altered the earlier sociolinguistic profile of the English language and the processes of transplanting it: it introduced English to South Asia; to Southeast Asia; to Southern, West, and East Africa; and to the Philippines.

It is primarily this phase of the diaspora on which I shall concentrate. It has four major cross-linguistic and cross-cultural characteristics. First, it implanted English within linguistic contexts where no English-using communities existed and no large-scale English-speaking populations were relocated. Second, English gained contact with genetically and culturally unrelated major languages: in Africa with especially the Niger–Congo languages, in Asia with the Dravidian languages, and in Southeast Asia with the Altaic languages, to give just three major examples. Third, rather than one consistent pedagogical model, there were diverse contexts, methods, and inputs in imparting English education, often with no serious input from the native speakers of the language. Fourth, though the arms of the Raj maintained a distance from the native cultures, and from native people, the language of the Raj was going through a process of acculturation. It was being influenced by the non-Western cultures and their sociolinguistic contexts. The pluricentricity of English, thus,

Introduction

is not merely demographic; it entails cultural, linguistic, and literary reincarnations of the English language. These sociolinguistic "reincarnations" may be viewed as processes of liberation, as it were, from the traditional canons associated with English.

The profile of this pluricentricity may be represented with reference to the Three Concentric Circles of English discussed in the Figure 1.1.[5]

The list of countries included in the circles, particularly in the Outer and Expanding Circles, is merely illustrative and is not intended to be complete; for example, South Africa, Ireland, Hong Kong, and Jamaica are not discussed here. These three circles have a message about the codification and diversification of English and provide motivation for various types of institutionalization of the language (B. Kachru 1985b). There are now three types of English-using speech fellowships: *norm-providing, norm-developing,* and *norm-dependent.*

In the Outer Circle and the Expanding Circle, the ecstasy generated by the power of English has several dimensions: demographic, ideological, societal, and attitudinal. English is not only an access language par excellence, it is a reference point for paradigms of research and methodology. In research, areas such as second language acquisition, first language acquisition, stylistics, bilingual and monolingual lexicography, and theories of translation are closely related to English studies. In theory construction, generalizations about natural languages, their structural characteristics, and possible categories of language universals usually begin with analysis and examples from English.

And across languages and literatures, the impact of World Englishes is Janus-like, with two faces. One face is that of ENGLISHIZATION, the process of change English has initiated in the other languages of the world (see, e.g., Viereck and Bald 1986; B. Kachru 1994b). The second face is that of the NATIVIZATION and ACCULTURATION of the English language itself, the processes of change that localized varieties of English have undergone by acquiring new linguistic and cultural identities (see B. Kachru 1986a [reprinted 1990]; also Cheshire 1991). This explains the use of terms such as the *Africanization* (Bokamba 1982 [1992]) or *Indianization* (B. Kachru 1983b and earlier) of English, or the use of terms such as *Singaporean English, Nigerian English, Philippine English,* and *Sri Lankan English.*[6]

Whatever reactions one might have toward the diffusion and uses of English, one must, however, admit that we now have a cross-cultural and cross-linguistic universal language. And with it, what John Adams saw in his crystal

---

[5] Population figures are taken from the United Nations website www.undp.org/popin/wdtrends/ p98/p98.htm, which lists world population figures for 1998. The statistic for Taiwan is from "Taiwan" Encyclopredia Britannica Online. www.eb.com:180/bol/topic?eu=1 15301&sctn=1.

[6] For references on these varieties, see McArthur (1992).

The Agony and Ecstasy

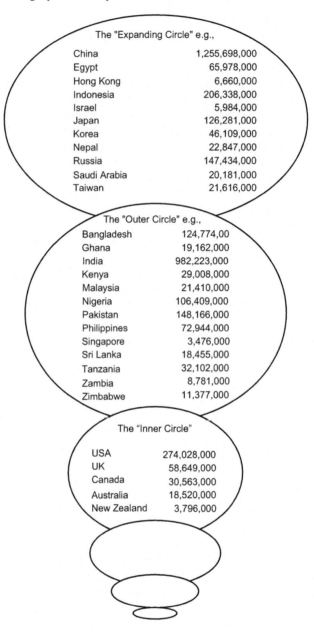

Figure 1.1 *The concentric circles of English*

Introduction 7

ball in September 1780 has come true. Adams (cited in Mathews 1931: 42) prophesied that "English will be the most respectable language in the world and the most universally read and spoken in the next century, if not before the close of this." (When Adams said "English" he actually meant "American English.") Adams's prophecy is evident in such recent claims as "The sun never sets on the English language" (though, after 1940, the sun did set on the empire), or "English is the language for all seasons," or "English has no national or regional frontier."

This demographic distribution of English surpasses that of Latin in the medieval period, of Sanskrit in what was traditional South Asia and parts of Southeast Asia, and of Spanish, Arabic, and French. And now no competing languages exist, not at present – not French, nor any artificial languages such as Esperanto. In other words, English continues to alter the linguistic behavior of people across the globe, and it is now the major instrument of initiating large-scale bilingualism around the world – being a bilingual now essentially means knowing English and using English as an *additional* language, as a language of wider communication, with one or more languages from one's region. This unparalleled spread of English has resulted now in an attitude of triumphalism about the language.

It is, however, difficult to determine how many people know English. The answer depends on whom you ask. A conservative figure gives us two non-native speakers for every native speaker.[7] The liberal figure (Crystal 1985b: 9 and Strevens 1982) gives us roughly four nonnative speakers for every native speaker.[8] In China, there are many more English-using Chinese than the total population of the United Kingdom, if we estimate just 5 percent of the Chinese use English. In the case of India, if we count only 10 percent of the population as English-knowing, it is the third largest English-knowing country after the United States and the United Kingdom. I have stated elsewhere (see e.g., B. Kachru 1994a and earlier) that my earlier estimated figure of more than 60 million users of Indian English speakers is already out of date. The current profile is substantially different. A survey conducted in India (*India Today*, August 18, 1997) claims that "contrary to the [Indian] census myth that English is the language of a microscopic minority, the poll indicates that almost one in every three Indians claims to understand English although less than 20 percent are confident of speaking it." If viewed in a larger context,

---

[7] That gives us an estimated figure of more than 750 million nonnative users of English.

[8] This optimistic estimate equals about 2 billion users. Crystal believes that "if you are highly conscious of international standards, or wish to keep the figures for World English down, you will opt for a total of around 700 million, in the mid-1980s. If you go to the opposite extreme, and allow in any systematic awareness whether in speaking, listening, reading or writing, you could easily persuade yourself of the reasonableness of 2 billion." However, he hastens to settle for a lower figure, saying, "I am happy to settle for a billion. . ." See also Strevens (1982).

8   The Agony and Ecstasy

these figures are staggering: The estimated population of India is almost 1 billion. The preceding figures indicated that almost 333 million Indians understand (some) English and almost 200 million have some spoken competence in the language. According to these figures, then, India now has an English-using speech community equal to the population of the major Inner Circle countries combined (the United States, the United Kingdom, and Canada). The Indian Constitution actually recognizes English as an "associate" official language.[9] And China is not far behind. Yong and Campbell (1995) tell us that there are now 200 million students in the People's Republic enrolled in programs in English as a foreign language. These figures of the two Asian giants add up to 533 million. What is impressive indeed is that this profile of English has developed within this century, particularly after the 1930s.

The question remains: How many people use English around the world? As outlined earlier, no one seems to have a well-researched answer to the question, since we actually have no reliable figures on which an answer to this crucial question could be based. Nor do we know how to define an English "knower" to separate him or her from a "semiknower" of the language. However, there is no argument about one fact concerning English: even if we accept the most conservative figures, there are now two nonnative speakers of English for every native speaker. And if we accept an extremely optimistic figure of 2 billion users of English out of the total world population of more than 5 billion, we have roughly every third person using some variety of English as a nonnative speaker.

In those regions that have felt no direct impact of English – the formerly Francophone countries, for instance – the indirect impact has been no less real, and has been difficult to arrest. This impact occurs through "invisible" channels that bypass the strategies devised by language planners. The influence of English penetrates indirectly from the models of creativity, the international media, processes used for translation, and now electronic media and computer technology.

We see the hegemony of English across cultures in the domains of education, administration, literary creativity, and both intranational and international interaction. But, more important, we see it in the attitudes toward English and its users. It is the only natural language that has considerably more nonnative users than native users. And it is the nonnative users who are now responsible for its spread and teaching, and its extended cross-cultural functions. Interactions involving English in non-Western countries are mostly carried on by nonnative users with other nonnative users, not, as one would suppose, by nonnative users with native users. In its extent and impact on other cultures,

---

[9] India's Constitution recognizes English as an "associate" official language.

Paradigms of Research and Paradigm Lag

languages, and literatures, this, then, is a unique phenomenon in the history of language diffusion. One therefore has to ask, Do we have appropriate theoretical and methodological tools to account for this phenomenon?

Paradigms of Research and Paradigm Lag

This global initiation of bilingualism in English, its range and depth, and the implications of its stratification have not been followed by accommodating, modifying, and refining paradigms of research and methodology. In fact, research for understanding this remarkable phenomenon of our times – and all times – and its implications have yet to be clearly worked out and presented.

Dell Hymes (personal communication), a sociolinguist, reminds us, "We have methods highly elaborated for addressing the process of genetic relationships, but very little for addressing the process of diffusion, contact, etc." He goes on to say that the methods for typological classification, which involve the least use of language, are more developed, while "the functional classification, which involves the most use of language, is the least developed."

The resistance to a paradigm shift is not purely intellectual; there are other strategies in action here that are ideologically based and very subtle.[10] However, traditionally, three main paradigms have been used to describe and analyze World Englishes.

Descriptive

The descriptive approach in the study of the diffusion of English has been attitudinally neutral. One notices it in some lexicographical work, which I have termed "Raj lexicography" (see B. Kachru 1996c).

Prescriptive Paradigms

The prescriptivists' primary yardsticks were the "native speaker" and the manuals of English based on the native varieties.[11] Originally, this standard was applied to linguistic deviation at any level: grammar, lexis, discourse. The term "deviation" entails uses of language not consistent with the prescriptive "native" norms.

---

[10] A number of reasons for resistance to paradigm shift are discussed in, for example, Phillipson (1992), Fairclough (1989).

[11] For a detailed discussion of various attitudes toward idealization of the "native speaker" see Paikeday (1985).

10 The Agony and Ecstasy

Purist Paradigm

The purists' attitude involves more than *linguistic* purism. It also sees language as a medium for cultural, religious, and moral refinement and enlightenment. This attitude is well articulated in the Orientalist vs. Occidentalist debate concerning the language policy for what was "the Jewel in the Crown," South Asia. In the 1830s, proposing English for India's language planning, Macaulay (cited in Grant 1831–1832: 60–66) said:

I have no knowledge of either Sanskrit or Arabic. But I have done what I could to form a correct estimate of their value. . . . A single shelf of a good European library is worth the whole native literature of India and Arabia.

Again,

The true curse of darkness is the introduction of light. The Hindoos err, because they are ignorant and their errors have never fairly been laid before them. The communication of our light and knowledge to them would prove the best remedy for their disorders.

In the former U.S. president McKinley's view, the solution to the problems in the Philippines was "to educate the Filipinos and uplift and civilize and Christianize them and fit the people for the duties of citizenship" (cited in Beebe and Beebe 1981: 322).

The phenomenal spread of English cannot be understood within these three approaches: in all of thems English is seen essentially as a colonizer's linguistic arm, without any identity or name. Any non-English linguistic indicators – cultural, social, and religious – have been viewed as the markers of deficiency and not merely of difference. The manifestations of language contact were viewed as *interference.* That term acquired an immense attitudinal load: one has to be cautious about the implications of such undesirable labeling, as has been shown in several studies.[12]

Institutionalization and the Sacred Cows

The institutionalization of English in the Outer Circle – in Africa and Asia – raises a variety of theoretical, methodological, and ideological questions that go beyond the concerns of simple pedagogy. Answering such questions within the new contexts and functions of English and their implications has meant slaughtering several types of sacred cows: theoretical, acquisitional, sociolinguistic, pedagogical, and ideological. I shall briefly discuss some of these in the following.

---

[12] This caution particularly applies to the use of English in bi- or multilingual contexts.

The theoretical concerns relate to four cardinal concepts in language study: the SPEECH COMMUNITY, the NATIVE SPEAKER, the IDEAL SPEAKER–HEARER, and the MOTHER TONGUE. In linguistics literature, the definition of *speech community* varies from Leonard Bloomfield's vague definition ("a speech community is a group of people who interact by means of speech") to the rather complex definitions of La Page and Gumperz (B. Kachru 1994c; see also discussion in Hudson 1980: 25–30). The underlying presupposition here, and certainly in earlier conceptualizations of the spread of English, is that monolingualism is the normal communicative behavior in which the mother tongue has a crucial function. Yet, the sociolinguistic reality is that, as Ferguson (1982 [1992]: vii) reminds us,

much of the world's verbal communication takes place by means of languages which are not the users' "mother tongue," but their second, third, or nth language, acquired one way or another and used when appropriate.

The consideration of monolingualism as normal linguistic behavior leads to yet another trap, that of considering the "native speaker" as a vital linguistic primitive. It was as a reaction to this reification of "native speaker" that Paikeday (1985) wrote his provocative book *The Native Speaker Is Dead!* But not quite. In 1991 Davies reincarnated the native speaker in *The Native Speaker in Applied Linguistics,* although, more than a decade earlier, Ferguson (1982 [1992]: vii) had warned us that

the whole mystique of native speaker and mother tongue should probably be quietly dropped from the linguists' set of professional myths about the language.

Sociolinguistically speaking, Chomsky's (1965) abstract idealization of the "speaker–hearer" presents unique problems with reference to World Englishes. What are the shared conventions of the users? How does one account for the variation that is characteristic of every level of language in each variety, e.g., the variation ranging from acrolect to mesolect to basilect, or, in South Asia, educated English to "Babu English," "Butler English," and "Bazaar English"?[13]

In acquisitional paradigms the dominant explanatory concepts with reference to the users of English in the Outer Circle are INTERFERENCE, ERROR, FOSSILIZATION, DEVIANCE, and INTERLANGUAGE. First, "interference" results in "error," which, if institutionalized, becomes "fossilization." "Fossilization" refers to those linguistic features that are "deviant" from the target language norm and are part of the linguistic performance of the user. These linguistic features are a part of what is termed an "interlanguage": the teachers' goal and learners' ideal is, of course, to attain nativelike competence. The

---

[13] For a brief description of these varieties of English see McArthur (1992) and B. Kachru (1994a).

12   The Agony and Ecstasy

attitudinal and other connotations of "interference" show the extension of a monolingual paradigm to contexts of contact. This attitude continues, in spite of the recognition that interference varieties

are so widespread in a community and of such long standing that they may be thought stable and adequate enough to be institutionalized and hence to be regarded as varieties of English in their own right rather than stages on the way to a more native-like English. (Quirk 1985: 27–28)

The sociolinguistic concerns relate to ideology and construction of identities. David Crystal rightly says that "all discussion of standards ceases very quickly to be a linguistic discussion, and becomes instead an issue of social identity" (1985b). This indeed is particularly true of English, since it has played an "integrative" role among the elite in the Third World: it has provided a perspective that is both "inward-looking" and "outward-looking," a role diametrically opposed to the aims and political agenda of the colonizers. English turned into an effective resource for understanding the dialectics of anticolonialism, secularization, and panregional communication for nationalism, regional identities, and communication across linguistic and cultural boundaries.

The paradigms of pedagogy (teaching methods and materials) have yet to catch up with the new challenges that World Englishes provide. This lack is specifically noticed in the conceptualization of, for example, communicative competence, English for Specific Purposes (ESP), and construction of evaluation tests of international competence in English.[14]

The ideological concerns open a well-discussed can of worms with a range of perspectives. The metaphor "killer English" symbolizes the overwhelming ideological power of English, which is further expressed in terms such as *genocide, inequality, imperialism, Anglocentricity, cultural nationalism,* and *neocolonialism,* all ideologically loaded terms. The symbolization of power depends on how one sees the medium and its message. The symbolic label depends on what kind of identity one establishes with the language.[15] The following labels are illustrative.

The Kenyan author Ngugi (1986: 5) is one of the most articulate writers in expressing the power and the resultant agony of English:

African countries, as colonies and even today as neocolonies, came to be defined and to define themselves in terms of the languages of Europe: English-speaking, French-speaking or Portuguese-speaking African countries. Ngugi (1986: 5)

---

[14] The issues related to communicative competence and intelligibility have been discussed, for example, by the following: L. Smith (1987), Nelson (1985 [1992]), and Berns (1990). For ESP and World Englishes see Chamberlain and Baumgardner (1988). For World Englishes and testing, see Lowenberg (1992) and Davidson (1993a).

[15] For a detailed discussion see Phillipson (1992).

Institutionalization and the Sacred Cows 13

Labels Used to Symbolize Power of English

Positive	Negative
National identity	Antinationalism
Literary renaissance	Anti–native culture
Cultural mirror (for native cultures)	Materialism
	Vehicle for Westernization
Vehicle for modernization	Rootlessness
Liberalism	Ethnocentricism
Universalism	Permissiveness
Secularism	Divisiveness
Technology	Alienation
Science	Colonialism
Mobility access code	

Note: See also Chapter 3.

English is a "cultural bomb," and

the effect of a cultural bomb is to annihilate a people's belief in their names, in their languages, in their environment... It makes them want to identify with that which is farthest removed from themselves, for instance, with other people's languages, rather their own.

He (cited in Jussawalla and Dasenbrock, 1992: 30) believes that

African thought is imprisoned in foreign languages. African literature and African thought, even at their most radical, even at their most revolutionary, are alienated from the majority.

On the other hand, Chinua Achebe expresses a contextual concern different from that of Ngugi. In Achebe's view (1966: 27–30; see also Mazrui 1975):

If you take Nigeria as an example, the national literature, as I see it, is the literature written in English; and the ethnic literatures are in Hausa, Igbo, Yoruba, Effik, Edo, Ijaw etc.

Ngugi suggests *distance* from the language, Achebe *complete identity* on his functional terms. However, Achebe asks, "Can an African ever learn English well enough to be able to use it effectively in creative writing?" And his answer is "Certainly yes." But he hastens to qualify the statement: "If on the other hand you ask: Can he [an African] ever learn to use it like a native speaker? I should say, 'I hope not. It is neither necessary, nor desirable for him to be able to do so.'" Achebe's attitude to English is essentially pragmatic. For him (1976: 11), English has to be

a new English, still in communion with its ancestral home but altered to suit its new African surroundings.

14   The Agony and Ecstasy

Does this, then, show that Achebe is completely free of linguistic agony concerning his identity with English? The answer is yes and no. Only a decade later after the first quote, Achebe expresses his agony concerning the paradigm trap: the application of European paradigms for discussion of African literature:

I should like to see the word *universal* banned altogether from the discussion of African literature until such a time as people cease to use it as a synonym for the narrow, self-serving parochialism of Europe. (Achebe 1976: 11)

Now, take another example. The Indian metaphysical novelist Raja Rao shows an entirely different kind of identity with the English language. He gives English a status equal to that of Sanskrit in the Indian context.

Truth, said a great Indian sage, is not the monopoly of the Sanskrit language. Truth can use any language, and the more universal, the better it is. . . And as long as the English language is universal, it will always remain Indian. (Rao 1978: 420–422)

Rao (1978: 420–422) accepts English "not as a guest or friend, but as one of our own, of our caste, our creed, our sect and of our tradition."

I said Raja Rao gave English a status equal to that of Sanskrit; for a Brahmin, from the South of India, that entails complete identity with the language: English becomes an Indian language. Raja Rao's language. And Lawrence Durrell is effusive in his praise of Rao's creativity in English:[16]

"Hurrah for you! You not only do India great honour, but you have honoured English literature by writing it in our language."

However, Durrell's "our" shows a different attitude to English, namely, that Rao's identity with the language is suspect; Rao is shown his place and we go back to *we* vs. *them*. Durrell is consistent in using his monolingual paradigm for creativity in English. Perhaps Anita Desai would have puzzled him more, as she says that, until she heard critics discussing problems of Indians writing in English, she (1996: 223) had

not been aware that there were problems. In fact I had been so misguided, or naive, to think it a distinct advantage to be able to delve into more than one language, more than one culture. In my own home, we tended to snatch at whatever word or phrase seemed appropriate to the moment or situation without stopping about which part of the world it belonged to. Pedants may shudder, and it was indeed a patchwork of languages, but was not all of Indian life a patchwork?

Salman Rushdie's personal experience as a writer from the Commonwealth is insightful. At a Conference on English Studies in 1983, he was told that "for

---

[16] This was conveyed to Raja Rao in a personal communication by Lawrence Durrell in 1960 after the publication of Rao's *The Serpent and the Rope*.

the purposes of our seminar, English studies are taken to include Commonwealth Literature" (1991: 61).

At all other times, one was forced to conclude, these two worlds would be kept strictly apart, like squabbling children, or sexually incompatible pandas, or, perhaps, like unstable, fissile materials whose union might cause explosions. (Rushdie 1991: 61)

An often repeated question is, Why do these writers (e.g., Achebe, Rao, Desai) write in English? Rao's answer (cited in Jussawalla and Dasenbrock 1992: 144) is

Historically, this is how I am placed. I'm not interested in being a European but in being me. But the whole of the Indian tradition, as I see it, is in my work. There is an honesty in choosing English, an honesty in terms of history.

And then, Rao (cited in Jussawalla and Dasenbrock 1992: 147) talks of authenticity:

The important thing is not what language one writes in, for language is really an accidental thing. What matters is the authenticity of experience, and this can generally be achieved in any language.

Multiidentities and the Canon

The elevated status and a wide functional range of English across cultures came at a price. Its multicultural identities resulted in deep sociolinguistic changes: a shift of traditional interlocutors, expansions of the canon, changes in discoursal organization, and the demythologization of canonical English.

Shift of Traditional Interlocutors

The international users of English have unrelated linguistic and cultural backgrounds (e.g., Dravidian, Bantu, Altaic), often with minimal or no shared linguistic and cultural conventions: a Japanese with a Taiwanese, a Nigerian with a Saudi Arabian, an Indian with a Scot. The *intranational* users have minimal interaction with the native speakers. The questions here are, What are the norms of intelligibility? What are the presuppositions concerning the shared knowledge of conventions of interactions? (See also B. Kachru 1982b, Y. Kachru 1991c, and L. Smith 1987.)

The Expansions of the Canon

The process of "opening up the canon" (Fiedler and Baker 1981) has taken place in English to an unparalleled extent, though it has yet to be seriously recognized. The processes of language change initiated by language contact

16   The Agony and Ecstasy

are not restricted to grammar, lexis, style, and discourse. They go beyond these levels and cross over to literatures across cultures. In the writing of Wole Soyinka, Chinua Achebe, Raja Rao, Catherine Lim, Chitra Fernando, Shashi Tharoor, Edwin Thumboo, and Vikram Seth, to name a few, English is used as a medium to present canons unrelated to traditional associations of the language. In the Outer Circle, then, there is a shift from the earlier European sociocultural and literary canons of the language, and a conscious attempt to relate English to local traditions of culture and creativity.[17] There is also a rethinking about such earlier uses of English, particularly during the colonial period of Asia and Africa.

In Nigeria, Kenya, Singapore, India, Pakistan, and the Philippines, bilinguals' creativity is considered now part of the national literatures. These literatures are *national* first and *universal* second, as long as the term "universal" is defined within Western parameters. The local English literatures are part of the local canons of creativity. Achebe (1966: 47) emphasizes that his vision is "necessarily local and particular." In understanding and interpreting Wole Soyinka and Amos Tutuola, the worldview of their ontology, mythology, and oral tradition is central, and Judeo-Christian traditions are peripheral. In interpreting Rao's *The Serpent and the Rope* or *The Chessmaster and His Moves,* a multilingual and Vedantist view is vital, and Vikram Seth's *A Suitable Boy* is completely embedded in North Indian sociocultural traditions.

The text, then, has its own context within the new canons of creativity: a context of sociocultural canons and canons of creativity. The reader has to be aware of this linguistic and contextual crossover. The traditional paradigms have yet to provide insights for exploring in such texts the "meaning potential" (cf. Halliday 1975). At present, contextually and linguistically, our yardsticks for intelligibility and interpretability of creativity in Englishes are based on one specific canon and the processes of monolingual creativity. In contact literatures in English, the multicultural and multilingual processes of organizing the text are reflected in Yorubization, Sanskritization, and so on. This raises an important question: My language, your culture – whose communicative competence (see Nelson 1985 [1992])?

Changes in Discoursal Organization

Discoursal organization in various interactional contexts – both literary and spoken – reflects the African and Asian canons of English. One reason for such textual reorganization is that English is now recognized as part of national and local literary traditions. The concerns of Chinua Achebe or R. K. Narayan may

---

[17] Recent good examples of such creativity are e.g., Tharoor (1989) and Seth (1993).

be universal, but the medium of the expression of those concerns is nativized; the contextualization of the text and its formal manifestations are not shared with other varieties: in that necessary sense, the text is regional and national

Demythologization of Canonical English

The preceding processes lead to the demythologization of canonical English in a number of ways: a) by dissociating the language from earlier sociocultural and historical assumptions, b) by considering World English literatures beyond the Judeo-Christian tradition, and c) by recognizing non-Western literary traditions.

What Price Ecstasy?

The ecstasy and its bounty – linguistic, nationalistic, integrative, and literary – had a certain price. Before I identify the reasons for the agony, I must note that all the reasons refer to spheres of power and control. Linguists have yet to provide a framework to structure the power of a language. The five linguistic models generally used to discuss such power are the Correlative Model, the Domain Model, the Conflict Model, the Functional Model, and the Verbal Repertoire.

Model

These models only capture part of the interplay of power, politics, and control. There is as yet no rigorous theoretical and methodological framework in which to understand the all-pervasive power of English. While considering the question of power, one naturally is reminded of Michael Foucault's discussion on this topic. Foucault, of course, does not directly address the issue of languages and power; however, he does confirm that "power and its strategies, at once general and detailed, and its mechanisms have never been studied." In Foucault's view, power is "an organ of repression" (1980). The question is, how is this "organ" of repression used in language, and what are the manifestations of linguistic power in a speech community?

The following manifestations of linguistic power come to mind: crude linguistic power, indirect psychological pressure, and what may be termed pragmatic power; these three are not mutually exclusive.

One finds numerous examples of crude linguistic power, as in the imposition of Japanese on the Koreans, Singaporeans, and Malays during World War II. A subtle psychological pressure is evident in claims that a particular language has "spiritual" power, as, in the ritualistic context, the recitation of Sanskrit hymns, the power of Japa, the other-worldly rewards of the reading of the holy *Quran*. In these contexts, however, the inherent power of language is accepted without question.

18   The Agony and Ecstasy

Pragmatic power may be interpreted in terms of a particular language's gain of control over a wide range of functionally crucial domains – political, religious, caste, class, and commercial. At present, English has abundant pragmatic power across cultures.

What Foucault (1980) suggests as "methodological precautions" entails asking the following types of questions: What is the "ultimate destination" of power at its "extremities"? What are the aims of the possessors of power? What is the network of power? Who are the agents of power? And what are the "ideological" productions of power?

Two of these questions deserve particular attention with respect to language. The first is, what are the channels used for linguistic control? It seems to me that linguistic control essentially means acquiring the power to *define*. As Tromel-Plotz (1981) warns us, "only the powerful can define others and can make their definitions stick. By having their definitions accepted they appropriate more power." The power to define shows in the use of channels of codification and the control of those channels.

The power to define also shows in the power to *authenticate* the uses and users of English in the Outer Circle. This power is reflected in attitudes toward linguistic innovations – lexical, grammatical, discoursal, and stylistic – and in the mixing and switching of languages. Current paradigms of power interpret any shift in paradigm as a manifestation of "liberation linguistics," and therefore "revolutionary" and undesirable.

Quirk (1988) has suggested that "liberation linguistics" is an extension of "liberation theology." In Quirk's view (1989: 236), then, the result of the ideological underpinning is that

the interest in varieties of English has got out of hand and has started blinding both teachers and taught to the central linguistic structure from which varieties might be seen as varying.

Quirk emphatically rejects the distinction between the Outer Circle (ESL) and the Expanding Circle (EFL). He ignores this sociolinguistically valid distinction, as he says, "because I doubt its validity and frequently fail to understand its meaning" (1988: 236).

If we accept Quirk's position, it entails the following assumptions and assigns writers from the Outer Circle to "a position on the periphery" by rejection of or indifference to the following:

1. dynamics of language contact and change;
2. sociolinguistic, cultural, and stylistic motivations for innovations;
3. existence of a cline of variation within a variety;
4. endocentric or localized norms;
5. emerging canons of creativity and cultures in English;

6. language and identity;
7. centrality to writers from the Outer Circle (B. Kachru 1991).

The rejection of a paradigm shift, and misinterpretation of what Quirk calls "liberation linguistics," are partly motivated by another unprecedented dimension of power, the economic power of English as an export commodity. The economic power of English can only be sustained if other strategies are kept under control: the paradigms of teaching, the authentication of creativity, and the guarding of the canon. We are told that "the Worldwide market for EFL training is worth a massive £6.25 billion a year" *(EFL Gazette,* London, March 1989).

The search for stable consumer markets has resulted in a competition between the United States and the United Kingdom, and to a lesser degree Australia. The competition is in promoting specific models of English, in marketing methodologies for the teaching of English, and in recruiting trainees for teacher training programs. The British ESL expert Christopher Brumfit seems to seek solidarity and alliance between the United States and the United Kingdom indirectly (1982: 7):

There is already evidence that varied sources of English are being exploited by countries in their attitude to learning English... The English-speaking world can be played politically by the non-English-speaking World.

There are now several power blocs, and their enthusiasm may be reflected in attitudes noted by Phillipson (1992: 8):

As the director of a dynamic worldwide chain of English language schools puts it: "Once we used to send gunboats and diplomats abroad; now we are sending English teachers."

Fallacies about the Forms and Functions of World Englishes

The issues discussed above have resulted in a variety of perceptions and fallacies about World Englishes: one can think of several reasons for such fallacies, for example, unverified hypotheses, partially valid hypotheses, or simple Anglocentricity. A number of these fallacies are also due to what may be termed leaking research paradigms. But that is only part of the story; the other is the motive of launching so-called paradigms for profit primarily for economic gain. Let me discuss some of these fallacies here.

Fallacy 1   Interlocutors, Us vs. Them

A major fallacy is that English is primarily learned to interact with native speakers of the language. Actually, English has both intranational and international functions, e.g., in Nigeria, India, Kenya, Singapore, and the

20   The Agony and Ecstasy

Philippines. Additionally, English has become the main language for people of diverse cultural and linguistic backgrounds: Japanese interacting with Pakistanis, Nigerians with Germans, and Singaporeans with Indians. These interactions take place in localized (nativized) discoursal strategies of, for example, politeness, persuasion, and phatic communion modeled after the speech acts of a dominant local language transcreated into English (B. Kachru 1983b).

A number of recent studies from written and spoken texts clearly demonstrate use of such strategies (Rushdie 1991, B. Kachru 1992b, see also K. Sridhar 1989). This research area has immense potential that has yet to be explored, and such research should provide valuable insights for creativity and pragmatics, processes of transcreation, and language function.

Fallacy 2   Judeo-Christian Canon vs. Multicanons

The second fallacy is that English is learned primarily to understand and teach American and British cultural values and Judeo-Christian traditions. In reality, in the Outer Circle, English is essentially used to recreate and embody local cultural values. Why English? There are several reasons, the major one being the pragmatic success of English – its extensive currency across linguistic, religious, and cultural boundaries – and attitudes toward the language.

Fallacy 3   Endocentric vs. Exocentric Models

The third fallacy is the claim that the goal of teaching English is to adopt exocentric models (e.g., Received Pronunciation, or General American). This view has no empirical validity and is pragmatically counterproductive.

Fallacy 4   Interlanguage vs. Institutionalized Varieties

The fourth fallacy is that the users of English in the Outer Circle and Expanding Circle actually use what is called an "interlanguage" in terms of their language acquisition, with their ultimate acquisitional goal "nativelike" control of the language. An interlanguage is thus an approximative system that differs from the native norms of Englishes. It has been argued that this generalization with reference to World Englishes is flawed on several counts.

Fallacy 5   Native Input vs. Local Initiative

The fifth fallacy is that native speakers of English provide substantial input in the teaching, policy formation, and administration of the spread of English around the world. There was some – actually very little – validity to the belief

Conclusion

in "native input" during the colonial period, but it has practically no validity during the postcolonial period. Actually the leadership in the policy formation, administration, and spread of bilingualism in English is in the hands of the local people – Asians, Africans, and others. It is also true that motives for retaining and encouraging the spread of English are often challenged by various groups in their own countries. That certainly is the case in India, Malaysia, and Nigeria, to give just three examples.

Fallacy 6 Deficiency vs. Difference

The last fallacy is that the diversity and variation in English, and innovation and creativity in the Outer Circle, are indicators of the *decay* of English. This concern about the *decay* of English, as of other languages of wider communication, is not new, and linguistic Cassandras have been vocal since language teaching – perhaps the second-oldest profession – began.

Conclusion

What I have outlined here is just the tip of the iceberg of a complex situation of World Englishes with a variety of academic dimensions. I believe that World Englishes provide a challenging opportunity to relate several areas of academic interest: language, literature, methodology, ideology, power, and identity. The contexts for inquiry involve diverse cultures, and varied situations of contact and creativity. There is a cross-cultural arena with one linguistic constant: English. In recent years, data from World Englishes have provided a refreshing corpus for asking questions and challenging established paradigms in areas such as the following:

1. Bilingual/multilingual language use (see B. Kachru 1986b)
2. Contact and convergence
3. Cross-cultural discourse (B. Kachru 1994d: 9)
4. Models of language acquisition (B. Kachru 1994d: 9)
5. Communicative competence (B. Kachru 1994d: 9, L. Smith 1987)
6. Language attitudes (B. Kachru 1994d: 9)
7. Intelligibility
8. Test construction
9. Process of nativization and acculturation
10. Language change
11. Typology of prestige languages (Kahane 1986, Kahane and Kahane 1979)
12. Lexicography

As Henry Kahane (1986: 495) observed, "English is the great laboratory of today's sociolinguist." And he tells us that "we are aware of the role of English in our time, 'the other tongue' on a global scale" (1986: 495). The sobering message that Kahane gives us is that "the event is not new. Like everything else in our time, it is larger in size, but in principle the situation of English is no different from earlier case histories" (1986: 495). The profile is larger, the power is much greater, and implications – linguistic, ideological, political, and sociolinguistic – are immense indeed.

The success story of English, its alchemy and the resultant ecstasy, has unleashed a variety of issues related to identity, elitism, and attitudes toward and perceptions of its users. In his novel *A Suitable Boy,* the Indian writer Seth (1993: 501) captures one attitude toward English in a conversation between a farmer and another Indian:

"Do you speak English?" he said after a while in the local dialect of Hindi. He had noticed Maan's luggage tag.
"Yes," said Maan.
"Without English you can't do anything," said the farmer sagely. Maan wondered what possible use English could be to the farmer.
"What use is English?" said Maan.
"People love English!" said the farmer with a strange sort of deep-voiced giggle. "If you talk in English, you are a king. The more people you can mystify, the more people will respect you." He turned back to his tobacco.

Then there is the other side of English, the *otherness* of the language, the agony and schizophrenia it produces. That side again has a long tradition, a long story. And thereby hangs a linguistic tale of cross-cultural attitudes about the forms and functions of World Englishes. What is viewed as deficit by one group of English users indicates pragmatic success to other users. What causes linguistic agony to one group is the cause of ecstasy for the other.

2 The Second Diaspora

Introduction

In this chapter a new dimension of the English language is outlined that has added *multicanonicity* to the language, specifically in diasporic contexts: English in nonnative sociolinguistic contexts. Let me begin the discussion of this important dimension of English with an issue raised in Chapter 1, namely the question of how many people use English around the world. The issue relates to the speakers of the language, their relationship to the changing sociocultural context of English, and the development of World Englishes.

The question is: How many people use English around the world? No one seems to have a well-researched answer to the question, since we actually have no reliable figures on which an answer to this crucial question could be based. Nor do we know how to define English "knowers" to separate them from "semi-knowers" of the language. However, there is no argument about one fact concerning English: Even if we accept the most conservative figures, there are now almost 800 million users of English. And if we accept an extremely optimistic figure of 2 billion users of English out of the total world population of more than 5 billion, we have roughly every third person using some variety of English as an additional language in bi- or multilingual contexts. Whether the figure of 1 billion or 2 billion is correct or not is unimportant. What is significant is that these figures, conservative or optimistic, are indicative of an unprecedented linguistic fact about the spread of the language.[1] However, the spread involves a first phase that was restricted to the British Isles and to a sociolinguistic context that had numerous shared characteristics and traditions. The second phase of the dispersion of English takes us to the far-flung parts of the

---

[1] The optimistic estimated figure of 2 billion users has been given by Crystal (1985b: 9). He believes that "if you are highly conscious of international standards, or wish to keep the figures for World English down, you will opt for a total of around 700 million, in the mid-1980s. If you go to the opposite extreme, and allow in any systematic awareness whether in speaking, listening, reading or writing, you could easily persuade yourself of the reasonableness of 2 billion." However, he hastens to settle for a lower figure, saying, "I am happy to settle for a billion..." See also Strevens 1982.

24   The Second Diaspora

world, to North America (e.g., see Mencken 1919), to Australia, to New Zealand (e.g., see Eagleson 1982), and to Canada (see Bailey 1982). During this phase, English was implanted on two distinct continents. However, these varieties of English were different from what may be termed the second-diaspora varieties. Though transplanted on other continents, the American, Australian, and New Zealand varieties were essentially the result of the movement and transplanting of English-speaking populations from one part of the globe to another. Thus, these varieties initially only partially entailed change or modification of linguistic behavior of local speech communities. And in terms of numbers, this expansion did not significantly contribute to the numerical superiority of English. When Australia, Canada, the United States, and New Zealand adopted English as the language of new nations, it became one of the major languages of the world with Arabic, Spanish, Hindi, and a handful of other languages. However, it was yet far from being a global language, as it is now.

It was the third phase that resulted in the second major diaspora and altered the earlier restricted sociolinguistic profile of the English language. This second diaspora introduced English to Asia, to Africa, to Latin America, and to the Philippines. It is this phase of the diaspora on which I concentrate in this chapter.

This diaspora of English is characterized by various cross-linguistic and cross-cultural features. The first characteristic refers to the new linguistic contexts. The regions in which English was transplanted had practically no users of the language initially. Thus, in terms of language acquisition, the teaching and learning of English entailed change in the linguistic behavior of speech communities of the users of other languages, Asian and African. To begin with, the English-using speech communities in these regions were small, but as time passed and as the colonies stabilized, these communities expanded. This is evident, for example, in the histories of English in Africa, Asia, and the Philippines.

The second aspect of this diaspora was that it put English in contact with genetically and culturally unrelated major languages. In Africa, for example, English came in contact with Niger-Congo languages, in Asia with Dravidian languages, and in Southeast Asia with Altaic languages. Historically this was an unprecedented and varied language-contact situation for English. This situation invariably left its mark and contributed to the development of regional contact varieties of English.

The third aspect of the diaspora relates to the traditions and distinct contexts of imparting English education. There was no one "native" model presented to the new learners. A number of teachers of English were from regions where they themselves had learned English as a nonnative language. A large number of missionaries were from Ireland, Wales, Scotland, and even from other parts of Europe (e.g., Belgium). They had inadequate linguistic training for imparting English education. Thus, many learners were not exposed to the native varieties, as is generally believed.

The final aspect of this spread was that English came in contact with a variety of major non-Western cultures and sociolinguistic contexts. That these points have relevance to present world varieties of the language will become clearer in this chapter. However, I am specifically thinking of the current "pluricentricity" of English, which is a result of all the developments specified. I shall return to this point at the end of this chapter.

In retrospect, we see that the story of the spread of English and its consolidation as a world language has actually resulted in three Concentric Circles, as discussed in Chapter 1, Figure 1.1.

There are several sociolinguistic, linguistic, and acquisitional motivations for separating these circles. They correspond to the types of spread, the range of functions of English in a region, the types of literary creativity and experimentation, the patterns of acquisition, and the depth of penetration of English at various societal levels. Note that the preceding circles do not include South Africa (pop. 39,357,000) and Jamaica (pop. 2,538,000). There is a reason for this: In these countries the sociolinguistic situation is very complex, and an accurate estimate of the English-using population is difficult to make.

Dimensions of the Second Diaspora

The sociolinguistic implications and various dimensions of the second diaspora cannot be fully grasped without seeing them in historical, political, and sociological contexts. The major initiator of the diffusion of English was the desire for colonial expansion and an urge to gain strategic control in various parts of the world, first by Britain, and later by the United States. But these two motives were sometimes related to yet another two motives: proselytization and cultural imposition. In attaining these nonlinguistic goals, the English language became a primary tool of communication, administration, elitism, and, eventually, linguistic control (B. Kachru 1986a [1990] and 1986d). English acquired an elitist position through the power it provided its users. As the colonial governments established stable foundations, English acquired vital domains of use. In each part of the colonial empire, the British administrators gave the language status and functional power. What Thomas Babington Macaulay (1800–1859) did in the Indian subcontinent as a senior representative of the Raj in initiating and implementing English education was done by administrators with Macaulay's zeal in other parts of the expanding British Raj (see quote in Chapter 1). One finds many examples of such zeal in Africa and in Southeast Asia.

It is true that often there was a segment of the local elite who supported such moves. And this local support for English was given for pragmatic reasons. In some colonies the local elite saw English as a window to the scientific and technological developments of the Western world. They wanted to partake of

26 The Second Diaspora

the bounty that the Industrial Revolution (1750–1850) had made possible for Europe. Additionally, English was considered a great literary resource, which opened the door to the rich literary traditions of other European languages such as French, German, and Russian through translations.

There were also some missionary groups who supported the cause of English as the language for proselytization. This was, of course, not the position of all the missionary groups. A large portion of missionaries, both in Asia and in Africa, advocated the use of local vernaculars for the spread of Christianity.

And slowly, with the power of the expanding empire behind it, English became a link language for elite populations in multilingual Asia and Africa. English contributed to the creation of a cross-linguistic and cross-cultural network of people who began to use it in the domains of science, technology, military, panregional business, and creative writing (see, e.g., McCrum et al. 1986; Fishman et al. 1977; B. Kachru 1982b and 1986a [1990]). It is primarily for these reasons that English eventually acquired its present status as a global language. However, the universalization of the language exacted a price, primarily that of linguistic and cultural diversification. This diversification increased as the second diaspora of English intensified and increased in terms of functions and social penetration of the language.

In geographical terms, the second diaspora covers a vast territory of the globe. First, it includes those parts where English was introduced during the political colonization of the regions and became a vital colonial linguistic tool (e.g., South Asia, West Asia, Southeast Asia). Second, it covers those parts where historically there are no colonial associations with Britain or the United States, but English is learned as an important additional language (e.g., Nepal, Thailand, Vietnam). A partial list of the second-diaspora countries is provided in the following.[2]

Africa
Botswana (2,155,784); Cameroon (22,534,532); Gambia (1,882,450); Ghana (27,043,093); Ethiopia (99,465,819[1]); Kenya (45,010,056); Lesotho (2,067,000); Liberia (4,503,000); Malawi (16,407,000);

---

[2] Salikoko S. Mufwene: The original figures provided by Braj Kachru were terribly out of date, the latest of them reflecting censuses or estimates of the year 2000. His health and eventual death before the publication of the book prevented him from updating them. Under time constraints, I have turned to Wikipedia to update them, with the earliest estimates or censuses reported in 2009 (in one case) or 2012 in a couple of others. Most of the others are from 2014 or 2015. Some are even from 2016. I have also divided the old Sudan into Sudan and South Sudan, and substituted Dominican Island for the Dominican Republic, since English is not listed as one of the official languages for the latter. Changes in the geopololitics of the Balkans have likewise prompted me to remove Yugoslavia from the list, as it has broken into a number of independent nation-states, which are not listed here, because Kachru did not intend his list to be exhaustive after all.

Mauritius (1,261,208); Namibia (2,113,077); Nigeria (182,202,000); Seychelles (92,000); Somalia (10,816,143); South Africa (54,956,900); South Sudan (12,340,000); Sudan (40,235,000); Swaziland (1,119,000); Tanzania (51,820,000); Uganda (37,873,253); Zambia (16,212,000); Zimbabwe (12,973,808)

South Asia
Bangladesh (171,700,000); Bhutan (742,737); India (1,293,057,000); Nepal (26,494,504); Pakistan (202,971,003); Sri Lanka (20,277,597); the Maldives (393,253)

West Asia
Afghanistan (32,564,342); Bahrain (1,378,000); Israel (8,541,000); Kuwait (4,348,395); Oman (4,441,448); the United Arab Emirates (5,779,760)

Southeast Asia
Brunei (415,717); Myanmar (51,486,253); Hong Kong (7,234,800); Malaysia (31,160,000); Indonesia (255,461,700); the Philippines (102,877,000); Singapore (5,535,000); Thailand (67,959,000); Vietnam (91,700,000)

The Americas and the South Atlantic
Argentina (43,417,000); Ascension Island (880); Belize (368,310); Bermuda (64,237); the Falkland Islands (2,932); Guyana (735,554); Honduras (8,249,574); Nicaragua (6,167,237); Panama (3,929,141); St. Helena (4,255); Suriname (573,311)

The Caribbean
Anguilla (13,600[1]); Antigua and Barbuda (91,295); Bahamas (392,718); Barbados (277,821); the Cayman Islands (56,732); Domica (72,660); Grenada (109,590); Jamaica (2,950,210); Montserrat (4,900); Puerto Rico (3,474,182); St. Kitts and Nevis (54,961); St. Lucia (183,600); St. Vincent and the Grenadines (103,000); Trinidad and Tobago (1,349,667); the Turks and Caicos Islands (31,458); the Virgin Islands (American and British) (144,632)

Oceania
Cook Islands (14,974); Fiji (909,389); Hawaii (1,431,603); Kiribati (103,500); Nauru (10,084); Papua New Guinea (7,059,653); the Solomon Islands (523,000); Tonga (103,036); Tuvalu (10,640); Vanuatu (243,304); Samoa (American and Western) (249,839)

28   The Second Diaspora

Western Europe
The Channel Islands (163,857); Cyprus (1,141,166); Ireland (6,378,000); Malta (445,426)

This list does not include China (1,376,049,000), Western Europe, or what were until recently called the "iron-curtain countries," e.g., Russia (144,192,450), Bulgaria (7,202,198), Czech Republic (10,553,443), Hungary (9,855,571), Poland (38,483,957), Romania (19,511,000), and so on. In these countries the profile of English has suddenly changed, and it is acquiring the status of an important foreign language, replacing Russian.

Diaspora and Diversification

The diaspora naturally resulted in diversification, which resulted from two underlying linguistic processes: *nativization* and *acculturation*. As introduced in Chapter 1, nativization refers to the linguistic readjustments a language undergoes when used by members of another speech community in distinct sociocultural contexts and language contact situations. A language contact situation entails convergence of two or more languages in a bi- or multilingual context. This is a very common linguistic phenomenon in most of the world. In other words, nativization is the approximation of a language to the linguistic and discoursal characteristics of one's native (or dominant) language. On the other hand, acculturation refers to reflection of one's sociocultural identities in a nativized language. It is these two processes that resulted in, for example, the Indianization (B. Kachru 1983b), Africanization (Bokamba 1982 [1992]; Kujore 1985, Zell and Silver 1971) and Singaporeanization (D. Bloom 1986; Foley 1988; Platt and Weber 1980) of English.

In the second diaspora, as these two processes of nativization and acculturation intensified, the English language developed several distinct varieties (see e.g., Bailey and Görlach 1982; B. Kachru (ed.) 1982d; Platt et al. 1984; Cheshire (ed.) 1991). A number of these varieties are already well institutionalized and will be discussed in the following section.

The two diasporas resulted in two types of Englishes: the native transplanted Englishes (e.g., American, Australian, Canadian, New Zealand), and the non-native Englishes (e.g., West African, South Asian, Southeast Asian). However, a caveat is appropriate here: The term "native" that I have used with the "native varieties" is controversial. This term is much less meaningful in multilingual contexts in which the English language is used as one language among two, three, or more. A good discussion on this topic is presented in Paikeday (1985), with arguments from various perspectives.

In Quirk et al. (1985; see also 1972) the question of varieties of English has been discussed in great detail, using a number of descriptive labels. One label

Diaspora and Diversification 29

that is particularly appropriate to the second diaspora varieties of English is "the interference varieties." We must note two major points concerning the concept of INTERFERENCE.

First, this concept manifests the monolingual's view of a language, in this case, that of English. That is not necessarily the view held in multilingual societies. In multilingual contexts all the languages in the verbal repertoire of a user are in some sense "interference varieties." Although the degree of contact and convergence may vary, nevertheless it is present in all the languages used in such societies. The difference is only of degree.

This linguistic fact is significantly articulated in what is known as a linguistic area. It is on the basis of such evidence that characteristics of convergence have been presented in the Balkan linguistic area, the South Asian linguistic area (J. D'souza 1987; Emeneau 1956; Masica 1976), and the Ethiopian linguistic area (Ferguson 1976), to name just three such areas. Interference, then, is the pull of languages toward establishing similarities, and "leveling" in terms of linguistic structures. In the native contexts, too, in the Inner Circle (B. Kachru 1985b), there have been several levels of "interference," but these have been primarily from the European languages, such as French, Spanish, and German. This interaction of European linguistic and literary trends has resulted in what has been called the "European literature" and, in a broader sense, "European civilization." Whether or not pan-Europeanism exists is another question.

The second aspect of the diaspora varieties relates to their acculturation. With the spread of the language and its increased uses in social and literary domains, the process of new non-Western cultural identities is intensified. The impact of such new multicultural identities is particularly marked in the second diaspora of English. The "multicultural" identities of English warrant an explanation here.

Shift of Traditional Interlocutors

English is one of the few languages that are used by a majority of people who speak them as a second, a third, or an nth language. The users have a wide variety of linguistic and cultural backgrounds: an Indo-Aryan language speaker communicating with a Dravidian language speaker, a Japanese with a Taiwanese, and a Nigerian with a Saudi Arabian. Often English is used by groups of nonnative speakers to communicate with other nonnative speakers. There are historical parallels of this situation, but these do not measure up to English in the depth of societal penetration and functional allocation: Latin in medieval Europe (see Kahane and Kahane 1979, 1986); Sanskrit in traditional South Asia, Arabic for religious purposes in the Islamic world, and French in the Francophone countries are some other

30   The Second Diaspora

examples. The traditional belief that English is used by the nonnative speakers only to communicate with the native speakers is a linguistic myth.

The Expansions of the Canon

A language represents a canon of cultural, social, and literary traditions. For example, in the case of Sanskrit the tradition includes more than two thousand years of history, philosophy, and the types of creativity embodied in the *Mahabharata* and the *Ramayana,* the two celebrated epics originally written in Sanskrit. The tradition draws on the *Pali*, the *Prakrtas*, and other classical works. In the case of Persian, the tradition includes the impact of Turkish and Arabic, and the Sufi and Islamic canon. In the areas of cultural and linguistic convergence the traditions blend in the same way that Sanskrit did in Southeast Asia (e.g., Indonesia) and Persian in South Asia (e.g., Bengladesh, India, Pakistan). When English was implanted in Africa, the Philippines, and Asia, the process – typically of such language and cultural contact situations – was repeated. But with English much more happened than mere repetition of the historically established process of convergence. The language was used as a tool to recreate the local sociocultural traditions.

Let me quote here a passage from an Indian metaphysical novelist, Raja Rao (Kanthapura 1938 [1963]: 10), and try to show how it entails contextualization at several levels.

'Today', he says, 'it will be the story of Siva and Parvati.' And Parvati in penance becomes the country and Siva becomes heaven knows what! 'Siva is the three-eyed', he says 'and Swaraj too is three-eyed: Self-purification, Hindu–Moslem unity, Khaddar.' And then he talks of Damayanthi and Sakunthala and Yasodha and everywhere there is something about our country and something about Swaraj. Never had we heard *Harikathas* like this. And he can sing too, can Jayaramachar. He can keep us in tears for hours together. But the *Harikatha* he did, which I can never forget in this life and in all lives to come, is about the birth of Gandhiji. 'What a title for a *Harikatha?*' cried out old Venkatalakshamma, the mother of the Postmaster. 'It is neither about Rama nor Krishna.'- 'But,' said her son, who too has been to the city, 'but, Mother, the Mahatma is a saint, a holy man.'-'Holy man or lover of a widow, what does it matter to me? When I go to the temple I want to hear about Rama and Krishna and Mahadeva and not all this city nonsense', said she. And being an obedient son, he was silent. But the old woman came along that evening. She could never stay away from a *Harikatha*. And sitting beside us, how she wept! ...

The same cultural and literary "ecosystem," to use Thumboo's term (Thumboo 1985b), is found in the following passage of R. K. Narayan's *The Man-eater of Malgudi* (1961: 101):

There was Ravana, the protagonist of Ramayana, who had ten heads and twenty arms, and enormous yogic and physical powers and a boon from the gods that he could never

Diaspora and Diversification 31

be vanquished... Still he came to a sad end. Or take Mahisha, the asura who meditated ... and ... secured an especial favour that every drop of blood shed from his body should give rise to another demon in his own image and strengthen ... the goddess with six arms ... came riding ... on a lion which sucked every drop of blood dropped from the demon ... or think of Daksha, for whom an end was prophesied through the birth of a snake, and he had built himself an island fortress to evade this fate...

This passage is replete with allusions to the epic *Ramayana*; here again there is departure from a shared European canon. One notices greater linguistic demands on the reader who is not part of the extended traditions of English when local aphorisms, proverbs, and idioms are used in English. The message is subtle, and at the same time overwhelming for the reader. Let me give some examples in which the collocations, stylistic conventions, and interpretations depend on understanding the underlying Vedantic philosophy of India. These are from *The Serpent and the Rope* (1960), a metaphysical novel by Raja Rao: *I do not believe that death is* (p. 9); *Resurrection is not because death is, resurrection is because life is* (p. 11O); *God is, and goodness is part of that is-ness* (p. 113); *Water is. So something is. And since is-ness is the very stuff of that something, all you can say is "is is"* (p. 202).

In G. V. Desanis's *All about H. Hatterr* (1951: 102–103) the rich storehouse of Sanskritic compounding provides a source for formations such as *"Ruler of the firmament!; Son of the mightiest bird!";* ... *"thy sister my darling, thy name?";* ... *"Son of thy ill-begotten mother! know, I have no sister. Thy accursed name?"*

In the work of the Nigerian writer Chinua Achebe, as in that of other writers, the translated proverbs contribute to such stylistic identity, e.g., *I cannot live on the bank of the river and wash my hands with spittle; if a child washed his hands he could eat with kings; a person who chased two rats at a time would lose one.*

Okara (1964: 137) is therefore right when, talking about the African writer in English, he says:

For, from a word, a group of words, a sentence and even a name in any African language, one can glean the social norms, attitudes and values of a people.

Thumboo (1985b: 219) further elaborates Okara's point:

Okara and others in a similar situation are neither the first nor the last to attempt a language for their tribes. It is not a question of purifying it. English has its history, culture, and environment, a powerful literary tradition from Chaucer to Ted Hughes, with a connotative reach that does not always apply in the Outer Circle. The denotative provides a substantial common base for all Englishes; the connotative will have to be re- constructed to accord with our individual ecosystems.

It is that "reconstruction" of the language that we find in the previous examples, and in other localized uses of English in its second diaspora.

32   The Second Diaspora

In the second diaspora, English was used as a tool to present distinct canons unrelated to the traditional canonical associations of English; however, this was not always done consciously. The situation was different from that of American English or Australian English, which made attempts to declare "independence" from what may be called "mother English" (see, e.g., B. Kachru 1981a). In spite of an urge for linguistic independence, the first diaspora varieties (e.g., American English, Australian English) were part of the Judeo-Christian tradition and shared the norms of cultural and literary traditions. This was not so for English in Africa, in South Asia, in Southeast Asia, in the Philippines, and elsewhere.

The reasons for this difference are many; the major reason is that English became part of new linguistic, cultural, and philosophical traditions in these parts of the world. The process of establishing such a new identity was slow, but the results eventually were manifested in the language, and the types of creativity for which English was used (see L. Smith 1987). Such uses of English had a great impact in the Outer Circle, both integrative and disintegrative.

It has been well illustrated in several studies that a distinct African and Asian canon was established in the second diaspora of English. What we actually find here is not a break from the earlier European literary and sociocultural canons of the language, but an expansion of the canon: English acquiring multiple canons with distinctly unrelated traditions. It is for this reason, as was discussed in Chapter 1, that a singular designation "English" is less appropriate to refer to the language now than is the plural "Englishes," hence *World Englishes*, which makes more pragmatic and sociolinguistic sense. McArthur has gone even further and suggested the term English "languages," which has an earlier history (McArthur 1986: 213). And so far as the English "literatures" are concerned, the term seems to have been accepted even by those who are unhappy with the pluralization of *English* (see, for example, the subtitle of Quirk and Widdowson 1985: *Teaching and Learning the Language and Literatures*). In this sense, then, English is not only an international language, but it is also one of the most *internationalized* languages.

Discoursal Organization

A linguistic convention in discourse and speech acts reflects the conventions of culture: English in England, Scots in Scotland, and White American and African American in the varieties of English. This also is true of other varieties of English in Australia, Canada, and New Zealand.

What has to be recognized now is that the same phenomenon is repeated in the second diaspora varieties of the language. In recent studies on contrastive

Diaspora and Diversification   33

discourse, several factors about the diaspora varieties have been highlighted. These include:

(1) Recreation of local (e.g., Nigerian, Indian) speech acts, e.g., those of abuses/curses, persuasion, greeting: In fiction, such translated speech acts are particularly used to contextualize the characters. It is true that the frequency of certain types of such translated speech acts is much lower in the spoken varieties of English.
(2) Recreation of cultural and local symbolism: for example, the cultural symbolism associated with words such as *chest, shadow, head, eyes, stomach, mouth,* and *heart* in African English varieties as discussed in Chishimba (1983). The same is true, for example, of the words *touch, defile,* and *pollute* in Indian English, where *touch* has a socio-logical and caste connotation and *defile* and *pollute* have ritualistic connotations.
(3) Presentation of cultural "meanings" that are essentially not shared with the native speaker of the language. Consider, for example, the use of *caste mark, sacred thread, communal attitude, intermarriage* in Indian English.

In other words, the mutual expectancy between the medium and the message has been altered from the traditional conventions. This is done by the use of several stylistic devices. Some common devices are use of nativized similes and metaphors – for example, Chinua Achebe's use of *like a bushfire in the harmattan, like a yam tendril in the rainy season,* or Raja Rao's use of comparative constructions, *as honest as an elephant, as good as kitchen ashes,* and *lean as an areca-nut tree.* A number of such other devices are discussed in B. Kachru (1982a, 1986a).

What are the reasons for this alternation? The major reason is that creativity in English is recognized as part of the national literary traditions. The literary message is universal, as in Chinua Achebe's novels; but the contextualization of the text and its formal manifestations are not necessar-ily shared with other varieties – the text is localized and acquires a national identity. The underlying textual presuppositions establish bonds that are shared within speech fellowships, and not with an extended English-speaking speech community.

Because the speech fellowships are African, South Asian, Southeast Asian, and so on, the discourse strategy adopted must be within the literary and cultural contexts of that fellowship. The Nigerian writer Chinua Achebe in his *Things Fall Apart* (1960: 20) very eloquently explains the motivations for nativizing discourse. He provides two alternate texts and explains why text *A* is more appropriate than text *B*, though *B* is closer to the Western discourse strategies, while *A* is Africanized.

34   The Second Diaspora

In the following short excerpt, the chief priest is explaining to one of his sons the importance of sending him to church. The preferred Africanized version is as follows (Achebe 1960: 20):

I want one of my sons to join these people and be my eyes here. If there is nothing in it you will come back. But if there is something then you will bring back my share. The world is like a mask, dancing. If you want to see it well, you do not stand in one place. My spirit tells me that those who do not befriend the white man today will be saying "had we known", tomorrow.

Now, Achebe asks (1960: 20), "Supposing I had put it another way. Like this for instance":

(b) I am sending you as my representative among those people – just to be on the safe side in case the new religion develops. One has to move with the times or else one is left behind. I have a hunch that those who fail to come to terms with the white man may well regret their lack of foresight.

And Achebe reaches the conclusion that "the material is the same. But the form of the one is in character and the other is not. It is largely a matter of instinct but judgment comes into it too." In other words, the non-Africanized version is not consistent with the linguistic and cultural ecosystem of Africa.

(De)mythologization process

The preceding processes – conscious or unconscious – lead to demytholo-gization of canonical English in more than one way. The concept of DEMYTHOLOGIZATION has various manifestations. For the present purposes it is necessary to explain that canonical English is demythologized first by dissociating the language from the sociocultural and historical assump-tions used in earlier histories of the English language and literature (cf., e.g., Craig 1950; Daiches 1960). Second, it is by considering the Judeo-Christian tradition as only one part of the traditions embodied in world English literatures and linguistic varieties. And third, it is by recognition of non-Western literary traditions and use of these traditions in literary creativity. Such creativity does not now draw only from the European circle of lan-guages, but also from the classical and modem languages and literatures of Asia and Africa (e.g., Bantu, Sanskrit, Chinese), as is evident from the experimentations in Singapore, India, and the Philippines (see, e.g., Thumboo 1985b). Such experimentation also draws from the rich oral traditions of Yoruba, and Swahili, and from the mythologies that are embedded in the literary and oral traditions of Asia and Africa. We find this experimentation in writers such as Raja Rao, Amos Tutuola, and Cathrine Lim, of India, Nigeria, and Singapore, respectively.

The preeceding discussion makes it clearer that "interference" in the diaspora varieties of English has "meaning" if viewed within the sociolinguistic contexts of the diaspora varieties while it appears to be "deviation" if seen without that context (B. Kachru 1982b).

Creativity, Identity, and Sociolinguistic Context

The use of modifiers such as *African, Indian,* and *Singaporean* with English is thus one way to express the relationship and constructs among creativity, identity, and the changed sociolinguistic context of the English language. It has been shown that the closer relationship there is between context and creativity, the greater identity a variety acquires. The issue of identity, of course, is a double-edged sword. The more Asian and African contextualization a variety of English acquires, the greater issues of intelligibility there are at each linguistic level (see, e.g., Nelson 1985 [1992]).

The second diaspora varieties reveal institutionalization in new sociolinguistic contexts in several other ways. First, English is institutionalized by assigning an important role to it in the linguistic repertoire of a speech fellowship. In such repertoires English functions in pluralistic linguistic and cultural contexts. English must, therefore, be viewed as an added member in partnership with other languages. In such sociolinguistic situations, one views language use in terms of domains of function.

In the Outer Circle, English has acquired four vital domains of functions:

- instrumental
- regulative
- interpersonal
- imaginative/innovative

It has an instrumental function as a tool for imparting specialized education (e.g., science, technology); a regulative function in the higher courts and panregional and national administration; an interpersonal function as a link language across linguistic, ethnic, and religious groups; and an imaginative/innovative function in developing local literatures in English (e.g., Nigerian writing in English, Indian writing in English).

The second point takes me back to the imaginative/innovative function of English, especially its role in literary creativity. The most important development concerning the identity of English is the recognition of the creative potential of the language as part of the national literatures in the countries where it is in its second diaspora. Such identity with English, and reflection of the attitudes of identity, shows in numerous ways: in the governmental recognition of English in its integrative roles, for example, as an "associate" official language in India; as the language of administration and education in Singapore; as a language of

36   The Second Diaspora

regional and panregional communication in South Asia, Southeast Asia, and West Africa; in the attitudes that educators, literary writers, and the historians express about English; and in the histories of literatures of the region.[3]

The governmental attitude and the attitude of academies and learned societies are further shown in India by recognizing literature written by Indians in Indian English for annual awards of the National Academy of Letters (Sahitya Academi). In Pakistan the same policy toward English is adopted by the Pakistan Academy of Letters. In other parts of Asia, identical acceptance is given to native English literature, for example, by the Singapore National Book Development Award, the Southeast Asian Writers Award, and the award of the Cultural Medallion for Literature.

A considerable body of literature has developed pleading for the recognition and acceptance of local creativity in English as part of national literary traditions. In several parts of the globe where English is in its second diaspora, there are now histories of local English literatures written by local scholars. What such recognition shows is that English is viewed as an integral part of a nation's extended literary tradition. In some cases, such a tradition dates back more than fifteen decades. In South Asia, to take just one example, the first known Indian poetic work in English, entitled *The Shair and Other Poems,* was published in 1830 by Kasiprasad Ghosh, and the first novel, by another Bengali, Sochee Chunder Dutt, was published in 1845.

However, as we saw in Chapter 1, there is no paucity of writing strongly denouncing the use of English for literary creativity in Asia or Africa. One of the most articulate among these is the work of Ngugi wa Thiong'o, whose position was mentioned in Chapter 1 (see Ngugi 1986).

Commenting on those who "encountered literature in colonial schools and universities," he says their "entire way of looking at the world, even the world of the immediate environment, was Eurocentric" (1986: 93). His book *Decolonising the Mind* was his "farewell to English as a vehicle for any of my writings. From now on it is Kikuyu and Kiswahili all the way" (1986: xiv).

In India, no one has bid farewell to English in Ngugi's style; however Buddhadeva Bose, a distinguished creative writer and critic, was not presenting only his own views when he wrote:

It may seem surprising that Indians, who have always had a firm poetic tradition in their own languages, should ever have tried to write verses in English. That they did so was an outcome of the Anglomania which seized some upper-class Indians in the early years of British rule. (quoted in Lal 1969: 3–4)

---

[3] See Gokak (1970), Iyengar (1962 [1985]), Kandiah (1971), and Wijesinha (1988).

Creativity, Identity, and Sociolinguistic Context 37

However, Bose's view is not a generally accepted one. Iyengar (1962: 3) is closer to the generally accepted attitude when he asks, "How shall we describe Indian creative writing in English?" And he answers: "Of course, it is Indian literature, even as the works of Thoreau or Hemingway are American literature. But Indian literature comprises several literatures ... and Indian writing in English is but one of the voices in which India speaks. It is a new voice, no doubt, but it is as much Indian as others."

In an earlier section, I mentioned that English is one language among many in a multilingual's code repertoire in Asia and Africa. That statement needs further elaboration. In the sociolinguistic contexts of these countries, English has become an integral component in code alternation, that is, in the choice of one linguistic code out of many available to an interlocutor. Code alternation manifests itself in two ways. One manifestation occurs when an interlocutor switches from one language to another depending on the context and the participant(s). For this strategy of a multilingual, the term "code-switching" is generally used.

The following is an example of code-switching from Raja Rao's *The Chessmaster and His Moves* (1988):

"Ça va?" answers Jayalakshmi, adjusting her necklace.
"Est-ce qu'on va le trouver aujourd'hui," he continues, the last word said with such heaviness.
"Si le seigneur le veut." "Mais quel seigneur?"
"Lui," she said with a mischievous smile, as if thinking of someone far away. "Qui donc?"
"Son Altesse le lion." Of course she was speaking a lie. "Le tigre?"
"Non," she said and turned to her father, asking if the mail had come.

Now consider this example of switching to Hindi: "Maji kahan gaye hain?-Acha. Suno. Vo kab arahi hai?-Agaye? Kapada badalke arahi hai? Acha, Padu. Bye-bye" (175). Rao makes no concessions to monolinguals. No clues are given to those who do not know French or Hindi or Sanskrit, and thus linguistic and cultural interpretations of sentences such as the following demand much of the reader: "Our alaya, the true home, is forever the Himalaya" (46); "It is all prarabdha, it's written on our foreheads" (49); "For either you touch suffering, and so suffer, or reach to the other side, and be it. One is kashta and the duhkha" (84); "I bhago-1run" (130); "A Brahmin should not touch jhoota, especially, my jhoota" (130); "And so you and your beads, and the sorrow. Duhkh me duhkh milaja" (108).

The point worth stressing here is that a bilingual or multilingual competence in understanding a text is taken for granted, and in the construction of such texts the monolingual speaker of English seems to have become irrelevant. This is evident even in the newspaper headlines and captions of national and international newspapers. Consider the following from South Asia:

38   The Second Diaspora

(1) Devi Lal leads "Delhi chalo" padyatra (*The Statesman,* New Delhi, December 1985).

(2) Lok Adalat settles 20 (*The Times of India,* December 9, 1985).

In these captions, local lexical items are preferred to their readily available English equivalents, *Delhi Chalo* ("march to Delhi"), *padyatra* ("walk"); *Lok Ada /at* ("people's court"). In these newspapers, the announcements of death in English are equally culture-specific; one has to understand the context and how the English language is used to convey it. A person leaves "for the heavenly abode" *(Hindustani Times* May 20, 1979), because of "the sad demise." There will be, for example, "kirtan and ardasa for the peace of the departed soul" (*Hindustani Times* June 30, 1979). Another way to present such news is that "the untimely tragic death ... of ... happened ... on ... uthaoni ceremony will take place on ..." (*Hindustani Times* June 30, 1979). The cultural and religious pluralism reflects in another way, too. If the dead person is a Muslim, then "his soyem Fateha will be solemnised on ..." and "all the friends and relatives are requested to attend the Fateha prayers" (*Dawn* March 14, 1979). In the case of a Sikh "... kirtan and Antim Ardas will be held at ... " (*Tribune* March 15, 1985), or "bhog of Sri Akhand" path in the everlasting memory of our beloved "will be performed on ..." (*The Tribune March* 15, 1985). And if it is a "holyman," there will be a "homage on the first nirvana anniversary," and "thousand salutations to His Holiness ... who became a part of the Param Tatav on ..." (*Tribune* March 15, 1985).

Another way this method is adopted is to use one language at home, another in the office with one's colleagues, and yet another in the market. We notice this often in Singapore, where the language of home may be Chinese, Tamil, or Malay; that of the office is English; while one might use the English basilect in the market for shopping in inexpensive shopping areas or in what are locally called "hawker centres." In the metropolitan cities of South Asia and Africa the same situation exists.

In such texts what we see, then, is that in the stream of discourse a multilingual user of English may mix two or more languages within a sentence, a clause, a verb phrase, or a noun phrase in which English is one of the constituent languages. Consider the following examples from different parts of the world:

Kiswahili-English
Wambie wakupe *up-to-date image* ya yalitiyotokea *so that you can go ahead with it*

(Tell them to give you an up-to-date image of what happened so that you can go ahead with it.)

(2) Spanish-English
I told him that p'a que la trajera ligero

(I told him that so that he would bring it fast.)

Creativity, Identity, and Sociolinguistic Context

(3) Kannada-English

... nanu *use* madida *strong language-u* eshto *control-madock* nodde adre nanu *educated-u, man of culture-u, broadminded-u* ...

(I tried so much to control the strong language that I used. But forgetting that I am educated, man of culture and broad-minded ...)

(4) Edo-English

Director: *Dial enumber* naa, *n'uiriform'en* Mr. Oseni ighe a *approve encountracti* nii ne. *But* khamaa ren ighe ogha ye *necessary* n'o *submit-e photostat copies* oghe *estimate* n'o ka ya *apply* a ke *pay* ere. *You understand?*

(Dial this number, and inform Mr Oseni that we approved the contract already. But tell him to submit photostat copies of the estimate that he applied with before we pay him. You understand?)

Secretary: *Yes, Sir!* Deghe e irr *office*, ni *dial his house?*

(Yes Sir! If he is not in the office; should I dial his house?)

(5) Chinese-English

Zhege jianglai geke laoshi douhui jiaode: ruhe yong *reference*, ruhe yong *bibliography*, shenme shihou yiao *quotation*, yige *point* yinggai ruhe lai *argue* huozhe *counter-argue*. Zhege numen douhui zhuyide.

(How to use reference, how to use bibliography, when it is appropriate to use quotations, how to argue and counterargue a point, all these your instructors will tell you. And these are the things you ought to pay attention to.)

(6) Filipino-English[4]

I'm sorry saka *nagreduce* ako ngayon e...

(I am sorry but I'm trying to reduce [i.e., diet] today...)

The use of the strategies of code alternation has serious and often far-reaching linguistic attitudinal implications that have been insightfully discussed within the context of English across languages in, for example, Bhatia and Ritchie (1989).

One major implication of the preceding code-alternation with English has resulted the "Englishization" of the world's languages, in the sense of being heavily influenced by English (Kachru 1994). This aspect of English in its second diaspora has yet to be described and discussed across languages, particularly of Asia and Africa. What it involves is the investigation of the

---

[4] Several examples of code-mixing and code-switching given in this chapter are from "Code-Mixing across Languages: Structure, Function, and Constraints" by Nkonko M. Kamwangamalu, Ph.D. dissertation submitted to the University of Illinois at Urbana-Champaign, 1989(a). Actual sources of each example and their sociolinguistic and syntactic analyses are given in Kamwangamalu's dissertation.

40 The Second Diaspora

impact of English on phonology, grammar, morphology, and lexis of the major languages of the world. But the impact goes beyond these traditionally recognized linguistic levels: It has also contributed to developing the style and register-range of languages across the globe and on literatures in these languages (see, e.g., Bhatia and Ritchie 1989, B. Kachru 1982a and 1987a).

Hierarchy of Varieties

The diaspora varieties of English are not homogeneous; nor are they as yet fully documented in terms of their phonological, grammatical, and discoursal characteristics. But their nondocumentation is not a major limitation for our recognition of this sociolinguistic fact. After all, British English and American English existed before these varieties were authenticated by describing their linguistic characteristics. And even now, after years of aggressive attempts to describe the world's languages, there remain hundreds of languages undescribed. But that really makes no serious difference to the users of such languages. It is true that linguistic descriptions make it easier to compare the range of differences in the varieties of a language and contribute to developing pedagogical aids, but that is a different question from the one I am addressing.

It is now recognized that each diaspora variety of English in Asia and Africa has an educated variety and a range of subvarieties. Again, the aspect of a range of subvarieties is not unique, as these sociolinguistic characteristics are shared with the INNER CIRCLE varieties of the language.

A number of variables have been used to determine the subvarieties. The differences in the varieties may be related to the society in two ways, vertically and horizontally. One might, for convenience, vertically categorize the differences in terms of the competence in the use of English. One could use the parameters of education as a variable. Using education as a parameter, sociolinguists have divided some OUTER CIRCLE varieties into three groups: *acrolectal, mesolectal*, and *basilectal.* If we view language varieties as a continuum, acrolectal speakers rank highest on the continuum, since they are normally considered the speakers of the educated or standard variety of the language. Mesolectal speakers rank somewhere in the middle, and the basilectal speakers rank the lowest. In terms of social prestige, the acrolect is considered highest. But that does not mean that the acrolect is necessarily used by the largest number of speakers of a language. It is well established, for example, that although the Received Pronunciation (RP) was for a long time recognized by some as the prestige variety of British English, the total number who actually used it did not exceed 3 percent of the British population.

It has been shown in the literature that this hierarchical classification is not without its problems. In functional terms, the lectal range, a term used for these three lects (or varieties), has well-assigned domains of use. However, an acrolectal speaker may switch among lects, depending on the context. The following example from Malaysia illustrates this point. In the play *Caught in the Middle,* the following strategies have been used: A major part of the dialogue is in English, but there is mixing among three local languages, Bahasa Malaysia, Cantonese, and Tamil. What actually happens in the excerpt is that "'Malaysian English' spoken especially marks a progression toward more realistic language in more realistic settings – the home, the pub."

Mrs. Chandran: Aiee-yah, mow fatt chee ka la (can't do anything about it.) Clean it up, Ah Lan. The rubbish-man will be coming soon, and you know he doesn't take rubbish that isn't nicely packed and tied up.

Ah Lan (the amah): Rubbish is rubbish-lah. Supposed to be dirty, what. Real fussy rubbish-man, must have neat rubbish to take away.

Lloyd Femando explains the motivation for the use of this method, namely, that Malaysian English provides realism to the play (*Caught in the Middle*), and

it explains that with good humor. Malaysian English is now a dialect, recognized as such. In some situations, if you don't speak like that, you are regarded as a foreigner. By using it [viz., Malaysian English] the playwright draws us into the magic circle. (*Asia Week,* May 24, 1987: 64)

Context of Conflict and Rivalry

In its second diaspora, English has naturally not been accepted without resistance. There is a long history of linguistic conflict and rivalry. On the one hand, there has always been a group of scholars who accept this historical fact of the addition of English to the local linguistic repertoire with enthusiasm. On the other hand, there are others who continue to consider English an intruder, slowly nibbling away the linguistic domains that in their view rightfully belong to local languages.

The controversy started when English was introduced in Africa and Asia some two centuries ago and has continued ever since. Furthermore, the positions concerning the continuation of English have not changed much since that period. At present, what we have, on the one hand, is the visible diffusion of English, and, on the other hand, there are well-articulated slogans for the curtailment of English. One sees these positions about language, for example, in Shah (1968), and in Bailey (1990 and 1996).[5] Even in countries where the

---

[5] Over the years a vast body of literature presenting various viewpoints and attitudes on this topic has developed. Shah's collection and Bailey's paper are just illustrative.

42   The Second Diaspora

educators and politicians adopt the public posture of curtailment of English, no effort is made to curtail its "invisible" spread.

Diaspora Varieties and Issues of Standards

The concerns about the standards of English in its second diaspora date back to the period when English was introduced in the colonies. These concerns were not much different from those expressed earlier about the models for standards in Britain or the United States or in Australia. Let me give just one example here. In 1863, the Very Reverend Henry Alford, D. D., Dean of Canterbury, in his "Plea for the Queen's English" said, "Look at the process of deterioration which our Queen's English has undergone at the hands of Americans. Look at those phrases which so amuse us in their speech and books, at their reckless exaggeration and contempt for congruity" (cited in B. Kachru 1981a: 23).

The case of English in the Asian and African colonies was, however, different in one respect. As discussed in Chapter 1, there was no significant population of native speakers who were part of the second diaspora of the language; that is, there was no serious input from the native speakers to stabilize an exonormative standard for the language. Nor were there many societal interactional contexts, in which the local English knowers and the native speakers interacted in English. In fact, chances for such encounters were minimized as much as possible. Naturally, given the limited local uses of English in the beginning, the main yardstick concerning standards was intelligibility with the native speakers. That this yardstick is presently misleading in several sociolinguistic contexts and is based on several fallacies has been the focus of many studies in recent years. The major positions on the issues of international and intranational standards and norms for English are presented in Quirk (1988 and 1989), and in B. Kachru (1991).

By now it is obvious that the sociolinguistic profile of English outlined in this chapter is significantly different from that assumed in traditional literature and assumptions on this topic. Let me review three major points of difference here. The first concerns pluricentricity, which includes centers in the regions where English is in its second diaspora. Earlier, English had only one recognized center for the norms of standard, literary creativity and linguistic experimentation. That center continued to be England during the peak of the colonial period. Then, slowly and, I might add, reluctantly another center was recognized: the United States. The struggle for the recognition of American English, and literature produced in it, is a fascinating study in understanding crosscurrents in language attitudes. But now, the norm-providing centers of English – as nodes of its creativity and experimentation – have multiplied during the past half-century and now include non-Western, non-Judeo-Christian,

Conclusion 43

multilingual, and multicultural societies. I have used the terms *multilingual* and *multicultural* with special intent, for these two contexts have serious implications for the creativity and thus for the development of world varieties of English.

The point of pluricentricity and the "shifting" of the center of English is recognized by Steiner (1975: 4), who is introduced in Chapter 1, but quoted here more fully:

The first, most obvious point to make is that the linguistic centre of English has shifted. This is so demographically. Great Britain now makes up only a small portion of the English-speaking totality. 'Totality', furthermore, is quite the wrong word. The actual situation is one of nearly incommensurable variety and flux. Any map of 'world-English' today, even without being either exhaustive or minutely detailed, would have to include the forms of the language as spoken in many areas of east, west and south [ern] Africa, in India, Ceylon, and United States possessions or spheres of presence in the Pacific. It would have to list Canadian English, the speech of Australia, that of New Zealand, and above all, of course, the manifold shades of American parlance. Yet, although such a catalogue would comprise hundreds of millions of English-speakers whose idiolects and communal usage would vary all the way from West Indian speech to Texan, or from the cadences of Bengal to those of New South Wales and the Yukon, it would be very far from complete.

The second point takes us back to the question of multicultural identities of English in diaspora, which I have briefly discussed earlier. This aspect of the English language today has not been well recognized in the literature, but it is an important aspect and has serious implications for understanding the issues of intelligibility, pragmatics, and cross-cultural discourse (for a detailed discussion, see Y. Kachru 1991a; Nelson 1985 [1992]).

The third point concerns the overused term *native speaker* and the acceptance of this term as a cardinal concept. The diaspora varieties of English raise several theoretical and functional questions concerning this concept.

Conclusion

The importance of the second diaspora to the sociolinguistic profile of English language and literature has been studied seriously during the last two decades. We still do not have more than marginal descriptions of what are erroneously termed *New Englishes*. It seems to me that the expansion of English, particularly in its second diaspora, has not reached its climax; nor are there any indicators as yet that increasing ethnic and linguistic nationalism has arrested the spread of English in a serious sense. What we see is that the present political developments around the world, and particularly those of the 1980s in Eastern Europe and China, have further opened up large regions for world Englishes.

44   The Second Diaspora

The leaders of nationalist movements in Asia and Africa have two faces about English, a public anti-English face and a private pro-English face. And so far, numerically and functionally, the spread of English has not been affected. If one country adopts an anti-English attitude, there are two countries that recognize English in their policies and open their institutions and purses for the teaching of the language. Such language policy shifts occur both in Asia and Africa.

In the second diaspora of English, a large number of bilingual/multilingual speech communities have adopted and recognized it as a vital additional language. The sociolinguistic implications and effects of such an adoption are that the English language has emerged from its traditional Western fold and has imbibed many new linguistic conventions and cultural and literary traditions. One has to recognize this unparalleled linguistic change, since the role of English in its social context will be only partially understood if the contexts of convergence and change of World Englishes are not viewed in appropriate sociolinguistic and pragmatic contexts. What is needed is a perspective that is integrative and considers function as crucial to our understanding of language dynamics.

3   Culture Wars

Introduction

This chapter addresses two issues currently debated internationally about the presence of the English language in the global context: one of celebration and truimphalism, and the other of the use of the language as part of the arsenal in what has been termed civilizational *culture wars*.*

The spread of English is characterized in subtle and not-so-subtle tones as a triumphalistic march of the language, which has gained global currency over other major languages (see e.g., Crystal 1997, and for another perspective, Kachru 1986a). In this triumph of English across cultures, it is now generally recognized that the Hydra-like language has many heads: the heads representing diverse cultures and identities. The language, as I have said elsewhere (e.g., B. Kachru 1994e), represents the legendary status of the "Speaking Tree." This legend goes back at least two millennia, to the period of Alexander the Great. It is said that the great warrior king was taken in India "to an oracular tree, which could answer questions in the language of any [one] who addressed it" (Lannoy 1971: xxv).

The tree was unmatched, says the legend – the trunk of the tree was made of snakes and animal heads, and its branches "bore fruit like beautiful women, who sang the praises of the Sun and Moon" (xxv). The tree acquired a special status in the Islamic tradition and in the Mughal miniature, and is called the Waqwaq Tree (i.e., "the Speaking Tree"); there are versions of this legend in other cultures, too. The Waqwaq Tree is viewed with feelings of awe and attraction. The metaphor of the Speaking Tree, therefore, represents many sentiments: fear and celebration, aversion and esteem, and, indeed, agony and ecstasy.

The trunk of the English language tree, the Inner Circle, continues to evoke reactions of suspicion, of conspiracies, and of mistrust (see, e.g., Fettes 1991;

---

* This chapter is a somewhat modified version of my Sir Edward Youde Memorial Fund Lecture, delivered on November 30, 1998, at the University of Hong Kong, Hong Kong. It incorporates some major points discussed in some other papers, particularly B. Kachru (1994e, 1996a, and 1996b).

46   Culture Wars

Fishman et al. 1996; B. Kachru 1996b and 1998a; Pütz 1995). There continues to be a lingering Trojan horse association with the language and its managers, not only in Asia and Africa but even in the United Kingdom and the United States.

There is, however, another reality that has haltingly, but certainly, emerged since the 1950s. After a long and agonizing wait, the branches of the Waqwaq Tree are bearing a delectable fruit: the fruit of accessibility to a variety of methetic functions through the language, in a shared medium of pluralistic identities. It is in this sense of multiplicity and pluralism that English has become a "global access" language. What Salman Rushdie says of his much-discussed *The Satanic Verses* (1989: 394) by extension is actually true of World Englishes. It stands for "change-by-fusion, change-by-conjoining. It is a love song to our mongrel selves." It actually is a celebration of syncretism.

This takes me to the first part of the title: the concept of WORLD ENG-LISHES.[1] This concept entails a distinction between language as a "medium" and language as a "message." The medium refers to the *form* of language – its phonology, morphology, and syntax – and the message embodies the *functions* in which the medium is used. There are indeed a variety of underlying theoretical, functional, pragmatic, and methodological reasons that demand this pluralization of the language: Englishes and not English (see e.g., Kachru 1994e).[2]

The concept of WORLD ENGLISHES, then, emphasizes the pluricentricity of the language and its cross-cultural reincarnations. This conceptualization about the functions and multiidentities of English has, therefore, become a loaded weapon for those who view the spread of the language exclusively in terms of the celebration of the Judeo-Christian mantras of the language – the view that the "global," "international," and "world" presence of the language is essentially a victory of what is perceived as a monocultural Western medium, and that the language is the English-using West's weapon in the clash of civilizations.[3] That view, as I will discuss later, does not represent the current global state of the language or the identities English has created across cultures. These discourses and narratives of the global triumph of the language need serious reevaluation in terms of functional pragmatism – especially that of multiple canonicity in Englishes – British, North American, African, and

---

[1] For a state-of-the art survey of the history and conceptualization of World Englishes, and a selected list of annotated references on this topic for research and teaching, see B. Kachru (1998a).

[2] See, for example, Bautista (1996 [1997]) for the Asianization of English. See also Burchfield (1994), Butler (1996), Cheshire (1991), and B. Kachru (1992d) for extensive references on cross-cultural and cross-linguistic functions and identities of World Englishes.

[3] It is, of course, an oversimplification to use hyphenated cover terms such as *Judeo-Christian*, and to claim that there is a monolithic Western tradition and that all Western countries share that one tradition. That would be a broad and misguided generalization.

Asian. In other words, what we need is a conceptualization of World Englishes in a framework of pluricentricity and distinct cultural canon formation.

The issue of canonicity is critical here, since canons, as Kermode ([1979], cited in Altieri 1990: 22) rightly reminds us, are essentially "strategic constructs by which societies maintain their own interests." And canons also provide two types of control. First is the control over the texts that "a culture takes seriously," and second is control "over the methods of interpretation that establish the meaning of serious."

The "loose canons" of English, to use the term of Henry Gates Jr. (1992), have yet to acquire this control, because the major paradigms in English studies, literary or linguistic, have not initiated any meaningful discussion of the global presence of English from these perspectives – the perspectives that the cultural identities and their *interpretations* have also become pluralistic.[4]

In the discourse on English outside the Inner Circle, references to Caliban, both as a symbol and as a metaphor, are frequent. So now let me draw Caliban into this discussion; I shall decontextualize Caliban from its territorial contexts of colonized human beings in a part of the Western Hemisphere. Whatever happened on that island symbolizes what has happened in the colonized world, irrespective of languages and cultures. In all colonial contexts, Caliban is assigned a space by control and submission. Caliban is told:

> I pitied thee,
> Took pains to make thee speak, taught thee each hour
> One thing or other: . . .
> I endowed thy
> purposes
> With words that made them known.

And Caliban answers:

> You taught me language, and my profit on't
> Is I know how to curse. The red plague rid you
> For learning me your language!

This metaphor, then, is central to these ongoing, vibrant, and often acrimonious and provocative debates about the canons that are at linguistic and literary peripheries and continue to be associated with Caliban's curse. The users of such canons, as Salman Rushdie warns us, are

kept strictly apart, like squabbling children, or sexually incompatible pandas, or, perhaps, like unstable, fissile materials whose union might cause explosions. (1991: 61)

---

[4] See e.g., B. Kachru (1996b) for a detailed discussion and relevant references.

48   Culture Wars

The debates about these Calibans' voices, their status, and the location of such voices within the canonicity of Englishes have become increasingly articulate. The questions these voices raise in West, East, and Southern Africa; in South and East Asia; in the Philippines; and even in the United States and United Kingdom, are not unrelated to the broader debate on "opening of the borders" and what Gates Jr. has termed "loose canons" (1992). These are significant linguistic, attitudinal, and ideological questions.

And when Levine (1996) addressed this question, he was essentially providing counterarguments to Bloom (1987) and to a string of books by D'Souza (1991), Bennett (1992), and Bernstein (1994), to name just four authors who articulate a need to guard the borders of the Western canon.

The concerns of Bloom and D'Souza are not necessarily related to Caliban's uncontrollable tongue; nor are they directly related to the discussion in this chapter. Rather, it is the underlying conceptualizations basic to these two approaches, to canon and canonicity, to language and language ownership, and to identities, that are relevant here.

This issue, then, takes me to the question regarding the ongoing "culture wars" of our times and the agendas for the new millennium. In these culture wars we see that language, the English language, is now a major issue. It has indeed become a vital weapon for articulating various positions and visions.

The issues in this debate touch us, all of us, as members of the English-using speech community, irrespective of the variety of the language we use or the speech fellowship of English with which we identify. These speech fellowships of English cover all the continents, all major cultures, and almost all the major geographical groups.

It is in that diverse, cross-cultural sense that English is *international*. And note that I have avoided the term *international language* with reference to English. The use of the term "international" with "English" is misleading in more than one sense: it signals an *international* English in terms of acceptance, proficiency, functions, norms, and creativity. That actually is far from true; that is not the current international functional profile of the language.[5]

Cassandras of English

The English language is now the most sought-after medium for initiating and accelerating bilingualism or multilingualism. This crossover of borders has given various strands of pluralism to the language. The need, then, is for the reconstruction and rethinking of what pluralism implies with

---

[5] I believe that the much-abused term *lingua franca* is also misleading – and functionally inappropriate – when applied to the sociolinguistic profile of World Englishes. I have discussed this point in Kachru (1996a).

reference to creativity in the language and its functions and in our conceptualization of English around the world.

And now, at the beginning of a new millennium, this reconstruction of English has taken several forms. And more Cassandras have appeared on the scene with their messages and visions of the doom and decay of the language. This soothsayer's enterprise has developed into a variety of genres. Their sociolinguistic speculations about English are based on what they see in their ideological crystal balls and crystal gazing for now, and beyond the end of the millennium. And English is vigorously being related exclusively to Western civilization and to the conflicts in the "remaking of world order." In their view – the Cassandras' view – the major concerns about the English language are varied. I will, however, discuss just two such concerns to illustrate my point.

Demographic Shrinking and Decline

The first concern regards what is perceived as the demographic shrinking of the English language. This concern is quite contrary to the current statistical profile of the language, and to the increasing worldwide perception that the juggernaut of English is rolling over cultures and languages, major and minor, across the world.

One example of Cassandra's cry about the decline of English is provided by Bailey (1987), who argues that

popular journalism, and academic inquiry have all conspired to obscure a remarkable basic fact ... [that] ... English, too, is *declining* in proportional numbers of speakers and in the range of its users. [Emphasis added]

Bailey's concern for the decline in the numbers of users and the functional range of English is based on five phenomena:

First, the initiatives to "foster multilingualism" in the USA, UK, and Australia;
Second, the efforts – in the USA and internationally – in linking "mother, mother tongue, and motherland" as "persuasive arguments" to declare that languages other than English will better serve *democratic* and *economic* goals" (1987: 6);
Third, the national language policy reversals and reassessments that entail shifts toward languages other than English (e.g., in Malaysia, the Philippines, and Singapore);
Fourth, the "cultural resistance to English in East and West Africa;
And *fifth*, the increasing "pluricentricity of English": that is the multiple centers in Asia and Africa where the language has developed institutionalized norms.

Bailey, of course, is not the first Cassandra of the language and certainly not the last.

A later articulation of this view is that of Huntington, a distinguished Harvard political scientist, in his provocative book *The Clash of Civilizations and the*

50   Culture Wars

Table 3.1 *Huntington's assessment of the world's major languages in percentages speakers.*

Year	1958	1970	1980	1992
Language				
Arabic	2.7	2.9	3.3	3.5
Bengali	2.7	2.9	3.2	3.2
English	9.8	9.1	8.7	7.6
Hindi	5.2	5.3	5.3	6.4
Mandarin	15.6	16.6	15.8	15.2
Russian	5.5	5.6	6.0	4.9
Spanish	5.0	5.2	5.5	6.1

Remaking of World Order (1996a). A more accessible, and somewhat alarming, summary of the book appeared in *Foreign Affairs* (1996b, vol. 75: 6), with the sweet and sour title "The West Unique: Not Universal." The parts that specifically interest me relate to the English language. I do, however, share Huntington's broad concern when he says that

in recent years Westerners have reassured themselves and irritated others by expounding the notion that the culture of the West is and ought to be the culture of the world. (1996a: 28)

In his view, as he says, "this conceit manifests itself in two forms. One is the Coca-colonization thesis... The other has to do with modernization." And he believes that

both these project the image of an emerging homogeneous, universally Western world – and both are to varying degrees misguided, arrogant, false, and dangerous. (28)

Huntington provides the profiles of speakers of major languages represented in Table 3.1 (in terms of percentages of the world's population). The profile leads him to two conclusions relevant to English: first, "that significant declines occurred in the population of people speaking English, French, German, Russian, and Japanese" (1996a: 60); second, that "a language foreign to 92 percent of the people in the world cannot be the world's language" (1996a: 60).

Severing the Umbilical Cord

The second concern relates to yet another type of perceived decay – the "decay" of the language as it is appropriated by the Anglophone African and Asian countries, who are severing their umbilical cord from the Inner Circle, or the original native speaking countries, and are, thus, making English a culturally pluralistic world language. This appropriation, in their view, colors the

Severing the Umbilical Cord 51

language in a variety of ways – linguistic, literary, and ideological – rendering it alien to its Occidental "owners." Even worse, they believe a *hybrid English* is becoming institutionalized and recognized as a viable vehicle for African and Asian norms for linguistic innovation and creativity. And yet another expression of the concern over this phenomenon is an epilogue entitled "Alice's Unvisited" by Felipe Femandez-Armesto (1995). In his peep into futurology, Femandez-Armesto's regret is that communications have been unable to "homogenize culture." A most "surprising example" of this, according to him, is that of the English language,

which, until recently, was widely hailed or feared as the world medium of the future; in fact, in defiance of the predicted effects of global broadcasting, *the English of the English-speaking world is breaking up into mutually unintelligible tongues, as happened with Latin in the dark ages.* (1995: 730; emphasis added)

This, for Fernandez-Armesto, is not a reassuring future, and his pessimistic interpretation of the horoscope of English is that

Krio, Pidgin, and Negerengels are already unintelligible to speakers of other forms of post-English. The street patois of African-American communities has to be translated for residents of neighbouring streets. The specialized jargon of communication on the Internet is a hieratic code, professed to exclude outsiders. Copy editors and authors on either side of the Atlantic sometimes keenly feel the width of the ocean. (1995: 730–731)

This agony is identical to Bailey's earlier concern when he saw "English at its twilight." The metaphor "twilight" is like a double-edged sword, which can be a harbinger of "bright morning" for the English language or can be frightening and murky to the tower builders at Babel (1990: 84).[6]

One has to agree with Huntington's (1996b: 62) more forthright and pragmatically correct observation:

The people who speak English throughout the world also increasingly speak different Englishes. English is indigenized and takes on local colorations which distinguish it from British or American English and which, at the extreme, make these Englishes almost unintelligible one to the other, as is also the case with varieties of Chinese.

That English has been "indigenized" is certainly true; however, that "these Englishes" have, therefore, become "almost unintelligible one to the other" is certainly empirically doubtful (see e.g., Smith 1992). In terms of functional and pragmatic uses of the English language, what actually happens is that English is used effectively for "thinking globally" and used, by choice, "to live locally," thus establishing a pragmatic link between the two identities.[7]

---

[6] I have responded to some of these issues in B. Kachru (1996b).
[7] This observation has been made by the Indian critic and educator C. D. Narasimhaiah (1991: viii).

52   Culture Wars

I do not intend to respond to each point raised by Bailey and Huntington here. One major point, however, must be addressed, and that is Huntington's observation that a language not used by "92 percent of the people" is not entitled to the label a *world language*.

There are four problems with this assumption. The first relates to the total percentage of English users. Recent estimates of users of English worldwide, as stated earlier, vary from 1 to 2 billion. If we take the lower number, then of the 5.63 billion people in the world, 18 percent use English. If we take the higher number, the percentage of English users jumps to 36 percent. In either case, the important point is that, whichever figure is used, the nonnative users of English outnumber the native users. Huntington does not, for whatever reason, address that vital point about global English. This is an unparalleled linguistic phenomenon and has a number of theoretical, methodological, pedagogical, and indeed ideological implications.

The second point is that the communicative functions of English across cultures (see Table 3.2) are distinctly different from those of Mandarin, Hindi, and Spanish – some of the competing languages listed by Huntington. The English language has developed a unique functional range and unique identities on every continent. In India now, an estimated figure of English users is about 333 million, and there are more than 200 million students enrolled in English programs in China.[8] It is a reality that the sun has already set on the empire, but it does not set on the users of English.

The third point is that Huntington and Bailey – to name just two writers – do not make a distinction between the COMPARATIVE FUNCTIONAL DOMAINS of languages and their number of speakers: they do not rank languages in terms of their RANGE of functions (what one can do with a language) or in terms of their social PENETRATION (how deep the language use is in the social hierarchy), particularly in what are generally labeled "nonnative" contexts.

The functional domains of English across the three circles are as follows: as mentioned earlier, the Inner Circle represents countries such as the United States, Britain, and Australia, where English is widely used as a first language;

---

[8] My earlier figure of more than 60 million users of English in India is already out of date. A survey by *India Today*, Delhi (August 18, 1997), shows that "contrary to the [Indian] census myth that English is the language of a microscopic minority, the poll indicates that almost one in every three Indians claims to understand English, although less than 20 percent are confident of speaking it."
The estimated population of India is is more than 1 billion; almost 200 million of them have some spoken competence in English, and 333 million say they understand the language. Thus, India's English-using speech community is estimated to be numerically equal to the total population of the United States, the United Kingdom, and Canada. The total English-using populations of India and China add up to 533 million. For China, see Yong and Campbell (1995); see also B. Kachru (1998b). [The demographics of English speakers provided here by Braj Kachru have not been updated, as the sources are not available to the editor. SSM]

Table 3.2 *Communicative functions of English in the Inner, Outer, and Expanding Circles.*

Function	Inner Circle	Outer Circle	Expanding Circle
Access Code	+	+	+
Advertising	+	+	+
Corate trade	+	+	+
Develo_Q_ment	+	+	+
Government	+	+	
Linguistic_im_Q_act	+	+	+
Literacy creatiy Y	+	+	+
Liter_renaissance	+	+	+
News broadcasting	+	+	+
New ers	+	+	+
Scientific higher edu.	+	+	+
Scientific research	+	+	+
Social interaction	+	+	+

the Outer Circle represents countries such as India, Nigeria, and Singapore, where English is institutionalized; and the Expanding Circle represents countries such as China, Japan, and Korea, where the diffusion of English has come about relatively recently.

Now, compare this overwhelming range and depth with those of other languages of wider communication, e.g., Mandarin, Hindi, Spanish, Arabic, and so on. No other language is close to English in its penetration in various social levels. This is clearly reflected in varieties that have developed within a variety, as in Singapore, Nigeria, and India, to give just three examples.

The fourth point relates to the life of English in the postimperial period. Bailey, for example, says that in Malaysia, the Philippines, and Singapore there are language policy *reassessments* toward languages other than English. This statement is only partially correct. In fact, the direction of the reassessment is in favor of English.

In Malaysia in the 1990s, for example, the reversal of the national language policy in favor of English indicates "compromise over its cultural convictions" (*Economist*, January 15, 1994).

"There would have been riots over this ten years ago," says Rustum Sani, a leading member of the pro-Bahasa lobby... Dr. Mahathir, ever the pragmatist, has said *that English is necessary if the country is to stay competitive.* [Emphasis added]

Malaysia's senior educator, Asmah Haji, puts this pragmatism in the right cultural context when she says:

Attitudes toward English have changed most significantly among the Malays. English is looked at *as an entity which can be separated from English culture.* This is evident in

54   Culture Wars

the urging *"to learn English but not to ape the Western* [meaning Anglo-American] *culture."* (Fishman, Conrad, Rubal-Lopez, 1996: 532) [Emphasis added]

In the Republic of Singapore, English always had the status of a dominant language. Now English is gradually being elevated to the status of *first* language by the younger generation, who do not hesitate to consider English their "mother tongue."

In the Philippines, the debate about English is also vibrant. A venerable English writer of the Philippines, Francisco Sionil Jose, says that "English has not colonized us but we have colonized the language," by using it as an exponent of the Philippine culture. There are a new revival, and a fresh awakening, about the use of a liberated English in the Philippines (see Bautista 1997).

The message here is that statistics and the numerical profiles provide some indicators of VISIBLE language and educational policies but tell us almost nothing about what Edwin Thumboo and Anne Pakir, for example, have called INVISIBLE policies, about attitudes and about identities in the context of Singapore. The invisible trade in the spread of the English language is extensive and has developed into a multibillion-dollar industry, under the name of "the ELT Empire" (Butler 1996), with ELT meaning "English Language Teaching."

The recent document by David Graddol (1997) entitled *The Future of English? A Guide to Forecasting the Popularity of the English Language in the 21st Century* is yet another attempt at the crystal gazing initiated by the British Council. The patron of the council, Prince Charles, in his foreword to the volume, accurately contextualizes it by saying that the council's "task is to promote Britain and the English language throughout the world." Prince Charles adds that, as part of this effort, the British Council's English 2000 project "aims to forecast the use of English and help develop approaches to the language which will meet new demands and challenges."

I will not comment on this document here. But it is relevant to point out that it is essentially a political document. It hardly has any reference to the most vibrant debate about the constructs of identities and functions of English by any African or Asian scholar. There is no discussion on the issue related to identity, innovation, and creativity, as well as to distinct canon formation, which resulted in Achebe's emphasizing that his vision of creativity in English is "necessarily local and particular." That process of "opening up the canon" in Asia and Africa is part of the vision Graddol ignores. There are perhaps two reasons for this. First, the document was essential as a part of "scare tactics" against the serious threats of budget cuts for the council from the then-Thatcher governnment.

Second, that vision of the English language would not be consistent with the prince's articulated position at the English 2000 function that the volume celebrates. At that function, Prince Charles declared that the American version of the language was "very corrupting" and the English version was the "proper" one. And he encouraged the British Council:

We must act now to ensure that English – and that to my way of thinking means English English – maintains its position as the world language well into the next century.

And we must be fair to Prince Charles: he is not alone in taking this position. There are others – politicians, scholars, publishers, and so on – very zealously guarding what is perhaps the major export commodity of Britain. It is said that "Britain's real black gold is not North Sea oil, but the English language" (Romaine 1992).

Medium (*Madhyama*) vs. Message (Mantra)

In the preceding perceptions there is an underlying concern about Caliban's linguistic curse: the way Caliban contextualizes and recreates the medium. In its new incarnations, English has become a repertoire of culturally specific African and Asian messages (mantras). It is true that this distinction has existed from the preimperial period. But now, in the postimperial period, it is being articulated more vigorously.

The pluralism of the message is partly indicative of crossovers from what is perceived as the center of English. It is with reference to the center that the peripheries were traditionally defined. It is a shift, then, from the Judeo-Christian and Western identities of the English language toward its African, Asian, and African American visions. In these multiple identities of the language the pluralism of World Englishes – the *madhyama*, the medium – is shared by us, all of us, as members of the World Englishes community. The mantras, the messages and discourses, represent multiple identities and con-texts and visions. The mantras are diverse, cross-cultural, and representative of a wide range of conventions. It is precisely in this sense that the medium has indeed gained international diffusion; it has broken the traditional boundaries associated with the language.

When we use epithets such as *global, international*, and *universal* with English, we are not necessarily talking of homogeneity and uniformity. We should not. The messages have to be learned, acquired, absorbed, and appreci-ated within the appropriate cultural contexts of the mantras. The medium provides a variety of shifting cultural "grids" through which we gain access to the multiple canons of the language: American, British, West African, East African, South Asian, East Asian, and so on.[9]

---

[9] For further discussion of this topic see papers in Hardgrave (1998).

56   Culture Wars

Exponents of Multiple Canonicity

The multiple canonicity of World Englishes manifests itself in many subtle ways: formal and attitudinal, one overlapping with the other, and in turn, each contributing to distinct canons with one shared thread – that of the medium (mantra). The divergence and crossovers of these varieties of English are of the following types:

1. *Identification specific to a variety* e.g., Nigerian English, Singaporean English;
2. *Acculturation of the variety* e.g., reflection of sociocultural, religious, and interactional contexts;
3. *Institutionalization of discourse strategies, speech acts, and genres;*
4. *Recontextualization of icons of identity* e.g., relating creativity to local literary and cultural traditions (*parampara*); and
5. *Alteration of textual texture*, e.g., by embedding devices of "mixing," etc. (B. Kachru 1998c).

In these shifts and crossovers, the boundaries of the center, as embodied in the language, are permeable. The periphery increasingly moves into the foreground. This crossover results in a reconstruction of the language in "accord with our individual ecosystems," as Thumboo (1985b) sees it. The attempt here is to establish a relationship between formal characteristics of the text – that is, its linguistic texture – and the contexts in which the language functions.

These crossovers entail recognition of three realities:

First, that the medium is shared by two distinct types of speech communities: those that perceive themselves as monolingual and those that are *multilingual* and *multicultural*.

Second, that there is a long tradition of distinct literary and/or oral traditions and mythologies associated with these communities; and

Third, that they represent distinct repertoires of stylistic and literary creativity.

Toward a Historiography of Canonicity

The historiography of the canonicity of Englishes in Asia and Africa, indeed in all the peripheries, has yet to be written in any serious sense. The peripheries have traditionally been ignored by literary historians.

A recent example of such neglect is *The Cambridge History of the English Language*, Vol. V, devoted to "English in Britain and Overseas." The planning of the volume, we are told, began in 1984, and the volume was ultimately published in 1994. The introduction tells us:

Toward a Historiography of Canonicity   57

It was the notable lack of professional scholarship at the time on the English of African countries such as Kenya, Nigeria, Tanzania and so on ... that led to the exclusion of these varieties [from the volume]. (Burchfield, 1994: 4)

The editor patronizingly assures us that "their turn will come one day." It is worth mentioning, however, that the volume edited by Bailey and Görlach, published in 1982, found no lack of such "professional scholarship." They were able to include surveys on English in East, West, and Southern Africa. In the same year, in putting together an edited volume, *The Other Tongue*, I had no problem in obtaining a scholarly survey of the Africanization of English and another study on "Kenyan English." The moral seems to be "Look and you will find." In contrast, the don't-look-and-you-won't-find attitude is also evident in many scholarly books meant to assess "the state of the language" – the English language.

One such book in particular comes to mind, perhaps because of its title: *The State of the Language*. This book was edited by Leonard Michaels and Christopher Ricks, was published in 1988, and had a 1990 edition by the same editors with the names reversed. The latest edition, the jacket tells us, provides *"new observations, objections, angers, bemusements, hilarities, perplexities, revelations, prognostications, and warnings for the 1990s."* The learned editors apparently, however, did not find any such aspects of English language use in Africa and Asia that would characterize the state of the English language or literature. These two volumes are the results of projects initiated by the English-Speaking Union, San Francisco; and the publication of the 1990 volume is, we are told, "supported by a generous grant from the George Frederick Jewett Foundation." The omissions made in these volumes are clear indicators of the attitudes toward Caliban's creativity (see also Kachru 1992d: 1–15, particularly pp. 2–3).

The stirrings for canonicity in World Englishes have a long history. These issues of identity and innovations in creativity are not extensions of the "liberation theology" of the 1960s, resulting in articulation of "liberation linguistics," as is argued in the literature.[10]

Nor did this institutionalization begin with the "Rushdiesque language" or "Rushdie's technique," attributed to Salman Rushdie. In reality, the "hybrid form" and "radical linguistic operation" (Langeland 1996: 16) associated with Rushdie follow in the tradition of much earlier linguistic innovations and creativity in African and Asian English.

The earliest conceptualizations of indigenization go back to the 1870s. And later reformulations, and more specific characterizations, began after the

---

[10] For different perspectives on the major issues and attitudes, particularly on "liberation linguistics," see papers in Tickoo (1991), especially section III.

58   Culture Wars

1930s. We see characterizations of African Englishes in Nigeria's Chinua Achebe, T. M. Aluko, Buchi Emecheta, Amos Tutuola, and, of course, Wole Soyinka; in Kenya's Ngugi wa Thiong'o; in Somalia's Nurudin Farah; of Indian English in Raja Rao, Mulk Raj Anand, Anita Desai, and R. K. Narayan; and of other regional or national Englishes in a long list of writers from Malaysia, the Philippines, Singapore, and Sri Lanka.

In South Asia the first well-articulated conceptualization of such crossover – linguistic and contextual – was presented in 1937 (published in 1938) by Raja Rao, in his novel *Kanthapura*. Rao's was, however, not the first attempt to give the South Asian voice to English. In his novel *Bengal Peasant Life*, published in 1874, Lal Behari Day almost apologetically presents the dilemma in contextualizing English in Bengal:

Gentle reader, allow me here to make one remark. You perceive that Badan and Alanga speak better English than most uneducated English peasants; they speak almost like educated ladies and gentlemen, without any provincialisms. But how could I have avoided this defect in my history? If I had translated their talk into the Somersetshire or the Yorkshire dialect, I should have turned them into English, and not Bengali, peasants. You will, therefore, please overlook this grave though unavoidable fault in this authentic narrative. (Bailey 1996: 305)

Approaches for Redefining Identities

The shift from the norms of the center has been slow and gradual. And the approaches for establishing linguistic and literary identities adopted by each writer, in each region, and each linguistic group are not identical. One sees several major approaches for establishing local literary and linguistic identities for English.

Ritualistic and Metaphysical

In this approach, as we will see, there is no Caliban's sting. There is no Caliban saying:

> You taught me language, and my profit on't
> Is I know how to curse.

In *Kanthapura*, Rao provides five perspectives to authenticate the crossover of English in the South Asian context in terms of the following:

1. The relationship between the medium *(madhyama)* and the message (mantra).
2. Reconceptualization of the contextual appropriateness of English as a medium of creativity.

Strategic Linguistic Weapon 59

3. The relevance of hybridity and creative vision and innovation.
4. The relevance of language variety, linguistic appropriateness, and identity.
5. Stylistic transcreation, cultural discourse, and their relationship with local *parampara* (Kachru 1998c: 66–67).

In his often-cited "author's foreword" of just 461 words, Rao did not sing the song of linguistic liberation for his innovative and nativized style or his Kannadization and Sanskritization of English. He argued on the basis of convergence, cohesion, and assimilation of the language, and thus moved English within the mainstream of India's linguistic and cultural *traditions – parampara*.

And in a later paper, "The Caste of English" (Rao 1978), as I have discussed elsewhere (Kachru 1998c), Rao placed English on the same elevated pedestal of Truth on which Indians have traditionally kept Sanskrit ("The Perfected Language") for thousands of years:

Truth . . . is not the monopoly of the Sanskrit language. Truth can use any language . . . and so long as the English language is universal, it will always remain Indian.

Rao confers on the discourse on English a certain mystique; he even involves the gods in his approach to the language:

We in India welcome everything outlandish and offer it to gods, who taste it, masticate it, and give it back to us as prasadam ["offerings to the gods returned to man sanctified"]. When our English will have come to that maturity it might still achieve its own nationhood. Till then it will be like Anglo-Norman, neither French nor English, an historical incident in the growth of culture.

And Rao responds to India's linguistic chauvinism by declaring English "of our caste, our creed and of our tradition." This is a subtle and sensitive way of including the language within the canon. This statement has a symbolic meaning too; it is like performing the initiation, the *samskara*, of the English language, and putting around it the symbol of initiation, "the sacred thread."

Strategic Linguistic Weapon

This second approach to English views the colonial medium as a strategic "linguistic blade," to be used as an effective weapon and turned back on the colonizer. The most passionate and skillful articulation of this position is by Wole Soyinka. Soyinka recognizes that, in the sociolinguistic context of Africa, English plays "unaccustomed roles" as "a new medium of communication," in "a new organic series of mores, social goals, relationships, universal awareness – all of which go into the creation of a new culture." And what did the African people do with this colonial weapon? Soyinka answers:

60 Culture Wars

Black people twisted the linguistic blade in the hands of the traditional cultural castrator and carved new concepts into the flesh of white supremacy. (1993: 88)

The result, says Soyinka, is "the conversion of the enslaving medium into an insurgent weapon." The medium now has a message: it is an *African* message. Thus, on the African continent the English language was put to a "revolutionary use" by Du Bois, Nkrumah, and Nelson Mandela. And says Wole Soyinka:

The customary linguistic usage was rejected outright and a new, raw, urgent and revolutionary syntax was given to this medium which had become the greatest single repository of racist concepts. (1993: 88)

This is a different path than the one adopted by Ngugi, who considers English a racist language and abandons the medium.

Contrastive Pragmatism

The third approach to English was lucidly articulated by Chinua Achebe in 1966. He provides a cogent argument for the stylistic Africanization and acculturation of English by explaining how he approaches the use of English in a contrastive way. He compares the *Africanized* and *non-Africanized* versions of creativity and then, contrasting the two styles, he argues:

The material is the same. But the form of the one is in character [of the Africanized style], the other is not. It is largely a matter of instinct but judgment comes into it too. (Achebe 1966)

And Okara (1964: 137) conveys an identical message:

From a word, a group of words, a sentence and even a name on any African language one can glean the social norms, attitudes and values of a people.

Despite their different attitudes and positions on the acculturation of English, these approaches converge in their underlying unity. In all these approaches one underlying motive is shared, and that is to move away from the Western canons of power and control – from the deemed center – and design yet another path for creativity in Asian and African English, and to use the medium for their mantra.

The tradition of such bilinguals' creativity is not new in multilingual societies. The crossover to another medium forms an integral part of such societies. It has been done for literary creativity, and for discourses on philosophic, epistemological, and religious topics. There has always been yet another language, yet another code, yet another style for such universes of discourse: Sanskrit for three thousand or more years, Persian after the thirteenth century in South Asia, and the High varieties of dominant regional languages such as Arabic, Greek, Tamil, Bengali, and Kashmiri. The newness is in the extension of this tradition of creativity to a Western medium – to English – to a medium that has recent colonial associations and presumed external centers of power and control. All these approaches are for redefining the medium, and contextualizing English in yet other sociocultural and linguistic context.

The metaphor of Caliban applies to other voices in English – not only to African and Asian and to other types of canonicity and formal experimentation. When Henry Louis Gates Jr. uses the term "loose canons" he is actually talking of such voices, such canons, and of multiple identities of English. Gates warns us:

> Cultural pluralism is not, of course, everyone's cup of tea. Vulgar cultural nationalists – like Allan Bloom or Leonard Jeffries – correctly identify it as the enemy. (1992: xvi)

And he continues:

> These polemicists thrive on absolute partitions: between "civilization" and "barbarism," between "black" and "white," between a thousand versions of Us and Them.

And for us – some of us – Gates is reassuring when he says that "but they are whistling in the wind."

The Outward Sign of Inward Fires

One might then ask what, in this context, are the outward signs of these "inward fires"? The liberated creativity of English in Africa and Asia has resulted in two major responses from the West.

One response views this creativity, and stirrings for canonicity, as "liberation linguistics" – in ideological terms – as loaded as "liberation theology," as mentioned previously. The second response considers such creativity as an indicator of what may be called "dehomogenizing creativity," i.e., creativity that is not contributing to "homogenize[ing] cultures." To Fernandez-Armesto (1995: 730; see also Fishman 1998–1999):[11]

> Communications seem to be unable to homogenize culture; the most surprising example is that of the English language, which, until recently, was widely hailed or feared as the world medium of the future.

In Fernandez-Armesto's view, there is only one space for English, and only one representation – one cultural definition – of the medium. However, that is not all. This creativity and articulation of cultural, linguistic, and regional identities are additionally viewed as a *"managed and revolutionary shift from*

---

[11] Note, for example, Fishman's concern about "strong regional *idiosyncrasies* that English acquires" (emphasis added) in contexts where English is used as an additional language.

62   Culture Wars

English to something more local" (Bailey 1990: 86; emphasis added). They are presented almost as a linguistic conspiracy. In this context, Bailey gives the example of Emeka Oreke-Ezigbo, who defends Nigerian Pidgin English as

a partial, viable, flexible language distilled in the alembic of our native sensibility and human experience. (1990: 86)

This discussion reminds one of the recent controversy over Ebonics in the United States, which soon ceased to be a sociolinguistic issue and became a political one. In Bailey's view, the decay of English has yet another dimension. He makes a distinction between English for "outward-looking aspirations" and English for "inward-looking patriotism." And he mourns that "English as a purely mental instrument of human expression is dying" (1990: 86). The concern is about local identities of English – the African, the Asian, and so on – and its acculturation. These are, then, some of the "language coming apart" hypotheses.

The War of Cultures and Canons

What I have said previously provides just an overview of the major strands of the ideological and power-related issues that are central to the debate on culture wars. But this is just the tip of the proverbial iceberg of World Englishes. There are two other issues that deserve our attention and provide some explanation for current attitudes toward Caliban's creativity.

The first issue concerns our sociolinguistic conceptualization of the architects of the canon, our view of who composes the speech community of English, the strands that constitute the canon, and our view of who can initiate changes and modifications in the canon. In other words, the questions are: What establishes the foundation of the canon? And who are the makers of the canon? It is by answering these questions in certain ways that we establish the territory of canonicity. The second issue, of course, relates to the economics of English, viz., English as a commodity, with an immense value in the international language market. Those with *ownership* of the commodity want to safeguard it and preserve it in terms of pounds and dollars.

The sociolinguistic issues relate to the linguistic, literary, and attitudinal sacred cows in the culture of the speech community. These attitudes ultimately shape our views about what constitutes a harmonious, cohesive, integrated, and motivated speech community. In the case of English these attitudes determine how we view multilinguality or bilinguality, individual and social bilingualism, and indeed the multilinguals' literary creativity (see B. Kachru 1988b).

And when we talk of creativity in World Englishes, particularly in Asia and Africa, we are talking of the world of creativity essentially based on various types and levels of hybridity, both linguistic and cultural. We are talking of the

The War of Cultures and Canons   63

type of hybridity in which African and Asian interculturalism and linguistic innovations and experimentation play a vital role. This type of hybridity is in conflict with the traditional conceptualization of canons. There seem to be three reasons for suspecting the acquired hybridity of World Englishes. The first reason relates to the *type of diversity* introduced in the text by, for example, Asian and African writers. The second reason is the traditional *negative attitudes* toward bilingualism and pluralism in Western societies. The third reason, as Lefevere (1990: 24) says, is the "monolingualization of literary history by Romantic historiographers."

This negativity toward diversity and bilingualism has been abundantly expressed in earlier research on bilingualism, specifically in the cases of the United States, the United Kingdom, and Australia.[12] These negative views are expressed by a wide range of social scientists and humanists. And the attitude is articulated in several ways, including perceptions such as the following:

(a) Pluralistic societies are complex and their descriptions present explanatory complexities;
(b) Homogeneity and uniformity need to be emphasized in linguistic and cultural descriptions;
(c) Diversity – social, cultural, and linguistic – essentially leads to chaos;
(d) Bilingual groups are marginal and problem-generating;
(e) Bi-/multilingualism retards economic growth; and
(f) Bilingualism has serious negative implications for educational progress.

And this is indeed a long list of problem areas. These questions have resulted in an acrimonious debate, in the United States and elsewhere. I will not go into that digression. One must, however, ask, What are the implications of such perceptions regarding bilingualism for our attitudes to the bilingual's creativity? Forster (1970: 7) argues that:

we have all been brought up to believe that each language has its mystery and its soul, and that these are very sacred things, in whose name indeed much blood has been shed.

And Lefevere (1990: 24) adds to this discussion yet another perspective, that of the *monolingualization* of literary history as an ideological and identity tool of the state. He points out the emphasis by romantic historiographers on "creating 'national' literatures preferably as *uncontaminated as possible by foreign influences*" (emphasis added).

In this conceptualization, then, African and Asian creativity is not only essentially "contaminated" and contextually "foreign" to the perceived tradition of the "Western canon," it is also threatening to that canon. And equally

---

[12] See B. Kachru (1996b), especially section 2: "Paradigm Myopia" (p. 242).

64   Culture Wars

crucial to the debates on the multilingual's creativity is the generally held view that literary creativity primarily occurs in one's *mother* tongue; creativity in another language is an exception, in the sense that it is contrary to the norm. This view is not uncommon in the scholarly community. Let me give here two examples of such views: one from a social scientist, Edward Shills, and one from a linguist, David Crystal. Shills (1988: 560) believes that

The national language of literary creation is almost always the language of the author's original nationality.

The exceptions Shills thinks of are Conrad, and, at a lower level, Nabokov and Koestler, Apollonaire and Julien Green. Even if we accept his assessment of Nabokov and the others, it is clear that Shills did not look beyond Europe. If he had, he might have changed his mind. And Crystal (cited in Paikeday 1985: 66–67), says that

it is quite unclear what to make of cases like Nabakov and the others [that] George Steiner *(Extraterritorial Papers)* talks about as having no native language.

Crystal obviously considers these "marginal cases."

The views of Shills and Crystal clearly reflect attitudes about multi-linguals' creativity. The distinction Crystal makes between a *native* and a *non-native* speaker is based on "the fact that there are some topics that they [non-native speakers] are 'comfortable' discussing in their first language. 'I couldn't make love in English,' said one man [a non-native speaker] to me." In reality, the facts are quite the opposite; creativity in English is no exception to the multilingual's creativity in many other languages. The list is long and it has an impressive tradition in South and East Asia, in East and West Africa, and, indeed, also in Europe.

In linguistic paradigms, too, bilinguality and the bilingual's creativity are still on the periphery. For example, describing grammars of bilinguals is considered extremely complicated. The emphasis is on homogeneity and uniformity. In 1950, Haugen articulates this concern when discussing bilin-gualism in general and the bilingual as a person:

The subject was for many years markedly neglected in this country [USA], and we might say that both popularly and scientifically, bilingualism was in disrepute. Just as the bilingual himself often was a marginal personality, so the study of his behavior was a marginal scientific pursuit. (272)

It is true that in recent years we as professionals have begun to ask questions and propose solutions for the complex issues concerning the forms and functions of World Englishes, and have done exciting research on various aspects of bi- and multilingualism. However, we are still hesitant to cross the threshold and face the complexities of multilinguals' language behavior and the impact of those language data on our hypotheses and our attitudes. We are reluctant to modify, reformulate, revisit, and reassess our favorite paradigms. And the result of this attitude is the marginalization of the multiple voices heard in World Englishes.

Conclusion

What we see, then, is that in creativity in World Englishes we have "the interplay of diverse voices" (Dissanayake 1989: xvi). We have multiple cultural visions, discourses, and linguistic experimentation. We have an unparalleled multicultural resource through one medium with many mantras. We have to ask ourselves how to make use of this rich resource. And this concern raises important theoretical, methodological, ideological, and pedagogical questions.

In looking at the resource in World Englishes, we need a perspective of "variousness," as I argued earlier in the context of the mythology associated with the teaching of English (B. Kachru 1995c). Perhaps Geertz (1983: 234) has a message for us when, addressing anthropological researchers, he says that "the world is a various place" in many ways:

various between lawyers and anthropologists, various between Muslims and Hindus, various between little tradition and great, various between colonial thens and nationalist nows.

And Geertz continues:

much is to be gained, scientifically and otherwise, by confronting that grand actuality rather than wishing it away in a haze of forceless generalities and false comforts.

The need now is to recognize the "variousness" and ask the right questions of the Speaking Tree. It means seeking answers for the "curatorial" and "normative" functions of canon, to use Altieri's words (1990: 33). These, then, are the types of questions we must ask if we do not want to continue walling up the world visions – including African and Asian – in this unique cultural and linguistic resource of our times: World Englishes.

4   Standards and Codification

Introduction

It is perhaps not coincidental that the fiftieth anniversary of the British Council in 1985 looked back on a span of fifty years that had witnessed a linguistic phenomenon of unprecedented dimensions in language spread, language contact, and language change. It is particularly noteworthy since these phenomena can be seen in relation to the diffusion and internationalization of one language, English, across cultures and languages. This anniversary, therefore, is an appropriate milestone to review the past, and to gaze into the crystal ball for future linguistic and other indicators for English in the new millennium.

Earlier research, especially after the 1950s, provides some perspective about the international diffusion of English, the attitudes toward it and other languages of wider communication, its formal and functional characteristics, and its impact on major world languages. We now have both satisfactory and not-so-satisfactory case studies of the *nativization* of English, and the *Englishization* of other world languages.

As we have seen, the sociolinguistic aspects of English in its international contexts are still not well understood; they have not been fully researched for a variety of attitudinal, theoretical, and logistical reasons. Attitudinally, there is a conflict between perceived linguistic norms and actual language behavior. Theoretically, as mentioned earlier, linguists are still conditioned by a monolingual model for linguistic description and analysis, and have yet to provide a framework and descriptive methodology for description and analysis of bi- or multilinguals' use of language and linguistic creativity. In logistical terms, such an investigation entails enormous empirical work by researchers who are multilingual and to some extent multicultural as well. I shall elaborate these points later.

What further complicates the task is the sheer magnitude of the spread of English: the variety of global contexts in which English is used and the varied motivations for its acquisition and use in the erstwhile colonial regions after the political phase of the Colonial Period. There are also some who believe the post–Colonial Period has ushered in a phase of *decontrol* of English, as it were, from earlier, reasonably well-accepted and not generally challenged standards for the language. The impression now is that with the diffusion of and resultant innovations in English around the world, universally acceptable standards are absent. In addition, the situation becomes even more involved as a result of the lack of a precise methodology for understanding and describing English in international sociolinguistic contexts.

The aim of this chapter is to discuss some implications of the global diffusion of English, focusing in particular on the issues of standardization and codification of linguistic creativity and innovations in its institutionalized nonnative varieties. But before I begin, a digression is necessary, to outline the main concentric circles within which the world varieties of English are presently used.

Three Concentric Circles

The initial questions about the universalization of English are: What is the major stratification of use due to the internationalization of English? And what are the characteristics of such stratification? The spread of English may be viewed in terms of three "concentric circles" representing the types of spread of English around the world, the patterns of its acquisition by different users, and the functional domains in which it is used across cultures and languages. This concept was briefly outlined in Chapter 1; I elaborate it here. I have tentatively labeled the circles as follows: the *Inner Circle*, the *Outer Circle* (or *Extended Circle*), and the *Expanding Circle*. In terms of the users, the Inner Circle refers to the traditional bases of English: the regions where it is the primary language and functions as the dominant vernacular.

The Outer Circle needs a historical explanation: it involves the earlier phases of the spread of English and its institutionalization in non-Western contexts, typically in former British exploitation colonies. The institutionalization of such varieties has linguistic, political, and sociocultural explanations, some of which I shall discuss later.

The political histories of the regions where institutionalized varieties are used have many shared characteristics: these regions have gone through extended periods of colonization, essentially by the users of the Inner Circle varieties. The linguistic and cultural effects of such colonization are now a part of their histories, and these effects, both good and adverse, cannot be wished away. It is, however, important to note that numerically, the Outer Circle forms a large speech community with great diversity and distinct characteristics. The major features of this circle are that (a) English is only one of two or more codes in the linguistic repertoire of such bilinguals or multilinguals, and (b) English has acquired an important status in the language policies of most of such multilingual nations. For example, in Nigeria it is an official language

68   Standards and Codification

(Bamgbose 1982); in Zambia it is recognized as one of the state languages (Chishimba 1985; in Singapore it is a major language of government, the legal system, and education (Platt and Webber 1980; Lowenberg 1984); and India's Constitution recognizes English as an "associate" official language and as one of the required languages in the Three Language Formula implemented in the 1960s (Kachru 1983b).

In functional terms, the institutionalized varieties have three characteristics: first, English functions in what may be considered traditionally "un-English" cultural contexts. And, in terms of territory covered, the cross-cultural spread of English is unprecedented among the languages of wider communication used as colonial languages (e.g., French, Portuguese, Spanish), as religious languages (e.g., Arabic, Sanskrit, Pali), and as lingua francas for trade and commerce (e.g., pidgins or bazaar varieties). Second, English has a wide spectrum of domains in which it is used with varying degrees of competence by members of society, both as an intranational and as an international language. Third, and very important, English has developed nativized, or indigenized, literary traditions in different genres, such as the novel, short story, poetry, and essay. In other words, English has an extended functional *range* in a variety of social, educational, administrative, and literary domains. It also has acquired great *depth* in terms of users at different levels of society. As a result, there is significant variation within such institutionalized varieties.

The Expanding Circle gives English yet another dimension. To understand this, one must recognize the fact that English has a global presence, having already outcompeted rivals such as French, Russian, and Esperanto, to name just two natural languages and one artificial language. The geographical regions lumped in the Expanding Circle do not necessarily have a history of colonization by populations of the Inner Circle (Ituen 1980). This circle is currently expanding rapidly and has resulted in numerous performance varieties of English, also identified as English as a foreign language (or EFL) (Kachru and Quirk 1981).

It is the users in this circle who actually further strengthen the claims of English as an international or universal language. This circle encompasses vast regions and countries such as China (pop. 1,376,049,000), Russia (pop. 144,192,450), and Indonesia (pop. 255,461,700). A partial list of other countries, where such performance varieties of English are used includes Greece (pop. 11,000,000), Israel (pop. 8,541,000), Japan (pop. 127,110,047), Korea (pop. 76,497,881), Nepal (pop. 26,494,504), Saudi Arabia (pop. 30,770,375), Taiwan (pop. 23,508,362), and Zimbabwe (pop. 12,973,808).

The Outer Circle and the Expanding Circle cannot be viewed as clearly demarcated from each other; they have several shared characteristics, and the status of English in the language policies of such countries changes from time to time. What is an ESL region at one time may become an EFL region at

Three Concentric Circles

another time, or vice versa. There is another difficulty: countries such as South Africa (pop. 54,956,900) and Jamaica (pop. 2,950,210) are not easy to place within the concentric circles since in terms of the English-using populations and the functions of English, their situation is rather complex. I have, therefore, not included these in the lists.

During the last fifty years, the spread of English has been characterized by several political and sociolinguistic factors that deserve mention. At present, English is fast gaining ground in the non-Western countries, and the mechanisms of its diffusion have significantly altered. The initiators of its diffusion are people who use it as an additional language – often as an alternative language – in multilingual and multicultural contexts. In a socioeconomic sense, a large number of English-using countries fall in the category of "developing" nations; their needs for the use of English are determined, on the one hand, by considerations of modernization and technology, and, on the other hand, by linguistic, political, and social "fissiparous tendencies," to use an Indian English expression.

These regions are geographically distant from English-speaking nations of the Inner Circle, and this factor has serious implications for the learning and teaching of English. A significant number of such nations are quite different in their religions, beliefs, cultural patterns, and political systems from those of the Inner Circle.

As an aside, one might add here that all the countries where English is a primary language are functionally democracies. The Outer Circle and the Expanding Circle do not show such political preferences. The present diffusion of English seems to tolerate any political system and the language itself has become rather *apolitical*. In South Asia, for example, it is used as a tool for propaganda by politically diverse groups: the Marxist Communists, the China-oriented Communists, and what are labeled the Muslim fundamentalists and the Hindu rightists, as well as various factions of the Congress Party. Such varied groups seem to recognize the value of English in fostering their respective political ends, though ideologically some of them seem to oppose the Western systems of education and Western values. In Singapore and Malaysia, English has become a medium for Asian values. In the present world, the use of English certainly has fewer political, cultural, and religious connotations than does the use of any other language of wider communication.

These three circles then confer on English a unique cultural pluralism and a linguistic heterogeneity and diversity that are unrecorded to this extent in human history. With this diffusion, naturally, are scores of problems concerned with codification, standardization, nativization, teaching, and description – and, of course, a multitude of attitudes about recognition of various varieties and subvarieties.

70   Standards and Codification

The diversity, in terms of both acquisition and use of English and different political, social, and religious contexts is, for example, evident in the following ten major English-using nations of the world:

USA	324,720,797
UK	65,110,000
India	300,000,000
Canada	36,286,425
Australia	24,251,400
Bangladesh	40,000,000
Nigeria	35,000,000
Pakistan	40,000,000
Tanzania	10,000,000
Kenya	45,010,056

Speech Community and Speech Fellowships of English

The pluralistic global profile of English, then, has multiple implications for our understanding and description of the language in a global context: first, in a theoretical sense, one faces a dilemma now in defining an "ideal speaker–hearer" for English (Chomsky 1965: 3), and in explaining what constitutes its "speech community." One might ask: Are all users of English in the three circles part of a single English-using community? If not, what are the differences?

It is evident that linguists, language planners, and language teachers have never had to confront the question of these dimensions and to this degree before, with so many theoretical, applied, and attitudinal implications. Answers to such questions are relevant to the description, analysis, and teaching of English. Furthermore, an answer to this question is basic to our discussion of the standards, codification, and norms of English. Prescriptivism – even of a mild form – must be based on some linguistic pragmatism and realism.

Before I elaborate further on this point, let me go back to the concept of ENGLISH-USING SPEECH COMMUNITY. It is now rightly being realized that the term "speech community" – a cardinal concept in theoretical and applied linguistics – needs some reconsideration. In pedagogical literature this term has acquired a special status for providing a "norm." In the linguistic literature, a speech community is generally seen as an abstract entity consisting of an "ideal speaker–listener." Here, of course, the focus is on *la langue*, associated with competence rather than performance.

Whatever the theoretical validity of this term and its traditional uses, the present global spread and functions of English warrant a distinction between *speech community* and *speech fellowship,* as originally suggested by Firth (1959: 208). The distinction identifies, as Firth says, "a close speech fellowship and a wider speech community in what may be called a language community comprising both written and spoken forms of the general language."

I believe that the term *speech fellowship* moves us closer to the pragmatic contexts, functions, and attitudes toward World Englishes, their underlying distinct differences, and their shared characteristics. One might find that the genesis of each such speech fellowship in English is unique, or there may be typologies of general patterns of development.

We certainly find such distinct patterns of linguistic and sociolinguistic development in the speech fellowships that use what Quirk et al. (1972: 26) have termed "interference varieties." Borrowing their words, I can observe that in the last fifty years such varieties of English have become

so widespread in a community and of such long standing that they may be thought stable and adequate enough to be institutionalized and regarded as varieties of English in their own right rather than stages on the way to a more native-like English.

What we see here, then, is that the nonnative English-using speech fellowships are using Englishes of the world in their divergent *situations* and *contexts* and with various linguistic and ethnic *attitudes*. Let me explain what I mean by these three terms: *situation* includes the linguistic, political and sociocultural, and economic ecology in which the English language is used. *Context* refers to the roles of participants in these situations and to the appropriateness of varieties of language used in these roles. And *attitude* is specifically used here for the overt and covert attitudes toward a language, its varieties, and the uses and users of these varieties.

Types of English-Using Speech Fellowships

In a normative sense, then, the speech fellowships of English around the globe are primarily of the following three types:

1. *Norm-providing varieties (the Inner Circle)*: These varieties have tradition-ally been recognized as models, since they are used by the "native speakers." However, the attitudes of the native speakers and nonnative speakers toward such native varieties are not identical. One might say that traditionally the British variety was generally accepted as the model, and it is very recently that the American model has been presented as an alterna-tive model. There is, however, still resistance toward accepting Australian or New Zealand varieties. The history of the battle of attitudes toward native English is an interesting story itself (see Kachru 1982d and 1984a).
2. *Norm-developing varieties (the Outer Circle)*: In regions using these var-ieties there has been a conflict in both the linguistic norm and the linguistic behavior. They are both endonormative and exonormative.

72   Standards and Codification

3. *Norm-dependent varieties (the Expanding Circle)*: This circle is essentially exonormative. I should, however, mention that in pedagogical literature, in popular literature (e.g., in newspapers), and in power-elite circles, only the Inner Circle varieties are considered "norm makers." The other two are treated as the "norm breakers." Even in the Inner Circle only a specific elite group is considered as "norm makers" or as models for emulation. We see this attitude, for example, in the writing of Newman (1974 and 1976) and Safire (1980), whose work has exerted a significant impact on the "linguistic etiquette" of the general public (see also Eble 1976, and Baron 1982, especially pp. 226–241).

In my discussion that follows, I am primarily concerned with the Outer Circle, which includes the institutionalized varieties (Kachru 1982d: 38–39). However, as I explained previously, it is evident that these categories are not necessarily mutually exclusive. Gray areas between the latter two do exist and we might as well recognize them.

Descriptive Issues and Prescriptive Concerns

The questions and controversies that have emerged as a result of the universal spread of English during the last fifty years may be reduced to four types. These questions repeatedly occur in theoretical literature, in applied and pedagogical discussions, and in the training of professionals. The first question concerns the codification of English, viz., who controls the norms? The second relates to the innovations that are formally and contextually *divergent* from the norms of the users of the Inner Circle, viz., what types of innovations and creativity are acceptable? The third question is about the pragmatics of selecting a norm, viz., what are the factors that determine a norm for a region? And finally there are issues surrounding the *de-Englishization* of the cultural context of English in the institutionalized nonnative varieties, viz., what are the parameters for the acculturation of English? I will now discuss these and related questions under four labels: codification, innovation, de-Englishization, and the nonnative bilingual's creativity.

Codification In spite of the attitudes expressed by and the vehement debates of linguistic purists, English actually has no authoritative channels of linguistic regulation other than the indirect ones: dictionaries, social attitudes, educational preferences, and discrimination in professions on the basis of accent. However, the need for some standards in written and spoken English for intranational and international intelligibility is well recognized (see e.g., Nelson 1982 and 1984; Smith 1983).

Innovation This is an offshoot of the question of codification, since the latter does imply standards for innovation. In the case of English, there are two types

Descriptive Issues and Prescriptive Concerns 73

of innovations: those initiated by users of the Inner Circle, and those that are essentially initiated by users of English in the Outer Circle. An innovation in the Outer Circle, then, refers to linguistic formations that are contextually and/ or formally distinct from language use in the Inner Circle. In the literature, various pejorative labels have been used for such innovations, including "mistakes," "errors," "peculiarities," "linguistic flights," and so on. It is only recently that studies of sociolinguistic appropriateness that encompass the discoursal level, speech acts, and functionally determined regional variation have been undertaken. In this case, then, codification implies determining the bounds of such innovations or creativity – in other words, the "allowable" divergences from the native norms.

At the formal levels, one is thus able to provide a schema for "error gravity," as has been done from native speakers' perspectives in the case of several nonnative varieties of English. The concept of "error" or "error gravity" has some use in morphologically or syntactically "divergent" constructions. However, a serious problem arises when one turns to the functional characteristics of such varieties because the formal divergences cannot be isolated from their functions. As several studies have demonstrated, the term *transfer* (or *interference*) is handy in discussing their characteristics. The degree and function of transfer may be seen as a *cline:* a cline of competence, lectal range, and domain assignment to English. Functionally, then, we find at least three marked varieties of Englishes on this cline:

(1) educated variety (*acrolect*): not to be confused with ambilingualism or "nativelike" competence;
(2) semieducated variety (*mesolect*);
(3) bazaar variety (*basilect*).

Within each variety, of course, further distinctions are possible, and an educated speaker may switch among two and more varieties, or mix varieties with other languages. Consider, for example, the following functionally appropriate innovations from Africa (A), South Asia (SA), and Southeast Asia (SEA).

(a) **Contextually determined collocations:** *tiffin carrier* (SA: a carrier for a snack or a light meal), *Himalayan blunder* (SA: a grave or serious mistake), *military hotel* (SA: a nonvegetarian hotel), *waist-thread* (SA: a ritualistic thread worn around the waist), *communal question* (SA: a question related to Hindu–Muslim relationships), *bush child* (A: child born out of wedlock), *funeral beer* (A: beer brewed and drunk after a funeral), *grave diggers* (A: people who are cousins of the dead person, traditionally responsible for digging the grave), *tight friend* (A: a close friend), *backward class* (SA: "deprived" groups), *small room* (A: a toilet), *cowife* (A: the second of two

74   Standards and Codification

wives), *minor wife* (SEA: a mistress), *knocking-fee* (A: a bribe), *chewing-sponge* (A: a twig for cleaning the teeth), *been-to-boys* (A: "been to England", cf. SEA: "England-returned"), *cop-shop* (A: police station), and *snatch boys* (A: "pickpockets").

(b) **Hybridization:** *kraalfamily* (A: family sharing the same enclosure), *lobola-beasts* (A: enemies who use bribe-price as a means of exploiting while feigning friendship), *swadeshi hotel* (SA: a native, vegetarian restaurant), *lathi charge* (SA: use of bataan for control [by police, etc.]), and *lovemuti* (A: a charm to entice people to love).

(c) **Idioms** (all from African varieties): *like a bushfire in the harmattan, like a yam tendril in the rainy season, where there is dew there is water, wisdom is like a goat skin – everyone carries his own, like a lizard fallen from an iroke tree, like pouring grains of corn into a bagful of holes, to eat each other's ears* (to talk privately), *to whisper together* (to talk privately), *to have no shadow* (to have no courage), and *to have no bite* (to have no courage).

(d) **Comparative constructions:** *as honest as an elephant, as good as kitchen ashes,* and *lean as an areca-nut tree* (all from South Asian varieties). In addition, consider, for example, *roaring silence* as used in Southern Africa, or *pin-drop silence* used in India, both meaning *dead silence.*

The third question about the pragmatics of selecting a norm has been in the forefront since the "Inner Circle" developed its transplanted native varieties (e.g., in Australia and the United States) and nonnative varieties (e.g., in Africa, South Asia, and Southeast Asia). These issues have been discussed in detail from various perspectives in, for example, Baron (1982, especially pp. 7–40), Finegan (1980), Kachru (1976, 1982d, and 1984a), and Strevens (1982).

The question concerning de-Englishization is related to the functional deviation and raises wider – and frequently debated – issues. One might ask: What relationship is there between language and culture? To what extent is a language acculturated in a new context in which it functions? And attitudinally important: How do native speakers of a language, e.g., English, react to such a situation? The innovations above sentence level take us to more interesting aspects of the linguistic creativity in the Outer Circle: the organization of nativized discourse strategies, registers, and speech acts (see Chishimba 1985 Kachru 1983b; Y. Kachru 1983; Magura 1984; Lowenberg 1984). In such innovations, there are clear relationships among the linguistic patterning of the text, transfer of underlying culturally determined strategies, and culturally intended effects.

These questions are important since, with its diffusion, English ceases to be an exponent of only one culture – the Western Judeo-Christian culture; it is now perhaps the world's most multicultural language, a fact that is, unfortunately, not well recognized. The present multicultural character of

Typology of Innovations 75

English is clearly revealed in its uses around the globe, especially in creative writing. In the writing of, for example, Cyprian Ekwensi, Gabriel Okara, Amos Tutuola, and Chinua Achebe, English represents Nigerian culture; in Alan Paton, it represents South African culture; in R. K. Narayan, Raja Rao, and Salman Rushdie, it represents South Asian culture; in James K. Baxter, Witi Ihimaera, and Frank Sargeson, it represents New Zealand culture; and in Edwin Thumboo, Ismail Sharif, and Fadzilah Amin, it represents Southeast Asian culture. In other words, English is now the language of those who use it; the users give it a distinct identity of their own in each region. As this transmuting alchemy of English takes effect, the language becomes less and less culture-specific (see Kachru 1984a).

This takes me to the fourth aspect, the worldwide literary and other types of creativity in English. This includes, for example, aspects of creativity by its nonnative users that are appropriate in the context of 1) creative writing (short stories, novels, poetry, etc.), 2) regional uses (newspaper, legal, administrative, etc.); 3) international and interpersonal uses (social interaction, letters, obituaries, etc.), and 4) the visual and spoken media (radio, television, etc.). To give just one example here, India is now the third largest book-producing nation in English after the United States and the United Kingdom. This fact cannot be ignored in discussing the diffusion of materials produced in English.

Typology of Innovations

In several earlier studies, attempts have been made to analyze both formal and functional characteristics of such innovations. Because of limitations of space, I will not discuss these here. However, on the basis of variety-specific (e.g., Singaporean, Indian) or region-specific (e.g., African, Southeast Asian, South Asian) studies, tentative typologies have been suggested about the shared characteristics of the institutionalized nonnative varieties. Again, I must avoid a digression here and not go into the details. The main claims of such studies are:

(1) The sociolinguistic context of language use determines such innovations and language change;
(2) The productive linguistic processes used for such innovations are shared with other such varieties, though the lexical realization in the varieties may be different (e.g., hybridization, context-dependent modes of reference and address, degrees of politeness, and strategies reflecting such deference).

What an outsider, then, views as an extreme linguistic divisiveness in the Outer Circle of English in reality is not so alarming and unusual. A surface judgment of this phenomenon is actually misleading; there are an underlying pattern and shared direction in the linguistic nativization of English.

76   Standards and Codification

Prescriptivism and Innovations

When we talk of prescriptivism in terms of innovations, we are primarily thinking of formal (lexical, phonological, syntactic), contextual, and discoursal divergences. What prescriptivism implies, then, is that with the spread of English we also expect the learners to acquire norms of behavior appropriate to the users of the Inner Circle. The expected behavior patterns characterize what one might call an "educated Englishman" (or American). This hypothesis is based on the assumption that language spread entails spread of cultural and social norms, or what has been termed in the pedagogical literature an "integrative motivation" for language learning. This hypothesis certainly is not fully applicable to the users of the institutionalized varieties of English. It is also doubtful that in a serious sense such integration was the aim of introducing English in the far-flung colonies. In any case, the present uses of English have clearly shown that an initially Western code has acquired numerous non-Western cultural incarnations and messages.

In understanding the present spread of English – and in looking for possible answers to our questions – what guidance can the other past and present languages of wider communication provide? Perhaps very little. We have already seen that the diffusion of English differs substantially from that of other languages of wider communication in terms of the vast territories it has covered in the process, the depth of its penetration into different societal levels, and the range of functions allocated to it. The earlier spread of Latin and Greek was restricted to only selected regions. The spread of Arabic, Sanskrit, and Pali outside their traditional territories was again geographically and functionally constrained: these were basically languages of religion.

The other languages of colonization – Spanish, French, Dutch, and Portuguese, to name just a few – have not approached the extent of the spread of English as both a vernacular and a lingua franca. Only one artificial language, Esperanto, gained some users and acceptance, but its present 2 million speakers around the world, and the ten-thousand-odd publications in it after almost one hundred years of existence do not compare in extent, range, and depth to those of World Englishes. The past cannot, therefore, guide us in terms of providing equivalent situations, but it does reveal some tendencies that are associated with languages of wider communication. These lessons are as follows: 1) the spread of a language invariably results in increased variation both in its functions and in terms of proficiency; 2) the displacement of a language from its traditional locale entails new acculturation; and 3) attempts at codification in such contexts may be psychologically uplifting for the purists, but the actual results of these attempts are very limited.

Arms of Codification

Since the past provides no insights, given the present international sociolinguistic profile of English, what are the possible arms for such codification – that is, if codification (or standardization) is the main concern? I shall consider four types here in order of their importance:

> First, *authoritative codification*: This entails a recognized codification agency for English, such as those established for Italian in 1582 (the Academia Della Crusca, in Florence), for French in 1635 (the Académie Française), for Spanish in 1714 (the Real Academia Espanola), and more recently, for Hebrew in 1953 (the Academy of the Hebrew Language), and for Bahasa Indonesia in 1975 (the Pusat Pembinaan dan Pengembangan Bahasa). As we know, the corresponding attempts made for English, in Britain in 1712 and in the United States in the 1780, did not succeed (see e.g., Baron 1982).
>
> Second, *sociological* (or *attitudinal*) *codification*: This requires strengthening a rigorous "accent bar" as discussed by Abercrombie (see Kachru 1984a). The term *accent* must be interpreted here in a wider sense and extended to other linguistic innovations and divergences.
>
> Third, *educational codification*: This refers to determining codification by instruments of education – dictionaries, the media, teachers' attitudes, and indirect references to "proper" and "acceptable" use of language. This type of codification is, of course, related to sociological codification and has always been present in the case of English.

Finally, *psychological codification*: This has been used in ancient times for languages such as Sanskrit, where a hymn, if not recited in the prescribed manner, would result in the wrath of the gods and "get the reciter ... destroyed by god Indra [the chief Vedic god, also the god of rain and thunder]" (see Kachru1984b). In this case, language is associated with a specific "power" and that power diminishes if the authoritative norms for its use are not obeyed. However, in the case of English, the psychological pressure is not God-induced; it has other, more worldly channels; nonetheless, the psychological pressure or power is felt.

What, then, are the choices for responding to the present complex international dynamics of English? The first choice seems to be to recognize the present variation in English in terms of the three circles and the variation within each circle. Such recognition will help in developing appropriate theoretical approaches, in initiating applied research, and in producing relevant

78   Standards and Codification

pedagogical materials for each situation. This will also mean reconsidering claims for the universal applicability of particular methods and approaches for teaching and learning English.

The second choice is to adopt various authoritative means for controlling the "divisiveness" and multiplicity of norms. This would naturally entail undertaking corpus planning with reference to innovations and creativity, and status planning with reference to the varieties within a variety. This, as we know, is not an easy task. But, then, "purists" have always had visions of doing this.

The third choice is to recognize the concept of a SPEECH COMMUNITY in the case of English as an abstract concept, while accepting that of SPEECH FELLOWSHIP as applying to the actual norm-producing linguistic groups. In a way, such norms are specific to speech fellowships and do not apply to the whole speech community. The intelligibility of English among members of a speech fellowship and across speech fellowships will depend on several sociolinguistic parameters: age, education, role, and so on. The types of variation that we find in the native varieties cannot be overlooked in the case of the nonnative varieties of English. Consider, for example, the following observation made by Ida Ward almost a century ago about English in Britain (Ward 1929: 5):

It is obvious that in a country the size of the British Isles, any one speaker should be capable of understanding any other when he is talking English. At the present moment, such is not the case: a Cockney speaker would not be understood by a dialect speaker of Edinburgh or Leeds or Truro, and dialect speakers of much nearer districts than these would have difficulty in understanding each other.

In Ferguson and Heath (1981), we see that in the United States the situation is even more complex. Hence, there is no reason to expect homogeneity in the multiethnic and multilinguistic societies of Africa, South Asia, Southeast Asia, or the Philippines.

Is this, then, a picture of desperation in which one throws one's hands up in the air and proclaims that the battle is lost? The answer depends partly on the depth of a person's linguistic cynicism. Let me indulge here in a nonlinguistic observation: the mental makeup of the English-using nations is not such that they will accept linguistic codification from above. The users in the Inner Circle will most likely not accept the formal authoritative means that they rejected more than two hundred years ago. Such users will continue to rely on subtle psychological, attitudinal, and sociological codifications. But more important, resistance to even such subtle codification has already developed, as we have seen, in many nonnative English-using countries.

Nevertheless, despite this resistance to deliberately imposed norms, what is emerging in the diverse native and nonnative English-using speech fellowships is an *educated variety* of English (or, shall I say, educated varieties of English?)

Collaborative Research on International Englishes 79

which is intelligible across these many varieties. This point leads me to Daniel Jones's cone-shaped concept of a speech community. It is actually a cone of variation; as one goes up on the scale, an extended level of intelligibility is acquired.

As I have stated elsewhere (Kachru 1984a: 70):

there is a pragmatically refreshing side to all these situations. What appears to be a complex linguistic situation at the surface, in Britain, in America, in Africa, or in South Asia, is less complex if one attempts to understand it from another perspective. In his cone-shaped diagram (reproduced in Ward, 1929: 5 *et seq.*), Daniel Jones has graphically shown that "as we near the apex, the divergences which still exist have become so small as to be noticed only by a finely trained ear" (Ward, 1929: 6). Ward rightly provides the argument of "convenience of expediency" (p. 7), suggesting that "the regional dialect may suffice for those people who have no need to move from their own districts." In this I find a clear case of parallelism between the native and institutionalized non-native varieties of English. Intelligibility is functionally determined with reference to the sub-region, the nation political areas within the region (e.g., South Asia, Southeast Asia), and internationally. True, educated (standard) Indian English, Singapore English, Nigerian English, or Kenyan English is not identical to RP or GA (General American). It is different; it should be different. Do such educated varieties of non-native Englishes create more problems of intelligibility than does, for example, a New Zealander when he or she talks to a Midwestern American?

What is needed, then, is to move from linguistic authoritarianism of the "native-speaker says" variety to a speech fellowship–specific realism. In such an approach, pedagogical prescriptivism is valid; so is the concern for acquisitional deficiencies, but with the realization that the functional and sociocultural distinctiveness of each speech fellowship cannot be arrested. In other words, there is a need for attitudinal change and linguistic pragmatism; these are not easily attainable and require a sustained effort and supporting research.

Collaborative Research on International Englishes

This takes me to my final major point: I believe that the time is more than ripe now for an international institute for the study of and research on English across cultures. I am not suggesting an academy for "correcting, improving and ascertaining the English tongue," as did Jonathan Swift in 1712, but a research center that has the functions of a clearinghouse, archive, think tank, and graduate teaching program.

Is this a utopian idea? What would be the organizational structure of such an institute, and its launching base? Is it financially feasible to undertake such an enterprise? These and related questions naturally crowd one's mind. The idea of such an institute has been discussed informally for the last five years. I believe that we should now discuss it more seriously and also take some

80   Standards and Codification

initiative in this direction. Broadly speaking, the institute should have the following components:

(1). Archives for English across cultures
(2). Graduate teaching programs
(3). Research programs
(4). International exchange programs

Let me elaborate on these components one by one. The first component, comprising the archive, may include source and research materials of the following types:

a). *Empirical studies*: resource and background studies, e.g., sociolinguistic profiles of English in the Inner Circle, the Outer Circle, and the Expanding Circle. These include profiles of the composition of English-using speech fellowships, the status of English in the language policies of different English-using countries, functional domains of English in ESL regions, and attitudinal studies concerning varieties and their subvarieties.
b). *Functional domains*: types of Englishes as they have developed in terms of various culture-specific roles of the language: localized norms, variational (lectal) range within local norms, and types of language contact and their impact (e.g., borrowing and "mixing").
c). *Formal studies*: the characteristic formal features of nativized uses of English from various text types, including registral (e.g., administrative, newspaper, and legal), interactional (e.g., nonnative norms for interaction in English), and creative (e.g., localized literatures in English).
d). *Survival registers*: studies of what may be termed *international* survival registers of English with their localized variants, e.g., medical, legal, Seaspeak, and aviation.
e). *Pedagogical studies*: comprehensive cross-cultural data for the teaching of English, including methods for the teaching of the English language and literature at various educational levels; curricula for the English language teaching specialists; and texts, teaching aids, and supplementary materials.
f). *Resource materials*: these include background materials of the following types: major agencies for the coordination of training and research within each region (e.g., the Regional English Language Center (RECL), Singapore; the Central Institute of English and Foreign Languages (CIEFL), Hyderabad); resources and research appropriate for each English-using region, specifically regional surveys of English (e.g., aspects of literature or language); and surveys and critical studies of the development of literatures in English (see e.g., Narasimhaiah 1976).

The second component concerns the graduate training program. I am not suggesting that a new graduate program be initiated. We need to extend the focus of current curricula leading to master's degrees in English studies. In such courses, a graduate student clearly has to be exposed to the internationalization of English and its linguistic, sociolinguistic, literary, and pedagogical implications. Ideally, such a curriculum should include the *multicultural* and *multinorm* contexts of the World Englishes, and the consequences of these varied contexts for teaching methods, discourse and stylistic strategies, pedagogical materials, cultural contexts of texts, and lexicography.

The third component, which involves research programs, cannot be isolated from the second. In a way, this component may be seen as an extension of the curricula for graduate teaching programs. The research should be seen in terms of the priorities established in the agenda for the first component.

The last component aims at providing for international exchange of researchers in the field of English studies. The goal is to establish serious links for scholars in the field to interact (better) with each other. This may be a step toward collaborative research among the centers. One hopes that the well-established data banks for description and analysis of English will make their resources available to such an institute. The insightful work done at such centers as the following may, then, be made available for shared research undertakings: the Survey of English Usage, University College, London; the Standard Corpus of Present-Day Edited International American English, Brown University; data available at Stanford University, California; RELC, Singapore; Central Institute of English and Foreign Languages, Hyderabad; lexicographical projects in the West Indies, South Africa, and so on.

I envisage that a project of this nature will be an extension of one of the present centers of TESL training and research. The organization and extension of an existing center will be easier than establishment of an altogether new one. The other components discussed may be added to such a center as a collaborative undertaking with English-using countries.

This chapter, of course, is not a blueprint for such a center; it simply articulates an idea. More important, this is not an idea for codifying English – even if that were possible – but a suggestion for initiating collaborative efforts between the native and nonnative users of English for monitoring, as it were, the direction of change in English, the uses and usage, and the scope of the spread and its implications for intelligibility and communication. I believe that it is through such collaborative attempts that a clearer picture of the forms and functions of English will emerge.

By the term *collaborative*, I do not imply collaboration merely between the British Council or other British institutions and interested agencies in the United States. Such an undertaking will have to be globally collaborative in the sense that those who use the English language in Africa, in Asia, and elsewhere, must feel involved in it. They must realize that at one level, there is a stake in maintaining an international standard for English, and, at another

82   Standards and Codification

level, there is a need to describe the uses of English with reference to diverging English-using speech fellowships. If there is concern for standards, the collaborating countries must contribute toward maintaining and staffing such an international institute.

Will-0'-the-Wispish Concerns vs. Linguistic Pragmatism

The preceding outline is, of course, programmatic, but the idea behind it deserves some attention: my main suggestion is for a collaborative effort, for the exchange of ideas, and for the establishment of a think tank where concerned scholars can discuss the shared issues and their implications. But with this outline, all the bees are not out of my bonnet. A number of other issues and concerns emerge, particularly within the context of the post-1950s developments. I shall merely mention some of them here.

First, in terms of exporting English language (and literature) experts, we are witnessing a new phenomenon: the users of the institutionalized varieties are now not only "norm-developing," as I obverved earlier; they also function as the channels for the diffusion of their respective norms to the Expanding Circle of English (the EFL contexts). This function is performed in various roles: as teachers of English, as engineers, as doctors, and so on. Sri Lankans, Malaysians, and Indians, to name just three Outer Circle speech fellowships, are now involved in academic planning and teaching of English in, for example, Egypt, Saudi Arabia, Iran, the Gulf countries, and Southeast Asia, in addition to their own countries. The figures, for example, for the export of teachers of English and mathematics from South Asia are impressive. One only has to take a look at the faculty lists of the universities and colleges in the EFL regions. Moreover, this import of nonnative English users as educators does not apply only to the Expanding Circle, but also to several countries that belong in the Outer Circle, where English has been institutionalized (e.g., Singapore, Malaysia, Nigeria, Kenya). The need for these expatriates as teachers and professors is immense and fast increasing. There is at present, as Cooper (1982 and 1985) observes in Israel, a "hunger" and "indecent passion" for acquiring English. But this is not restricted to Israel. The teaching of English has become everybody's business: it has developed into an international commercial enterprise and every English-using country is capitalizing on it in its own way.

The second issue has pedagogical implications. In the international context one must ask, What does the term *communicative competence* mean for English? In other words, competence within which context or situation? The question is especially applicable to the institutionalized varieties of English.

The third issue takes us to the core of some recent paradigms of research in second language acquisition, particularly with reference to English. A number of key concepts in this research deserve a serious second look, including the

Conclusion 83

concepts ERROR ANALYSIS, FOSSILIZATION, and INTER-LANGUAGE. The universal use of the term *error* for all divergences from native-speaker norms was incorrect and diverted attention from serious sociolinguistic research for at least two decades, until such research in "error analysis" arrived at a dead end. We are only now, as it were, recovering from it (for a discussion, see Lowenberg 1984).

The fourth key issue relates to the models and methods used for research on institutionalized varieties of English. I have discussed this issue elsewhere (see Kachru 1985a), but let me reiterate a few points here. It is useful to consider, for example: What is the state-of-the-art of research on nonnative Englishes? What approaches have been used for such research? What lines of research would be useful to follow? The answers to these and related questions are vital for the study of changes and their directions in the English language. Until very recently the dominant paradigm for such research was what I have termed the *deviational* model. It is only recently that other approaches have been used, such as the *contextualization* model, the *interactional* model, and the *variational* model.

The fifth issue takes me to ELT as a profession and as an area of inquiry. Let me stick my neck out a little further now and ask, for example: Has our profession realized its responsibilities within the new contexts in which English is used? Has it incorporated the insights with which the long tradition of teaching, learning, and nonnative creativity in English has provided us? It seems to me that the answer is no. (For further discussion see e.g., Tickoo 1991.)

One interpretation of this situation is that the current approaches to TESL reveal indifference to the pragmatic context of the present status of English as a world language. A harsher interpretation is that our profession has not been able to shake off the earlier evangelical and rather ethnocentric approaches to its task. One might add, then, that this ostrichlike attitude is not the correct response to the international ecology of English. What is needed is both attitudinal change and professionalism based on pragmatism and linguistic realism.

Conclusion

If this chapter has given the impression that I am a linguistic cynic lamenting that we have reached a state of linguistic helplessness, that impression is wrong. If I have given the impression of preaching linguistic anarchy, that impression is wrong as well.

My position is that the diffusion of English, its acculturation, the establishment of its international functional range, and the diverse forms of literary creativity it is accommodating are historically unprecedented. I do not think

84 Standards and Codification

that linguists, pedagogues, language planners, and the purists – if I might include them here – have ever faced this type of linguistic challenge before. I do not believe that the traditional notions of CODIFICATION, STANDARD-IZATION, MODELS, and METHODS apply to English anymore. The dichotomy of its *native* and *nonnative* users seems to have become irrelevant. We may talk of "standards" for our linguistic satisfaction, but we seem to be at a loss to explain what we mean by them, and equally important, how to apply them. I do not think that in discussing standards for English, the sociolinguistic reality of each English-using speech fellowship can be ignored.

In my view, the global diffusion of English has taken an interesting turn: the native speakers of this language seem to have lost the exclusive prerogative to control its standardization; in fact, if current statistics are any indication, they have become a minority. This sociolinguistic fact must be accepted and its implications recognized. What we need now are new paradigms and perspectives for linguistic and pedagogical research and for understanding the linguistic creativity in multilingual situations across cultures.

5   The Power and Politics

Introduction

When we use the term *power* with regard to language, we are creating a potent metaphor to characterize language as "the loaded weapon," to use Bolinger's (1980) phrase. The targets of the weapon, the range of linguistic ammunition one can use, and the aftermath of such use of language have yet to be studied in depth by linguists.[1] There are, of course, exceptions to this general apathy of language specialists to this aspect of language: in the past, the language of religion – and its power – attracted considerable attention.[2] More recently, the use of language in the domains of law, medicine, advertising, and so on, has developed into a special field of applied linguistics (e.g., see Alatis and Tucker 1979; Di Pietro 1982; Geis 1982; Leech 1966; Leibowitz 1976). The story of the study of language and politics, however, is much different. There have been several case studies on this topic, both general discussions and specific case studies (e.g., see Edelman 1964; Fishman et al. 1968; Friedrich 1962; Knappert 1968; Mazrui 1967; O'Barr 1976; Salisbury 1976; Sankoff 1976; Tambiah 1967).

In this chapter, however, I have a modest aim: to provide a blueprint for the discussion of selected issues related to the power and politics of the spread of English in a global context. While addressing the specific issues concerning English, an aside on the frameworks for the theoretical conceptualization of the relationship between language and power – and its politics – will be helpful. This aside will, I hope, contribute to our understanding of how complex the relationship between language and power is.

I will briefly explore several other interrelated issues connected with language and power. These include the concept of POWER and its application for language; the motivation for acquiring linguistic power; presuppositions for a power base; strategies used for power and politics; linguistic power and its

---

[1] The following observation by Tromel-Plotz (1981: 74) is very apt: "linguists who are so concerned with language and still so far removed from an analysis of language which truly promotes human rights and concerns."

[2] For references on language and religion see e.g., Samarin (1976).

86   The Power and Politics

implications for linguicide, that is, direct or indirect causes of language death; the politics of language in the Inner Circle (e.g., the United States and United Kingdom); and, finally, a revisitation of the issue of a framework for the study of power.

However, let me start with a warning: questions about language and power need not necessarily involve linguistic issues. The issues extend beyond linguistics into the realms of history, sociology, attitude studies, politics, and very mundane and complex economic considerations. Thus this topic has many faces, and the power of English has yet to be studied from all of these perspectives. This chapter, then, reveals only part of the story.

The two crucial terms in this chapter, *power* and *politics* of English, are linked in more than one way; the first implies an attainment of various types of "control," and the second signifies the processes and strategies used for this control (see e.g., Kramarae et al. 1984: 9–22).

Once a language attains power, it does not follow that political strategies are necessarily abandoned – far from it. Rather, it is a vicious circle: in order for power and control to be maintained, political maneuvering must continue, and it then develops into various situations of *conflict*.[3]

How do power and politics relate to language? The power of language is intimately connected with societal power of various types. The dimensions of power and resultant politics include the spread of a language to expand the speech community numerically;[4] the use of language as a vehicle of cultural, religious, and other types of "enlightenment" (this applies to English in several ways, which I will discuss in a later section); and the use of language with one or more of the following motives: to deculturalize people from their own tradition (e.g, the use of Japanese in Korea and Malaysia during World War II, and the use of Persian in parts of northern India); to gain economic advantage; to control various domains of knowledge and information; to use the language for deception (e.g., see Bolinger 1980, particularly chap. 10; Bosmajian 1974; Rank 1974; Tromel-Plotz 1981); and to create a circle of dependency on a country, nation, ideology, culture, and so forth.

The concerns for power, and its reflection in the types of politics, show up in different ways at different times. For example, almost five decades ago, when George Orwell addressed the issues of the politics of the English language, his concern was to provide a "catalogue of swindles and perversions" (Orwell and Angus 1968: 162) that had entered the English language – especially in political writing. And he chose his targets appropriately – Harold Laski,

---

[3] For discussions of case studies of language conflict, see for example Bourhis (1984), Brass (1974), and Das Gupta (1970).

[4] For an excellent treatment of language spread, its various manifestations, and case studies, see Cooper (1982).

What Is "Linguistic Power"?

Lancelot Hogben, and so on. As we know, Orwell was not the first to address the "decay" of the English tongue; nor will he be the last: Cassandras predicting the doom of English are still alive and active.[5] The concern of this chapter, however, is not identical to that of Orwell: it is not to show that the "present political chaos is connected with the decay of language" (Orwell and Angus 1968: 169). If it is connected, that connection is not relevant here.

The two key terms, *power* and *politics*, are used here in the context of their interplay within the three Circles of English. As explained in the preceding chapters, these three circles represent three distinct types of speech fellowships of English, phases of the spread of the language, and particular characteristics of the uses of the language and of its acquisition and linguistic innovations. There is, of course, an interplay of politics – and conflicts – within each circle; that aspect of English merits a detailed study in its own right, as does the study of the politics that countries in the Inner Circle are playing against the Outer Circle.

What Is "Linguistic Power"?

The study of linguistic power is not exactly of the same type as the study of the use of power by the state, in the legal system, for religious commands, and so on. Linguistic power has to be understood essentially through symbols and manipulation of the symbols. On the other hand, the understanding of linguistic power is concerned with both "relations of power" and "relations of meaning," as has been shown in several studies, including Brown and Gilman (1960), Kramarae et al. (1984), and Rubin (1976).

Linguistic power may manifest itself in the modification of linguistic behavior in one or more of the following ways: First is adding a code to the linguistic repertoire of a speech community or a speech fellowship. This may be done by the use of one or more of the following power strategies: persuasion, regulation, inducement, and force. Second is by the suppression of a particular language variety and the elevation of another variety. The arms of suppression need not be very obvious (see e.g., Wolfson and Manes 1985). The strategies for the "imposition" and "elevation" of a language need not be direct; they are often psychologically very subtle.

All of the strategies indicated have been used in the case of the spread of English. However, in order to see this relationship, one has to start, as it were, from the beginning: provide a conceptual framework, discuss some case studies, and attempt certain generalizations. This chapter will attempt to provide, at least partially, such an overview.

---

[5] For references and discussion see Greenbaum (1985), especially the chapters by James C. Stalker, Randolph Quirk, Julia Penelope, Edward Finegan, and Ian Pringle.

88   The Power and Politics

Is Linguistic Power "Intrinsic" or "Acquired"?

There are two hypotheses concerning language power, in this case, the power of English: the "intrinsic-power" hypothesis and the "acquired-power" hypothesis, The first claims that English intrinsically has certain linguistic – and other – characteristics that make it a preferred language for international roles. The noted linguist Otto Jespersen goes beyond this and claims that "it must be a source of gratification to mankind that the tongue spoken by two of the greatest powers of the world is so noble, so rich, so pliant, so expressive and so interesting" (Jespersen 1905). He is not alone in holding this view, although for some, this position is tantamount to claims of racial superiority.

The second hypothesis is, in contrast to the first, easy to understand. It emphasizes various ways through which language eventually acquires power: historical, societal, and functional. Once a language acquires power, maintaining this power indefinitely is not always easy. The range and depth of a language seem to pass through a life cycle.

Prerequisites for Linguistic Power

The interplay of power and politics in relation to language entails certain prerequisites, which I characterize as "sociolinguistic." The contexts described in the following provide an ideal situation for the growth of language-related politics. This fact is well attested by a number of sociolinguistic case studies across languages and cultures.

Linguistic Hierarchy

A linguistic hierarchy may be of the following types: first, that of traditionally multilingual societies (e.g., South Asia, West Africa, the Philippines, and Indonesia); second, that of societies where monolingualism is recognized as the norm, and diversity within a language, or linguistic pluralism, is generally ignored or even suppressed (e.g., the United States, Great Britain, and Japan); and, third, that of monolingual societies where an outside language may be imposed on people for relatively short periods.

Hierarchy of Use

A society with a linguistic hierarchy normally develops another type of hierarchy, that of functional allocation for each language and/or dialect. This situation often becomes explosive and results in language riots. We have witnessed such situations in India, Sri Lanka, Bangladesh, Canada, the United

Prerequisites for Linguistic Power 89

States (in Miami and California), and Nigeria, to give just some examples (see e.g., Pandit 1972; and B. Kachru 1982a and 1984a for further discussion and references).

Attitude toward Users

The attitude toward language use is a valuable clue for understanding the imagined or "real" power of language, in this case, that of English. The attitudes reveal positive, negative, or neutral feelings toward a language, its varieties, and types of innovations. In many cases, attitude is partly determined by perceptions of the language as it is used by "outsiders" and "insiders."

The attitude toward "mixing" English with elements from other languages provides a good indication for the cross-cultural and cross-language power of English. This aspect of English has been discussed with ample illustration in numerous studies (see B. Kachru 1983a: 193–207, where most of the studies are cited).

Domain Control in Terms of Roles

Competition for extending the roles of English in the Outer Circle has developed in the past and continues to develop in various linguistic conflicts. The conflicts are initiated typically by kinds of situations listed in the following. In these situations, the users of *competing* languages feel that English is playing one or more of the following roles in a multilingual situation:

(1) Dislocational role;
(2) conflictive role; or
(3) parallel role.

In the acquiring of any of these roles in the Outer Circle, it is believed – and sometimes rightly – that the interests of local languages are at stake. The preceding role-acquiring situations may be described as follows:

The *dislocational* role of English is seen, for example, in Singapore, where English is slowly displacing the other recognized languages (especially Hokkien, Malay, and Tamil) from their assigned roles. It is not uncommon to find young college-attending Singaporeans claiming English as their first language.

When the *conflictive* role is evident, politicians seem to exploit a linguistic situation by playing one language group against another. In India, for example, there are many such cases at the state level and at the national level. The situation of parallel roles is rather rare, though traditionally Switzerland is presented as a case of this type: but even in Switzerland there is some competition, particularly between French and German.

90   The Power and Politics

These linguistic situations typically result in serious political maneuvering and in the formation of linguistic groups.[6] However, the resultant conflicts do not necessarily involve only two distinct languages (e.g., Hindi vs. English). The conflict may be between varieties of the same language (e.g., between dialects of Hindi, as discussed by Y. Kachru and Bhatia 1978). Among others, these may involve situations of the following types: 1) in the Inner Circle, one may cite the case of Scottish vs. English English, the Received Pronunciation vs. other varieties of educated English, and "ethnic" varieties such as African American English and Chicano English vs. white middle-class English in the United States; 2) in the Outer Circle, the case of acrolectal vs. basilectal English varieties in Singapore.[7]

On Approaches to Understanding Language and Power

The concepts of POWER and POLITICS have been discussed in various disciplines, as pointed out already by O'Barr and O'Barr (1976). However, so far, the discussion of the relationship between these two concepts and language in general, and English in particular, has been based on very few descriptive case studies, some anecdotal statements in literature, and some quantitative studies of attitudes. To be sure, there is no paucity of frameworks used to establish a relationship between language and society. A number of such approaches have a long tradition in the linguistic sciences. But not all of the approaches listed in the following focus on linguistic data. Some have other orientations: political, sociological, and so on. Let me briefly mention five instances here:

1) *The correlative model*: This model establishes covariation between the formal linguistic features and sociological contexts of various types (e.g. caste, class, status, and sex; for further discussion, see Dittmar 1976: 195–224 and Labov 1970). The correlative model is not necessarily meant to establish a language and power relationship. However, such studies (e.g., of caste, class, and economic status) do provide good indicators for power-related interpretations.
2) *The domain model*: This model studies the use of a language or a speech variety with reference to preferred domain allocations. This model has been used both in monolingual societies (as in style and register shift) and in multilingual societies (as in language shift; for further discussion see Fishman 1971).

---

[6] For a discussion of language policy and the linguistic situation in various parts of the world, see Kaplan (1982). The following case studies discussed by Kaplan are of particular interest: East Africa (Carol Myers Scotton), Australia (Michael Walsh), Republic of China (John Kwock-Ping Tse).

[7] For particular case studies, extended discussion, and bibliographical references, see e.g., Das Gupta (1970), Edelman (1964), Kramarae et al. (1984), and O'Barr and O'Barr (1976).

On Approaches to Understanding Language and Power   91

3) *The conflict model*: This model, as Nichols (1984: 36) observes, emphasizes the economic basis of class divisions and sees them as organized in relation to the model of production: it stresses exploitation, oppression, and social conflict as important factors in social organizations.

The terms *exploitation* and *oppression* are vital here. Within this approach, language may be seen as an instrument of exploitation and oppression, and this perception – correct or not – may result in conflict (see e.g., O'Barr and O'Barr 1976; Edelman 1964; Leibowitz 1969; McDougal et al. 1976).[8]

4) *The functional model*: The functional model has been associated with several schools of linguistics. One major characteristic of these schools is that language is seen essentially as an instrument of social interaction (see e.g., the work of the British linguist J. R. Firth, discussed in B. Kachru 1981c and 1981d, and M. A. K. Halliday's work: e.g., Halliday 1975; see also the section entitled "Functional Studies" in Dittmar 1976: 224–235, and Pride 1979). The "interactionist model" usually used by sociologists may also be subsumed by this approach. According to this view, "social organization places relations between people at the center and recognizes that human interaction is a shaping process in its own right" (Nichols 1984: 38). Consider the following observations of Mead (cited in Nichols 1984: 38):

> There is . . . a range in our use of language; but whatever phase of this range is used is a part of a social process, and it is always that part by means of which we affect ourselves as we affect others and mediate the social situation through this understanding of what we are saying.

5) *The verbal-repertoire model*: The verbal-repertoire concept recognizes the linguistic and functional coexistence of languages, language varieties, and styles within the repertoire of one person or speech community. The choices of codes depend on the perceived power of a code in terms of functions, participants, situations, and so on. In the verbal-repertoire model, the power of a code is seen as much in *establishing* an identity by the use of a particular code as in *suppressing* it by the use of another code. One sees this phenomenon, for example, in using English for the neutralization of identities in several multilingual societies. In recent studies on "code alternations" ("mixing" and "switching"), several such cross-cultural generalizations have been made about the perceived power of English (B. Kachru 1982a).

One might ask, What is the relevance of the preceding approaches to the study of language and power? There are several ways in which these approaches can

---

[8] Note that both of these terms have been used with reference to English and its varieties.

92   The Power and Politics

be applicable to our understanding of this relationship: first, to provide validation for extralinguistic indicators of *power* or lack thereof regarding the distribution of language features, as has been shown in studies on caste and class (B. Kachru 1982a); second, to study the power basis for attitudes to and preferences for a language, its varieties, styles, and registers; third, to understand the question of language and identity; fourth, to see whether language change, especially in multilingual contexts, has a relationship with the perception of *power, domination,* and *imposition* of a language; and fifth, to study the phenomenon of language modernization and its relationship to a particular language (see e.g., Krishnamurti and Mukherjee 1984 for the impact of English on news and media in India).

The preceding approaches are not mutually exclusive; the difference is in the underlying assumptions and the focus of each approach. Some of the models discussed previously are primarily language-centered (e.g., the correlative model and the functional model), while some are not (e.g., the conflict model). But none of these approaches has been used to interpret linguistic power per se; nor is it the primary goal of the language-centered models to do so. However, several "socially realistic" linguistic studies do provide vital insights into the understanding of linguistic power in terms of language use. This is true of, for example, the approaches by J. R. Firth, M. A. K. Halliday, William Labov, and Dell Hymes, to name just four. The problem is not just that linguists have generally ignored this aspect of language as practice; there is also serious terminological confusion, since each discipline interprets POWER differently and offers different methodologies for the analysis and interpretation of the concept.

Foucault's Approach to Power

The preceding brief discussion shows that in linguistics there still is no clear grasp of power-related issues, for these issues have not been the concern of main paradigms of linguistics or of sociolinguistics. In order to identify the issues in a broader sense, one might find it useful to go beyond the traditional boundaries of the linguistic sciences, and explore the approaches of scholars in other areas.

In doing so, one immediately thinks of the insightful discussion by Michel Foucault on topics related to power. However, even Foucault (1980) confirms that "power and its strategies, at once general and detailed, and its mechanisms have never been studied." What do we mean by the strategies of power? Let me go back to Foucault (1980) to seek some illumination. In his view, "strategies are the exploitation of possibilities which [power] itself discerns and creates." There are two assertions about power: one, that power is exercised and exists in action; two, that power is a relation of force. Following Foucault's interpretation, then, power is "an organ of repression." In this framework, the schemas for the analysis of power are contact–oppression

Language Spread and Motivations for the Acquisition of Power 93

schema and domination–oppression schema. Before we proceed further in exploring Foucault's assertions about power, it is necessary to answer questions closer to linguistic concerns:

(1) Is Foucault's basic assertion applicable to the understanding of language?
(2) Is linguistic *power* always an instrument of oppression?
(3) How does linguistic power manifest itself in a speech community?

The answers to the first two questions vary from one case study to another. The manifestations of linguistic power have a wide range: crude linguistic power, indirect psychological pressure, and pragmatic power. An example of crude linguistic power is the imposition of Japanese on the Koreans and the Malays during World War II. Indirect psychological pressure is evident when languages make claims of "Other-World" power. This power is attributed to a language in the context of religion, e.g. the recitation of Sanskrit hymns, power of *japa,* the "reward" for the reading of the Qur'an, and so forth. This power of language is unique since it must be accepted without question; one accepts it as an *inherent* power of language. The pragmatic power of a language has been experienced by all of us. In fact, one aim of education is to teach us the pragmatic success and failure of various languages, varieties of languages, and styles. At present, English has the greatest pragmatic success in a wide variety of domains across cultures. I return to this topic later.

And now let me digress again and revisit Foucault (1980: 96ff) to summarize his suggestions for what he terms "methodological precautions" for the study of power. These are given in Chapter 1, but are repeated here. One has to ask, as Foucault suggests, questions such as the following:

(1) What is the "ultimate destination" of power at its "extremities"?
(2) What is the aim of someone who possesses power? In other words, who has power and what does that person have in mind?
(3) What is the network of power? In Foucault's view (1980: 98), power "must be analyzed as something which circulates, or rather as something which only functions in the form of a chain."
(4) What are the agents of power?
(5) What are the "ideological productions" of power?

In the sections that follow, I will address some of the questions raised by Foucault, with specific reference to English.

Language Spread and Motivations for the Acquisition of Power

Motivation for the acquisition of various types of power has been particularly strong for the languages associated with colonial expansion: Arabic, English, French, Persian, Portuguese, and Spanish, to name six major languages.

94   The Power and Politics

Turning to English, during its expansion in various continents, its speakers have claimed – and sought – different types of power for it. The language has also been perceived by others to symbolize such powers. Consider, for example, the following:

1) *Enlightenment in a religious sense*: The term *enlightenment* is used here in the context of religious indoctrination, proselytization, and other-worldly reward. Note the observation about "the true curse of darkness" of the Hindus in Chapter 1 of this volume, which, as Grant (1831–1832: 60–66) states, motivated "the communication of our light and knowledge to them." In Sri Lanka the situation was no different. There, a "Christian Institution was set up in 1827 to give a superior education to a number of young persons who from their ability, piety, and good conduct were likely to prove fit persons in communicating a knowledge of Christianity to their countrymen" (Barnes 1932: 43).

The American approach to the Philippines was identical to the approach to South Asia, as esplained in Chapter 1. It was one way of conscience soothing, using power with the motive of other-worldly reward. This resulted in the emergence of a " power elite" of a type previously unknown to the regions of Asia and Africa. Mazrui rightly asserts that "Christianity in Africa ... is the religion of the power elite in the majority of countries south of the Sahara" (Mazrui 1975: 11–12).

2) *Marker of the "civilizing process"*: One might use a broad label here to refer to the claim of the "civilizing process" as the development of material and intellectual potential through various processes of Westernization. The literature is full of examples of this attitude on the part of many Westerners in Asia and Africa (see e.g., Narasimhaiah 1986, in which reference is made to the use of formulations such as the "White Man's burden" in England, the "Mission civilisatrice" in France, "Kultur" in Germany, and the "Great Society" in America). I cannot resist the temptation to cite the following two examples from a Ph.D. dissertation entitled "Papua New Guinea English" (A. Smith 1986), which includes two quotations from important scholars teaching English in Papua Guinea. One scholar took the position that "English *per se* is the most valuable gift we can bestow on the native" (cited in A. Smith 1986: 11), and the other, who became the first vice-chancellor of the University of Papua New Guinea, said in 1958, "Teach them English, English, and more English: this is what they want" (cited in A. Smith 1986: 14).

3) *Distancing from native cultures*: This claim is interrelated with the motivation of the "civilizing process." An extreme example of this is T. B. Macaulay's (1800–1859) observation. The United States, as Zentella (1981: 219) observes, tried to Americanize Puerto Rico "with a vengeance during the

fifty years of its occupation." The aim was the following, as the then–commissioner of education, Victor Clark (cited in Zentella 1981: 219), saw it:

> If the schools became American and the teachers and students were guided by the American spirit, then the island would be essentially American in sympathies, opinions, and attitudes toward government.

This attitude change would result in an immense social change, and the ultimate result would be similar to what we have seen in Africa and South Asia: the creation of "Afro-Saxons" (Mazrui 1975: 11) and "Brown Sahibs."

4) Acquisition *of various spheres of knowledge*: English has now become a major tool for acquiring knowledge in the sciences, technology, and humanities. Its "vehicular load," to use the term suggested by Quirk et al. (1972: 2), is indeed unprecedented for a human language: "Vehicular load" refers to the extent to which English is "a medium for science or literature or other highly regarded cultural manifestations – including way of life" (*ibid.*). English does not represent only "the way of life" of the Inner Circle but that of countries within the Outer Circle, too. And there lies its strength as an international language.

5) *Vehicle of pragmatic success*: The pragmatic success of English is not restricted to international contexts only. Its success is evident in the Outer Circle, in its various intranational roles. This aspect has been widely discussed in literature and the terms *link* and *complementary* language have been used to refer to this function of English. And here the term *link* is used for a medium of communication both *within* a country and *across* countries.

6) *Marker of modernization*: The modernization and development effect of English is primarily determined by the attitude people have toward the users of this language, and their worldly success.

7) *Masters' code of control*: In the multilingual and multiethnic contexts of colonial Asia and Africa, English was used to serve the new master. It was, as Chishimba says (1985: 59), "introduced in Africa for the functional goal of making the African serve his master, not in order to assimilate him into the English way of life." A long list of reasons can be given for this attitude.

Strategies for Power and Politics: "Range" and "Depth"

In the global context, the two important indicators of the power of English are its "range" and "depth." "Range" refers to the total domains of function and the types of functions that the language has acquired around the world. At present, English dominates the largest spectrum of functions in the widest possible register range, as shown in Chapter 3.

As time goes by, this domination by the functional domains of English is increasing in spite of the outcry against language imperialism and other such

96   The Power and Politics

anti-English slogans. I present in the following some parameters of the power of English, which attest to the present (and expanding) *range* and *depth* of the language.

The Parameters of the Power of English

(a) *Demographical and numerical*: Its unprecedented spread across cultures and languages, on practically every continent (see e.g. Fishman et al. 1977 and Crystal 1985b).

(b) *Functional*: It provides access to most important scientific, technological, and cross-cultural domains of knowledge and interaction.

(c) *Attitudinal*: It symbolizes – certainly to a large group across cultures – one or more of the following: neutrality, liberalism, status, and progressivism.

(d) *Accessibility*: It provides intranational accessibility in the Outer Circle and international mobility across regions (cf. "link language" and "complementary language").

(e) *Pluricentricity*: This has resulted in the nativization and acculturation of the language. These two are, then, responsible for the "assimilation" of English across cultures.

(f) *Material*: It is a tool for mobility, economic gains, and social status.

The term *depth* is viewed in a horizontal sense – the societal penetration of English – in educated and other varieties. In the case of South Asia, we see "penetration" in terms of the hierarchy of the caste. However, the demography of language "penetration" – in a societal sense – is only marginally important. It is the societal and educational levels of the users of English that seem to carry more weight.

One just has to ask the following types of questions to understand the power of English across cultures:

(1) What is one's reaction toward a competent and proficient user of English in the Outer or Expanding Circle?

(2) Are the roles acquired by English users emulative?

(3) What are the economic motivations for learning English?

(4) What are the uses of English in terms of intranational and international mobility?

Is there any way to mark the indicators of the depth of English – linguistic and societal? The depth of language in terms of social penetration is rather difficult to assess. However, there are two indicators for it: first, the pluricentricity of English; and second, the development of varieties within an educated variety, particularly in the Outer Circle. Regarding the pluricentricity of English, and the "shifting" of the center of English, Steiner's observation (1975: 4) is very apt. Steiner, referring to Great Britain, observes that it "makes up only a small portion of the English-speaking totality."

And then he (1975: 4) explains:

> "Totality," furthermore is quite the wrong word. The actual situation is one of nearly incommensurable variety and flux. Any map of "World Englishes" today, even without being either exhaustive or minutely detailed, would have to include the forms of the language as spoken in many areas of east, west, and south[ern] Africa, in India, Ceylon, and the United states possessions or spheres of presence in the Pacific. It would have to list Canadian English, the speech of Australia, that of New Zealand, and above all, of course, the manifold shades of American parlance. Yet although such a catalogue would comprise hundreds of millions of English-speakers whose idiolects and communal usage would vary all the way from West Indian speech to Texan, or from the cadences of Bengal to those of New South Wales and the Yukon, it would be very far from complete.

Pluricentricity has further led to pluralism in incorporating other cultural and literary traditions: African, Southeast Asian, South Asian, and so on. And the result is that English, as we have seen, is no longer an exponent of only the Judeo-Christian traditions and Western concepts of literary creativity. The varieties within an institutionalized variety in the Outer Circle have provided access to various strata of society. Such varieties may be mutually exclusive, or not so exclusive, or may involve lectal shifts (as, for example, in the case of the basilect in Singapore, Nigerian Pidgin in Nigeria, and bazaar English in India).

Though the demography of English cannot be underestimated, it should be mentioned that the "range" of functions is a better indicator of the power of English than is its depth. One can think of many reasons for this. Consider, for example, the following:

First, English seems to have gone through a *filtration* process: the varieties within a variety have contributed to the expansion of the range of English (though not necessarily in its educated variety). The subcodes have acquired important roles that motivate a *variety shift* among the users of English. Again, a case in point is Singapore-Malaysian English. Not-so-standard varieties have been used by, for instance, Arthur Yap (who wrote poetry in Singaporean basilectal English), Nassim Ezekiel (whose poems are in "Indian English"), and Chinua Achebe (some of whose characters speak Nigerian Pidgin English).

Second, in multilingual contexts we have seen that the most viable codes tend to acquire most vital domains. One, however, has to explain – even tentatively – what one means by a "viable" code. There are two ways to determine the *viability* of a language: what one thinks the language (in this case, English) will do for a person, and what others think of a person when he or she uses the language (again, in this case, English).

There is, thus, a relationship between the range of a language and language "abandonment" under the impact of English, and in favor of English. One may – on this count – accuse English of causing functional "dormancy" in the number of major and minor languages of the world. The "maintenance" of

98   The Power and Politics

other languages under the overwhelming power of English must be seen within this perspective. Note that this accusation is often presented as an argument against the use of English. One, therefore, sees that the policies of a government – or the recognition of a language for a particular role (as, for example, in India) – do not seem to be effective under the "power" of English. While emotional attachments may be to one language, pragmatic needs motivate not only the continued use of English, but also its further expansion. It is indeed a vicious linguistic circle.

We find evidence of this in the attitude (and use of language power) of the new emerging elite in the Outer Circle. They are generally English educated; they exploit the power and symbols that such education bestows upon them and they see to it that their children go to the best English medium schools and seek admission to Western universities. And then, they proclaim – both in English and in local languages – the ills of English, and the evils of its power, and they protest against the continued domination of the language. On the one hand, such groups are exploiting the current pragmatic power of English as far as they and their families are concerned. On the other hand, they are attempting to create a power base for another language – interestingly, through the medium of English!

How English Acquired Depth and Range

How did English acquire its unprecedented depth and range? A number of answers have been given in the literature. The major reason is the historical role of England as a colonial power, with English being the linguistic tool of that political might. Other strategies – not always consciously planned – come to mind.

1) *The camel-in-the-tent strategy*: This strategy was typically applied in parts of Africa and South Asia. In these regions, English first gained a highly restricted foothold and later, with political maneuvering and other tactics, expanded its range. In some cases the role of missionaries had been substantial. (See, for example, the case of East Africa; in South Asia the role of the missionaries varied from one part of the region to another.)
2) *The linguistic elitism strategy*: The political power naturally attributed a "power" to the language of the Raj.
3) *The "close-the-ranks" strategy*: This was essentially a language solidarity strategy. Those who wanted to identify with the political power first had to establish an identity of a shared code.
4) *The information control strategy*: The power of English is not exclusively due to information "control" in the domains of science and technology. In the Outer Circle, for example, information control had other manifestations,

Spheres of Power and Control

too. English was – and continues to be – the language of the legal system, the language of higher education, the language of a panregional administrative network, and now of information technology, and so on (see e.g., Bailey and Görlach 1982 and B. Kachru 1984a).

5) *The marketability strategy*: English is already a major language of trade, commerce, banking and international advertising. In the Outer Circle, English additionally performs several localized roles, either because the indigenous languages are not equipped for these roles – as they have not been used in such contexts before – or because the use of English is considered prestigious, more appropriate, or "powerful." This attitude has bestowed more power upon the language. I will not dwell on this point here since I have discussed it in detail elsewhere (see B. Kachru 1984a; see also Phillipson and Skutnabb-Kangas 1986).

Spheres of Power and Control

What are the current domains – and spheres of control – that provide evidence of an interplay of power and politics related to the English language? And what are the pressure groups that control the strings of power?

The answer to the first question is perhaps easier than to the second question. There are four basic areas in which the power of English manifests itself: linguistic, literary, attitudinal, and pedagogical. The manifestation of this power has been described – and, of course, attacked – under different provocative labels: *discrimination* (e.g., Leibowitz 1969), *imperialism* (e.g., Haugen 1985 and Read 1974), *genocide* (e.g., Day 1981 and 1985), *inequality* (e.g., Sato 1985), and *death* (e.g., Dressler and Wodak-Leodolter 1977), to list only a few such terms.[9]

First, let us consider the question of linguistic control. This is reflected in the following ways, among others:

(1) The use of channels of codification and the control of these channels;
(2) The attitude toward linguistic innovation by those who are not part of the Inner Circle. (This is, however, not restricted to the Outer Circle; there are "linguistic lames" in the Inner Circle, too, as has been shown in several studies, notably by William Labov 1972a, 1972b);
(3) Lexicographical research and the choice of dictionary-worthy entries (see e.g., McArthur 1986; B. Kachru and Kahane 1995).

The three channels of linguistic control listed here are most powerful since they can *define* and, again, as Tromel-Plotz (1981: 76) reminds us, "Only the

---

[9] Note that all these studies do not necessarily focus on English, though a majority do.

100   The Power and Politics

powerful can define others and make their definitions stick. By having their definitions accepted they appropriate more power."

The second aspect to consider is the ethnocentric attitude toward literary creativity in the English language in the Outer Circle (see Dissanayake 1985 and Thumboo 1985a). This attitude is expressed in subtle ways by establishments in departments of English language and literature, in professional journals, and in professional organizations. There is already an impressive body of data available on this point. The result of such control is that the *authentication* of nonnative writers of English primarily depends on the Inner Circle.[10]

The third aspect is attitudinal. Here we become involved in complex psychological and sociological issues concerning the identities of individuals, of speech communities, and of speech fellowships. One would like to believe that issues of attitude apply only to the Outer Circle; actually, this is not the case. We now have an abundance of literature to show that the power and politics of some selected groups have equal sway in the Inner Circle on some "disadvantaged" segments of society (see, e.g., Nichols 1984 and Smitherman 1984).

The fourth aspect is concerned with the "pedagogical issues" in the teaching of English in global contexts. In other words, it refers to the power that a limited number of agencies in the Inner Circle have acquired about the teaching-related (classroom-oriented) aspects of English. Because of space limitations, I will not list all of the concerns here. Note, however, that these are not unrelated to the economic aspects that I shall enumerate later.

A list of such pedagogical concerns includes, for example:

(1) The model for the teaching of English and its sociological and pragmatic validity;
(2) the bandwagons of methods (often commercially motivated), which seldom take into consideration the local needs and the various limitations in the Outer Circle;
(3) the teacher-training programs for ESL that have been developed in the Inner Circle for the training of "specialists";
(4) The fast-developing industry of tests for evaluating competence and proficiency in English, and the underlying culturally biased assumptions for the construction of such tests; and
(5) the approaches and research paradigms for English for Special Purposes (ESP).[11]

---

[10] There is another side of this aspect. I will not address it in this chapter.

[11] For a detailed critique of ESP from the perspective of the Outer Circle see B. Kachru (1986c).

These pedagogical aspects are just illustrative. One can add to this several other areas, for example, the pragmatic inadequacies of research on communicative competence, approaches to syllabus design, and research in applied lexicography. The last aspect relates to economics: the economic motivations resulting in underlying conflicts. These economic aspects cannot be isolated from the other three aspects. However, they do deserve highlighting, since in recent years the economics of English has resulted in significant competition among the countries in the Inner Circle and the Outer Circle.

"Killer" English

"Killer" English is a rather complex and emotional issue. The use of linguistic *power* and *politics* invariably results in the suffering of language minorities – and not uncommonly in the devouring of the smaller "linguistic fish" by a powerful language. This phenomenon has been described as language "death" or "linguicide." The smaller "linguistic fish" are those languages that have a restricted number of speakers and limited depth and functional range.

In discussing language death, a distinction is desirable between what one might call an *inevitable* language death and a death due to the motivated power (and politics) of another language. The ominous word *inevitable* here refers to the following: a demographically insignificant number of speakers, the pragmatically highly restricted domains of a language, and economic and societal discrimination against the use of a language.

The question is, Have the global uses of English become the main instruments of linguicide? One might also ask, What are the implications of the spread of English and its power on the linguistic rights of the speakers of not-so-powerful languages? Consider here, for example, the case of speakers of American Indian languages, Australian Aboriginal languages, and African and South Asian minority languages; the list can go on and on.

The relationship between language and international human rights has been succinctly discussed in McDougal et al. (1976), which also provides an excellent bibliography. In other studies, too, a direct case has been made blaming English for linguicide (cf. Phillipson and Skutnabb-Kangas 1986).

However, the accusing finger cannot be pointed only at English for causing language death, for local Asian and African languages also play roles in this linguicide, although the power and politics of English are immense and the implications are extensive. Itis well documented now that in this battle of languages English seems to have been gaining ground, certainly since World War II. As a consequence, it has left behind a trail of dead or dying languages and dialects, or languages that are not able to develop to their full potential in terms of gaining a functional range.

102   The Power and Politics

The Politics of English and the Power Feud between the Cousins

The Inner Circle is not immune from this power struggle. Thus, the United States, the United Kingdom, and, to a lesser degree, Australia are competing with each other in making gains from the English language. The competition is, in many ways, to sell a particular model of English, to make a market for teachers (or "experts") from one's own country, to seek foreign students from particular regions of the world for the study of English, and so on.

Achieving victory in the competition for selling a model has both material and other – more abstract – advantages. If a country outside the Inner Circle accepts a particular model of English, this naturally results in the creation of a market for pedagogical and technological materials, and equally important, for live human beings as "experts."

The rivalry among the cousins for selling a particular variety of English, or a particular method of teaching the language has also resulted in what one might call "linguistic paranoia." There is the feeling that the Outer Circle is playing the countries in the Inner Circle against one another, as illustrated by the observation of the British ESL expert Brumfit (1982: 7), who sees division between "the English-speaking World" and "the non-English-speaking World." In his view:

American English may be preferred to British by countries wishing to express their independence from a traditional British connection: countries too closely connected by geography or history to the States have been known to turn towards Britain for a change in model and teaching policy for their English. Perhaps the same is happening in contact with Australia or New Zealand.

One cannot fail to see this rivalry between the United States and the United Kingdom in the ESL-related professional organizations. However, on one point there seems to be agreement: that is to present a front of solidarity among the members of the Inner Circle. This is particularly true in the organizations that claim to serve the cause of English "internationally."

Foucault's Approach and Linguistic Power: Seeking Parallels

Let me allude to an earlier mention of Foucault's insights on power, though, as noted previously, Foucault's concerns are not specifically related to language. In his view, power is interested in "relations," and language focuses on "meaning." Even if we agree with his distinction, it seems to me that Foucault's discussion of various aspects and agencies of power, his conceptualization of this phenomenon, and his insights concerning methodologies for understanding power raise many language-related questions. One also finds many insightful parallels between those issues that concern Foucault (e.g., the use of power by the state, or by the agencies of the state) and those related to language, its manipulation, abuse, codification, and so forth.

The language-related issues motivated by various types of power include, for example, first, the use of various types of manipulation for the spread of a language with the aim of gaining political, caste, economic, and class power. The goal of such application of power is to acquire control over a vital aspect of human behavior – language. Second is the use of subtle or not-so-subtle linguistic devices for deception and propaganda – political, religious, and commercial. It was due to this concern that a short-lived school of semantics developed after World War II (e.g., see the work of Alfred Korzybski, Samuel Hayakawa, and Stuart Chase). This concern is further evident in the current movements for "plain English" and in studies of abuses of language in the media (see e.g., Redish 1985; Dayananda 1986; and Maher and Cuffs 1986 for discussion of "plain English," and see relevant chapters in Bolinger 1980 regarding the media).

Foucault's "methodological precautions," briefly mentionedearlier, provide a useful framework for describing the power of language. Of course, Foucault provides only broad suggestions not specifically pertaining to linguistic power. But language does not create power for itself; the agents of linguistic power are its promoters and its users, who develop a power base for its functions. This is done by assigning "powerful" and significant roles for a language, by providing an important position to it in language planning, and creating a context in which its user acquires an attitudinal status.

In other words, the strategies for gaining linguistic power have several similarities with other power-developing strategies, for example, in politics. Thus, taking the five methodological guide points of Foucault, one might rephrase his questions specifically with reference to the power of English. One has, then, to ask, for example:

(1) What is the "ultimate destination" of the power of English?
(2) Once the English-knowing elite acquire the power of language – at whatever level – what are their goals?
(3) How has the network of the power of English been created?
(4) Who are the agents who work within this network?
(5) What kind of "ideological" change does English produce?

These questions must be asked within the context of the global networks of English. The network has distinct characteristics within each circle of English. The symbols of power, the motivations for power strategies, the relationships of power, and the ultimate goals to be achieved understandably differ within each circle; they are often even in conflict with each other. The reality and the myth of the symbols have to be seen within. The Outer Circle is perceived to use the language for domination of various

104   The Power and Politics

types – cultural, economic and political. It is seen, as the argument goes, to cause both conscious and unconscious linguicide and dislocation of native cultural traditions by introducing or spreading Westernization. This is the position taken by various groups in, for example, Iran, Pakistan, Nigeria, and India. But, most important, English is seen as a tool of economic exploitation and domination.

This perception presents only one side of the story. The Outer Circle sees the other dimensions of the legacy of English, too: as a tool of national identity and political awakening, a window onto the world, a "link language," and so on. The Expanding Circle sees it as a vehicle for entering the twenty-first century. In the same country the English language is characterized by different labels representing power. The list of labels used to symbolize English (and its power) in Chapter 1 includes examples of this. The power of English is symbolized by labels such as "modernization" and "rootlessness," "national identity," "antinationalism," "Westernization," and so on. Often the same term (e.g., *Westernization*) may be used both in a positive and in a negative sense, depending on who uses it.

Ideological Change and English

The most important question Foucault asks is, What are the ideological products of power? Let me make this question appropriate to our present concern and ask, What kind of ideological change does English produce? Now, this naturally raises a host of concerns. The answers depend on the beholders' perceptions.

There is now a large body of literature – political, attitudinal, and of other genres – claiming that English is the most potent (shall we say powerful?) instrument of social, political, and linguistic change. (See e.g., Masavisut et al. 1986 for the power of English in Thai media). There is no doubt that the current power of English lies in this multiperception. Within each circle, groups of various political and other ideologies – the fundamentalists, the socialists, the nationalists, the communists, and so on – are exploiting this "multisymbol" characteristic of language for their own goals. Discussing this relationship between language and change, the Indian historian Panikkar (1953 [1961]: 329) argues:

Philosophy and religious thinking, however much they may influence the people in general, are the special interests of intellectuals... It is the change in the language that is in many ways the most far-reaching transformation in Asia, for it is not merely the reflection of the changed mind but is itself the instrument of continuing changes, for the new languages of Asia represent a new semantics, a new world of ideas and thought which is reaching a larger and larger circle every day.

Conclusion   105

The power bases of English, then, have to be seen in both material terms and psychological terms.[12] In psychological terms, English now has support groups in the Outer Circle that have given it credit for cultural renaissance, the spread of nationalism, panregional literary creativity, and neutrality. It is due to these psychological reasons that there is a strong emotional attachment to the language: this type of attachment is unprecedented in the history of language spread. It is interesting that the native speakers of English in the Inner Circle have as yet not recognized this psychological factor. A total profile of the present power of English cannot underplay the psychological factors. These factors are vital for creating an "identity" with the language and for contributing to the belief in the "alchemy" of English (B. Kachru 1986a [1990]) and functionally considering it a "language for all seasons." What we need, then, is to develop typologies for the power and politics of English for the three circles. It is through such typologies that one can understand the current power and politics of English, and its effects – good and not so good – on other societies and cultures.

Conclusion

This chapter essentially raises questions and does not necessarily provide answers. Concerning the global functions of English, as yet not many meaningful questions have been asked. It is not that one does not think of such questions since most of these are rather obvious. It seems to me that perhaps in the suppression of such questions, if one looks very carefully, one might find an interplay of "power" and "politics."

---

[12] Note that there are several other accidental and not-so-accidental reasons that helped the Inner Circle to create a power base for English: the Inner Circle used both overt and covert strategies for the spread and power of English. One factor that contributed to the pluricentricity of English was the absence of an academy and a recognized codifying agency for English. One could only "revolt" against an organized body with the mission of codification, but, as we know, for English there was no such organized academy. The most subtle strategy adopted was the "psychological bar," which is effective and, at the same time, elusive. This is true in the Inner Circle as well as in the Outer Circle.

Part II

Context and Creativity

6   The Speaking Tree

Introduction

The Speaking Tree analogy in the title of this chapter is relevant in more than one sense.[1] The legend of the Speaking Tree has historical depth – it actually dates back at least four millennia – and has been mentioned with reference to Alexander the Great, who, we are told, was taken in India "to an oracular tree which could answer questions in the language of any [one] who addressed it" (Lannoy 1971: xxv). The trunk of the tree, it is claimed, was made of snakes and animal heads, and the branches "bore fruit like beautiful women, who sang the praises of the Sun and Moon" (xxv). In the Moghul miniature, following the Islamic tradition, the Waqwaq tree – the Speaking Tree – is viewed with both awe and attraction.[2]

The trunk of the English language – the Inner Circle – evokes mixed responses, as did that of the Speaking Tree, but the branches are bearing delectable fruit. The linguistic Speaking Tree is blooming, for we believe it answers all our questions: those related to access to knowledge, those of pragmatic functions, and those of creative functions. In short, we have a unique oracle with many faces.

As explained, the concept WORLD ENGLISHES demands that we begin with a distinction between English as a medium (*madhyama*) and English as a repertoire of cultural pluralism (mantra): the former refers to the form of the language and the latter to its function and its contents. It is the medium that is designed and organized for multiple cultural – or cross-cultural – conventions. It is in this sense that one understands the concepts GLOBAL, PLURALISTIC, and MULTICANONS with reference to the forms and functions of World Englishes. What we share as members of the international English-using speech community is the medium, that is, the vehicle for the transmission of

---

[1] This chapter is a slightly modified version of my plenary talk at the Georgetown University Round Table in Languages and Linguistics, GURT 1994, and is dedicated to James E. Alatis, whose own professional career represents an active commitment to promoting the three dimensions of the 1994 meeting's theme.

[2] Anne Pakir tells me that in Baba Malay there are references to the Waqwaq tree.

110   The Speaking Tree

the English language. The medium per se, however, has no constraints on what message – cultural or social – we transmit through it. And English is a paradigm example of medium in this sense.

When we call English a global medium, it means that those who use English across cultures have a shared code of communication. And the result of this shared competence is that, in spite of various types of crucial differences, we believe that we communicate with each other – one user of English with another. It is in this broad sense of interlocutors that we have *one* language and *many* voices. The Speaking Tree responds to our culture specificity and moves us beyond.

It is this cross-cultural function in education, in business, in tourism, in personal interaction, and in literary creativity that has given English an unprecedented status as a global and cross-cultural code of communication. And the evidence for such unparalleled roles acquired by one language has been documented in several ways in numerous studies.[3] It is for this power that English is presented as an Aladdin's lamp for opening the doors to cultural and religious "enlightenment," as the "language for all seasons," a "universal language," a language with no national or regional frontiers, and the language on which the Sun never sets, or, to use McArthur' s (1994) term, "the organized Babel."

Medium versus Message

The cross-cultural functions and globalization of English have, however, had a price. How high the price is depends on the person to whom one talks. The English language and literature have slowly ceased to be exclusively Eurocentric, Judeo-Christian, and Western.[4] There is, as it were, a diffusion of other traditionally unaccepted canons; it is not that other canons are as yet necessarily accepted or recognized – far from that. It is, however, evident that the language and literary creativity in English have acquired many faces, of many colors, regions, and competencies.

And now at least in some circles, the use of the term *English literature*, in the singular, is considered rather restricted and monocultural. Instead, the term *English literatures*, in the plural, is steadily gaining acceptance (see Quirk and Widdowson, ed., 1985), and the term *Englishes* or *World Englishes* does not raise eyebrows in every circle. This terminological feud is not innocent; it is loaded with ideologies, economic interests, and strategies for obtaining power.[5]

---

[3] For references see, for example, Bailey and Gerlach (1982), B. Kachru (ed., 1982d [1992d], 1986a [1990], and McArthur (1992).

[4] I must hasten to add that I am aware of the hazards and oversimplification of using these broad cover terms, for example, combining the Judeo-Christian tradition, and considering the Western tradition as if they uniformly shared one tradition.

[5] For various perspectives on this debate from a linguistic perspective see relevant papers in Tickoo (1991), especially papers by Honey, Quirk, and B. Kachru.

By looking at English as a pluralistic language, we are actually focusing on its layer after layer of extended processes of convergence with other languages and cultures. And this convergence, a by-product of contact with other languages, is unique, since it has altered the traditional patterns of acknowledged contacts in its history, for example, with French, German, Italian, and Scandinavian languages. English has opened up itself, as it were, to convergence with the non-Western world: that part of the world that was traditionally not a resource for English. It is territories in this non-Western world, for example, West Africa, East Africa, South Asia, West Asia, and the Philippines, that have become relevant and contributors to and partners in the pluralism of the spreading language.[6] The opening up of the language and the multiculturalism expressed in it do not mean that these multistrands, from the Inner Circle or the Outer Circle, have been accepted by the power elite. That has yet to happen. The canons in the Outer Circle, the African American, the Chicano, and the Asian American, continue to be "loose canons," and the result is "the culture wars."[7]

And now, returning to our topic, by pluralism we mean the multiple identities that constitute a repertoire of cultures, linguistic experimentation and innovations, and literary traditions. And they havea variety of sources. It is in this sense that English embodies multiculturalism. And it is in this sense also that English is a global language. The input to this multiculturalism, then, is from all three types of users who constitute the aforementioned three Concentric Circles (B. Kachru 1982b,Smith, ed., 1987, and Y. Kachru 1991b).

Exponents of Multiculturalism

The strands of multiculturalism in World Englishes are of several types, but all have one feature in common: they manifest the multilinguals' creativity. As explained previously, this creativity is not necessarily consistent with the traditionally accepted norms of English, particularly when the violation of the norm is by the Outer Circle. The first strand is that of cultural identity of a variety – Nigerian, Indian, Singaporean – that is distinct from the Judeo-Christian identity of the language. Again the example of *The Serpent and the Rope* by Raja Rao comes to mind. The Sanskritized style of that novel has an ideological and metaphysical context e.g., "God is, and goodness is part of that is-ness." Or, again, for stylistic appreciation of G. V. Desani's *All About*

---

[6] For an extended discussion and some examples see B. Kachru (1994b), and papers on this topic in the "symposium" issue of *World Englishes* 13.2 (1994) titled *World Englishes in Contact and Convergence*.

[7] For further discussion, again from a linguistic perspective, see e.g., Dissanayake (1985) and Thumboo (1985a, 1992).

112   The Speaking Tree

H Hatterr (1951), knowledge of Sanskrit compounding *(samasa)* certainly facilitates interpreting constructions such as "Ruler of the firmament"; "Son of the mighty-bird," and "Thy sister my darling, thy name?" Naipaul believes that K. Narayan's novels are "religious books ... and intensely Hindu" (Naipaul 1977: 13).

A recent excellent attempt in this direction is Shashi Tharoor's *The Great Indian Novel* (1989): a contemporary story woven around the *Mahabharata,* an epic of ancient India and the longest poem in the world, dating back to the fourth century BC. We see the same types of strands in, for example, the works of Gabriele Okara, T. M. Aluko, and Onuora Nzekwu in West Africa.

The second aspect includes appropriate acculturation of the language, to mold it to function in the sociocultural, more specifically religious and inter-actional, context of Africa or Asia. We notice this in culture-specific personal interactions, in the news media, in matrimonial advertisements, in obituaries, and in letters of invitation. The matrimonial columns reflect African or Asian sensitivity and prejudices regarding color, caste hierarchy, regional attitudes, and family structure.

The third aspect relates to discourse strategies and speech acts. These are transcreated into English to approximate the Asian and African backgrounds, religious subgroups, and interactional contexts of a variety of African and Asian languages: they include culture-specific patterns of apologies, compliments, condolences, persuasion, politeness, and requests. These contextualized strategies are skillfully exploited by, for example, Mulk Raj Anand, Raja Rao, Ahmed Ali, and Anita Desai in India, and by Chinua Achebe, Wole Soyinka, and Nuruddin Farah in Africa.[8] We have yet to raise relevant questions about the canon expansion of English.

The reason is that our current paradigms of teaching continue to be based on monolingual and monocultural notions of creativity and canon formation or canon expansion. I will return to this issue in the following section.

Canon Expansion

When we talk of "canon expansion," it takes us to a complex question of what is meant by the concepts of CANON and MULTICANON. This, of course, is an elusive question, like defining the term *standard* or *norm*. "Standard," as Abercrombie (1951: 15) has warned us, provides "an accent bar," and "the accent bar is a little like color-bar to many people; on the right side of the bar, it appears eminently reasonable." And this is true of canon formation. As for norms and standards, one has to recognize "the politics and ironies of canon

---

[8] See, for examples, B. Kachru (1982b), Smith (1987), and Y. Kachru (1991b).

Canon Expansion

formation," as Gates (1992: 32) clearly does, in defining the canon of African American literature. Following Kermode, one might say that

canons are essentially strategic contracts by which societies maintain their own interests, since the canon allows control over the texts a culture takes seriously and over the methods of interpretation that establish the meaning "serious." (cited in Altieri 1990: 22)

In connection with canon formation, several questions come to mind. The first, what are the defining characteristics of a canon? Now, keeping in mind what has been said about the notions of STANDARD and NORM, a canon is both a symbol of self-identification and power and a strategy for exclusion. However, a canon does presuppose a cultural identity and tradition, a linguistic experimentation and innovation, and an extended period of creativity, which make it possible to compare creativity within a canon and across canons, in spite of the gatekeepers of canons. It is in this sense, then, that one talks of the "masterpieces," the "classics," and the "standard works." I have used the words "self-identification" and "power." A good example of this is provided by Said (1993: 37), when he refers to the rather acrimonious debate on the curriculum changes at Stanford University.

Bernard Lewis, a senior Orientalist – and, as Said says, "an authority on Islam" – entered the debate about changing the "Western canon." Commenting on Lewis's observation, Said writes:

[Lewis] took the extreme position that "if Western culture does indeed go a number of things would go with it and others would come in their place." No one had said anything so ludicrous as "Western cultures must go," but Lewis's argument, focussed on much grander matters than strict accuracy, lumbered forward with the remarkable proposition that such modifications in the reading list would be equivalent to the demise of Western culture; such subjects (he names them specifically) as the restoration of slavery, polygamy, and child marriage would ensue. To this amazing thesis, Lewis added that "curiosity about other cultures," which he believes is unique to the West, would also come to an end.

This position of a distinguished Orientalist is not much different from William Bennett's (1992) call for "reclaiming our heritage" and my compatriot Dinesh D'Souza's (1991) alarm about multiculturalism.

The question, however, becomes more complex when other dimensions are added to what is believed to be one medium and primarily one canon (the Western canon), ignoring the linguistic and cultural crossover of the language.

- That English as a medium is used by two distinct types of speech communities, those that perceive themselves as monolingual and monocultural and those that are multilingual and multicultural;
- that these speech communities represent distinct literary and/or oral traditions and mythologies;

114   The Speaking Tree

- and that the norms of literary creativity and linguistic experimentation are not necessarily shared.

A number of creative writers from Africa and Asia, and Chicano writers in the United States, have addressed this complex question.

The second question is, What are the implications of canon expansion? I believe that canon expansion is an indicator of two processes: divergence and convergence. Divergence marks the differences between two or more varieties of English, and convergence indicates shared *Englishness* in World Englishes. It is the shared features that mark, for example, Nigerian English, Kenyan English, or Indian English as a variety of what we know as Englishes. In the Outer Circle, the divergence is conscious, as in, for example, the work of Achebe, Rao, and Anand, and is a result of multilinguals' creativity. Ngugi refers to this multilingual context when he says that in Kenya, there is Swahili as the lingua franca, and there are "nationality languages" such as Gikuyu and Luo. And "by playing with this language situation, you can get another level of meaning through the interaction of all three languages" (interview in Jussawalla and Desenbrock 1992: 34).

Multicanons as Symbols and Substance

We must view canon expansion as more than mere linguistic experimentation, since multicanons in English have symbolic and substantive meaning: symbolic in the sense that one's identity is symbolic, and substantive in the way the identity is expressed, articulated, negotiated, and preserved in language.

How we respond to these symbols and articulations of identities is not just an issue of attitude toward another canon within World Englishes; it also becomes an issue of ideology and of power. And it is the ideological issues that are reflected in the selection of paradigms of inquiry and models for research. These issues determine how one conceptualizes a speech community, how one constructs the barriers for *us* and *them*, for *insiders* and *outsiders* (see e.g., Phillipson 1992, B. Kachru 1994a).

And if we look at global language use, norms of language interaction, and literary creativity across societies – Asian, African, and European – it is evident that the majority of the world's population is either bi- or multilingual, or, at least, diglossic. The diglossic users of a language choose between a formal and a colloquial variety of language, as do, for example, Arabic, Tamil, and Greek speakers.

And from a multilingual's perspective, even the concept second language learning is in reality somewhat restrictive and misleading. The concept second language learning and teaching does not have pragmatic validity in West Africa, East Africa, South East Asia, and South Asia. In these regions, as in many other regions, bilingualism or trilingualism is a part of daily interaction, and it is in such interactional contexts that English has emerged as yet another linguistic code interfacing in Nigeria with Yoruba, Hausa, and Igbo; in Singapore with Chinese, Malay, Tamil, and Panjabi; in Kenya with Swahili and several "nationality languages"; and in India with at least eighteen major languages recognized by the republic's Constitution. It is in such culturally and linguistically pluralistic contexts that, for instance, African English, South Asian English, and Philippine English have developed. I purposely used the modifiers *African, South Asian,* and *Philippine* with *English* and have done so throughout this volume. The modifiers are markers of change and adaption: change due to contact with indigenous languages and adaption in terms of acculturation.

I have so far tried to unfold a dimension of English that looks at language variation, linguistic creativity, and linguistic identity from a pluralistic perspective. I believe that the global dimension of creativity in English, its recognition in the classroom, in the curriculum, and in teacher training, has relevance to educational linguistics.

However, before we take that step, we must seek liberation from consciously cultivated myths or fallacies about World Englishes. These myths are the result of flawed hypotheses, a lack of empirical and sociolinguistic links with the contexts of language use, or deliberate myth making.

World English Literatures and Transcultural Canon

We have traditionally discussed literary creativity in English within the framework of monolingualism and the native tongue, monolingualism being the norm and literary creativity an artistic manifestation of it – in other words, within the impact of the preceding four myths. And, as we have seen, the result of this monolingualism myth is that Conrad and Nabokov, for example, have been viewed as "exceptions" to this cherished norm (see e.g., Crystal cited in Paikeday 1985: 66–67, and Shills 1988: 560). These assumptions not only cloud our view of creativity in World Englishes but also distract us from the study of World Englishes as transcultural and multilingual canons. As a result, we have ignored the fact that this manifestation of literary creativity – more widespread than the monolingual's – reveals that bi- or multilingualism is normal activity and bilinguals' creativity is a normal manifestation of such linguistic competence.

This situation is well illustrated in Forster (1970), to give just one example. The author traces multilingualism in European literatures through the Middle Ages and the Renaissance, and he illustrates it even with the writers of the twentieth century. He skillfully demonstrates (1970: 7) that "the idea of polyglot poets" is less strange than we believe. And he argues that it is due to the influence of the romantics that

116   The Speaking Tree

we have all been brought up to believe that each language has its mystery and its soul, and that these are very sacred things, in whose name indeed much blood has been shed in our own lifetime and is still being shed ... If we put sentiment aside, there are very many people and very many situations for which different languages are simply tools appropriate to certain definite purposes, analogous to the different stylistic levels within any one language.

In the global context, from the earliest period, what has been considered elitist literary creativity has been carried on in nonnative languages. In Europe, we see such creativity in, for example, Latin and Greek; and in South Asia, in Sanskrit and Persian. In essentially monolingual contexts, or where the mother tongue has been the primary language for creativity, there generally are diglossic situations. In such situations, traditionally the High variety was used for literary creativity: *sadhu bhasa* in Bengali; *granthika* in Telugu; the formal variety in Tamil; Persianized or Sanskritized varieties in Kashmiri. The High varieties have always been distant from the common varieties used by the speakers of these languages: so much for the claims of Crystal and Shills.

In transcultural creativity in the "other tongue," we have seen several distinctive characteristics. Such creativity entails formal "patterning" – conscious or unconscious – from more than one language. However, there is one language that provides, as it were, the scaffolding and the raw formal apparatus for transcreation of the texts. In establishing such an equivalence, the creative writers obviously have to make several decisions. The writer can do what Mulk Raj Anand and Amos Tutuola have done in terms of equivalence: keep the text in English close to Punjabi and Yoruba, respectively.

A writer may take another track, that of Raja Rao. What Rao does is not to establish equivalence at the lexical level or in terms of just the speech functions. He goes much beyond that; he recreates a distinct discourse. One type of strategy is evident in Rao's *Kanthapura,* and another type in *The Serpent and the Rope*: one representing the vernacular style of the mother tongue and the other, of Sanskritization. It is almost recreation (or transfer) of the diglossic situation into English. In such literary creation, much depends on how close the bilingual writer wants to remain to the formal patterning of the *other* language.

Does this, then, mean that in characterizing creativity in World Englishes, for example, in speech acts, we have three broad classes of writers, as D'Souza (1991: 309) has proposed for Indian English: the Minimizers (e.g., Anita Desai, Amitav Ghosh, Kamala Markandaya, R. K. Narayan); the Nativizers (e.g., Mulk Raj Anand, Bhabani Bhattacharya, Khushwant Singh); and the Synthesizers (e.g., Meena Alexander, Upamanyu Chatterjee, Bharati Mukherjee)? At one level this categorization is insightful; but, then, once we discuss, for example, *Clear Light of Day* by Anita Desai, the Minimizer category creates problems in interpreting the vital functions of "the fourfold pattern," and the significance of the number 4 in the Indian tradition (Zimmer 1972: 13). At the lexicogrammatical level, Desai is a Minimizer, but not so at the higher level at which the text has a sociocultural meaning.

Perhaps, in comparison with Raja Rao's *The Serpent and the Rope,* Desai is less complex. Rao' s book, a metaphysical novel, is said to have four distinct voices. This requires contextualizing the text in the sociocultural and religious milieu of Vedanta, and an understanding of the complexities of the Vedantic doctrine.

What we see, then, is that World Englishes literatures raise a variety of theoretical, descriptive, and pedagogical issues concerning culture and its interpretation and comprehension of a text across cultures. One must ask, for example:

- How does one approach this totality?
- How does one approach the distinct parts of this totality?
- What is universal in such a body of creativity?
- What is specific?
- How does one apply the methodology of educational linguistics for teaching this body of culturally pluralistic creativity?

The preceding discussion moves to the forefront a string of broad points concerning transcultural literary creativity in English and the cultural component in such creativity, and issues related to interpretation.

I believe that there are other emerging interconnected issues that deserve attention. One major point concerns the recognition of an unprecedented event of our times: the development of World Englishes as a vital multicultural resource. This resource has established itself as multiplicity of canons, which incorporate several regional, sociocultural, linguistic, and literary identities. The process of canon formation is an ongoing one, an evolving one. In building this canon, in its distinctiveness, linguistic, discoursal, and stylistic, various linguistic processes, including that of translation, play a vital role. But this is only one part of canon building.

There is, as it were, "the interplay of diverse voices" (Dissanayake 1989, xvi): polyphony, multivocality, and heteroglossia. This view is precisely that of Bakhtin (1981: 262 cited in Dissanayake 1989). It is this process

whereby the unified meaning of the whole is structured and revealed. In comprehension and interpretation of a text and the canon which it belongs to, the notion of intertextuality provides a good theoretical backdrop.[9]

One might ask, Why is there a resistance to view literatures in World Englishes within this perspective? Is it, again, an extension of "monolingualization"? As we have seen, Lefevere (1990: 24) believes it is.

---

[9] Kristeva (1969: 146) defines intertextuality as a "sum of knowledge that makes it possible for texts to have meaning: *meaning of text as dependent on other text that it absorbs and transforms*" (cited in Sareen 1989: 42).

118   The Speaking Tree

World Englishes and Educational Linguistics

And now, let me turn to the question of the relevance of World Englishes to "educational linguistics." In this brief discussion, I will not go into the controversies concerning this subfield, but will instead accept the outline and boundaries of the subfield as presented in Stubbs (1986).

In the United States and elsewhere, MULTICULTURALISM as a societal or as a pedagogical concept has been perceived both as a divisive practice and as an enriching experience. It has been seen as a step toward national balkanization and as a laboratory for mutual understanding. In literature and language, the variationist approaches have been applauded for social realism and attacked as "liberation linguistics," an offshoot of "liberation theology." However, we must agree with Hughes:

> In society as in farming, monoculture works poorly. It exhausts the soil. The social richness of America, so striking to the foreigner, comes from the diversity of its tribes. Its capacity for cohesion, for some spirit of common agreement on what is to be done, comes from the willingness of those tribes not to elevate their cultural differences into impassable barriers and ramparts. (cited in Gates Jr. 1993: 115)

And commenting on this, Gates is right when he says that Hughes "provides one of the most gruffly appealing defenses of genuine multiculturalism that we have" (1993: 115). That this literature is a product of multilingualism and of multiculturalism has yet to be empirically demonstrated. The use of such literature(s) as a resource in the classroom has as yet to be fully explored. The difficulties in doing so are not only that appropriate pedagogical resources are limited. That may be true, but that is only part of the problem. A more serious difficulty is that we have still not shaken off the "romantic historiographer's" view of the English language, and the literature legacy continues, as suggested by Lefevere.

What is more frustrating, we have marginalized such creativity and multicultural dimensions of English by using terms such as "Commonwealth literature" or "Third World literature." In an illuminating observation, Rushdie says:

> When I was invited to speak at the 1983 English Studies Seminar in Cambridge, the lady from the British Council offered me a few words of reassurance. "It's all right," I was told, "for the purposes of our seminar, English studies are taken to include Commonwealth literature." At all other times, one was forced to conclude, these two would be kept strictly apart, like squabbling children, or sexually incompatible pandas, or, perhaps, like unstable, fissile materials whose union might cause explosions.

And Rushdie continues,

> A few weeks later I was talking to a literature don – a specialist, I ought to say, in *English* literature – a friendly and perceptive man. "As a Commonwealth writer," he

suggested, "you probably find, don't you, that there is a kind of liberty, certain advantages, in occupying, as you do, a position on the periphery?"

One does not have to quote Rushdie here: one also sees this attitude about the African American canon and the Chicano canon. And not many years ago – a little more than half a century ago – the same attitude was expressed about American literature in Britain. The great Pandit of the American language H. L. Mencken summarizes well the British attitude to American English when he writes that "this occasional tolerance for things American was never extended to the American language." This was in 1936.

Let me summarize the ways in which the preceding discussion relates to educational linguistics. I believe that literature in World Englishes and linguistic innovations from diverse cultural contexts provide refreshing texts for interdisciplinary debate and research. I have discussed these in detail elsewhere (B. Kachru 1992a and 1992b). These include:

- Cross-cultural discourse
- The bilingual's creativity
- Language contact and convergence
- Language acquisition
- Intelligibility
- Lexicography
- Language, ideology, and power

The teaching of World Englishes, then, entails a paradigm shift in several ways. The following points deserve attention for training professionals, and for teaching advanced students:

- sociolinguistic profile of the forms and functions of English;
- variety exposure and sensitivity;
- functional validity of varieties within a variety (e.g., Nigerian Pidgin, the basilect, and bazaar English); range and depth of uses and users;
- contrastive pragmatics;
- and multiculturalism in content and creativity.

The application of educational linguistics for exploring the crosscultural dimensions of World Englishes entails three interrelated steps:

- *Selection of a model,* that is, choosing a linguistic approach that is relevant to various dimensions of World Englishes. It has to be one of the models that provide a framework of socially realistic linguistics, e.g., Michael Halliday's and Dell Hymes's.
- *Identification of domains,* that is, demarcating the domains in which the distinctiveness of a canon is articulated and characterizing the innovations within a linguistic framework.

120   The Speaking Tree

- *Development of materials,* that is, developing pedagogical and, resource materials for the functions identified in the previous two.

There is also a provocative ideological facet to English teaching: Why is English considered a language of power? What ideology does English represent? Why do, for example, Ngugi – and some others – consider English a "culture-bomb," and, to quote Ngugi again, "probably the most racist of all human languages" (1981: 14)? Why does English evoke – or symbolize – positive or negative labels, which range from "cultural-bomb" and "killer English" to language of "liberalism," and "universalism"?

Conclusion

These are some of the provocative and challenging questions for discussion around one language in its various global incarnations, in its multicanons. I believe that we are depriving ourselves – as teachers and students – of an immense resource of cross-cultural perspectives and strategies of multilinguals' creativity if World Englishes are viewed exclusively from a Judeo-Christian and a monolingual perspectives.

By marginalizing the global uses of English, we are walling up an important world vision. And this reminds me of what an Indian pragmatist and wise man, Mohandas K. Gandhi (1864–1948), said so well in another context: "I do not want my house to be walled in on all sides and windows to be stuffed. I want cultures of all lands to be blown about my house as freely as possible. But I refuse to be blown off my feet anyway" (cited in K. K. John n. d.: epigraph).

The medium of English now provides that cross-cultural house. What is needed is a pluralistic vision to use this resource with sensitivity and understanding. And we must ask the right questions of the Speaking Tree to get appropriate answers for our linguistic, pragmatic, and pluralistic concerns and challenges. It means seeking answers for "curatorial" and "normative" functions of canon (Altieri 1990: 33). These are, then, the types of question I am raising in this chapter.

7   Creativity and Literary Canons

Introduction

This chapter argues that the generally held view that the "mother tongue" is the main medium for literary creativity is only partially true and that the role of "translation" or "transcreation" in the bilingual's creativity has usually been underestimated. The texture of the bilingual's creativity is essentially the result of the processes of translation and transcreation, and insightful approaches to stylistics – its theory and methodology – must take this fact into consideration. This is particularly true of the multilingual's transcultural creativity in World Englishes.

In recent years there has been a vibrant debate on literary creativity in the *mother* tongue, as opposed to the *other* tongue. The debate is essentially concerned with the "transculturational process," its manifestations in World Englishes, and the resultant canon formation. At the root of this debate is the generally held view that literary creativity is essentially undertaken in one's mother tongue, and that creativity in the other tongue is an exception, a rare activity, and a break from the norm. This characterization of creativity is prevalent in the societies that prefer to view themselves as monolingual, as opposed to bi- or multilingual societies. This perception is also present in what may be termed the folk view of literary creativity.

The view that literary creativity in the other tongue is an exception is not restricted to laypersons – that would perhaps be understandable – but it is also a widely held view in the scholarly community. The positions of the social scientist Edward Shills and the linguist David Crystal discussed earlier in this book illustrate the point. But their views only partially reflect the contexts of literary creativity across speech communities, particularly in multilingual societies. The attitude toward one's mother tongue (however the term is defined) depends on a variety of factors, including the role of the mother tongue in various domains, the status of the mother tongue in the hierarchy of languages, and questions of identity.

Let me illustrate the question of identity from my own mother tongue – a minority language of India, Kashmiri. One might ask, Why has the Kashmiri

122   Creativity and Literary Canons

language traditionally not been used in literary creativity? Why have the creative writers in Kashmir preferred another language for such creativity, for example, Sanskrit, Persian, Urdu, Hindi, or English? It is not for lack of a literary tradition in Kashmiri. Actually, good specimens of literary creativity in Kashmiri date back to the fourteenth century, in Lalleshwari's (born c. 1335) *vaks* "verse-sayings." A partial answer to the question is found in a *masnavi*[1] composed by Jalāl ad-Dīn Muhammad Rūmī (in the thirteenth century), who adopted Persian for composing poetry:

> Writing verse in Kashmiri
> is groping in the dark.
> If you would shine as candle-flame,
> write in Persian verse;
> You merely waste your talent if
> you write in Kashmiri.
> For you would not let the jasmine
> hide in a nettle bush,
> nor edible oil or spices waste
> on a dish of mallow wild.
> But times have changed and Persian is
> no longer read,
> and radish and loaf-sugar is
> relished alike.[2]

It is not only that at one time the language of literary creativity was Persian in Kashmir (see Tikku 1971), but that Persian also provided the standards of comparison for Kashmiri writers, a sort of a literary yardstick: Mahmud Gami of Shahbad, a Kashmiri poet, was called the Nizami of Kashmir, and Wahab Pare, another poet of Kashmiri, was considered the Firdausi of Kashmir (B. Kachru 1981b: 34–35).[3]

In such multilingual societies, as the language of creativity changes, the models for creativity and experimentation also change. One sees this in the creativity of Kashmiris in Sanskrit, Hindi, Urdu, and English. Kashmiri, of course, provides an example of a minority language. But what applies to Kashmiri can also be seen on a larger scale in several major languages in South Asia or other multilingual regions of the world. The language of literary creativity – even a transplanted language – has traditionally been elitist, and in most of the world an elitist language has generally been the mother tongue of a mere fraction of the population of the users of that language.

---

[1] *Masnavi* is a Persian literary form borrowed by Kashmiri writers.
[2] See Kaul (1945: 175), from which this translation is taken.
[3] The yardsticks for comparison provide valuable clues to the attitudes toward one's own language and the language of comparison.

Transcultural Creativity and Types of Cultural Crossover

In transcultural creativity, cultural crossover entails a cline. There are essentially three types of crossover. The first type occurs within a speech fellowship. The members of a speech fellowship generally have shared underlying sociocultural resources. The linguistic resources may be somewhat different, though to a large extent there is mutual intelligibility (e.g., between the speakers of Dogri and Punjabi, Hindi and Awadhi,[4] regional dialects of English, and educated English).

The second type of crossover occurs within speech communities sharing broadly identical literary, cultural, and religious canons, as is generally the case between the Dravidian South and the primarily Indo-Aryan North in India. One might label this situation as linguistic divergence underlying cultural identity. In such contexts, although there are linguistic differences, several processes of convergence may be identical, as is the case with the processes of Sanskritization, Persianization, and the ongoing process of Englishization in this region, which was initiated mainly after the 1830s.

The third type of crossover takes place within speech communities that are culturally, sociolinguistically, and linguistically divergent. Their cultural, linguistic, and literary canons are distinct. The transcultural creativity in the Outer Circle of World Englishes is of this type.

Measuring Intercultural Crossover

The existence of intercultural crossover and its various manifestations in transcultural creativity is not in doubt. The question that is not yet answered fully satisfactorily is how to measure intercultural crossover.

A number of criteria have been used to characterize the complexities of such crossover in a literary text. Smith has proposed the use of three key concepts: INTELLIGIBILITY, COMPREHENSIBILITY, and INTERPRETABILITY (see L. Smith 1992; Smith and Nelson 1985). The Smith triad may be explained as follows.

The term *intelligibility* refers to surface decoding of a linguistic utterance. It has been shown that in several varieties of World Englishes a number of lexical items present no problem in decoding the denotative meaning, but that what is essential is to comprehend the extended meaning, which involves the crossover in literary texts. Consider, for example, the following formations – *cow dung cakes, salt giver,* and *twice-born* – in their extended meaning in Indian English fiction.

---

[4] Dogri is spoken in the Jammu province of the Jammu and Kashmir state of India. Awadhi is traditionally considered a dialect of Hindi; it is spoken in eastern Uttar Pradesh.

124   Creativity and Literary Canons

The second stage of the triad is termed *comprehensibility* – that is, comprehension of a text of one variety of English within the context of situation of another variety. One has to go beyond the lexical meaning, from denotation to connotation. One has to focus on the culture-specific meanings that the preceding formations have acquired in Indian English. At this level, *cow dung cakes* has a functional and ritualistic meaning among Hindus; *salt giver* expresses gratitude in the sense that "one has done a good deed for you"; and *twice-born* conveys a vital stage in one's initiation into Brahminhood, from one's natural birth to a second "birth" as a Brahmin. In other words, an intelligible linguistic item acquires a function within a specific sociocultural context. Consider, for example, the translation of *hazur ka namak khate hain* in the Indian novelist Premchand's (1881–1939) short story *"Shantranj ke khilardi"* (The Chess Players).[5] Three renderings of this construction, in English, are as follows (see Gargesh 1989: 67–68):

a. We are your devoted slaves.
b. We have eaten your salt.
c. We are loyal to our master.

The third stage is that of *interpretability:* contextualization of the text within the variables that are appropriate for it within the context of its source language. This goal for making text explicit has traditionally been accomplished by adding commentaries to translations, for example, those of sacred texts such as the Bible and the Bhagavad Gita. It is at the level of interpretability that one establishes the relationship of a text with an appropriate context language seen as an exponent of culture. In the case of World English literatures, it would mean "reincarnating" English into the cultural contexts of Asia, Africa, and so on.

Text Types and Contexts

It is this "reincarnated" culture specificity of World Englishes that has contributed to the institutionalization of canons of English literatures in Asia and Africa. It is again due to these processes that claims of the "decolonization" of English have been made (see e.g., Dissanayake 1985; B. Kachru 1992e; Thumboo 1992). A number of aspects of such culture-specific texts, particularly of politeness, class and caste hierarchy, persuasion, and apologies in World Englishes, have been insightfully discussed by, for example, Y. Kachru (1991b). Let me go back to Kashmiri and present an example of the speech act of *greeting* in that language:

---

[5] Premchand was one of the most innovative novelists in Hindi and Urdu.

A. *kot chivi gatshan*

where are (HON.) going? 'where are you (HON.) going?'

B. *bas yot tam*

just here up to 'just up to here.'

C. *kyah kami?*

what to do 'For what?'

D. *bas yithay*

just for nothing 'nothing'

Contrast the examples of this speech act with American or British English greetings. This "inquisitive" and "probing" speech act not only is unacceptable, but also conveys "nosiness" from the English or North American perspective. And now, multiply a variety of such culture-specific speech acts in a large text, a short story, a novel, and add to that the underlying cultural and literary assumptions from India, Singapore, and Nigeria: the result is a shared medium but divergent cultural manifestations (see B. Kachru 1994e). One example of this divergence is Shashi Tharoor's novel *The Great Indian Story* (1989); another is the much-acclaimed novel of Vikram Seth *A Suitable Boy* (1993).

Linguistics and Cultural Issues in Transcreating a Text

Whatever underlying theoretical and methodological frameworks one adopts, it is clear that transcreating a text poses a variety of challenges. Let me again revert to Kashmiri to illustrate this point by giving a translation of a sonnet entitled "Zun" (The Moon) composed by Dina Nath Nadim (1916–1988). This translation illustrates that cultural and linguistic crossover is a cline and the linguistic and cultural "distance" of a text may increase or decrease in terms of the three variables in the Smith triad discussed earlier.

The Moon Rose Like a *Tsot'*
That day, the *tsot'*-like moon ascended
  behind the hills looking
wan and worn like a gown of Pampur tweed with a tattered collar and loose
  collar-bands, revealing
sad scars over her silvery skin.
She was weary and tired and lusterless
as a counterfeit pallid rupee-coin deceitfully given to an unsuspecting
  woman labourer
by a wily master.
The *tsot'*-like moon ascended and the hills grew hungry.

126 Creativity and Literary Canons

> The clouds were slowly putting out their cooking fires. But the forest nymphs
> began to kindle their oven fires.
> And steaming rice seemed to shoot up over the hill tops.
> And, murmuring hope to my starving belly, I gazed and gazed at the
> promising sky.

The task of contextualization becomes progressively complex as one crosses the shared and partially shared literary, cultural, and sociolinguistic canons, and the shared knowledge concerning such canons. One has to go through a process of, as it were, redefining and recontextualizing the text with each crossover.

The genre of sonnet in Kashmiri is patterned after English sonnet, and it is a recent literary innovation in Kashmiri in which Nadim excelled. The Kashmir-ization of the sonnet is obvious in many ways. First, by the use of what may be termed "culture-dependent" lexis: e.g., *tsot'* "'Kashmiri nan"; *tani* "collar-band"; *m ren* "a female laborer"; *thekdar* "contractor"; *gaj* "traditional place for cooking"; *vβthΞd/n* "traditional portable oven for cooking." Second, by the use of fixed collocations that entail shared knowledge of the local (in this case, Kashmiri) context, e.g., *popur pot* "tweed made in Pompur town." Third, by the use of language-specific fixed collocations and idioms. Consider, for example, the following:

Bat kulyi khasin	cooked rice trees (plural) to grow	"to have trees resembling cooked rice"
sech bavun	?	"to share a secret"
ech phir phir vuchun	eyes turn turn to see	"to gaze incessantly"
pan pan gatshun	thread thread to happen hungry	"to fall apart (to be very tired)"
phak phor	stomach	"to be hungry"

Fourth, the use of phonaesthetic features, as in the following line in Kash-miri: *ropi tani hani hani pani pani ga #Bmitspo #mpir 'po #t his* . There is no way this phonaesthetic (alliterative) effect can be created in a translation.

So much for the segmentation. Now let me explain some other features of the text. The metaphor *zun* "the moon" as *tsot'* (Kashmiri *nã;n* "bread") is very potent and suggestive. The personification of the moon is consistent with Indian mythology and literary tradition. But, with Nadim, there is a shift in such personification. In this sonnet, the depiction of the moon *as tsot'* acquires centrality. It evokes the feelings that are traditionally associated with the moon in Indian literature and folklore. But the similarity ends there. Consider also the range of lexis that occupies the modifier position: "the collar-bands are loose" is a sign of grief: Among the Kashmiri Pandits, "loose collar-bands" are indicators of mourning. The moon is lusterless "like a counterfeit pallid rupee-coin" deceitfully passed on with other coins to an unsuspecting woman laborer by a wily contractor. The skyscape further intensifies the suggestion of unsatisfied hunger: the clouds "put out their cooking fires," the forest nymphs "kindle their oven fires," and steaming rice seems to "shoot up the hill tops." And what does the laborer do? "Murmuring hope to starving belly, she gazes at the promising sky."

There are several questions one can ask about the underlying context of the sonnet. How relevant is it to mention that Nadim was an active member of the Progressive Writers Association, a leftist political and cultural organization, which dominated the literary scene of South Asia in the post-1930s? Furthermore, is it relevant to note that in this sonnet there is a conscious effort to neutralize his style – not to use Persianized or Sanskritized varieties of Kashmiri? And the major point is, How does transcreation in Punjabi, Hindi, Tamil, or, in our specific case in English, recreate the devices and strategies used for "foregrounding" by Nadim?[6] These questions have been faced by translators and creative writers since the first cross-linguistic translation was attempted, or since literary creativity in the *other* tongue was attempted.

The English version of Nadim's poem given earlier illustrates that the transcreation of the text results in marginal crossover; it is a mere approximation. The complexities are at the lexical, collocational, syntactic, phonaesthetic, and sociocultural levels. And this limitation of "translation" is generally well recognized.

And now, turning to transcultural creativity in World Englishes, we see that the "in-betweenness" of two or more languages and of two or more sociocultural contexts has not been explored with methodological rigor in stylistics.

World English Literatures and Transcultural Canons

Let me return to the observations of Shills and Crystal. Their claim actually is that literary creativity as an artistic manifestation is restricted to one's "mother tongue," or to one's "native language." This claim is close to the position of the romantics, who emphasized that "each language has its mystery and its soul, and that these are very sacred things" (Forster 1970: 7). In the romantic view, the secret to this mystery is available only to the "native speaker." That there is not enough evidence to support such a hypothesis about the "mother tongue" and its relationship to literary creativity is a different story, and I will not go into that here.

However, there is another manifestation of literary creativity – more widespread than the first type – that is common among bi- and multilinguals who engage in creativity in two or more languages. There are a number of creative writers who write in more than one language: their "mother tongue" and the "other" tongue. In India, for example, as Paranjape (1993: 5) observes, "most of

---

[6] The term *foregrounding* is used here in the sense in which it is used in the Prague School of linguistics.

128   Creativity and Literary Canons

the Indian poets in English have been bilingual or have at least translated from Indian languages." The creativity of such multilingual writers is based on the conflation of two or more languages, and the basic ingredients are "translation," "transfer," and "transcreation," used in the broadest senses of those processes.[7]

There are several explanations why, in linguistics, literary criticism, and stylistics, the "native language" and its "pure" form have been considered as the "norm" and as the "expected" tools for literary creativity. In reality, this view is in conflict with what actually has been the tradition of literary creativity in most of the multilingual world, and in large parts of Europe. In Forster's brief but well-argued study (1970: 7), he has shown that it is not difficult to see that "the idea of polyglot poets should seem rather less strange than it may well have done at first."

I have yet to explain what motivated my long digression on translation and transcreation, and on the Smith triad concerning intelligibility. My explanation is that there are several unique characteristics in transcultural creativity in World Englishes that may be explained with reference to these processes. In such texts, one first notices that there is an underlying scaffolding, as it were, for formal patterning of the text from another language. In the case of the Nigerian novelist Amos Tutuola, it is Yoruba, and in the case of the Indian novelists Raja Rao and Mulk Raj Anand, it is Kannada and Punjabi, respectively. One also sees that the formal patterning and linguistic conflation are not always conscious. In establishing such equivalence, a creative writer obviously has to make several choices. The writer can do what Mulk Raj Anand and Amos Tutuola have done in terms of equivalence to keep the English text close to Punjabi–Hindustani and Yoruba, respectively. A writer may adopt another approach, for example, that of Raja Rao, and establish equivalence not at the lexical level or in terms of just the speech functions: Rao goes much beyond lexis and creates a distinct discourse.

As discussed earlier, this strategy is evident in Rao's *Kanthapura* and *The Serpent and the Rope* – one representing the vernacular style of the mother tongue, and the other of Sanskritization. It is almost a case of recreation or transfer of the diglossic situation of his "mother tongue" into English. In such literary creation, much depends on how close the bilingual writer wants to remain to the formal patterning of the *other* language.

The third aspect of such texts relates to the type of link a creative writer desires to establish with the earlier native literary traditions, oral and/or written. In the case of Amos Tutuola, the link is essentially with the oral Nigerian

---

[7] Paranjape's list (1993: 5) includes the following names: Torn Dutt, Manmohan Ghose, Sri Aurobindo, Rabindranath Tagore, Puran Singh, Sri Ananda Acharya, Nissim Ezekiel, A. K. Ramanujan, R. Parthasarathy, Pritish Nandy, A. K. Mehrotra, Arnn Kolatkar, Jayanta Mahapatra, Dilip Chitre, Saleem Peeradina, and Agha Shahid Ali. The situation is not much different in Africa or other parts of Asia.

tradition, and in Raja Rao's *The Serpent and the Rope* the link is with the classical (High) Sanskritic tradition. In both cases, the desire is to establish an ancestral link between one's creativity and the past tradition. And this connection with the past is essential, as T. S. Eliot (1919 [1951]: 293–294) reminds us:

No poet, no artist of any art, has his complete meaning alone ... the best and the most individual parts of his work may be those in which the dead poets, his ancestors, assert their immortality most vigorously.

It is by establishing such a connection with the past – with the "ancestors" – that an African or Asian creative writer in English introduces the native literary and cultural tradition to the "other" language. It is through such strategies that the process of "decolonization" of English is initiated and accelerated, and its distinctness in terms of new canons is established.

Transcreation as a Tool of Power

The translator's task is far from innocent. We see translation as a tool of power in many contexts. FitzGerald's translation of the *Rubaiyat of Omar Khayyam* is a good example of the use of such power. In this translation he demonstrates immense artistic capacity for transcreation and reveals his attitude toward the Persians as people and as creative writers. FitzGerald's originality as an unsurpassed translator is widely acclaimed. However, what is less well known are his ethnocentricism and his disdain for the Persians as masters of the art of poetry.

While discussing the "liberties" he took in his translation of Omar Khayyam, FitzGerald (cited in Lefevere 1990: 19) wrote to a friend:

It is an amusement for me to take what Liberties I like with these Persians who (as I think) are not Poets enough to frighten me from such excursions, and who really want a little Art to shape them.

And, commenting on this outpouring of FitzGerald, Lefevere (1990: 19) warns us that "FitzGerald would never have taken the same liberties with Greek or Roman authors."

Perhaps not. However, Lefevere is making a broad generalization. That is evident when we read T. S. Eliot's attack on the translation of Euripides by Gilbert Murray (see Eliot 1920 [1960] and Murray 1910). Eliot strongly feels that in Murray's translation of *Medea*, "the Greek brevity" is sacrificed "to fit the loose frame of William Morris, and blurs the Greek lyric to the fluid haze of Swinburne" (cited in Das 1989: 34).

What a translator does to a specific text depends on the translator's creativity. Das (1989: 33), in discussing the English version of *Medea,* is right in saying that it "does not belong to English literature, nor does it belong to Greek, though in some sense it belongs to both." A translator functions among

130   Creativity and Literary Canons

languages, among two or more formal systems and their contextual connotations. The translator makes choices in creating a desired effect. In crossover and "blending" two or more systems a text is reincarnated.

The situation in creativity in World Englishes is not different from this. It is in this formal and contextual "in-betweenness" that a bilingual writer in World Englishes creates complexities in relation to Smith's three levels of intelligibility.

Transcultural Creativity As a Linguistic "Weapon"

The stylistic innovations in transcultural varieties of World Englishes have yet another dimension that remains to be studied in detail. That is using various stylistic devices as a linguistic "weapon," as it were, to alter the "colonial" language to give it a new identity and, as Soyinka says ([1988] 1993: 88), to turn English into "a new medium." It is in this sense that "a new medium," a colonial medium, is made to function in "the revolutionary use," as Soyinka ([1988] 1993: 88) would say.

The list of such "revolutionary" users is extensive indeed, both in historical terms and in terms of the countries it covers. The list includes African, African American, and South and East Asian writers, political thinkers, and social reformers. In their hands, we have seen what Soyinka ([1988] 1993: 88) calls "the conversion of the enslaving medium into an insurgent weapon" and "a linguistic blade."

In the perception of the colonized creative writer, then, the English language was to be redeemed from its exhaustion; it had to be revived with fresh linguistic energy, and it needed planned strategies for stylistic innovations to answer African, Asian, and Caribbean challenges. The linguistic "weapon" had to be redefined. In Bhabha's view (1994: 166):

Salman Rushdie's *The Satanic Verses* attempts to redefine the boundaries of the Western nation, so that the "foreignness of languages" becomes the inescapable cultural condition for the enunciation of the mother-tongue. In the "Rosa Diamond" section of *The Satanic Verses* Rushdie seems to suggest that it is only through the process of *dissemination* – of meaning, time, peoples, cultural boundaries, and historical traditions – that the radical alterity of the national culture will create new forms of living and writing.

Stylistic studies of transcultural texts have only marginally analyzed such writing in World Englishes from these perspectives.

World Englishes and Stylistics

The discussions – theoretical and applied – of transcultural creativity in non-Western World Englishes have yet to be conducted with appropriate theories and methodology. This fast-expanding and well-established body of writing

World Englishes and Stylistics 131

has yet to attain the status it deserves in departments of English language and literature, and in ESL curricula. The types of questions the translation of Nadim's "Zun" (The Moon) into English raise concerning cultural crossover are to a large extent identical to the issues we need to address in explaining the creativity of bilingual writers in World Englishes. The conceptualization of stylistics must go beyond the confines of monolingual paradigms. Literary creativity in Englishes is as much a part of the West African or South Asian canon as it is a part of World Englishes. In understanding these canons, various strategies of canon formation, one must not underestimate *translation* as one of the significant ingredients of such creativity.

One has to agree with Lefevere (1990: 24) that there are two major reasons why the role of translation in the creative process has generally been ignored or underestimated. The first reason is that "for the literary historian translation had to do with 'language' only, not with literature." That, of course, is a very restricted view of creativity. The second reason is "another pernicious outgrowth of the 'monolingualization' of literary history by Romantic historiographers intent on 'national' literatures preferably as *uncontaminated* as possible by foreign influence" (emphasis added).

And viewed within these perspectives, transcultural creativity in English is "contaminated" on many counts: It is not a part of a "national" literature as the term is generally understood; it shows deep linguistic and cultural convergence and contact – actually, it may reflect more than one "influence" – as is true of many literary traditions of South Asia and Southeast Asia, for example. These attitudinal concerns are only part of the story. A more fundamental reason for this inattention to processes of translation is that no interest has been shown in formulating approaches to stylistics that would account for the bilingual's creativity, and for transcultural creativity.

The story in this case is not much different when we compare it to our understanding of the bilingual's grammar. World Englishes literatures essentially manifest the diversity view of literary creativity and canon formation. Our approaches to the linguistic and literary creativity of bilinguals must be based on such perspectives. And I am using the term "diversity view" without any political connotations.[8]

---

[8] Discussing the creativity of the Indian writer C. V. Desani, Anthony Burgess (cited in Dissanayake 1989: xviii) refers to his use of language as "a sort of creative chaos." He says:

> It is the language that makes the book a sort of creative chaos that grumbles at the restraining banks. It is what may be termed whole language in which philosophical terms, the colloquialism of Calcutta and London, Shakespearean archaisms, bazaar writings, quack spiels, references to the Hindu pantheon, the jargon of litigation, and shrill babu irritability seethe together. It is not pure English; it is like the English of Shakespeare, Joyce, Kipling, gloriously impure...

Conclusion

In conclusion, then, this chapter makes three claims. The first is that the bilingual's creativity is the result of a textual and contextual blend of two literary and cultural canons: that of the "native" language and culture and that of the "other" tongue. The result of this bi-ness is another canon of creativity, as we see, for example, in West African English and South Asian English (see B. Kachru 1994e). The second claim is that the conscious or unconscious processes of translation at various levels play a very vital role in establishing the cultural and linguistic distinctiveness in the text. And finally, that the "monolingualization" of approaches to stylistics is inadequate to provide insightful analyses of texts in World Englishes. Our approaches have to be liberated from the prison of monolingual biases in order to provide theoretical and methodological answers to the challenges that the bilingual's creativity poses (B. Kachru 1992a, Y. Kachru 1994a, Sridhar and Sridhar 1986 [1992]).

Part III

Past and Prejudice

8   Liberation Linguistics

Introduction

In his important and provocative papers published more than two decades ago, Sir Randolph Quirk, former president of the prestigious British Academy, and founder of the Survey of English Usage, expressed several concerns about the current paradigms used for describing various issues related to the diffusion of English in the global context (see Quirk 1988 and 1989); he particularly addressed the question of standard and variation.

These concerns were actually first expressed by him in a somewhat different tone in 1985 at the 50th Anniversary Celebration meeting of the British Council in London (Quirk 1985).[1] I believe that the vital concerns expressed by Quirk, though specifically addressed to the global spread of English, are not peculiar to English. In the literature we see that more or less identical concerns have been expressed with reference to other languages of wider communication. These include languages restricted to a specific country (e.g., Hindi in India) and those that cut across national boundaries (e.g., Swahili in East Africa, Bahasa Malaysia in South East Asia, and French in Francophone countries).[2] The Quirk concerns are, then, worth considering, whether one is concerned with the language policy of a specific nation or with generalizations on language policies and attitudes that cut across languages and cultures.

The case of English is important to language policy makers for additional reasons, too. The global functions of English move to the forefront a number of variables that, I believe, have generally eluded language policy makers. These variables are rarely mentioned in the literature on language diffusion, language use, language shift, and language maintenance (B. Kachru 1988b; Phillipson and Skutnabb-Kangas 1986). I am thinking particularly of "unplanned" (or "invisible") policies as opposed to "planned" (or "visible") policies (Pakir 1988; Y. Kachru 1989). The Quirk concerns discussed here go much beyond specific

---

[1] Quirk and Widdowson (1985) contains the main papers presented at the conference and the discussion.

[2] For Hindi see S. N. Sridhar (1988); for other languages see e.g., Coulmas (1988).

136   Liberation Linguistics

issues, since Quirk has thrown his net very far and wide, covering a broad range of attitudes and issues: it is not possible to disentangle all the issues here.

I have briefly referred to Quirk's paper "Language Varieties and Standard Language" (1989), in which he expresses deep dissatisfaction with what he terms "liberation linguistics." To put it in other words, in Quirk's paper, there is a presupposition that "liberation linguistics" has an underlying ideological motivation, an unarticulated philosophical and political position. He says (1989: 21), "English was indeed the language used by men like Gandhi and Nehru in the movement to liberate India from the British Raj and it is not surprising that 'liberation linguistics' should have a very special place in relation to such countries." Quirk does not use any ideological term for his concerns; that does not, however, mean that his position cannot be related to an ideological position appropriate to them. After all, it is rare that there is a position without an ideological backdrop. It seems to me that Quirk's position is not much different from what in another context has been termed "deficit linguistics." What, then, is deficit linguistics? This concept has so far primarily been used in the context of language learners with inadequate competence in using vocabulary, grammar, and phonology of a language (e.g., Williams 1970; see also Phillipson and Skutnabb-Kangas 1986). It has also been used for "deficit" in organization of discourse and style strategies, and competence in manipulation of codes (e.g., Bernstein 1964ff.). During the past two or three decades a considerable body of literature has developed on this topic, both pro and con. A well-argued case against the deficit position, specifically with reference to African American English, is presented in Labov (1972a, 1972b). The Quirk concerns, of course, go beyond African American English and have global implications for research and the teaching of English.

The Quirk Concerns

First let me outline the major Quirk concerns. Those that he expresses are an attack on the positions that linguists (or, should I say sociolinguists?) have taken about the spread of English, its functions, and its multinorms,[3] in other words, on the recognition of pluricentricity and multiidentities of English discussed in earlier chapters. These concerns encompass a medley of issues, six of which I shall discuss here.

The first concern is that the recognition of the taxonomy of variation for English is a linguistic manifestation of underlying ideological positions. In Quirk's (1989: 20) view, "liberation theology" has led to the demand "Why

---

[3] These include positions by e.g., Ayo Bamgbose, John R. Firth, M. A. K. Halliday, Larry E. Smith, Peter Strevens, and Edwin Thumboo. My position in this connection is presented in papers published since 1962. A number of these are in B. Kachru (1982d, 1983b, 1986a).

not also a 'liberation linguistics'?" Quirk (1989: 15) therefore believes that the result of this ideological underpinning is that "the interest of varieties of English has got out of hand and has started blinding both teachers and taught to the central linguistic structure from which varieties might be seen as varying."

The second is that there is a "confusion of types of linguistic variety that are freely referred to in educational, linguistic, sociolinguistic and literary critical discussion" (1989: 15).

The third is that the use of the term "institutionalized variety" with the nonnative varieties of English is inappropriate. He says (1989: 18), "I am not aware of there being any institutionalized non-native varieties." Once he takes this position, he provides supporting evidence from a native and nonnative speakers' competence test for French (Coppieters 1987). The results of this test lead Quirk to the conclusion that there is

the need for non-native teachers to be in constant touch with the native language. And since the research suggests that *the natives have radically different internalizations,* the implications for attempting the institutionalization of non-native varieties of any language are too obvious for me to mention. (1989: 19; emphasis added)

One might mention here, as an aside, that this position is diametrically opposite to the position he expressed in Quirk et al. (1972: 26), and again in Quirk, Greenbaum, et al. (1985: 27–28), where it is stated that in the case of English, such [institutionalized] varieties

are so widespread in a community and of such long standing that they may be thought stable and adequate enough to be institutionalized and hence to be regarded as varieties of English in their own right rather than stages on the way to a more native-like English.

The reference here is to the speech fellowships of English in South Asia, West Africa, and Southeast Asia.

And now, returning to Coppieters's test for French, Quirk (1989: 19) concludes that nonnative teachers should be in "constant touch" with the native language. And he is concerned about the "implications for attempting the institutionalization of non-native varieties of any language."

However, there are problems with the conclusions. The solution of "constant touch with the native language" does not apply to the institutionalized varieties for more than one reason. First is the practical reason: it simply is not possible for a teacher to be in *constant* touch with the *native* language, given the number of teachers involved, the lack of resources, and overwhelming *nonnative* input. Second is a functional reason: the users of institutionalized varieties are expected to conform to the local norms and speech strategies, since English is used for interaction primarily within intranational contexts. And the last reason takes us to the psycholinguistic question of "internalization." The natives may have

138   Liberation Linguistics

"radically different internalizations" about their L1, but that point is not vital for a rejection of institutionalization. In fact, the arguments for recognizing institutionalization are that such users of English have internalizations that are linked to their own multilinguistic, sociolinguistic, and sociocultural contexts. It is for that reason that a paradigm shift is desirable for understanding and describing the linguistic innovations and creativity in such varieties (see B. Kachru 1987a).

A number of these points have been raised by Paul Christophersen with reference to Quirk (1989) in his comments published in *English Today*, 23 (1990) (vol. 6.3, pp. 61–63). Christophersen, however, is addressing his comments primarily to Quirk's mention of Coppieters's research on "native" and "nonnative" speakers of French; he rightly warns us that "we must not jump to conclusions regarding [its] possible implications." I cannot resist the temptation of presenting Christophersen's comments here. He says that Coppieters's research was

exemplary in the way it was conducted and presented, but, as I am sure René Coppieters would be the first to admit, a great deal more work and more thinking are required before we can draw any safe conclusions. Let me mention a few points.

In the first place, two groups of 20 and 21 people, respectively, can hardly be considered statistically significant in a matter that involves millions and millions of people.

Secondly, and more importantly, "native" and "non-native" speakers are not two precisely defined categories. Even among "natives," who might be thought to constitute a fairly homogeneous lot, one sometimes finds surprising variations, and an interesting example occurs among Coppieters's research subjects. One of four Italians was out of line with the other three in her perception of tenses (Italian and French), apparently because she came from a part of Italy where there is a regional difference. Yet we are told that all the subjects were well educated, so she must have learnt standard Italian in her Italian school. In the English-speaking world, where in some quarters the very word "standard" makes hackles rise, there are likely to be equally striking differences among the "natives." One wonders, too, how to classify people with an L1 learnt for only the first four or five years of life and since abandoned and largely or entirely forgotten. Some Welsh people fall into this category. And does a *Schwyzertutsch* speaker who has learnt High German in school qualify as a "native" speaker of German?

"Non-natives," being a negatively defined category, are bound to vary much more. A differently selected group of research subjects might well have produced a very different result. Coppieters's group contained the following L1 speakers: American, British, German, Italian, Spanish, Portuguese, Chinese, Korean, Japanese and Farsi. They were all engaged in academic or similar work; they had lived in France for an average of seventeen years and appeared to be fully at home in French and in their French surroundings, but only six of the twenty-one had no foreign accent. With two exceptions they had all had formal training in French, but none of them had specialized in French.

I wonder about the non-native's training in French. The questionnaire that was used in testing them covered mainly such things as *imparfait/passé composé, il* or *ce*, and the place of the adjective before or after the noun – relatively subtle distinctions, yet all of

The Quirk Concerns 139

them ones which should have formed part of their training. If they had been better trained in French, might they not have done better in the test? I tried one or two of the questions on my son, who had done a level of French, and he seemed to cope fairly well. And my own formal training in French, which I received in Denmark well over fifty years ago, also seems to have equipped me quite well. I have never lived in France; nor has my son.

What I am unhappy about is a tendency to assume that there is a mysterious, semi-mystical difference between two groups of people, natives and non-natives, a difference which affects forever the way their minds work when handling the language concerned – something to do with the way their minds are "wired," as some people would put it. This assumption is very similar to the Whorfian hypothesis in its outré form, in which we are all regarded as imprisoned within our respective languages and the thought forms that they impose upon us, with apparently no chance of escape across the language barrier. There is also, I fear, a link with ancient beliefs associating differences in language with tribal or national differences and assuming that these matters are all congenitally determined. Now a theory that implies unbridgeable mental differences should only be accepted as a last resort, if there is no other explanation available. And I believe there is an explanation; I think an escape route exists through improved language teaching and, most important of all, through improved language learning – because it must of course be realized that the learner himself will have to make a great effort if he is to rewrite his mind.

Quirk also seems to believe that institutionalization is a conscious process that is *attempted* with definite ends in mind – political ends not excluded. I am not so sure of that: institutionalization is a product of linguistic, cultural, and sociolinguistic processes over a period of time. Attitudinally, one may not recognize these processes and their linguistic realizations, but that does not mean that they do not exist.

The fourth concern is that there is recognition of variation within a nonnative variety. Quirk is concerned about the "disclaimer of homogeneity" and "uniform competence" (1988: 235) in such varieties of English. To Quirk, recognition of variation within a variety is thus confusing and unacceptable (B. Kachru 1986a).

The fifth concern is that there is a widely recognized and justified sociolinguistic and pedagogical distinction between ESL and EFL. Quirk ignores this distinction partly because, as he says, "I doubt its validity and frequently fail to understand its meaning" (1988: 236). However, in Quirk (1985), he recognizes the validity of this distinction and explains the differences within this "terminological triad" succinctly: the EFL users "live in countries requiring English for what we may broadly call 'external purposes'" (p. 1); the ESL countries are those "where English is in wide-spread use for what we may broadly call 'internal' purposes as well" (p. 2); and the ENL countries are "where English is a native language" (p. 2).[4]

---

[4] For a sociolinguistically and pragmatically motivated discussion of this triad see B. Kachru (1985b).

140   Liberation Linguistics

And the last concern is that there is recognition of the "desirability of non-native norms" (1988: 237). To illustrate his argument, Quirk says that "Tok Pisin is displaying gross internal instability and is being rejected in favor of an external model of English by those with power and influence" (1988: 237).

These six concerns do not exhaust Quirk's list of manifestations of "liberation linguistics"; however, they do capture the main arguments of his position. In articulating his concerns, Quirk, of course, is not presenting an alternate model for describing and understanding the diffusion, functions, and planning of a multilingual's linguistic behavior with reference to English. However, the arguments he presents do contribute to developing a framework for "deficit linguistics." What precisely does Quirk's "deficit linguistics" entail? I believe it entails the rejection of six important assumptions, namely:

(1) He reejects the underlying linguistic motivations for the taxonomy of variation, and finds such variational models motivated by an urge for linguistic emancipation, or "liberation linguistics."
(2) He rejects the sociolinguistic, cultural, and stylistic motivations for innovations and their institutionalization.
(3) He rejects the institutionalization of languages (in this case, specifically English) that are not native to their speakers.
(4) He rejects the natural cline of varieties within a nonnative variety.
(5) He rejects the endocentric norms for English in the Outer Circle.
(6) He rejects the distinction between the users of the Outer Circle (ESL) and the Expanding Circle (EFL), as he reduces all variation to a native vs. nonnative (L2) opposition.

Historical Context for Quirk's Concern

The concerns which Quirk has articulated in his usual elegant style are of course not new. Such concerns have been expressed at various periods not only about English, but also about other languages: Sanskrit, Greek, Latin, Spanish, Hindi, and so on. In addition, the deficit models have been used both in L1 and L2 situations.

It was in 1968 that Clifford Prator, a distinguished educator from the United States, took a more or less identical position to that of Quirk. However, there was a difference: in Prator's view the "heresy in TESL" was being committed by cousins on the other side of the Atlantic (Prator 1968). It was Britain preaching "liberation linguistics" (B. Kachru 1986a). There is, as Graeme Kennedy (1985: 7) says, referring to Quirk's 1985 paper, "a delicious irony" in that "Professor Quirk's paper reflects, in many respects, the position Prator advocated." Kennedy continues: "However, since the orthodoxy has changed, it might be argued that Professor Quirk articulates a new British heresy. You simply cannot win."

Kennedy (1985: 7) sees the question of standards as "fundamentally an attitudinal and especially an aesthetic one." Crystal (1985a: 9–10), commenting on the same paper, raises another important point of discussion when he writes, "What concerns me, however, is the way in which all discussion of standards ceases very quickly to be a linguistic discussion, and becomes instead an issue of social identity and I miss this perspective in his paper." Here Crystal has put his finger on a vital sociolinguistic point.

Myths vs. Multilinguals' Realities

The Quirk concerns are, of course, motivated by a venerable scholar's lifelong desire for maintenance of what he considers "standards" for international English and the world's need for a functionally successful international language. And there is no disagreement regarding English's being "the best candidate at present on offer" (Quirk 1989: 24–25). One indeed shares this concern with Quirk. However, it seems to me that in expressing this concern, Quirk has not only thrown out the bath water, but with it he has also thrown away the baby of many sociolinguistic realities. And to me, recognizing the sociolinguistic realities does not imply "an active encouragement of the anti-standard ethos" (Quirk 1985: 3); nor does it imply "to cock a snook at fashionably unfashionable elitism by implying (or even stating) that any variety of language is 'good', as 'correct' as any other variety" (Quirk 1985: 5).

Quirk seems to perceive the spread of English primarily from the perspective of monolingual societies, and from uncomplicated language policy contexts. The concerns he expresses are far from the realities of multilingual societies and negate the linguistic, sociolinguistic, educational, and pragmatic realities of such societies. I shall briefly discuss some of these realities here.

Linguistic Realities These provide a complex network of various types of convergence, which are more powerful in molding linguistic behavior than are outsiders' attitudes toward such modulated linguistic behavior (cf. Hock 1986: 498–512; Lehiste 1988). The basic criterion for marking pragmatic success is functional success with the members of the interactional network. This is particularly true of languages of wider communication or contact languages (e.g., the *bazaar* varieties).

Sociolinguistic realities, which move us closer to the functional context of language, attitudes, and identities. In Quirk's denial model the sociolinguistic realities have no place. In institutionalized nonnative varieties of English (and I know Quirk rejects this concept) this is particularly true,

142   Liberation Linguistics

as has already been demonstrated in a number of studies (e.g., see B. Kachru 1986a [1990] for more specific references).

Educational realities, which open up a can of worms in terms of problems such as classroom resources, equipment, teacher training, and teaching materials. One important point to be considered is the input that a learner of English receives in acquiring the language. The input for acquisition, the model to be followed, and the speech strategies to be used are provided by the peer group, the teachers, and the media. And there is an additional attitudinal aspect to it: the expectations of the interlocutors in an interactional context. The recognition of institutionalization of a language in language policies is only partly an attitudinal matter. To a large extent, it is a matter of the recognition of the linguistic processes, history, and acculturation of the language in a region, and functional allocation of a variety. All these aspects must be viewed in their totality. When the Indian Constitution stipulates English as an "associate official language," there is a message in it. When Chinua Achebe considers English as part of Africa's linguistic repertoire, his statement is indicative of a social, cultural, and linguistic reality. The claim that Indian English should be considered an *Indian* language (Kachru 1989a) on its functional basis is a recognition of several sociolinguistic realities. The reactions of an outsider who does not share these realities are only marginally useful here: they mark just that – the attitude of an "outsider."

Chinua Achebe's perspective or Raja Rao's positive identity with English is, of course, valuable from one perspective. However, equally valuable, if not more so, is the position of those Africans and Asians who are denigrating English, foreseeing its doom. They are suspicious of its immense functional power, its social prestige, and its "spell" on the people. Ngugi (1986: 5) is concerned that "African countries, as colonies and even today as neo-colonies, came to be defined and to define themselves in terms of the languages of Europe: English-speaking, French-speaking or Portuguese-speaking African countries." To him (1986: 3), the "biggest weapon" is "the cultural bomb," and

the effect of a cultural bomb is to annihilate a people's belief in their names, in their languages, in their environment, in their heritage of struggle, in their unity, in their capacities and ultimately in themselves ... It makes them want to identify with that which is furthest removed from themselves; for instance, with other peoples' languages, rather than their own.

Then, there is the voice of Pattanayak (1985: 400) from another continent, who says that the

English language in India has fostered western orientation and reduced the self-confidence of its users. Its dominant use in education has created a system which has bypassed the majority; in administration it has denied the majority participation in the socioeconomic reconstruction of the country and has made justice unjusticiable. Its use in the mass media threatens to homogenize cultures, obliterate languages and reduce people into a mass.

The recognition of realities of multilingual societies means relating policies concerning World Englishes to the complex matrix of identities and uses. The institutionalization and continuously expanding functions of English in the Outer Circle depend on several factors that demand demythologizing the traditional English canon. To restate them here briefly, the "invisible" and not often articulated factors are, for example:

(a) Emotional attachment to English. The result is that the *our* code vs. *their* code dichotomy, as suggested by Quirk, becomes very blurred. This attachment is evident in response to questions asked of creative writers who write exclusively in English or in English and their "mother tongue" (see e.g., Lal 1969);

(b) English as part of code extension in the verbal repertoire of a multilingual population. It is a question of code alternation not only in the sense of switching between codes but also in "mixing" codes (e.g., English and Indian languages);

(c) The recognition of English as a nativized and acculturated code that has acquired local non-Judeo-Christian identities; and

(d) The recognition of English as a contact code for intranational function, with marginalization of international functions.

World Englishes and Language Policies

What lessons does the spread of English have for our understanding of approaches to language policies and their formulation? There are several lessons that can help us in sharpening our conceptualization and formulation of language policies.

Pressure Groups and Change

The first lesson is that we should observe the close relationship between the various pressure groups and their influence on changes in policies. The parameters of language policies are only partially in the hands of the planners. The spread of English during the postcolonial period provides several case studies: India, Malaysia, Indonesia, and Bangladesh. In all these countries, the recommendations of the planners had to be changed to meet the real political demands or to project an ideological image (e.g., that of Islamization in Bangladesh, and the calming of Muslim fundamentalist groups in Malaysia).

144   Liberation Linguistics

Unplanned Parameters

The second lesson is related to the power of *unplanned* language planning, as opposed to that of planned (*visible*) language planning. Visible language planning refers to organized efforts to provide language policies by recognized agencies. On the other hand, unplanned language "planning" refers to the efforts of generally unorganized nongovernmental agencies for acquiring and using a language. This point is well illustrated in Pakir (1988) and Y. Kachru (1989). In fact, the invisible language policies are often contrary to the policies espoused by the state or other organized agencies. And such invisible pulls seem to be more powerful than the visible ones. Who are the initiators of invisible language policies? The studies on, for example, Singapore and Malaysia show that invisible language planning is determined to an extent by the attitude of parents toward a language, the role of the media, the role of peers, and societal pressures. What we notice, then, is the conflict between the *slogan* concerning the language policies and the *action* in actual execution of the policies: there is abundant cross-cultural evidence to support this point.

The other dimension of invisible language policies is the literary creativity in molding language policy. I am not aware of this aspect's being seriously considered in the literature on this topic. Two examples related to the use of English come to mind, one from Southeast Asia and the other from South Asia. In Singapore, the stated language policy is nonrecognition of what has been termed *basilect*. However, as Pakir (1988) shows, this variety plays an important role in the verbal repertoire of the Singaporeans. That this variety is a viable medium for literary creativity is demonstrated in the poems of, for example, Arthur Yap, and in fiction by Catherine Lim and others (see B. Kachru 1987b). The result is that, in spite of the language policy makers' efforts of open rejection of this variety, the basilect variety continues to function as a valuable linguistic tool in the verbal repertoire of a Singaporean.

In two South Asian countries, Pakistan and Sri Lanka, it is the efforts of literary writers in addition to other invisible planners who keep English a candidate in these multilingual settings. Hashmi (1989: 8) considers Pakistani literature in English "as a national literature," which is responsive "to the society in which it is created, and to the sensitivities that the society engenders." In Sri Lanka, English revived in a somewhat "unplanned" way since "the monolingual Sinhalese and Tamil had ... no means of communication with members of other communities" (Wijesinha 1988: i). And in India, as in other regions of the Outer Circle, as Narasimhaiah (n. d.: 14) argues, it was "a different racial and national genius and different social realities" that "called for departures from the normal English syntax, different intonational contours and made it inevitable for Indian writers to assimilate them into their own speech rhythms" (see also B. Kachru 1987a).

Invisible strategies are not used only in the context of an imposed colonial language, say English; the same strategies are adopted in multilingual societies as a reaction – in favor of or against – other languages of wider communication. Let me consider India's case again: in the Hindi belt of India (*madhya desa*), the speakers of what were considered the dialects of Hindi are establishing the rights of their own languages. The cases in point are those of Maithili in the state of Bihar and Rajasthani in the state of Rajasthan. What, then, are the motives for it? The main reasons for these vibrantly articulated trends are

(1) To establish an *identity* within a larger speech community,
(2) To mark *ingroupness*, in order to obtain and retain power in a democratic society,
(3) To establish a *pressure group* for economic and other advantages, and
(4) To assert *cultural separateness* in literary and other traditions.

In South Asia and Southeast Asia, for example, we have cases of numerous strategies used to frustrate the organized language policies. But that is not all. There are also cases of invisible language planners frustrating the unrealistic language policies: again one thinks of Singapore, or Bangladesh. In Bangladesh, when it constituted a part of Pakistan, the Pakistani policy of language imposition was repeatedly rejected, and in the process several people were killed during the language riots. February 24 is annually observed as Language Martyrs' Day in Bangladesh. These are important cases of explicit awareness of language and identity, which result in significant human sacrifice and suffering. The question of identity with language equally applies to English. It is in this sense that English has multicultural identities.

The Quirk Concerns and Language Policies

One might ask in what sense are the Quirk concerns relevant to the theoretical, sociolinguistic, and pragmatic issues related to language planning? The two papers of Sir Randolph Quirk are thought-provoking in more than one way. One very important contribution of the papers is that they lead us to ask some serious questions about language policies and attitudes that are not generally asked in the literature on the topic. Consider, for example, the following four questions.

The first question is of a theoretical nature: whether one is talking of a sociolinguistic theory or that of contact linguistics, can language policies be formulated and implemented in a theoretical vacuum?

The second question is related to attitudes and identities: can attitudes and identities be separated while discussing language policies, standardization, and the norm?

146   Liberation Linguistics

The third question takes us to the politics of language policies: what role, if any, is played by political leaders in issuing language policies, whether visible or invisible? The visible aspect is illustrated by Islamization and Arabization (e.g., in Bangladesh) or Hindu fundamentalism and Sanskritization (e.g., India). The invisible aspect is the concern for nativelike standards or about falling standards of English expressed by political leaders, as mentioned by Quirk (e.g., Mrs. Indira Gandhi of India and the prime minister of Singapore).

The fourth question takes us to the age-old topic in second language acquisition: What, if any, are the strategies that the influential and powerful native speakers use to control the direction of English, its innovations, and its acculturation?

In the three papers mentioned earlier, Quirk has not answered any of these questions; that he has raised some very provocative questions is, of course, in itself a contribution to an intense debate. These questions are closely related to contact linguistics, sociolinguistics, pragmatics, and literary creativity. These areas are vital for our understanding of language acquisition, and use and creativity in human language.

It seems to me that any language policy divorced from "a renewal of connection" (to use a Firthian term) with these theoretical areas is not going to be insightful. One cannot develop a language policy merely on attitudes. Attitudes may indeed be important exponents of an underlying motive for language policies as, for example, was the "Imperial Model" discussed by Quirk. But attitude alone cannot provide a sound base for developing a policy. In my view, Sir Randolph Quirk has presented a serious theoretical dilemma to us by suggesting that the spread of English, and its linguistic, sociolinguistic, and literary consequences, be seen purely from an attitudinal perspective. I believe that linguistic history is not on his side.

There seem to be several fallacies in conceptualizing World Englishes in the Outer Circle. These are primarily of four types: theoretical, methodological, linguistic, and attitudinal (cf. also Kachru 1987b and 1989a).

In Quirk's arguments, one notices a subtle rejection of the *deviational, contextualizational, variationist,* and *interactional* approaches for the understanding and description of the implications of the spread of English. While supporting the deficit approach, Quirk does not identify in any of his three papers the methods one might use to control codification around the world: I have discussed elsewhere in greater detail the four types of codification traditionally used for implementing language policies (cf. B. Kachru 1985b). These are *authoritative, sociological, educational,* and *psychological.*

Authoritative or Mandated Codification This category includes policies generally adopted by the academies. A good and classic example of this is the French Academy, established in 1635. As is well known, there were two attempts to establish such academies for English, the first in England in 1712, and the second in the United States in 1780, and both failed. Perhaps history has a lesson for us.

Sociological or Attitudinal Codification This is reflected in social or attitudinal preference for certain varieties. Abercrombie (1951: 14) has called it the "accent bar." However, this bar does not apply to "accent" only; it is often extended to other levels too: grammatical, lexical, discoursal, and stylistic.

Educational Codification This category refers to codification determined by the dictionaries, the media, teachers' attitudes, etc.

Psychological Codification A good example of this is the psychological constraints on the ritualistic use of Sanskrit. The *correct* use was a precondition for *effective* use of the language; incorrect use could result in the wrath of gods.

In the case of English, there is essentially no authoritative codification, unless, of course, we grant authoritative sanction to various dictionaries and language manuals; the codification for English is primarily sociological, educational, and, indeed, attitudinal. It seems to me that the deficit approach fails not only because it is based on several fallacies, but also because it is based on at least four false assumptions about the users and uses of English.

The first assumption is that in the Outer and Expanding Circles – that is, Quirk's ESL and EFL countries – English is essentially learned to interact with the native speakers of the language. This, of course, is only partly true. The reality is that in its localized varieties, English has become the main vehicle for interaction among its nonnative users, with distinct linguistic and cultural backgrounds – Indians interacting with Nigerians, Japanese, Sri Lankans; Germans with Singaporeans; and so on. The culture-bound localized strategies of, for example, politeness, persuasion, and phatic communion transcreated in English are more effective and culturally significant than are the "native" strategies for interaction.

The second assumption is that English is essentially learned as a tool to understand and teach the American or British cultural values, or what is generally termed the Judeo-Christian traditions. This again is true only in a restricted sense. In culturally and linguistically pluralistic regions of the Outer Circle, English is an important tool for imparting local traditions and cultural values. A large number of localized linguistic innovations and their diffusion are related to local cultural and sociopolitical contexts.

The third assumption is that the international nonnative varieties of English are essentially "interlanguages" striving to achieve "nativelike" character. This position has been taken by, among others, Selinker (1972). In reality the situation is, as Quirk et al. observed in 1972 and again in 1985, that such institutionalized varieties are "varieties of English in their own right rather

148   Liberation Linguistics

than stages on the way to more nativelike English." This is a sociolinguistically correct position (see Sridhar and Sridhar 1986; see also Lowenberg and Sridhar 1986).

The fourth assumption is that the native speakers of English as teachers, academic administrators, and material developers are intensely involved in the global teaching of English, in policy formulation, and in determining the channels for the spread of language. In reality, that is again only partially true.

In proposing language policies for English in the global context, the situation is indeed complex, and there are no easy answers. There is thus need for a "paradigm shift," as has been proposed in several recent studies. Paradigm shift entails reconsidering the traditional sacred cows of English, which does not necessarily mean, as Quirk (1985: 3) suggests, "the active encouragement of anti-standard ethos." The list of such sacred cows is long; I do not propose to list all of them here. But let me mention just three theoretical constructs that linguists and language teachers have considered sacred. As I have stated previously in this volume and further elaborate in Chapter 9, I am not sure that these are still sacred for English. I am thinking of concepts such as the SPEECH COMMUNITY of English, an IDEAL SPEAKER–HEARER of English, and a NATIVE SPEAKER of English (B. Kachru 1988b; Paikeday 1985).

In the context of World Englishes, what we actually see is that diversification is a marker of various types of sociolinguistic "messages." Let me again briefly mention some of these from an earlier study on this topic (B. Kachru 1987b): First is English as an exponent of distance from the Inner Circle – which may be social, cultural, and ideological. Second is English as a marker of "creativity potential." This aspect is clearly evident in the innovations used in creative writing by Ali Ahmad, Mulk Raj Anand, Raja Rao, Salmon Rushdie, Ngugi wa Thiongo, and Amos Tutuola. And third is English as a marker of the "Caliban Syndrome." This syndrome is a linguistic response to what Ngugi (1986) has called the "cultural bomb" effect of the colonial powers. There is no doubt that the "linguistic bomb" is somewhat defused by giving it a local identity and a new name.

The earlier diffusion of English, as Quirk rightly suggests, follows the imperial model of language spread. However, that historical fact has changed with later sociolinguistic realities, involving acculturation and diversification of the language. A rejection of this reality implies codification as a means of linguistic control. And that is a very "loaded weapon." This linguistic control is reflected in three ways: the use of channels of codification and the control of these channels; the attitude toward linguistic innovations, and their diffusion by those who are not part of such speech fellowships; and the suggestion of dichotomies that are sociolinguistically and pragmatically not meaningful.

And let us not forget that this subtle linguistic control provides immense power to those who have that power and are able to *define*. Again, one cannot,

Conclusion

therefore, ignore the warning of Tromel-Plotz (1981: 76), viz., "Only the powerful can define others and can make their definitions stick. By having their definitions accepted they appropriate more power."

And making these definitions stick is not power in an abstract sense only. As we have seen, there is more to it in economic terms. According to a recent report, "The worldwide market for EFL training is worth a massive £6.25 billion a year according to a new report from the Economic Intelligence Unit" (*EFL Gazette,* March 1989). The economics of determining and proposing language policies has never been so vital before. What effect the "liberation linguistics" may have in marketing English is just being studied.

There is no doubt that current debate on the "liberation model" vs. "deficit model," particularly with reference to English, is presenting numerous theoretical and pragmatic challenges to language policy makers. We have so far tackled issues of standardization and corpus planning in local and regional terms, except in the case of survival registers, where international codification has been proposed (e.g., Seaspeak). However, a concept of WORLD ENGLISHES raises questions about international standardization with new parameters: *us* vs. *them*. This, in my view, is an unprecedented challenge to language policy makers. It takes us across languages and cultures, practically on every continent. The Quirk concerns clearly articulate the dilemma, but, as Crystal has rightly pointed out (1985a: 9–10), completely miss the perspective of "social identity": the issues have been divorced from sociolinguistic and pragmatic concerns.

Conclusion

In conclusion, let me share with you a story, actually a true story, narrated to me by a former ambassador of India to the United States.[5] The story is a touching one, about a young American scholar who spent several years in a village in the Bihar State in eastern India. At the time of his departure for the United States, the village council (*panchayat*) gave him an Indian-style farewell. During the ceremony, one member of the village council, in his own dialect, requested the village headman to ask the young American guest whether there were water buffaloes in his country, the United States. The puzzled young American replied, "No." This response completely surprised, and somewhat shocked, the villager, and he innocently remarked that if the chief guest's country has no water buffaloes, it must be a poor country! And, lo

---

[5] K. R. Narayan told me this story in 1983. This has also been published in his book *India and America: Essays in Understanding* (1984: Washington, DC: Information Service of the Embassy of India, p. x. He writes, "I used to tell a story – a true story – to illustrate this peculiar mixture of goodwill and lack of understanding that characterizes our relationship [India and US]."

150   Liberation Linguistics

and behold, before the farewell ceremony concluded, the young American scholar was presented with two healthy water buffaloes. And the head of the village council was profusely apologizing for giving him just two buffaloes. But he reassured the puzzled young American with folded hands (an Indian gesture of respect) that he should rest assured: in course of time, after reaching the United States, these two healthy buffaloes would multiply and make his native America prosperous.

And thereby hangs a linguistic tale: in this well-meaning exchange there is a message for all of us who have suggestions for determining policies about English around the world. What is seen as "deficit linguistics" in one context may actually be a matter of "difference" that is based on vital sociolinguistic realities of identity, creativity, and linguistic and cultural contact. The questions are: Can sociolinguistic realities be negated? And can international codification be applied to a language that has more than 7 billion users across the globe? If the answer to the second question is "yes," it is vital to have a pragmatically viable proposal for such codification. We have yet to see such a proposal.

9   Sacred Linguistic Cows

Introduction

The increasing expressions of concern about the diversification and international standards of English, I believe, convey a serious sociolinguistic message. And it is clear that the reactions to the message, and its interpretations, vary from one receiver to another (cf. for example Quirk 1988). One encouraging interpretation of this concern regarding diversification is that the English language has now actually achieved a global penetration at various societal levels – an unprecedented feat in terms of "depth." And globally, English has attained extraordinarily wide functional domains – also an unprecedented phenomenon in terms of its linguistic "range." Sociolinguistically speaking, then, English has acquired multiple identities and a broad spectrum of cross-cultural interactional contexts of use – a purists' and pedagogues' nightmare though a variationists' blessing.[1]

The identities of English are multicultural in the sense that they involve linguistic interactions of three types of participants: native speaker and native speaker; native speaker and nonnative speaker; and nonnative speaker and nonnative speaker. The consequence is that the spread of English has resulted in a multiplicity of semiotic systems, several linguistic conventions that are not shared across the board, and numerous underlying cultural traditions.

And any speaker of English (native or nonnative) has access to only a subset within the patterns and conventions of cultures that English now encompasses. Within each subset, English has developed distinct functional varieties (e.g., basilect vs. educated variety in Singapore and Malaysia; bazaar vs. educated English in India and Pakistan; Nigerian Pidgin vs. educated Nigerian English in Nigeria). This, then, is the sociolinguistic reality of English in the global context.

---

[1] The "multiple identities" of English are not recognized by all scholars; there is resistance to the acceptance of sociolinguistic reality. See for example Quirk (1988), as also discussed in the preceding chapters.

152   Sacred Linguistic Cows

The reactions of language specialists to this sociolinguistic reality, and the resultant diversity, are of two types. One group derives satisfaction from the fact that, at last, we have an international language that provides access across cultures and national boundaries. In their view, the dream of a universal language has finally (almost) been realized, and diversity and acculturation are part of the blessing. There is, however, another group, which views diversity among Englishes as a marker of divisiveness, as a sign of the decay of the language, and – perhaps more upsetting – as a threat to the traditionally perceived Eurocentric, Judeo-Christian ethos of the language and a challenge to what English – in the perception of this group – would ideally represent. (This position – not, of course, in its extreme form – is articulated in Quirk 1988.) From this perspective, the cross-cultural linguistic innovations and various types of satisfaction in language use are seen as danger signals for the maintenance of an "international" and "universal" standard of English. And therein lie the concern and controversy, and the appropriateness of a special session of the 1994 Georgetown University Round Table on Languages and Linguistics devoted to "The Spread of English: Diversification and Standards."

I will not digress here to discuss the underlying causes for the spread of English. There is already an abundance of studies on this topic, though most of these studies address the subject primarily from a Western perspective: political, sociological, linguistic, sociolinguistic, and so on.[2] It seems to me that most such studies have yet to recognize one major point concerning the wider implications of the spread of English: that is, how the diffusion of English, its nativization and acculturation, have been instrumental in slaughtering many sacred cows of different types: linguistic, attitudinal, sociolinguistic, and pedagogical.

In this chapter my concern is with some of these sacred cows: how the global uses of English and its expanded and localized functions have affected several basic linguistic concepts, particularly those that have traditionally been accepted without serious questions. But, first, a crucial observation about conceptualizing the spread of English. Following Cooper (1982: 6), it may be said that it is not languages that spread; it is the increase in the number of users who acquire the language that marks the spread. In other words, English did not acquire its users; the users acquired English. And, ultimately, the uses of English resulted in the modification of linguistic behavior of individuals and social groups. This way of looking at the spread of English has two advantages: it emphasizes the focus on the *user,* and it sees language as an *activity* within a sociolinguistic context. It is these two

---

[2] For selected bibliographies, see Bailey and Görlach (1982); Fishman et al. (1977); B. Kachru (1986a); B. Kachru and Smith (1986); and Platt et al. (1984).

Nature of the Sacred Cows 153

perspectives that help us better understand the underlying reasons for the diversification of English and relate the diversity to two important functional concepts: the concept of MEANING POTENTIAL suggested by Halliday (1978) and that of VALUE-ADDED MEANING, as opposed to mere GRAMMATICAL and LEXICAL MEANING discussed by Quirk (1986: 9–10).

What we see, then, is that as English spreads, and as more people include it in their verbal repertoires, it continues to absorb – and unfold – "meanings" and "values" from diverse cultures, as both an international and an intranational language. The increasing demographic gains of the language and its immense current functional range (localized as in Singapore, regional as in South Asia and Africa, and international across the continents) certainly do not help arrest the diversification.[3] The English language has now acquired such important dimensions that the medium and its message have become the yardstick for the evaluation of other cultures and languages. However, this undaunted victory march of the language has also resulted in various theoretical and "real world" attitudinal questions. I am examining some of these questions here.

Nature of the Sacred Cows

I shall specifically focus on certain conceptual and terminological sacred cows within theoretical and applied areas of the linguistic sciences. Some of these are accepted on faith, and others, Hydra-like, have a way of vanishing and then reappearing in one form or another. I believe that these sacred cows have relevance to the issues related to the spread of English, and to our understanding of the daunting questions concerning diversity and standards. The issues are theoretical, acquisitional, sociolinguistic, and pedagogical. I shall first briefly discuss the acquisitional aspect, and then the others, ending with the theoretical aspects.

Acquisitional Sacred Cows

In second language acquisition research, the concept INTERFERENCE seems to have become pivotal, providing the current major paradigm of research. However, unfortunately, the way the term has been used distorts many facts about the forms and functions of varieties of English in the Outer Circle. This is particularly true in conceptualizing and describing the innovations and creativity in the institutionalized nonnative varieties of English. What is worse,

---

[3] A number of linguistic, sociolinguistic, and attitudinal reasons for diversification are given for example in B. Kachru (1986a) and Lowenberg (1986a, 1986b).

154   Sacred Linguistic Cows

the "interference paradigm" has created a conceptual trap – obviously unintended – from which a nonnative user of English seems to have no escape.

There is a cluster of other concepts too, though not all are related to INTERFERENCE: INTERLANGUAGE, ERROR ANALYSIS, FOSSILIZATION, to name just three. The uninsightful use of these concepts has resulted in various observations about the users and uses of English that have doubtful empirical bases if seen in the world context of the uses of English. The concepts per se are not necessarily to be questioned. Rather, we should seriously evaluate the validity of the generalizations made on assuming them uncritically.[4]

Sociolinguistic Sacred Cows

One might ask at least two sociolinguistically significant questions here: What has been the result of the "pluricentricity" of English? And what has English contributed as an instrument of ideological change? A corollary to the second question would be, What kind of ideology does English represent in the Outer Circle?

The pluricentricity, or, what Steiner (1975: 4) has termed the "shifting linguistic center" of English, has had far-reaching consequences. The most important outcome has been that the traditional English canon has been demythologized (B. Kachru 1987b), and new canons have been established with their own identities: literary, linguistic, and cultural. These results, of course, have been contrary to the visions of pundits like Thomas Babington Macaulay in his "Minute on Indian Education" (1835). It is evident that, ultimately, the function of English as a catalyst for creating "brown sahibs" and "Afro-Saxons" – to use Mazrui's (1973) term – only partially succeeded.

What actually has happened is that as an exponent of cultural and ideological contact and change, the English language acquired two faces: one face representing "Westernness," the Judeo-Christian tradition; the other face (more pertinent to the present discussion) reflecting local identities: African, Asian, and others.

It is the second face of English that has provided national and regional identities. In the former colonies it initiated a national discourse on what were the colonial extensions of the Western powers: their legitimacy and exploitation of various types. This discourse was not curbed by ethnic, caste, religious, or linguistic considerations. It is unfortunate that this second face of English – the face of local cultural revival, nationalism, collective soul searching, regional and national integration – has remained somewhat

---

[4] Detailed discussions of this topic are given in Sridhar and Sridhar (1986) and in Lowenberg (1984, 1986a, 1986b); see also B. Kachru (1987b) for a further discussion.

obscure. The nonnative users of English have underplayed it, and the native users of English did not want to recognize it. From the native users' perspective, it has been better not to recognize this face of English, since it provides serious reasons for authenticating the diversification of English.

It is this second face of English – the more obscure face – that has produced what, for some, is the elusive concept of AFRICAN or ASIAN identity, or for that matter, the THIRD WORLD identity, of the language (see for example Quirk 1988). What we see is that the Western-educated local elite turned the Western linguistic weapon into an effective tool of national uprisings against the colonizers. In ethnically diverse and linguistically pluralistic societies, English drew together the politically conscious local leaders who articulated local aspirations in a language that had international currency. At last, the linguistic weapon was backfiring! While English was used for fostering intercultural, interethnic, and interlanguage networks, the masses used numerous languages and dialects to participate in the national movements. In turn, the elite also used the local languages, when it suited them to facilitate mass communication, as did Mohandas K. Gandhi in India, in using Hindustani.

In the Outer Circle, then, the English-knowing elite provided a perspective that was both "inward-looking" and "outward-looking." The inward look of these English users contributed to creating a perspective of nationalism, which was by and large above traditional caste, class, and regional politics. (That English created another social class takes us to another story, which is too lengthy to take up here.)

This "integrative" role of English was diametrically opposed to the aims and political intentions of those who took the language to the colonies: to the dismay of the colonizers, English became a valuable resource for understanding the dialectics of anticolonialism, secularization, and panregional communication. It was indeed an important tool for "Westernization." What does the foregoing digression contribute to our understanding of "diversification" and "standards" of English? It shows that English became more and more localized as its regional roles expanded in the Outer Circle.

What, then, is the "cultural identity" of English in the Outer Circle? I am not claiming that pluricentricity has obliterated the British or American identities of English. Rather, the English language has succeeded in gaining other identities: cultural, social, linguistic. In some sense, these identities are endowed with great local power in the Outer Circle (see e.g., Chishimba 1985, B. Kachru 1986d; Lowenberg 1984, 1986a and 1986b; Magura 1984). Two related questions come to mind: Whose culture does the language represent for example in the African and Asian varieties? And who are the intended users of the texts – spoken or written – produced in these varieties? One answer to these questions is that English is now essentially an exponent of local cultures in the Outer Circle. In a majority of contexts, the shift is

156   Sacred Linguistic Cows

from the native speaker–oriented texts to the "localized" texts in which the
bilingual and bicultural competence of an interlocutor is taken for granted.
As such local contextualization increases, the diversity becomes more
marked (see B. Kachru 1986a). This sociolinguistic reality of English has
not as yet been taken into consideration by language specialists. The professionals have generally ignored it, and the reasons for ignoring it are varied:
economic, political, attitudinal (see Phillipson and Skutnabb-Kangas 1986;
B. Kachru 1986d; K. Sridhar 1986).

Pedagogical Sacred Cows

The complexities of the spread of English and specific local needs have not
always been recognized in the pedagogical paradigms; nor does educational
research generally show sensitivity to local sociolinguistic contexts. This
indifference to the pragmatics of teaching English internationally is evident
in the following areas, to give just a few examples: (1) models for teaching
English, (2) methods of teaching, (3) discussions of the motivations for
learning English, and (4) materials for what is called "communicative language
teaching," and for teaching English for specific purposes (see B. Kachru
1986c). A number of studies, particularly during the last decade or so, have
drawn attention to this aspect of English (Berns 1985 and 1990).

Theoretical Sacred Cows

And now, let me revert to what I mentioned as the first concern, that of the
theoretical sacred cows. In view of the ongoing diffusion of English, identity
with the language, attitudes toward it, its functions in the repertoire of multilingual societies, and creativity in it across cultures, three basic theoretical
concepts need further consideration:

(1) The SPEECH COMMUNITY of English,
(2) the IDEAL SPEAKER-HEARER of English, and
(3) the NATIVE SPEAKER of English.

Let me discuss these one by one. The concept SPEECH COMMUNITY continues
to be controversial in linguistic literature, and the use of this term with
reference to English has become particularly elusive. One has a choice, as
Hudson (1980: 25–30) illustrates, of at least six ways of looking at the concept
and defining it – from Bloomfield's (1933: 42) vague definition to Le Page's
(1968) complex and elaborate description (both cited in Hudson 1980: 27).

   Without embarking on an evaluation of the definitions of SPEECH COMMU-
NITY, one has to recognize now that as the uses of English are institutionalized
beyond the Inner Circle, as the multilingual populations consider English as

part of their verbal repertoire, as users of English in such societies identify with the language, and as English acquires non-Western cultural and interactional roles, the concept of SPEECH COMMUNITY for English acquires a new meaning. One must pause and recognize that the textual and interactional expectations for the language have acquired new pragmatic contexts. For the extended speech community, one has to assume that a member has, at least, a) bilingual competence in languages that have traditionally not been within the linguistic repertoire of the Inner Circle and b) multicultural competence, including cultural experiences not shared with the Inner Circle. These assumptions are not only useful for understanding the extended speech community of English; they are also insightful for investigating the challenging area of the bilinguals' competence and grammar.

The second concept, an IDEAL SPEAKER–HEARER (Chomsky 1965), is, of course, an idealization. However, it does have some relationship with the real world in that it entails sharing cultural and pragmatic conventions, or, in other words, sharing certain sociolinguistic bonds. What are the "shared conventions" of the users of English now? The spread of English shows two tendencies: first, a conscious attempt to resist identification with the "shared conventions" of the Inner Circle, and thus a desire to break such "bonds"; second, development of distinct linguistic and cultural conventions patterned after the social and cultural expectations appropriate to the Outer Circle. One cannot overemphasize the implications of these two underlying factors for the diversification of English.[5]

The third concept, the NATIVE SPEAKER, has become "a cardinal tenet of our linguistic faith" (Paikeday 1985: viii). This term is an age-old sacred cow carrying an immense attitudinal and linguistic burden. It has been used by linguists, pedagogues, generations of producers of teaching materials, essentially as an article of faith. Now, the spread of English has unleashed great cynicism about this venerable sacred cow as well.

The elusiveness of this "linguistic myth" is clearly shown in an illuminating discussion with "linguists, philosophers, psychologists, and lexicographers" by Paikeday (1985). The participants in the discussion include the historian A. L. Basham, the philosopher Willard Quine, and the linguists Noam Chomsky, David Crystal, Victoria Fromkin, M. A. K. Halliday, Raven McDavid, and Randolph Quirk.

Paikeday's discussions place at the forefront the conceptual and procedural difficulties in defining the term, specifically with reference to the Inner

---

[5] This position is, of course, not accepted by all. Consider, for example, two contrastive views. One is represented by Prator (1968) and Quirk (1985, 1988); the other is represented by B. Kachru (1985b, 1986a), Smith (1981, 1983), Strevens (1977), Pride (1981), and Thumboo (1985b).

158   Sacred Linguistic Cows

Circle. And, once the Outer Circle is included in the discussion, we have opened the proverbial can of worms. Consider, for example, complications of the following types.

The first is that the Outer Circle brings draws the fold those users of English who belong to "traditional" bi- or multilingual societies. In such societies, as Ferguson (1982) rightly warns us, "verbal communication takes place by means of languages which are not the users' 'mother tongue', but their second, third, or *nth* language, acquired one way or another and used when appropriate." And here the monolinguals' paradigm of looking at the users of English does not seem to be very insightful.

The second complication takes us to the multilinguals' creativity in English. Let me point out here that in spite of some linguists' beliefs, such creativity is not "marginal" (see Paikeday 1985: 67). And Vladimir Nabokov and Joseph Conrad, as David Crystal would like us to believe, are indeed not exceptions in their creativity in a "nonnative" language (see Crystal's comments in Paikeday 1985: 67). In traditionally multilingual societies, there is a long tradition of creativity in a "nonnative" language. Indeed, there is an abundance of examples – Sanskrit and Persian in South Asia, English in the Outer Circle, Hindi in the south of India, Swahili in East Africa, French in Francophone countries, and Bahasa Indonesia in Indonesia, to mention just a few.

The third complication is, of course, attitudinal: the attitudes both of those who consider themselves the "native speakers" of the language and of those who use the language as an "additional" code in their verbal repertoires. Here I provide two examples to illustrate the point. The first example, from Paikeday (1985), vividly shows that the "us/them" distinction in dividing the "native" and "nonnative" users is "directly linked with the nationality in the legal sense." Paikeday illustrates this point by an example of two Indian users of English with an excellent command of the language. Notice, however, the attitude toward their English, as narrated by Paikeday (1985: 72).

As members of "visible minorities," they are not supposed to sound any different from the stereotype of speakers of so-called Indian English. They would be accused of conspicuous consumption or something similarly bad. For the same reason, when they are among people of their own nationality, they would rather affect features of Indian English than be looked down on as foreigners. In the movie *Gandhi,* did you notice the marked change in Ben Kingsley's accent between South Africa and India? I thought that was quite true to life.

The other example is that of my wife, a speaker of Hindi, Bengali, Marathi, and English. As her parental language, she was exposed to a diaspora variety of Marathi, "Tanjore Marathi." However, she feels most comfortable with Bengali, Hindi, and English. In fact, those Bengali and Hindi speakers who do not know her linguistic background consider her a "native speaker" of

Bengali and Hindi, respectively. However, once they know her linguistic biography, they immediately call her a "native speaker" of Marathi, which, linguistically speaking, is far from the truth. In her case, then, the parental history seems to determine her "native language."

The multilinguistic contexts, and the use of English in such contexts, clearly show that Ferguson (1982: vii) has a point when he suggests that " the whole mystique of native speaker and mother tongue should probably be quietly dropped from the linguists' set of professional myths about language."

There is a message in the extended global uses of English. The presuppositions about English must take into consideration the following three implications of the spread of English: the change in the traditional linguistic periphery of English, extension of underlying shared and nonshared sociocultural conventions, and new norms for text organization and "interlocutor expectancy."

First is the change in the traditional linguistic periphery of English. Since the 1930s, there has been a marked shift in the traditional linguistic periphery of the language, its main and expected sources of syntactic, lexical, stylistic, and other borrowings and innovations.[6] The main reason for this slow shift, of course, is the past sociopolitical history, mainly of the United Kingdom.

In some sense, the "periphery shift" is one of degree. In the past, the Inner Circle Englishes were influenced by elements that may be considered nontraditional for the language. Two examples immediately come to mind: the impact of American Indian languages on American English and that of Maori on New Zealand English. These influences, however, have been marginal. The periphery shift not only entails the development of new varieties in the Outer Circle, it also involves the transfusion of the linguistic innovations from the Outer Circle into the Inner Circle.

Second is extension of underlying shared and nonshared cultural conventions of English. This is closely linked to the culture of the users of English. Quirk (1986: 19) appropriately reminds us about the close relationship between language and culture in the following words:

Even the simplest, shortest, least technical, least momentous texts have a structure involving profound *interactions* between language and the world, between individual

---

[6] This again is not unique to English. There is evidence from other "linguistic areas" (Emeneau 1956) and "sociolinguistic areas" (D'Souza 1987). For example, in South Asia as a linguistic and sociolinguistic area, one finds substantial evidence of this phenomenon, in both the Indo-Aryan and Dravidian language regions. The traditional linguistic periphery may be "violated" for cultural, historical, and political reasons, as happened to English. In the case of South Asia, these factors contributed to the Persianization of the local languages with the Muslim conquest and the Englishization of the languages soon after the East India Company established its roots in the subcontinent. The Arabization of the African languages is another such example, as is the Sanskritization of some South East Asian languages (e.g., Thai, Indonesian, Burmese). For further discussion and references, see Hock (1986).

160   Sacred Linguistic Cows

and culture in which they operate: involving extensive assumptions about shared knowledge and shared attitudes, reasoned inferences about the degree to which participants in even such simple communication are willing to cooperate [emphasis added].[7]

This fact and its implications for the institutionalized varieties of English are well documented in several studies (see for example Chishimba 1985; B. Kachru 1986a; Y. Kachru 1985a and 1985b; Smith 1981 and 1987). The range of textual presuppositions (intratextual, extratextual, and inter-textual) encompass a variety of cultures and linguistic traditions, as is evident in the works of Chinua Achebe, Raja Rao, Wole Soyinka, Puny-kante Wijayaratne, and others. Each institutionalized variety of English has developed its own linguistic resources appropriate to its cultural and sociolinguistic milieu.

Third are new localized norms for text organization and "interlocutor expectancy." The term *interlocutor expectancy* refers to shared knowledge of culturally appropriate conventions and awareness of identities that participants in a linguistic interaction desire to establish.

The diversification in textual organization often has a deeper meaning than merely that of minor stylistic adjustment. Additionally, a specific textual organization may be used as a device to reflect various types of "power": linguistic, metaphorical, symbolic, and so on. In other words, it is a well-organized stylistic device, which the Russian formalists have termed "making strange" (see Erlich 1965: 176–178).

A specific type of text organization may be chosen to send a signal that the "native speaker" is irrelevant to such stylistic experimentation. Indeed, an attempt is made to cross over the linguistic and cultural conventions tradition-ally associated with the Inner Circle of English. The text is "particularized." It is in this sense, then, that Achebe's creativity is "local and particular" (Achebe 1976: 69), Totuola works within "Yoruba thought and ontology" (Awoonor 1973–1974: 667), and Rao emphasizes his "Indianness" (see B. Kachru 1986b). It is again in this sense that in a provocative study, Dissanayake (1985) is asking for the "decolonization" of the language. However, the most forthright statement on localization is from Achebe (1976: 11): "I should like to see the word *universal* banned altogether from discussions of African literature until such a time as people cease to use it as a synonym for the narrow, self-serving parochialism of Europe." This statement may sound like a political credo, but it does reflect an attitude, a pragmatic motive for diversifi-cation. And linguists – even the purist kind – cannot easily sweep such attitudes under the rug.

---

[7] Note, however, that Quirk (1985, 1988) takes a somewhat different position.

Contexts of Diversification

What we see, then, is that the contexts of diversification of English are not just acquisitional deficiencies, as generally presented in literature. There are far deeper sociological, linguistic, and cultural reasons. The diversification often is symbolic of subtle sociolinguistic messages, including the following:

Exponent of "Distance"

The message here is "I am distinct from you – culturally, socially, attitudinally – and let my variety of English (linguistic creativity) say it." And equally important is the fact that one might want to convey that "I will use English as a tool for my culture, my identity, my conventions." In the Outer Circle, English is particularly used as an exponent of "distance" if one wants to create a semiotic system that does not fall within the traditional cultural and linguistic canons of English. We see such uses in literary creativity, in a conscious use of local accents, in lexical and other choices made in media, and in the use of code mixing and code switching. This position is also evident in statements such as that of Achebe quoted earlier.

Jvjarker of "Creative Potential"

Another reason for diversification is to exhibit, as it were, a linguistic chip on one's shoulder. However, that is a simplistic statement. Quirk (1986: 9) provides another explanation. He says that the "most abiding difficulty about human communication is that it is human." Further, he adds, "human communication is human too in its potential for creativity, for responsiveness to change, and to the demands of new conditions, new environments, new challenges." This "humanness" of language, emanating from multiple cultures from all the continents, is a major underlying motivation for the diversification of English.

Expression of the "Caliban Syndrome"

There is yet another side to "conscious" diversification, which may be termed the "Caliban syndrome." This is a linguistic reaction to what Ngugi (1986: 3) calls "the effect of a cultural bomb." For him, the effect of such a bomb, as reported earlier, is "to annihilate a people's belief in their names, in their languages, in their environment, in their heritage of struggle, in their unity, in their capacities and ultimately in themselves." However, in spite of such a reaction, one sees that the main carrier of the "culture bomb" – the colonizer's language – continues to be used for a multitude of local and external reasons.

162   Sacred Linguistic Cows

One may ask, What does this have to do with diversification and standards? The perception seems to be – at least, in some quarters – that the linguistic "bomb" is somewhat defused by giving it a local character of Indianized, Nigerianized, or Philippinized English. We have seen that the English language is well adapted to this cultural and linguistic localization.

However, this is not the whole story of the psychological responses to English. This language continues to provoke psychological resistance even from those nonnative users who have excellent – shall I say, "nativelike" – competence in the language, or those who make the best English instruction available to their children. I have discussed the reasons for this reaction elsewhere (B. Kachru 1987b).

Diversification vs. International English

At the outset I said that the optimists are grateful that, at last, we (almost) have a universal language with international and intranational roles: international as in aviation, seaspeak, multinational corporations, intellectual exchange (scientific, technological), literary creativity, and travel, to mention just a few domains; and intranational as a localized extralinguistic arm in the verbal repertoire of multilingual societies in the Outer Circle. English has now become a medium of cross-cultural expression and, one hopes, of intercultural understanding, too.

The internationalization of the language has, obviously, had a price. Several points come to mind: first, hesitation about – or indifference to – the acceptance of the traditional literary and cultural canons of the English language; second, development of multiple varieties of the language (e.g., performance, social, regional, ethnic) in the Outer Circle. These varieties have acquired a "cone-shaped" structure, showing considerable diversification at the base, or colloquial level, and less diversity as one advances to the apex, or educated level (see B. Kachru 1982c: 94–95). Third, the concepts related to communicative competence (e.g., acceptability, appropriateness) have acquired distinct meanings in various English-using speech fellowships. Finally, there is an attitude blended with cynicism toward the traditional sacred linguistic cows.

Managing Diversification

And now we come to the purists' nightmare: the need for management of diversification. This need may be traced to the following concerns. The first is well known and has resulted in shelves of the literature produced over several centuries. It is the alarm about the decay of the language, its careless use, and the ultimate danger of the loss of intelligibility among its users across cultures. The reasons for the decay of the language are generally traced to indifferent

Managing Diversification

teachers, irreverent media moguls, and sociolinguists. The second concern is directly related to the status of the language after its spread in the Outer and Extended Circles. These concerns are primarily related to the following issues:

Decay in Proficiency in English

A comparison is made with an idealized past of the English language in the Outer Circle. It is then concluded that the standards of acquisition and teaching have decreased. This hypothesis is faulty on many counts – there is no empirical evidence to prove the point. In fact, the contrary may be true. With the unprecedented diffusion in education, the core of the English-knowing and English-using population has substantially increased during the postcolonial period, as has the number of semiproficient speakers and ill-equipped English "teaching shops." And, equally important, the learning of English is no longer restricted to the privileged urban segments of society; all social classes are keen to learn English and have access to some kind of English instruction. If anything, the core of proficient users of English is fast expanding in the Outer Circle, as is, conversely, the number of those whose proficiency is highly restricted.

Decay in International Intelligibility

There certainly is merit in the argument that if English is needed for international interaction, the users of the language should have international intelligibility. This position, for example, is articulated in more than one paper by Quirk (for example, Quirk 1985 and 1988). The context for international uses of English, however, is complex. One has to accept this position with several caveats. First, in the Outer Circle, English has primarily localized intranational functions, the international roles are restricted to only a few domains, and the number of people involved in such domains is proportionately very limited. Second, the concept "intelligibility" has several levels, and the burden of international intelligibility is a shared undertaking in which education has to be imparted about what may be called "variety tolerance." Here I am thinking of the education of professionals, particularly of those working in the field of English studies. Third, the degree of linguistic pessimism about the failure of intelligibility in international communication in English is rather exaggerated. The monumental and successful role English currently plays in varied international contexts seems to be underestimated. The concern seems to be more about future (possible) danger of the loss of international intelligibility. Finally, there is a paradox in this concern. On the one hand, international uses of English are considered desirable; on the other hand, great concern is expressed about internationalization of the language. It is difficult to separate the two: the

164   Sacred Linguistic Cows

internationalization of a language is accompanied by nativization and acculturation, as we have seen in Europe as well as Asia.

Indifference to the Native Speakers' Role as the Guardians of English

It is believed that the recognition of regional endocentric norms as pedagogical standards, and as linguistic resources for creativity, has underestimated the role of the native speaker as a norm provider, and the native standard as the model for creativity. Acceptance of an endocentric norm, in a way, implies breaking away from an almost-sacrosanct dictum in language pedagogy that the "native speaker" is the norm. However, it seems to me that the case of English is in many ways unique in the history of human languages. In this respect, too, the remarkable evolution of English has slaughtered yet another sacred cow.

Conclusion

In the preceding discussion I have attempted to show that the reactions to the diversification of English are only partially linguistic. A number of these are essentially attitudinal and ethnocentric; it is difficult to find pragmatic and sociolinguistic justification for some of the extreme reactions.

It seems to me, as I have said earlier, that there is much to celebrate in the spread of English as a world language. Where more than 650 artificial languages have failed to gain global acceptance, English has achieved it; where many other natural languages with political and economic power to back them up have failed, English has succeeded. One reason for this success of English is its propensity for acquiring new identities: its power of assimilation, its adaptability to "decolonization" as its language, its manifestation in a range of lects, and, above all, its provision of a flexible medium for literary and other types of creativity across language and cultures. A major question is, As a result of this global power and hegemony of English, are the cultures and other languages of the world richer or poorer? This is indeed a very tricky question to answer (see B. Kachru and Smith 1986).

Finally, for those who are concerned about diversification and standards, the past has a lesson for us.[8] We have a continuous recorded history of language planning – both conscious and unconscious – that dates back many centuries. On the basis of past experience, let us ask ourselves the following questions.

---

[8] In Quirk (1988), several concerns are expressed. A number of these reflect personal attitudes toward "diversification" and "standards." However, he raises several other points, some of these specifically attributed to me. Quirk's interpretation of some of my earlier statements suggests misunderstanding, and consequently misinterpretation, of my position. I am not able to discuss these here, because of space limitations. I have, therefore, discussed them in B. Kachru (1989b), "World Englishes and Applied Linguistics."

First is a pragmatic question: What are the educational, psychological, and other results of the elusive attempts to curb diversity in English, and to provide an exocentric (British or American) model in the classrooms of the multilingual world? Second is a question of strategy: What methods, if any, do we have for controlling diversity (that is, of course, if we agree that it is possible and desirable to do so)? Third is a sociolinguistic question: Is it possible to control diversity, particularly when it is motivated by underlying reasons of cultural, social, regional, and group identities, and other sociolinguistic considerations? Fourth is a question of professional and social responsibility: What are our responsibilities as professionals, once we act as Cassandras and brood over the possible doom of the English language, its diversity, and the imagined decay of its standards?

In the vast body of the literature on this topic, especially the literature written by those who are concerned about the diversity of English and its multiple identities, these questions have yet to be answered in a responsible way.

10   The Paradigms of Marginalization

Introduction

In this chapter,[1] I would like to address a variety of issues that have traditionally not been articulated in the major forums of our profession. Our professional journals continue to pay rather muted attention, if any, to them. These issues are a consequence of the unprecedented and overwhelming phenomenon of the global spread and uses of English, and the results of these processes in World Englishes. We have actually witnessed this linguistic phenomenon particularly since the 1940s. The acquisition of English in its various varieties and canons is now a major motivation for the increase in multilingualism around the world. And this is undoubtedly an almost-universal fact. The implications of this spread and Englishization of the world's languages are not my concern in this chapter. I have addressed some of them earlier and especially in B. Kachru (1994b). My concern here is with the responses and reactions to this linguistic reality and varied perceptions about it.

It is only recently that researchers have begun to question the conceptual and methodological foundations of English language teaching (ELT). The refreshing challenges presented by the world profile of English in the "Three Concentric Circles"[2] and the search for responses to these challenges are almost absent from our professional agenda. The reality of functions of English in the

---

[1] This chapter was originally presented as the Annual James E. Alatis plenary address at the 1994 TESO convention in Baltimore (March 8–12) and is dedicated to him. Somewhat modified versions were presented at the Singapore Association for Applied Linguistics, Singapore (August 12, 1994), and JACET, Kyushu Chapter, Nagoya, Japan (May 28, 1995). I am grateful to several scholars who provided their comments, particularly Yamuna Kachru, Peter H. Lowenberg, and Cecil L. Nelson.

[2] McArthur (1993: 334) observes that B. Kachru "has not dissolved the trinity [ENL, ESL, and EFL], but he has re-named it, discussing first of all an 'inner circle' of those nations traditionally associated with the language, an 'outer circle' of those nations that are in effect in the process of NATIVIZING their forms of English, and lastly an 'expanding circle' of other nations which are in the process of adopting English in various ways for various purposes. This is a more dynamic model than the standard version, and allows for all manner of shadings and overlaps among the circles. Although 'inner' and 'outer' still suggest – inevitably – a historical priority and the

world has considerably altered since the 1940s; however, our perceptions of it have yet to be reconciled with these linguistic and pragmatic realities. I would like to include some of those perspectives in this discussion.

In presenting the story of the diffusion of English, we repeatedly remind ourselves that the second diaspora of English, in Africa and Asia, following its first diaspora in North America and Australia, has added several exhilarating, even overwhelming characteristics to the English language, particularly those related to its numerical size, its demographic composition, and its Asian and African functions. As mentioned earlier, there are now at least four nonnative speakers of English for every native speaker (to the extent that the distinction is significant), and most of the channels of spread are controlled and funded by the nonnative users of the language in Asia and Africa, and by agencies that they support. The innovations in paradigms of creativity, the range in types of English – from basilects to acrolects – and the functional allocation of the language increasingly reflect this cross-linguistic and cross-cultural nature of its uses and users. The question then is, What types of responses does this profile of World Englishes elicit from our profession (see Kachru 1994d)?

There are essentially two types of responses. One is to view this overwhelming linguistic phenomenon as an age-old process of language dynamics accentuated by the complex culturally and linguistically pluralistic contexts of language acquisition, language function, language contact, and linguistic creativity. This response demands questioning the earlier paradigms, asking new probing questions, and looking for fresh theoretical and methodological answers. The second response, from a number of active scholars, is to marginalize any questions – theoretical, methodological, and ideological – that challenge the earlier paradigms or seek answers appropriate to new global functions of English.

The Paradigms of Marginality

I propose to raise some questions here concerning this marginalization phenomenon – a very effective strategy of subtle power. I intend to address and revisit a variety of issues concerning the spread of English, and the implications of the marginalization of a majority of the users of the language. I will label clusters of these issues in three groups: *paradigm myopia, paradigm lag, and paradigm misconnection.* I shall use a cover term for these paradigms, which is the title of this chapter: *the paradigms of marginalization.*

---

attitudes that go with it, the metaphor of ripples in a pond suggests mobility and flux and implies that a new history is in the making."

168   The Paradigms of Marginalization

Paradigm Myopia

By the term PARADIGM MYOPIA I mean a shortsighted view of the fast-increasing English-using speech community in the new contexts of diaspora. This myopia in turn conditions the types of proposals, generalizations, and hypotheses presented in all three paradigms. One shared underlying characteristic of these paradigms is that they are based on a flawed assumption viz. that monolingualism and monolingual societies are the norms for hypothesis formation. This assumption is the result of societal attitudes toward multilingualism, partly formed by education – a cultivated state that crosses over to hypothesis formation. One must hasten to add that this "cultivated attitude" is far from the reality in the Inner Circle of English. The implications of this attitude are serious when they form bases for scholarly generalizations. It is this very attitude that Dell Hymes (1981: v) disputes when he observes that the United States is

a more interesting country than it sometimes lets itself admit. One does not have to go to India or New Guinea for diversity of language. To be sure, it may sometimes seem that there are only two kinds of language in the United States, good English and bad. Only one kind, if some people are to be taken literally: English, surrounded by something else that cannot be "English," or even perhaps "language."

In the case of Britain, Stubbs (1986: 15) rightly asserts that, though most individuals are monolinguals, "as a country Britain is socially multilingual." And a quick perusal of Trudgill (1984b), Dixon (1980), Alladina and Edwards (1991, two vols.), and Clyne (1982) shows that the perception of the monolingualism of Britain and Australia is contrary to the linguistic facts of these two Inner Circle countries.

This confusion between perception and reality concerning monolingualism vs. multilingualism results in several other fallacies about the uses and users of English in the Outer Circle. I will just mention three such fallacies here, which have directly influenced various types of hypotheses concerning World Englishes: the *interlocutor fallacy,* the *methodology fallacy,* and the *functional range fallacy.*

It is taken for granted that the goal for the acquisition of English is the nonnative speaker (NNS) interacting with the native speaker (NS); that use of Ll in L2 teaching is essentially hazardous for L2 acquisition; and that functions of English in the Outer Circle should be restricted to one function, the mathetic. These fallacies naturally result in proposals that lack observational adequacy, descriptive adequacy, and sociolinguistic realism. But more serious consequences of such proposals are that they establish what Foucault (1980: 131) terms "regimes of truth." Their implications become more serious when these hypotheses are used as foundations for curriculum design, teaching methodology, and teacher training.

The Paradigms of Marginality 169

One sees this in the case of language teaching methodology, for example in the rejection of Michael West's bilingual method for the teaching of English in South Asia. West's method was replaced with vigorous zeal by supporters of other approaches of doubtful validity and appropriateness in the South Asian context. This attitude is also reflected in the belief that L2 and L3 acquisition has a kind of linearity, and that it takes place essentially in some order of succession.

The reality in the traditional multilingual societies is much different from what is presented to the profession. One sees that simultaneous acquisition of two or more languages (or varieties) in nonformal contexts is generally much more common than either successive acquisition of languages or certainly monolingualism. And in linguistic interaction, language switching and mixing are among the most usual and preferred modes of communication out of the total repertoire available to a person.

Paradigm Myopia thus results in looking at linguistic creativity from a rather restricted perspective. Consider, for example, Chomsky's (1986: 17) observation on language "mixing":

The language of the hypothesized speech community, apart from being uniform, is taken to be a "pure" instance of UG [Universal Grammar] in a sense that must be made precise... We exclude, for example, a speech community of uniform speakers, each of whom speaks a mixture of Russian and French (say, an idealized version of the nineteenth-century Russian aristocracy). The language of such a speech community would not be "pure" in the relevant sense, because it would not represent a single set of choices among the options permitted by UG but rather would include "contradictory" choices for certain of these options.

It is this type of attitude toward multilinguals' behavior that has clouded major issues related to World Englishes, resulting in a PARADIGM LAG.

Paradigm Lag

The term *paradigm lag* designates resistance to taking into consideration linguistic and sociolinguistic contexts that entail modification or alteration of hypotheses: This resistance may be theoretically motivated, methodologically determined, or ideologically conditioned and may manifest itself in two ways: by claiming a theoretical status for terms that are attitudinally loaded, and by generalizing their use in contexts in which their theoretical or methodological value is doubtful. As an example of such lag, let us consider two terms introduced earlier that have acquired a vital position in current second language acquisition (SLA) paradigms: *fossilization* and *interlanguage*.

In recent years these two terms have become issues of growing debates, particularly with reference to World Englishes (see e.g., Davies 1989; B. Kachru 1995b; McDonald 1988; Mukattash 1986; Nelson 1988a and

170   The Paradigms of Marginalization

1988b; Sridhar and Sridhar 1986 [1992]; S.N. Sridhar 1996; and Williams 1987; see also Lowenberg and Sridhar 1986 and Singh, Lele, and Martohard-jono 1988). Adding to the discussion, Selinker has revisited the concepts INTERLANGUAGE and FOSSILIZATION in two recent studies (Selinker 1992 – reviewed by Y. Kachru 1993a – and Selinker 1993). I will not recapitulate the whole debate here; rather, I will focus on two key claims concerning these two concepts: the first is theoretical, the "completeness" issue; and the second is sociolinguistic, the "identity" issue – pertaining, respectively, to fossilization and to interlanguage.

The completeness issue, which, it is argued, is "theoretically important" (Selinker 1993: 199), was discussed earlier by Schachter (1990). On the basis of her investigation of the UG principle of subjacency, she claims that non-native speakers cannot have a "complete" grammar of a language, that is, grammatical "completeness" from the perspective of a monolingual grammar (for further discussion, see Selinker 1993: 23–24).

This, of course, raises a string of basic questions. One is whether the transfer of the assumption of *completeness* in monolinguals' linguistic behavior to the multilingual's behavior is actually relevant or insightful. One might ask, If one has functional competence in L2, L3, Ln, does that presuppose that the person has, structurally, three "complete" grammars corresponding to the three sets of grammars of the monolingual users of these languages? In other words, is a bilingual or a trilingual a composite of two monolinguals or three monolinguals, respectively?

A culinary analogy might be useful here: a cake baked only with one flavor – chocolate, coconut, or pineapple – will, of course, taste different from one cooked with two or more flavors, say chocolate and pineapple. In one there is distinctiveness of one ingredient; in the other, there is merging or "mixing" of distinctiveness of two or more flavors. In Chomsky's (1986: 17) terms, the chocolate–pineapple cake is not "pure" because "it would not represent a single set of choices," and from the perspective of interlanguage (IL), it is "incomplete." There is structural "incompleteness" if a monolingual's behavior is considered the norm. But, on the other hand, there is also structural expansion if multilinguals' behavior is taken into consideration – for example, the much-discussed phenomenon of convergence and mixing resulting in expansion. We see this "expansion," for example, in various institutionalized varieties of English. In the case of South Asian English, consider for example:

(a) Quotative constructions (e.g., The head of a cricket team is called a captain (S.N. Sridhar 1992));
(b) System of complementation (e.g., I want *that I should get leave* (Baumgardner 1995));

The Paradigms of Marginality 171

(c) System of tense-aspect, especially the present perfect and present progressive (e.g., I *have sent* two letters *last month* (Ayyar 1993; S.N. Sridhar 1992; and 1996)).

This "completeness" issue then, takes us to the daunting question of bilinguals' grammars. Ferguson, touching on this question, insightfully observes (1982 [1992]: xiv) that

[a] universal explanatory principle or a general theory of language should account for all linguistic behavior. Variation in structure as between L1 and L2 seems just as interesting a subject as dialect or register variation in a complete monolingual community.

In this debate on monolingualism vs. multilingualism we have yet to answer some fundamental questions, for example: Do bi- or multilingual speech communities reflect the patterns of "completeness" as these are understood to exist in monolingual societies? Does a bilingual's grammar necessarily reflect generalizations – theoretical and otherwise – made on the basis of a monolingual's linguistic behavior?

A major unanswered question, then, is, What do we mean by "a bilingual's grammar"? We do not know the answer, but we do know the linguistic contexts and aspects of linguistic behavior for which answers must be found. Ferguson (1978: 101), referring to such contexts, says:

There are speech communities in which a number of different languages are part of the linguistic repertoire of the community. Distinct languages exist side by side and are part of the whole scheme of variation of the speech community.

And, in the same paper, he further identifies the problem when he says that:

if we are going to write a grammar of what goes on in a speech community that uses – let us say – four languages, instead of writing four separate grammars and then writing rules for when people use one language or another, we should try to write a unified grammar in which all this variation fits somewhere. Instead of four separate structures which are variously used, we may have one linguistic structure with complex internal variation.

A number of partial attempts have been made in this direction – what Ferguson characterizes as "problem papers" (e.g., Denison 1968; Lavandera 1978; Nadkami 1975; Trudgill 1976–1977). Lavandera's study, based on bilingual Italian immigrants in Argentina, indicates that "for these speakers Spanish and Italian are not independent codes, at least not more so than the different registers of a monolingual speaker" (cited in Ferguson 1978: 103).

The limitation of transferring generalizations from one type of speech community to another e.g., the "completeness" issue is that we are imposing paradigms on language users whose linguistic repertoires are not identical to those of the communities on which the generalizations were based.

172   The Paradigms of Marginalization

The next issue, that of "identity," has been argued, for example, by Jane Zuengler. She is, of course, on the right path in arguing that the sociolinguistic issue of "identity" in second language acquisition is "not only a linguistic process... but social dynamics must be taken into account" Zuengler (1989: 80). Her paper is primarily a review of the sociolinguistic studies on identity-related issues, focusing on various types of language stratification – social, ethnic, gender, and so on. However, she goes off the track at the last section of her paper ("IL Settings versus NNV settings" 1989: 90–93). Here she extends her approach to the sociolinguistic and functional contexts of nonnative varieties of English (NNVE) by "normalizing" these contexts of Lowenberg (1986b) and Sridhar and Sridhar (1986 [1992]).

Zuengler's major disagreement seems to be based on four issues. The first, "the target language issue," relates to the NNVE users' "targets" for acquisition. The argument here is not that NNVE users do *not* have pragmatic, functional, and sociolinguistic preferences for "a target." Indeed, they do express a preference, but the preference is very marginally exonormative. Even those who claim an attitudinal preference for an exonormative model actually use a nativized model in their own performance. Within an institutionalized variety, the "variety shift" ranges from basilect to acrolect, or from a pidgin to educated English, as in for example Singapore and Nigeria. The question here is not about the target for acquisition, but the *type* of target.

The second concern is about the "input" and the "type of input" available to an NNV user. Zuengler is again right that "the input in NNVE settings is *richer* than that in IL settings" (1989: 91; her emphasis). But there is a catch here: the ingredients of the richness are not the same as those Zuengler has in mind. The multilingual contexts indeed provide multilingual input by convergence of languages – two, three, or more – which are often structurally and culturally unrelated to English; the functional contexts are different and the underlying assumptions for organizing the units of speech acts (e.g., apologies, flattering, persuasion, and condolences) are different. The expectations of the interlocutors are distinct from those in the Inner Circle, and mixing and switching are part of the repertoire. The "input," indeed, "is 'rich' enough to enable acquisition to take place" (1989: 91). But what kind of "input"? The answer is that it is the type of input that provides linguistic and sociocultural motivations for *nativization,* and that is a significant point of divergence.

The third issue is that of motivation: Is it "integrative" or "instrumental"?[3] I believe that Zuengler is right in claiming that motivation may be "a combination of instrumental and integrative" (1989: 93). But this observation does not

---

[3] This issue has been discussed in the literature for a long time, particularly in the context of SLA. In the context of ELT, Prator (1968) discussed it, as did Prator in B. Kachru (1976). It has been reproduced in B. Kachru (1986a, especially pp. 106–107).

address the vital – and more relevant – aspects of the questions: What types of channels are adopted for the realization of these two motivations, linguistically, pragmatically, and ideologically? The label "instrumental" is valid across the varieties of English, but the linguistic exponents of such functions are significantly altered in the Outer Circle – these functions are nativized by the use of devices such as mixing, switching, lectal blend, variety shift, and so on. The interlocutors in such NNE contexts must possess two types of competences to make a linguistic action meaningful: that of sensitivity toward a localized variety, and that of the range in which the variety is used. It is this multi-linguistic reorganization that provides the "meaning potential" and functional appropriateness to the instrumental use of the variety, as has been discussed and illustrated in several earlier studies.[4]

The integrative function very marginally – if at all – involves the cultures of the Inner Circle, including the canons of these cultures and the social assumptions associated with them. There is now a long tradition of using English for national and cultural integration within the countries in the Outer Circle – that is, integration within the Nigerian national and cultural context, the Indian national and cultural context, and the Singaporean national and cultural context, to give just three examples.

The final issue is whether nativization is a "group" issue or an "individual issue": it is, of course, both. It is the idiolects that give us the shared features of the dialects or varieties. What matters here, then, is whether the individual or the social group is under focus of attention, and what shared features articulate the identity.

The issue here is not whether pedagogically IL is a useful concept. Nor does this discussion intend to put IL in its grave prematurely. Rather, the issue is whether IL provides any interesting insights for our better understanding of the contexts of institutionalized World Englishes. Current research on this topic has not demonstrated any vital insight at all. What, then, are the reasons for these misplaced assumptions? I shall return to this question later.

Paradigm Misconnection

I believe that not unrelated to paradigm myopia and paradigm gap is the third issue, here labeled *paradigm misconnection*: This refers to misconnection between a hypothesis and its generalization, and the relationship of both to sociolinguistic contexts and the historical realities of language use.

---

[4] There is an increasing body of research, both conceptual and classroom oriented, on this topic. See e.g., B. Kachru (1982d [1992]), Y. Kachru (1991b), Bamgbose, Banjo, and Thomas (1995), and Owolabi (1995). See also the relevant issues of *World Englishes* and *English Today.*

174   The Paradigms of Marginalization

I will briefly discuss three perceptions that have developed in response to three distinct dimensions of the diffusion of English: one provides a rather provocative profile of the demographic and numerical status of the English language and creativity in the language by African and other writers; the second attacks the alleged motives of those who follow what has been termed *liberation linguistics*; the third attempts to motivate arguments for the characterization of English in the Outer Circle essentially in terms of the mathetic function – that is, English as a language of "knowledge paradigm."

These are, of course, serious perceptions, which raise important questions to members of our profession, as teachers, as researchers, and as policy planners.

The Shrinking Core and Linguistic Decline

I shall first discuss the perception that addresses a rather elusive issue, that of the demographic and numerical status of English. In more than one forcefully articulated paper Bailey (1987 and 1990) has claimed that (1987: 1)

popular journalism, and academic inquiry have all *conspired* to *obscure* a remarkable basic fact ... [that] ... English, too, is declining in proportional numbers of speakers and in the range of its uses [emphasis added].

The bases for Bailey's claims are, for example:

a.) That there are initiatives to "foster multilingualism" in the Inner Circle (e.g., the United States, United Kingdom, and Australia);
b) that the linking of "mother, mother tongue, and motherland" is a persuasive argument "to declare that languages other than English will better serve democratic and economic goals" (1987: 6);
c) that several major nations are reassessing their earlier policies toward English, and there is a shift to other languages (e.g., in Malaysia, the Philippines, and Singapore);
d) that there is a "cultural resistance" to English (e.g., in West and East Africa); and
e) that English has developed "pluricentricity," in which the language is not just undergoing changes due to "normal evolution" (1990: 85), but by "linguistic adaptation" (1990: 86) – language evolution is "taken to be a matter of fate; adaptation is a matter of choice" (1990: 86).

The metaphor of "twilight," which Bailey uses in his title "English at Its Twilight," can, as he recognizes, be a harbinger of "bright morning" for the English language, or be "frightening to the tower-builders at Babel" (1990: 84). Whether one views Bailey's speculations as sanguine or despairing, one must ponder some of the concerns expressed in the papers.

The Paradigms of Marginality   175

The first concern is about the acculturation and nativization of World Englishes. Bailey believes that nativization and the bilingual's creativity are "planned, managed, and promulgated by those who support a new tongue for new times" (1990: 86), for example in Emeka Okeke-Ezigbo' s defense of the Nigerian Pidgin as "a practical, viable, flexible language distilled in the alembic of our native sensibility and human experience." Bailey sees an anticipation of "something more than mere evolution. He [Okeke-Ezigbo] supports a *managed* and *revolutionary* shift from English to something more local" (1990: 86).

Bailey's next concern is that "English as a purely mental instrument of human expression is dying" (1990: 86), and another concern is that English "reflects an ideology of inward-looking patriotism" (1990: 90), as in Singapore, as opposed to the "outward-looking aspirations."

In making these claims about the shrinking core of English, Bailey provides an intriguing example of the "observer's paradox." There are four major problems with his English-in-twilight hypothesis: first, his claims are based on extremely selective sources, primarily those that he believes support his arguments; second, he makes no distinction between the "private face" and the "public face" in the statements made about English, in for example India, Malaysia, Nigeria, and Bangladesh; third, he does not recognize that in the spread of English, "visible" language planning is less important than "invisible" language learning and teaching; and finally, he considers bilinguals' linguistic creativity and innovations as linguistic markers of "twilight" and believes that multilingualism in the Inner Circle is a threat to the core of the English-speaking population (e.g., Spanish in the United States). (See also Bailey 1996.)

Liberation Linguistics and World Englishes

The second perception, equally forceful, is presented by Quirk in several of his papers (e.g., 1985, 1988, 1989). In his view, a rather disconcerting trend, which may have eventual drastic consequences for the English language, has gained momentum. As explained, Quirk terms this trend *liberation linguistics*. He believes that it is modeled on "liberation theology." The Quirk position has resulted in an extended debate reproduced in a useful volume edited by Tickoo (1991). The major points that Quirk makes are:

(a) That the emphasis on the range of variation in English, especially in the Outer Circle, is the linguistic manifestation of an underlying deep ideological position;

(b) that the use of the term "institutionalized varieties" – and what it implies – for nonnative Englishes is inappropriate (He says, "I am not aware of there being any institutionalized non-native varieties" (1990: 18));

176   The Paradigms of Marginalization

(c) that a number of uses of the term *variety* have resulted in "confusion" (his emphasis);

(d) that he does not accept that there is a range of variation within nonnative varieties;

(e) that the distinction between ESL and EFL is of doubtful accuracy ("I doubt its validity and frequently fail to understand its meaning" (1988: 236)); and finally,

(f) That he does not consider it desirable to recognize nonnative norms (1988: 237).

The first two perceptions, as articulated by Bailey and Quirk, address wide-ranging concerns, and touch upon a variety of theoretical, methodological, and sociolinguistic issues. The concerns of the third perception, outlined in the following, on the surface appear to be more specific and more focused – but that is an illusion.

The Mathetic Function as a "Knowledge Paradigm"

We see this perception for example in Prabhu (1989). It is related to Halliday's (1975: 3) distinction between the use of language as *doing* (the pragmatic function) and its use for *learning* (the mathetic function). In one function, language is seen as *action,* and in the other function, as *reflection.* On the basis of this underlying distinction, Prabhu (1989: 3) argues that

the prevalent view of the role of English in the Third World tends to focus primarily on the pragmatic function and secondarily on the aesthetic function, thus overlooking the mathetic function.

Prabhu (1989: 2–3) proposes a shift in the uses of language (in the Third World) toward the "cognitive aspect of language use, rather than the artistic one." English as a world language, says Prabhu (1989: 5), is

not just a transactional medium across large parts of the world, but more significantly the medium of a knowledge paradigm which has spread across the present-day world.

This shift in emphasis to the mathetic function is motivated by the following considerations. First, it would give the Third World a share in the "knowledge-generating" process; second, it would reduce the divide between "knowledge-generators" and "knowledge- receivers" – the former being the First World and the latter the Third World; third, if the "knowledge paradigm" of English is emphasized, we are emphasizing the pragmatic function, and if we emphasize the "knowledge-generating" process, we are emphasizing the mathetic function, which "can enable us to play a more equal or integral part in the future development of the knowledge paradigm or the eventual emergence of a new

The Paradigms of Marginality 177

paradigm" Prabhu (1989: 8–9); fourth, because the "current knowledge paradigm is accessible in the written mode, therefore it is crucial to learn this mode" Prabhu (1989: 12); and fifth, the advantages of this approach are, according to Prabhu, twofold: first, "It strengthens the case for a high priority for reasoning gap activities, since reasoning in English is clearly a good preparation for mathetic uses of language" (Prabhu 1989: 13). The second advantage is "in preventing (or at least reducing) the phenomenon of 'fossilization' in language acquisition" (Prabhu 1989: 13). This claim is based on the assumption that the mathetic function involves a "relatively high degree of deliberation and precision."

Prabhu (1989: 15) does recognize one communicative hazard of his proposal, viz, making "non-native speakers 'sound like a book' or move toward spelling-based pronunciation." Prabhu In his intriguing proposal, Prabhu (1989: 16) makes one major claim:

International English is of greatest value as the language of international collaboration in the mathetic endeavor, and it is by internationalizing that endeavor more and more that we can truly internationalize the language.

The underlying assumptions of this proposal are identical to those of Prator (1968) and Quirk (1988, 1989), with the difference that it emphasizes one type of function: the mathetic. We are, however, not told about the processes by which the functional allocation of a language may be controlled, or even restricted. In other words, when a natural language has a full range of functions – pragmatic, creative, and mathetic – how does one curtail those functions or withdraw them from a language? The question is who are to police the functions as gatekeepers of the language? The past histories of English and other languages have a lesson for us here.[5]

One cannot ignore the fact that the functions of World Englishes are related to cultural and intellectual identities in various parts of the world, particularly in Africa and Asia. And these localized functions – creative, pragmatic, and interactional – are international only in a marginal way. They establish regional, local, and class identities.

It is worth noting here that there were two reactions to Quirk's somewhat identical perceptions, first by Graeme Kennedy (1985: 7) and later by David Crystal (1985a: 9); these are discussed in Part III of this book. The uniqueness of institutional varieties of English – in terms of both identities and repertoires – makes them very different from Latin and Sanskrit (see B. Kachru 1985c).

---

[5] One immediately thinks of the fate of e.g. Basic English and Nuclear English. For details, see relevant entries in McArthur (1992).

178   The Paradigms of Marginalization

We must learn another lesson from linguistic history here. The proposal for developing artificial languages, including Esperanto, for mathetic or other functions did not survive in any serious sense. It was not for the lack of attempts; there have been internationally almost seven hundred such attempts. They just did not work.

From the perspective of a "paradigm of knowledge," World Englishes are already performing the "knowledge function" of various types at the inter-regional and international levels – and very well indeed. If this fact is not recognized, and if other functions – pragmatic and artistic – are considered peripheral, we are indeed escaping from a well-established sociolinguistic and literary reality. It is important to remember that the use of English in the artistic and pragmatic functions is not just precolonial, but that this use has over-whelmingly increased during the postcolonial period – that is during the last five decades.[6] This is a historical and literary reality.

It is obvious that these perceptions reveal the daunting complexities of English around the world from several intriguing and different perspectives. Bailey's perspective is that of unrestricted diffusion of English and the threat of increasing multilingualism to the Inner Circle of English, and the reduction in number of speakers within that particular circle. Quirk's is that of ideology and conflict resulting from multicultural identities of English – the processes of nativization and variation and multicanons in creativity. And Prabhu's is that of the "knowledge-generating" power of English and the need for some kind of functional control, though he does not use that term.

The recognition of these demographic, ideological, and power-related issues clearly demonstrates the range of questions, their intensity, and their significance for users of and researchers in World Englishes. And if English has 2 billion estimated users, we are talking of roughly one of every three people in the world. This number is simply mind-boggling.

In my brief discussion of paradigm myopia, paradigm lag, and paradigm misconnection, I briefly attempted to examine these issues and questions. I have presented a perspective from the Outer Circle, which I believe is rewarding when talking of a world language. Let me now go a step further, and again briefly indicate a number of shared features and iden-tities of these paradigms within the framework of the discourse of marginality.

---

[6] It should be noted that in most of the studies on SLA with specific reference to English, hardly any awareness is shown of the immense creativity in Asian and African literatures written in English. There is a long tradition of such writing, which has serious linguistic and sociolinguistic messages for us. See e.g., Y. Kachru (1991b) and later; for a literary discussion and relevant references see Ashcroft, Griffith, and Griffiths (1989).

Discourse of Marginality

The discourse of marginality has been discussed in several recent studies (e.g. Pennycook 1994; Phillipson 1992; B. Kachru 1986aff.; for a review of earlier literature see Tromel-Plotz 1981). We see that the paradigms outlined previously adopt several shared underlying strategies to, as it were, *depower* the counterarguments. These strategies include for example the psychologically disarming strategy of "derationalizing" the counterarguments. A good example is Selinker's discussion of "fossilization and simplicity" and his wonder at "why colleagues appear *emotional* about this topic" (1993: 22, emphasis added). In this comment the word "emotional" completely marginalizes the argument – the contrast is between rationality, objectivity, and, of course, emotion. The readers' focus is distracted – the emphasis changes from the validity of the argument to the psychological state of those who question the hypotheses.

The second is the use of NORMALIZATION STRATEGY when it is claimed that "IL settings are not very different from NNV settings" (Zuengler 1989: 93), and that "processes are similar" (93). We notice the two methods here. One defines the phenomena in a specific way, thus creating straw persons, and then attacks them. This method is evident in the discussion of terms such as *transfer, input, interlanguage*, and *identity*, terms that actually need context-specific application. The second method is to make the broad generalization that all NNV contexts are identical, and that what applies to contexts in New York and Puerto Rico must by implication apply also to traditionally multilingual societies in Asia and Africa.

The issues that the institutionalized varieties of English raise in South, South East, and East Asia and in West, East, and Southern Africa cannot in every case be compared with the use of Russian, French, and German in the same regions. Lowenberg and Sridhar (1986) have specifically addressed the theoretical and methodological issues concerning English NNVs, not NNVs of any language in any context. The Procrustean approach used in various paradigms is thus unrewarding for insightful research.

The third strategy is that of the SOCIOLINGUISTIC OSTRICH. This is revealed in for example nonrecognition of differences between ESL and EFL, and in accepting a broad dichotomy of *us* vs. *them* – native vs. nonnative. One notices the elements of the same strategy in the preceding positions taken by Bailey, Quirk, and Prabhu. Each strategy reflects the cynicism toward recognizing a linguistic process motivated by both sociolinguistic and multilingual contexts. The variational features and innovations are considered "managed ... revolutionary shift" (Bailey 1990: 86), "liberation linguistics" (Quirk 1989), and "a loud assertion or declaration of linguistic independence or secession – a self-conferment of linguistic status" (Prabhu 1989: 16).

180   The Paradigms of Marginalization

Conclusion

One major problem with these proposals, hypotheses, and generalizations is that their sociolinguistic, pragmatic, empirical, and pedagogical bases are questionable. The elephant is defined on the basis of individuals' limited perceptions, and a serious gap is evident between the perceptions and the reality of the whole beast.

And since we are celebrating stories of experiences, of research, of marginality and power, let me share with you an ancient Indian folktale (Ramanujan 1991: xiv) which, I believe, succinctly sums up both our problem and our dilemma:[7]

One dark night an old woman was searching intently for something in the street. A passer-by asked her, "Have you lost something?"

She answered, "Yes, I've lost my keys. I've been looking for them all evening." "Where did you lose them?"

"I don't know. Maybe inside the house." "Then why are you looking for them here?"

"Because it's dark in there. I don't have oil in my lamps. I can see much better here under the streetlights."

This simple yet insightful story tells us two things about the hypotheses, theories, sociolinguistic claims, and approaches to World Englishes. First, where a majority of English users use the language, we are warned that it is a multilingual jungle; it is the Tower of Babel, and it is too dark, too complex, to look for the "keys" of solution in that *real* world of English. One quick solution, therefore, is, Why not seek answers from in here, in the perceived harmony of monolingualism, where there is some "light," and then apply the generalizations we come up with to the Outer Circle? Second, our current paradigms are neither observationally nor descriptively adequate to account for the challenges of a language that has multiple identities. These identities appear threatening to some, a mark of "liberation" to others, and simply overwhelming to still others. In this confusion, we have generated – consciously or unconsciously – a bewildering variety of paradigms of marginality.

It is true that we as professionals have begun to ask questions and propose solutions for the complex issues concerning the forms and functions of World Englishes. In raising such questions we have gone almost to the borders of monolingualism and monoculturalism. We have done exciting research on various aspects of bi- and multilingualism. However, we are still hesitant to cross the threshold and face the complexities of multilinguals' language behavior and the impact of those language data on our hypotheses and our

---

[7] The theme of the 28th Annual TESOL Convention at Baltimore, Maryland, in the United States, March 8–12, 1994, was "Sharing Our Stories." It appears, therefore, appropriate to share this short South Asian story with the present readers.

Conclusion 181

attitudes. We are reluctant to modify, reformulate, revisit, and reassess our favorite paradigms. The answers to these questions demand both cynicism and optimism.

We need cynicism about our cherished views and attitudes about World Englishes, and about our current tools: theoretical and methodological frameworks. We need optimism for seeking answers to the challenging questions. We must look for the lost "key" of solutions where it actually is, in the multilingual and multicultural world where the World's Englishes are used. What Haugen said in 1950 still has a ring of truth to it. He observed that

> the subject was for many years markedly neglected in this country, and we might say that both popularly and scientifically, bilingualism was in disrepute. Just as the bilingual himself often was a marginal personality, so the study of his behavior was a marginal scientific pursuit. (272)

The study of bilinguals and their behavior continues to be "a marginal scientific pursuit." And the result of this attitude is the paradigms of marginality, which continue to be used as linguistic mantras.

Part IV

Ethical Issues and the ELT Empire

11 Applying Linguistics

Introduction

The choice of World Englishes as the starting point of this chapter calls for two types of explanations: one, that of terminology: why *World Englishes*, in the plural, and not just *World English*, in the singular? And two, that of justification of relationship: why choose World Englishes to address the issues related to applied linguistics? There is no simple or short answer to the first question, as is evident from my earlier discussions. An answer to this question, as we know, entails, more than pure linguistic issues, issues of attitude, and additionally several extralinguistic factors, as noted in previous chapters. During the last three decades, a reasonable body (cited in Chapter 14) of research has addressed this question. This chapter provides a perspective for the second question, that of justifying the relationship between World Englishes and applied linguistics, a perspective that is essentially that of the user of English who belongs to the Outer Circle of English.[1]

It seems to me that this perspective not only defines my approach to our understanding of the global spread of English but also defines the goals that I set for the field of applied linguistics. The relationship between World Englishes and applied linguistics as a field of research and inquiry is motivated by several types of issues: theoretical and applied, as well as societal, and ideological.

I will start with what I consider the theoretical issues. Since the 1950s there has been intense activity in the linguistic sciences for analysis and description of two main varieties of the English language: American and British. Extensive

---

[1] Population figures cited here are taken from the United Nations Web site www.undp.org/popin/wdtrends/p98/p98.htm (2010), which lists world population figures for 1998. The statistics for Taiwan are from "Taiwan" Encyclopredia Britannica Online. www.eb.com:180/bol/topic?eu=1 1530l&sctn=l. David Crystal provides an optimistic estimated figure of 2 billion users of English. He says, "If you are highly conscious of international standards, or wish to keep the figures for World English down, you will opt for a total of around 700 million, in the mid-1980s. If you go to the opposite extreme, and allow in any systematic awareness whether in speaking, listening, reading or writing, you could easily persuade yourself of the reasonableness of 2 billion." However, he hastens to add, "I am happy to settle for a billion" (Crystal 1985b: 9).

186   Applying Linguistics

data banks have been established on English at research centers at Brown University and the Universities of Birmingham, London, and Lund, to name just four. And such data banks are also being developed in Asia and Africa (see, e.g., Greenbaum 1990 and Shastri 1985). The largest number of applied linguists in various parts of the world are working in ESL/EFL-related contexts. And, at some places, the term *applied linguistics* is often wrongly equated with the teaching of ESL/EFL.

The research on second language acquisition, first language acquisition, and different aspects of sociolinguistics has to a large extent focused on English. Additionally, the interdisciplinary fields of stylistics and bilingual and monolingual lexicography have also concentrated on English. The major insights gained in the theory of translation are derived from translatiing English texts into other languages of the world and texts in those languages into English. Generalizations about natural languages, their structural characteristics, and the possible categories of language universals usually begin with analyses of and examples from English. In short, what we see, linguistically and sociolinguistically speaking, is that the field of linguistics and its applications are closely linked to one major language of our time: English. And almost the total spectrum of applied linguistics research, its strengths and limitations, can be demonstrated with reference to this language. One might say, then, that the last five decades have been the decades of English.

Moreover, English has acquired unprecedented sociological and ideological dimensions. It is now well recognized that in language history no language has touched the lives of so many people, in so many cultures and continents, in so many functional roles, and with so much prestige, as has English since the 1930s. And, equally important, across cultures English has been successful in creating a class of people who have greater intellectual power in multiple spheres of language use, unsurpassed by any single language before; not by Sanskrit during its heyday, not by Latin during its grip on Europe, and not by French during the peak of the colonial period.

The reasons for the diffusion and penetration of English are complex, and these have been extensively discussed in earlier literature (cited in especially B. Kachru 1985b, B. Kachru and Smith 1986, and Pride 1982). However, one dimension of the diffusion of English is especially important to us, particularly those of us who represent the developing world, who are directly influenced by the research in applied linguistics, and who are considered the main beneficiaries of the insights gained by such research. Again, it is the developing world in which the English language has become one of the most vital tools of ideological and social change, and at the same time an object of intense controversy.

It is this developing world that forms an important component of the three Concentric Circles of English: the Inner Circle, the Outer Circle, and the

Expanding Circle. These three circles, as has repeatedly been mentioned in the literature, give to the English language (and, of course, to its literature, too) a unique cultural pluralism, and a variety of speech fellowships. These three circles certainly confer on English linguistic diversity, and let us not underestimate – as some scholars tend to do – the resultant cultural diversity. One is tempted to say, as does Tom McArthur (1987), that the three circles of English have resulted in several English "languages." True, the purist pundits find this position unacceptable, but that actually is now the linguistic reality of the English language.

The World Englishes are the result of these diverse sociocultural contexts and diverse uses of the language in culturally distinct international contexts. As a result, numerous questions and concerns move to the forefront. Applied linguists, primarily of the Inner Circle, have articulated their positions about these concerns; they have interpreted vanous contexts of the uses of English, and they have provided research paradigms and methodologies.

The range of aspects of applied linguistics such scholars have covered in their paradigms is wide, e.g., sociolinguistics, stylistics, language teaching, and acquisition of English as an additional language. The impact of such research has been significant; it has raised daunting questions that have never been raised before, particularly concerning the standards, models, and diversification in English; concerning the functions of English in the Outer Circle; concerning the functional power of English; and concerning the social issues and – if I may add – the responsibility of applied linguists (see e.g., Quirk and Widdowson 1985; B. Kachru and Smith 1986; Lowenberg 1988; Conner-Linton and Caroline Adger 1993).

And here, two points need stressing: the terms *applied linguistics* and *social concern*. The dichotomy between "theoretical" and "applied" linguistics is essentially one of difference in focus rather than of distinct identities. Charles Ferguson, Michael Halliday, and William Labov – to mention just three names – have repeatedly warned us that the separation of the two is not very meaningful. However, applied linguistics, in whatever manifestation, is essentially an area that reveals certain concerns and certain responsibilities. And the term *social concern* introduces another dimension, though an extralinguistic one.

I believe that "social concern" refers to the responsibility of a discipline toward relevant social issues, and the application of an appropriate body of knowledge to seek answers to such issues. The term *social issues* naturally opens a Pandora's box: What is a social issue? And, how can a profession be evaluated on its response to such issues? These are, of course, controversial questions. As Bolinger (1973: 539) rightly says, the answers to them have to be rediscovered by each generation. However, now and then, a profession must address these questions as an exercise in the evaluation of the field and its direction.

188   Applying Linguistics

It is true that in the United States, during the 1940s and 1950s, we passed through a long phase "across the semantic desert." There was a feeling that "life had lost all meaning, except perhaps differential meaning" (Bolinger 1973: 540). We had stopped asking questions concerning "meaning" and "responsibility." And fortunately even in the United States, that phase is over now. During the last two decades, serious questions have been asked: questions about the evaluation of the field, about the applied linguists' responsibilities, and about the goals and areas of applied linguistics (see, e.g., Labov 1982 cited in Trudgill 1984b; Lakoff 1975).

However, a caveat is in order here: whenever such questions are asked, they are naturally concerned with issues related to the United States or the United Kingdom. Very rarely have questions of concern, of responsibility, and of linguistic pragmatism been raised with reference to World Englishes. In other words, to quote Bolinger (1973: 540) again, "the linguist up to very recently has been a more or less useful sideliner, but not a social critic." And, so far as World Englishes in the Outer Circle are concerned, that position of the linguist still persists.

Major Issues of Concern

Now, I do not propose to take up the role of a social critic here. What I propose to do is to select some of the issues related to World Englishes and applied research, and share with you my concerns about such research. I will, of course, not discuss all the issues and their ramifications. I will merely present a commentary on the following issue, which I consider vital for our understanding of English in its world context: 1) attitudes concerning the ontological status of the varieties of English, 2) generalizations about the creative strategies used for learning English as an additional language in multilingual and multicultural contexts, 3) descriptions of the pragmatic and interactional contexts of World Englishes and their relevance to pragmatic success and failure, 4) assumptions about the cultural content of the varieties of English and the role of such varieties as the vehicles of the Judeo-Christian (or, broadly, Western) traditions, 5) assumptions about the role of English in initiating ideological and social changes, and 6) assumptions about communicative competence in English and the relevant interlocutors in such communicative contexts.

I shall discuss these points one by one in the following sections. But before I do that, I must briefly discuss the current dominant and less dominant approaches to World Englishes to provide a theoretical perspective for the discussion. In recent years the following approaches have been used to study World Englishes: 1) the deficit approach, 2) the deviational approach, 3) the contextualizational approach, 4) the variational approach, and 5) the interactional approach.

However, of these five approaches it is the first two – the deficit and deviational approaches – that have dominated the field. And it is these two approaches that, I believe, are the least insightful. The following comments are thus a critique primarily of these two approaches, and the attitudes that such approaches reflect.

Ontological Issues: Conflict between Idealization and Reality

The initial question takes us to the core of the problem, the issues of attitudes and identity. The attitudes toward a variety of English are only partially determined by linguistic considerations. The other considerations are of assigning a place and a status to the user of the other variety, or marking the distance of a person in the social network. We see two major positions concerning the varieties of English in the Outer Circle: first, the "nativist monomodel" position; and second, the "functional polymodel" position.

The first position, perhaps in an extreme form, is well articulated in two paradigm papers, one by Clifford Prator (1968) and the other by Randolph Quirk (1988). These two studies were presented almost a generation apart. The Prator study was originally presented in 1966. Quirk presented his views first at the 1987 Georgetown University Round Table devoted to language spread (see also Quirk 1989).

The functional polymodel position entails the use of theoretical and methodological frameworks, which relate the formal and functional characteristics of English in the Outer Circle to appropriate sociolinguistic and interactional contexts. I have presented this position since the 1960s, and over time many studies have been written following this approach, at various centers. (For bibliographical references see Chapter 14.)

The Quirk papers, representing the first position, deserve special attention for several reasons: these papers are written by one of the most venerable and intellectually influential scholars of the English language during our time, and his papers take us back to some of the fundamental questions that concern all who are working in the areas of applied linguistics. Furthermore, the papers reopen some questions that some of us believed had been put to rest during the past rather productive years of research on World Englishes.

The main points of what I have called "the Quirk concerns" may be summarized as follows. Quirk sees language spread primarily with reference to three models: the *demographic,* the *econocultural,* and the *imperial.* The demographic model implies language spread with accompanying population spread. The econocultural model suggests language spread without an

190   Applying Linguistics

extensive population spread, essentially for scientific, technological, and cultural information. The imperial model applies to language spread as the result of political (colonial) domination.

The demographic model has resulted in several varieties of English in the Inner Circle (e.g., American, Australian, Canadian, New Zealand). The econocultural and imperial models have, over time, resulted in the endocentric varieties of English in Africa, Asia, and the Philippines (e.g., Bailey and Görlach 1982; B. Kachru 1982d, 1986a; Platt et al. 1984; Pride 1982).

However, Quirk's concerns are about the endocentric models in the Outer Circle and their implications for pedagogy, the international currency of English, and, generally, the good linguistic health of the English language. These concerns raise a number of questions relevant to serious practitioners of applied linguistics. Consider, for example, the following: 1) Do the Outer Circle varieties of English, primarily second language varieties, have an ontological status – that is, sociolinguistically speaking? 2) What communicative needs do they serve: econocultural or intranational? 3) What is the relevance of various types of ontological labels used for the varieties of English in the Outer Circle? 4) What is the relationship between the sociolinguistic identity of a variety of English and the available descriptions of the variety at various linguistic levels? and (5) What is the formal and functional relevance of distinctions such as ESL and EFL?

Quirk, in his usual elegant way, has not only raised these questions for the profession to ponder but moved into the open a concern that is shared by several scholars. In brief, his position on the preceding questions is as follows. Quirk rejects the sociolinguistic identity of the varieties of English in the Outer Circle and considers the recognition of such identity as "the false extrapolation of English 'varieties' by some linguists" (1988: 232). He sees the international needs of English essentially as econocultural – the econocultural model of language spread applied in our times more to English than to any other language (1988: 231). He rejects the use of identificational terms such as "Nigerian English," "West African English," "South Asian English," "Singapore English" and characterizes them as "misleading, if not entirely false" (1988: 234); he does not believe that the varieties of English are adequately described at various linguistic levels, and, therefore, these cannot be used as pedagogically acceptable (or ontologically recognizable) models. And finally, he rejects the generally recognized dichotomy between ESL and EFL. In his own words, "I ignore it partly because I doubt its validity and frequently fail to understand its meaning" (1988: 236).

In other words, for Quirk, among the English users of the world there is another kind of dichotomy: one between *us* (the Inner Circle) and *them* (the Outer Circle and the Expanding Circle). This dichotomy has serious sociolinguistic and attitudinal implications, one of which is that the power to define the

Acquisition and Creativity: The "Leaking" Paradigms

other group is with us and not with them. This is an interesting way of making a distinction between "inclusive" and "exclusive" members of English-using speech fellowships. I am not saying that that is what Quirk has in mind – far from that. However, we should not forget that labels have a value; they provide definitions. And Bolinger (1973: 541) is right when he says that "a loaded word is like a loaded gun, sometimes fired deliberately, but almost as often by accident."

I will not digress here to discuss why Quirk's major points cannot be accepted in terms of the sociolinguistic reality of World Englishes, and how they cannot be supported by the linguistic history of the spread of other major languages of the world. This has already been done in a number of studies, in particular B. Kachru (1986a) and Smith (1987). However, I do not want to give the impression that Quirk's concerns are not shared by other scholars. Indeed, there are several scholars of that persuasion in the United Kingdom and in the United States, as well as in Asia and Africa. (For further discussion of the "Quirk concerns," see Chapter 8.)

Acquisition and Creativity: The "Leaking" Paradigms

The second question relates to acquisition and creativity. The dominant paradigms of second language acquisition are "leaking" for more than one reason. The question of "bridging the paradigm gap" between the theory and functions of the institutionalized varieties of English has been discussed in several studies, in particular Lowenberg and Sridhar (1986). I am addressing here another aspect of the leaking paradigms: the misinterpretation or neglect of the creative aspects of uses of English in the Outer Circle.

This misinterpretation is essentially the result of undue emphasis on concepts such as INTERLANGUAGE and FOSSILIZATION. However, it is gratifying to note that, after dominating the scene for more than a decade, the error in institutionalizing "error analysis" as an insightful paradigm has finally been realized (see relevant studies in Robinett and Schachter 1983). But let me go back to the concepts INTERLANGUAGE and FOSSILIZATION.

Interlanguage is "the type of language produced by second- and foreign-language learners who are in the process of learning a language" (Richards et al. 1985: 145) and *fossilization* refers to

linguistic items, rules, and subsystems which speakers of a particular NL [native language] will tend to keep in their IL [interlanguage] relative to a particular TL [target language], no matter what the age of the learner or amount of explanation and instruction he receives in the TL. (Selinker 1972 in Robinett and Schachter 1983: 177).

Interlanguage, then, is a developmental process, and fossilization is a static condition. The first is developmental in the sense that it is model (or target)

192   Applying Linguistics

oriented, and suggests directionality in terms of attaining stages toward a goal. The second is static and indicates "freezing" with respect to creativity. There are at least three problems with these two concepts in relation to World Englishes.

Acceptance of a monomodel approach to creativity The creative use of language is seen with reference to the model provided by the target language, and the goal of acquisition is determined by the acquisition of an exonormative model.

Rejection of the contact features as undesirable interference This has even resulted in a failure to recognize subtle creative processes due to the influence of the contexts of contact. The effects of contact have only been viewed in a negative sense.

Emphasis on a "unidimensional" view of functions The "unidimensional" view" provides a misleading picture about the functions of English, and about the innovations in English. This view is misleading in more than one sense. First, it results in a serious corpus constraint. Variety-specific generalizations are made on one type of data (e.g., scripts provided by students), ignoring the implications of the cline of bilingualism. Second, the "interference" is not related to function: The result is that external discoursal and interactional norms are imposed on a variety. The "interference" in, for example, Singaporean English or Pakistani English is not always the result of acquisitional deficiency; there is sometimes a clear motivation for it. Often, in newspaper registers, for example, the aim is to establish, contextually speaking, an identity with readers (see e.g., B. Kachru 1982d for references).

The insightful dimensions of creativity in English, such as nonnative literatures in English, and intranational registers ("mixed" or "unmixed"), seem to have escaped the attention of second language acquisition researchers in English. In fact, as I have said elsewhere (B. Kachru 1987b), David Crystal is not alone among linguists who believe that "it is quite unclear what to make of cases like Nabokov and others" (see Paikeday 1985: 67; Kachru 1988c). It so happens that in bilingual societies, most literary creativity is done in a language or a variety that is not one's first language variety. The constraints of "interlanguage" and "fossilization" on such creativity are simply not applicable. If a text is not viewed in this broader context, the result is misleading generalizations of the type that we find in Bell (1976) and Selinker (1972). Bell (1976: 155) considers "Indianized English" and "Anglicized Hindi" to be "x-ized" varieties, because "the motivation for or possibility of further learning is removed from a group of learners" (155). How misleading!

It is essential to consider the multiple dimensions of creativity, and then make generalizations. By multiple dimensions I mean creativity of various types, appropriate to different contexts, genres, and so on. Consider, for example, the following:

Exponents of creativity

Figure: a three-dimensional box with the label "Exponents of creativity" along the top, its faces containing the following vertically-set text:

Mixing Elements various linguistic from languages

Switching within and between languages varieties

Transcreating discourse strategies: style: H vs. L and

Acculturating cultural-y-dependent interactions

Pragmatic Contexts: Success vs. Failure

The third question concerns the users and uses. Research on the pragmatics of English is – on the variables of pragmatic success and failure in World Englishes – basically determined in terms of 1) the formal characteristics of the code or its varieties, 2) the participants in an interaction, and 3) the "effective results" of verbal communication. Linguistic encounters in the Outer Circle are primarily viewed with reference to variables of the Inner Circle.

This, of course, raises several questions, because the underlying sociolinguistic presuppositions are mistaken. One basically wrong assumption is that nonnative varieties of English are primarily used for international purposes. As observed in previous chapters, that actually is not true. In the Outer Circle, the interaction with native speakers of English is minimal. In India, Nigeria, Singapore, and the Philippines, to give just four examples, the localized (domesticated) roles are more extensive, and more important, than are the international roles.

Another mistaken assumption is that when English is used internationally, a native speaker is usually involved. This emphasis on the native speaker of English in all interactional contexts is of doubtful sociolinguistic validity. The real-world situation is that, in the Outer Circle, the predominant functions of English involve interlocutors who use English as an additional

194   Applying Linguistics

language – Indians with Indians, Singaporeans with Singaporeans, Indians with Singaporeans, Filipinos with Chinese or Japanese, Nigerians with Kenyans, and so on. This point has been clearly elucidated in Smith 1987 with empirical data from several parts of the world.

In such intranational and Outer Circle encounters, the users of institutionalized varieties of English are certainly not using just one type of English; they expect an Indian to sound like an Indian and to use the discoursal strategies of an Indian, and they expect a Nigerian to correspond to their notion (however stereotypical) of a Nigerian user of English. The interlocutors in such interactions expect a functional range of varieties, and they certainly adopt the strategies of "mixing" and "switching" depending on the participants. It is thus the contexts of encounters that determine the international strategies used in a linguistic interaction.

I am certainly not advocating that we should not expect linguistically (and contextually) maximal pragmatic success in what have been claimed to be the "survival" registers. My claim is that, for determining the pragmatic success of the largest range of functional domains for English, the local (domesticated) pragmatic contexts are important, because it is these contexts that matter most to the largest number of English users in the Outer Circle. The interaction with native speakers is only marginal. In an earlier paper (B. Kachru 1986c), I have suggested that this claim applies to several subregisters – e.g., legal or medical – in India and Nigeria, to give just two examples.

In the Outer Circle, the members of English-using speech fellowships interact with a verbal repertoire consisting of several codes, and the use of each code has a "social meaning." We seem to have underestimated the linguistic manipulation of the multilingual contexts in which English is used. We see this manipulation when we watch a Singaporean doctor talking to a Singaporean patient, or an Indian or a Pakistani doctor interacting with a patient from his or her region. The manipulation takes place in lectal switch, code mixing, and so on.

And, while discussing the pragmatics of a code, let me introduce an aspect of World Englishes generally ignored by applied linguists: the use of subvarieties of English in, for example, literary creativity. This aspect has been ignored particularly by those linguists who work in the areas of applied or contrastive stylistics. What immediately come to mind are the nativized styles and discourse in the Englishes used in the Outer Circle (see e.g., Smith 1987). Consideration of this aspect of English is important, since the writer of English in the Outer Circle is faced with a rather difficult situation; he/she is a bilingual or multilingual, but not necessarily bi- or multicultural. And he/she is using English in a context that gives the language a new linguistic and cultural identity (see e.g. Dissanayake and Nichter 1987; Gonzalez 1987; B. Kachru 1983b, 1986b; Thumboo 1985a).

Now, the pragmatic success of such codes is not determined by the attitude of the native speaker toward the code, but by the effectiveness of such codes within the contexts of use, such as stylistic effectiveness, emotional effectiveness, and effectiveness in terms of identity. Let us consider, for example, the creative writing of three contemporary Singaporean writers of English: Kripal Singh, Arthur Yap, and Catherine Lim.

Singh's *Voices* and Yap's 2 *mothers in a hbd playground,* both poetic compositions, and Lim's stories *A Taxi Driver* and *A Mother-in-Law's Curse* exploit distinctly different stylistic devices to achieve what I believe is maximum pragmatic success in textual terms. In *Voices* Singh essentially uses mixed codes; Yap contextually, as it were, "legitimizes" the use of an attitudinally low variety and shows the effectiveness of various types of mixing; e.g., the poem contains *jamban* ("toilet bowl" in Malay), *toa-soh* ("drive a car" in Hokkien), *ah pah* ("father" in Hokkien), and constructions such as *What boy is he in the exam?, I scold like mad but what for?,* and *Sit like don't want to get up.* And Lim provides convincing examples of appropriate code alternation true to the the the sociolinguistic contexts of Singapore.

It is through such linguistic devices of diglossic switch and mixing (as in Yap's poem) that various local stylistic resources for creativity are exploited. True, there is a linguistic dilemma in this: On the one hand, if such creativity is evaluated within reference points provided by the Inner Circle, or taking the native speaker as the primary reader of such texts, one might say that there are "inappropriate" uses of varieties of English. On the other, if the creativity is viewed from the perspective of the code repertoire of a Singaporean creative writer and a Singaporean reader, the codes are appropriate in terms of use. And for those who are familiar with the Singaporean sociolinguistic contexts, the language has been used with maximum pragmatic success.

Another example is from the state bordering on Singapore: Malaysia. *Asia Week* (May 24, 1987: 64) tells us that "English-medium drama by local playwrights is a recent trend." In the play *Caught in the Middle,* there is an attempt to "go completely Malaysian." The strategies used are the following: the majority of the dialogue is in English, but there are switching and mixing among Bahasa Malaysia, Cantonese, and Tamil. We are told that "'Malaysian English', spoken, especially marks a progression toward more realistic language in more realistic settings – the home, the pub."

Consider the following excerpt:

MRS. CHANDRAN: Aiee-yah, mow fatt chee ka la (can't do anything about it.) Clean it up, Ah Lan. The rubbish-man will be coming soon, and you know he doesn't take rubbish that isn't nicely packed and tied up.

196   Applying Linguistics

AH LAN (THE AMAH):   Rubbish is rubbish-lah. Supposed to be dirty, what. Real
fussy rubbish-man, must have neat rubbish to
take away.

And Llyod Fernando's observation, quoted in the *Asia Week* article, is that
Malaysian English provides realism to the play:

It exploits that with good humor. Malaysian English is now a dialect, recognized as
such. In some situations, if you don't speak like that, you are regarded as a foreigner. By
using it [Malaysian English] the playwright draws us into the magic circle.

The point here is that the parameters for determining pragmatic success cannot
always be, and should not always be, determined by the Inner Circle. Achebe
(1976: 11), therefore has a point when he says that

I should like to see the word *universal* banned altogether from discussions of African
literature until such a time as people cease to use it as a synonym for the narrow, self-
serving parochialism of Europe.

Let me give another example here from the register of advertising in Japan. Of
course, Japan is not a part of the Outer Circle, and from my point of view that
fact makes this example even more significant. The example throws a different
light on our use of the term "pragmatic success," and I believe supports what
I have suggested.

The pragmatic success of English in advertising in Japan, as illustrated by
the following example, must be seen with reference to the attitude of the
Japanese toward English, and their "consuming passion for English vocabulary" (*Asia Week,* October 5, 1984: 49).

(1). Kanebo cosmetics: for *beautiful human life*
(2). Tokyo Utility Company: *my life, my gas*
(3). Shinjuk:u Station Concourse: nice guy making; multiple days autumn
fair; planning and creative; let's communicate.

Asia Week makes an apt observation about contextual justification of these
examples:

To the English speaker they [vocabulary items] may be silly, childish, or annoying.
Sometimes a double meaning makes them unintentionally funny. But the ubiquitous
English of Japanese ads conveys a feeling to Japanese. (p. 49)

The use of these phrases – deviant, from the native speakers' perspective – has
a deep psychological effect from the Japanese point of view, and, from a
commercial perspective, that is just what an advertisement should achieve.
This point is clearly emphasized in the following extended excerpt:

To produce one such phrase requires the expensive services of an ad agency as
sophisticated as anywhere. A creative director gathers the team and concepts are tossed

about, a first-rate copywriter works on the theme, a lengthy rationalization is prepared for the client, a decision eventually made to launch. Cost: maybe millions of yen. *Everyone understands that it is substandard English. Explains a copywriter at Dentsu: yes, of course we know it sounds corny to an American, even objectionable to some. But what the foreigner thinks of it is immaterial. The ad is purely domestic, a lot of market research has gone into it. It evokes the right images. It sells.* For product names, English words that seem dismayingly inappropriate to the foreign listener are sometimes chosen. The most frequently quoted example is a very popular soft-drink called *Sweat.* The idea of using a body secretion as an enticing name for a fluid to drink out of a can is just as unpleasant to a Japanese as to an Englishman, but *sweat* conjures a different image: hot and thirsty after vigorous activity on the sporting field. The drink's *Pocari* in Hongkong. Some English words enjoy a fad season. Currently very much in are *life, my, be,* and *city,* the last-named suffering from the phonetic necessity to render the *s* before *i* as *sh. My City* is a multi-storeyed shopping complex in Shinjuk:u where you can shop for *my-sports* things to take to your *my-house* in your *my-car. New* remains popular. If no suitable English word exists, nothing is lost, coin one. Some, indeed, are accidentally rather catchy: *magineer.* Others elicit only sighs. *Creap* is a big selling cream-powder for coffee. *Facom* was perhaps not such a felicitous choice considering the open back vowel for Japanese. Currently in season are words ending in *-topia,* presumable from *utopia.* There was a *Portopia,* a *Computopia* and a *Sportopia.* The brand-new Hilton Hotel boasts a splendid shopping annex called the *Hiltopia.* (Emphasis added; *Asia Week,* October 5, 1984)

Cultural Content of English

The fourth question is rather controversial: What is the culture specificity of English? There are two views on this point. One view holds that English is essentially an exponent of the Western Judeo-Christian tradition. It is believed that it is this association and cultural load of English that interfere in more than one sense with the native sociocultural traditions in Asia and Africa. Therefore, the second, non-culture-specific view, takes the position that "the English language is different from other languages in that it 'extends' the meaning of particular words beyond the culture-specific connotations because of the international demands made on it" (Lyons, quoted in Street 1984: 78).

The first, culture-specific, view seems to be used in more than one sense. A number of scholars in Britain and the United States feel that the culture specificity of English is its essential characteristic, and that the non-culture-specific view dilutes that position of the language. In the Outer Circle, those who oppose English use the culture specificity of English as a basis for arguing that the use of English is an intrusion into their native cultures. Thus, according to this group, English is an "alien" language not only in the sense that it does not belong to the linguistic stock of the region, but also in that it represents a culture alien to the local sociocultural traditions.

198   Applying Linguistics

It seems to me that the strength of English is not its culture specificity with reference to Britain or America, or lack of culture specificity in the sense in which Lyons presents it, and that Street (1984: 66–94) rightly rejects. The strength of English lies in its multicultural specificity, which the language reveals in its formal and functional characteristics, as in, for example, West Africa, South Asia, and the Philippines. These characteristics have given the English language distinct cultural identities in these regions, and recognition of this fact is essential for any insightful research on the world varieties of English. A good parallel example is that of Christianity and Islam in Asia: these two religions have become so much a part of the local cultural traditions that it is not very insightful to consider them now as "foreign."

Ideological Change

The fifth question is closely related to the preceding discussions, since culture specificity and ideological change seem to go hand in hand. I believe that in discussions of ideological change, undue emphasis seems to have been laid on one type of ideological change – the positive or negative aspects of Western-ization. The reality seems to be in between the two extreme positions (see Chapter 5). A process of rethinking and reevaluation is needed to see what English has contributed in the past and continues to contribute in the present in the Outer Circle – as indeed do other languages – toward self-identification and self-knowledge. A good example is again provided by Japan, as in the following excerpt from *JAAL Bulletin* (December 1986: 7):

Prof. Takao Suzuk:u of Keio university lectured on "International English and Native English – Is English Really an International Language?" Dividing English into Inter-national English and Native English, he criticized Japanese teachers of English for teaching Native English, dealing only with the literature, history and lifestyles of England and America. He urged us to recognize the fact that English is no longer the sole property of native English speakers. Japan's relations with Europe and America have changed from "vertical" (unidirectional inflow of advanced technology and culture) to "horizontal" (economical and cultural exchange on equal terms). Accord-ingly, he argued, English teaching in Japan should also change from emphasizing the conventional "receiver" type to emphasizing the "sender" type in order to express ourselves and our culture. While using English as the "form," he suggested, we should use as the "content" Japan and other non-English cultural phenomena such as Korean history, Arabic religion, or German literature.

The last question is about communicative competence, and it has many faces. My preceding discussion of pragmatic success, culture specificity, and ideo-logical change naturally leads us to the area, which is vaguely represented in "communicative competence" (for further discussion see Savignon 1987). In recent years, communicative competence has become one major area to which applied linguists have paid serious attention. A partial bibliography on communicative language teaching includes more than 1,180 items (see Ramaiah and Prabhu 1985; also Berns 1985). Again, considerable research on this topic has been done with specific reference to the teaching of English in the Outer and Expanding Circles of English, and this research has various vintages. The most popular and, at the same time, rewarding for the publishing industry is research on ESP (English for Specific Purposes).

Research on ESP, manuals for its use, lexical lists, and other aids are guided by the assumption of the culture specificity of English, in which "appropriateness" is determined by the interlocutors from the Inner Circle. I have shown in an earlier paper on this topic that this assumption is only partially correct (see B. Kachru 1986c).

However, as an aside, I would like to mention a recent paper by Frances B. Singh (1987) that insightfully discusses the role of power and politics in the examples chosen to illustrate various grammatical points in three grammar books used in the Indian subcontinent: Nesfield (1895), Tipping (1933), and Wren and Martin (1954). She, then, contrasts the examples used by these three grammarians with that of Sidhu (1976), an Indian teacher of English. The conclusions Singh arrives at are very illuminating. These four grammar books provide paradigm examples of power and politics as reflected in the genre of school textbooks. What we need now is a study of the same type for ESP texts. My guess is that the results concerning the underlying assumptions of such texts will be, to say the least, provocative.

Where Does Applied Linguistics Fail the Outer Circle of English?

And now I arrive at what to me is the heart of the problem. And it is naturally controversial. Where does applied linguistics fail the Outer Circle of English? It is true that the last three decades have been the decades of significant strides for the development of applied linguistics. True, we must recognize the fact that applied theory has been used in areas that have been almost unresearched before. And the result of this extension and application of the linguistic sciences has been insightful. It is now realized, though belatedly in the United States, as Lakoff (1975: 336) tells us, that "the theoretical linguist must deal with problems of the intellect and morality, with reality and sanity..." And, turning to applied linguists, Lakoff continues, "the applied linguist must concern himself with decisions among possible theories, universals of grammar, relations among grammatical systems." But, then, that is only one side of the coin. There is, naturally, another side, which has traditionally been left without comment and touches millions of users of English in the Outer Circle.

It is this side of applied linguistics that concerns educators, policy planners, parents, children, and, above all, a multitude of developing nations across the proverbial Seven Seas. The implications of applied linguistic research raise questions and result in various types of concerns. As I said at the outset, these are questions of theory, empirical validity, social responsibility, and ideology. Let me briefly present some of these here.

First, the question of ethnocentricism in conceptualization of the field of World Englishes. World Englishes in the Outer Circle are perceived from the vantage point of the Inner Circle. The perception of the users and uses of English in that circle is not only in conflict with the real sociolinguistic profiles of English but also conditioned by an attitude that has divided the English-using world into two large groups. One group, defined in most unrealistic terms, comprises those who seem to be expected to learn English for communication with another particular group. And the other group comprises those who continue to look at the diffusion of English essentially in pedagogical terms. This ethnocentric perception has created a situation that is obviously incorrect on many counts.

The second question relates to what has been termed in the literature "the Observer's Paradox." The paradox applies in several ways to observations on English in the Outer Circle. First, there is an idealization of contexts of use; second, the focus is on static categories of the lectal range as opposed to the dynamic interactional nature of the functions; third, the observer isolates the use of English from the total repertoire of the user; and fourth, the researcher does not recognize the confusion between the performance and the model.

The third question involves the "paradigm trap." The paradigm trap seems to constrain not only description of the varieties, but also discussion of creativity in the use of the language, models for teaching, and teaching methodology. One notices this constraint in several ways: in the theoretical and methodological approaches used to describe the sociolinguistic contexts, and in the data selected for analysis; in the description of the acquisitional strategies and the resultant description of such language, and the generalizations made from such data (e.g., interlanguage, fossilization); and in the evangelical zeal with which the pedagogical methods are propagated and presented to the developing Third World, often with weak theoretical foundations, and with doubtful relevance to the sociological, educational, and economic contexts of the Outer Circle.

The fourth question relates to the frustrating signs of excessive commercialization of professional minds and professional organizations. In professional circles, in ESL/EFL programs, there still is the syndrome that the English language is part of the baggage of transfer of technology to the Outer Circle. This one-way transfer-of-technology mentality is fortunately being abandoned by pragmatic and forward-looking social scientists working on the problems related to the developing world. But, unfortunately, in the ESL/EFL circles the old paradigm continues.

The preceding concerns do not exhaust the list; they are only indicative of the tensions that one notices in the literature. However, there are some other, in my view fundamental, concerns for applied linguistic research, which have broader significance. I would like to discuss these briefly. They concern conceptualizations about the users of English internationally, conceptualizations of the theoretical frameworks adopted for the description of the English-using speech fellowships in the Outer Circle, and the question of the "renewal of connection" between the theoretical frameworks and the uses and users of English (B. Kachru 1981d: 77).

First, let me discuss the conceptualization concerning the users of English internationally. In the post-1950s period, the dominant paradigms of linguistic research took monolingualism as the norm for behavior in linguistic interactions. This is particularly true of the United States. This position, unfortunately, has resulted in a rather distorted view of bilingual societies, and bilingualism in general. As a consequence, the manifestations of language contact have been viewed from the wrong perspective. Miihlhäusler (1985) is right in drawing our attention to the fact that language contact has been receiving less and less attention in linguistic literature.[2]

The concept that seems to have survived in applied linguistics is INTER-FERENCE. And here Joshua Fishman's observation (1968: 29) has, unfortunately, come to haunt us. According to him, linguists tend to see language in two ways, "the first being that of two 'pure' languages, and the second that of 'interference' between them." That observation may not apply to all linguists, but it is certainly true of most dominant research paradigms used for the study of World Englishes. The term *interference* has acquired a negative connotation, attitudinally very loaded.

What such statements convey, unfortunately, is that multilingualism is an aberration, and monolingualism is the norm. However, the reality is that monolingualism is the exception, and the largest number of users of English are bi- or multilinguals; such bi- or multilingual users of English give the English language a multicultural dimension, not only in the Outer Circle, but even in Scotland, Wales, Ireland, and so on (see e.g., Walker 1984).

It is not that the relationship between language and the sociocultural context is not recognized. Indeed it is, as for example by Quirk (1986: 19), when he says:

---

[2] As Miihlhäusler (1985: 52) correctly suggests, aspects related to language contact have been treated somewhat peripherally in introductory textbooks on linguistics. A random survey of such textbooks clearly proves Miihlhäusler's point, when he observes: "We can observe a marked decrease in the number of pages devoted to language contact phenomena." For a detailed discussion on language contact and for references, see Hock (1986).

202   Applying Linguistics

Even the simplest, shortest, least technical, least momentous texts have a structure involving profound *interactions* between language and the world, between individual and culture in which they operate: involving extensive assumptions about shared knowledge and shared attitudes, reasoned inferences about the degree to which participants in even such simple communications are willing to operate. [Emphasis added]

However, when it comes to recognizing the implications of the uses of English in, for example, the Asian or African contexts, the results of such uses on the form and functions of English, and the reflections of such uses in the literatures written in English, there is considerable resistance to the interrelation between language and the world, as we find in Quirk's observation: the important process of cross-over is missing. That is true of Quirk's own papers (see e.g., Quirk 1988 and 1989).

And related to this is the conceptualization of theoretical frameworks used for description and analysis of English in the Outer Circle. The types of models used for such descriptions by applied linguists have been rather uninsightful. What is needed is to view the uses and the users of English within theoretical frameworks that may be considered "socially realistic." What I have in mind are, for example, the frameworks presented by J. R. Firth, M. A. K. Halliday, Dell Hymes, and William Labov. Halliday (1978: 2) tells us:

A social reality (or a "culture") is itself an edifice of meanings – a semiotic construct. In this perspective, language is one of the semiotic systems that constitutes a culture; one that is distinctive in that it also serves as an encoding system for many (though not all) of the others...

And he adds:

The contexts in which meanings are exchanged are not devoid of social value; a context of speech is itself a semiotic construct, having a form (deriving from the culture) that enables the participants to predict features of the prevailing register ... and hence to understand one another as they go along.

The advantage of such frameworks as Halliday's is that they provide a content for description, they relate language to use, and, yet, they draw out the formal distinctiveness: they assign a "meaning" to what has merely been termed *interference* or *fossilization*. They provide a dimension to the description that many structural and poststructural paradigms have failed to provide. A socioculturally satisfactory description and theoretically insightful analysis must still seek the "renewal of connection with experience," as Firth (1957: xii) would say. And here, the crucial word is "experience."

It is not too much to ask that claims about the forms and functions of English in the Outer Circle be justified in terms of the renewal of connection. This implies that the observations about English in the Outer Circle should be valid in terms of the following: 1) the sociolinguistic contexts, 2) the functional contexts, 3) the pragmatic contexts, and 4) the attitudinal contexts.

What I have said previously is a broad generalization: it gives the impression that all current approaches to World Englishes have ignored these contexts. That actually is not correct. The earlier discussion may be summarized in terms of a bundle of fallacies that show in the dominant approaches to World Englishes. The fallacies are of the following types: theoretical, methodological, formal, functional, and attitudinal.

But all the bees are not out of my bonnet yet. The issues raised in this book, though restricted to applied linguistics and World Englishes, apply to other areas of applied linguistics too. Here, I must go back to the position that I presented at the beginning. I do not see applied linguistics divorced from the social concerns of our times, nor from the concerns of relevance to the societies in which we live. This view, of course, entails a *responsibility*. The question of responsibility pushes several other issues to the forefront: the issues of social identity, of attitudes, of cultural values, and of culturally determined interactional patterns and their acceptance, and, above all, of choosing of the most insightful paradigms of research.

In other words, the question of the whole semiotic system is involved here. And, more importantly, in answering questions about Englishes across cultures, we get only glimpses. True, these glimpses are tantalizing, but they do not present the whole truth about the users and uses of English. And here, once more, I must go back to Dwight Bolinger's (1973: 549) inspiring Presidential Address to the Linguistic Society of America (1973), in which, with reference to a different context, he says, "Truth is a linguistic question because communication is impossible without it." We, as applied linguists, cannot justifiably be just "social sideliners." And if I may continue with Bolinger's quote, the issue becomes more complex, since, as he aptly warns us, "a taste of truth is like a taste of blood."

Conclusion

The task of applied linguists working on various aspects of World Englishes is very intricate, and very sensitive, for the consequences of such research are immense. This research touches us all in very meaningful and far-reaching ways. A large segment of the human population is involved in using English across cultures, and across languages. In our task, we have to satisfy many gods. And most of all, we should remind ourselves, more often than we actually do, that the situation of English around the world is unprecedented in many respects, and approaches to it have to be unprecedented too, formally, sociolinguistically, and attitudinally. It seems to me that our present paradigms and attitudes are simply not up to the challenge that our discipline is facing.

Table 11.1 *Types of fallacies about World Englishes (The Outer Circle)*

Theoretical	Methodological	Formal	Functional	Attitudinal
*Paradigm trap *Ideal hearer– speaker *Monolingualism as the norm *Emphasis on static as opposed to dynamic	*Cynicism about ontological status of varieties *Nonrecognition of varieties within a variety *Ignoring sociolinguistic contexts (users/ uses) *Nonrecognition of <u>cline</u> of a. Bilingualism b. Intelligibility c. Acceptability *Nonrecognition of "verbal repertoire" *Ambilingualism as the norm *Directionality toward monomodel	*Variety-specific generalizations on one type of data *Nonrecognition of institutionalization *"Error"-oriented-approach *Unidimensional generalizations (developed / developing) *No distinction between acquisitional deficiency and creative deviation/ innovation *No attempt to contextualize nativization *Nonrecognition of "systemicness" *Nonrecognition of social identity with lectal shifts, discoursal strategies, mixing, switching, and the cline of "norms"	*No consideration of "range" and "depth" *Nonrecognition of "pluricentricity" *Nonrecognition of multiple sociocultural identities *Undue emphasis on international as opposed to intranational roles *Variables for the following, e.g., determined on the basis of Inner Circle a. Pragmatic success/failure b. Intelligibility/interpretability/ comprehensibility c. Communicative competence d. ESP	*Us/them dichotomy *Nonrecognition of historical depth *Emphasis on "integrative" as opposed to "instrumental" motivation *Stress on exocentric models without pragmatic justification

And the profession at large does not show that we are aware of the issues that confront the largest segment of users of World Englishes. We must be courageous and ask ourselves, as a Brahmin priest asked of Gautama Buddha more than twenty-five hundred years ago: "What are you then? Are you a god, a demigod, some spirit or an ordinary man?" "None of these," answered the Buddha; "I am awake."

The problem is that applied linguists have not been asked the question. We seem to have no accountability; therefore, we do not know whether we are "awake" to the challenges and the social implications of our research. Perhaps the time has come to ask ourselves some serious questions: questions of social concern and of social responsibility. In other words, it is time for questions concerning accountability.

12   Leaking Paradigms

Introduction

This chapter begins with a string of disclaimers. First, I do not propose to make yet another attempt to resolve the identity crisis that applied linguists express in identifying their field. There is a long tradition of such self-doubt, which is ritualistically articulated in various degrees at our meetings and in our publications.

Second, I do not plan to complicate matters further by suggesting yet another definition for the field; that again seems to have become a favorite professional endeavor in which we engage frequently. (See e.g., Kaplan 1980: 4–20; Kunnan 1990.) Third, I would like to mention at the outset that I will not attempt to separate applied theory in applied linguistics from an underlying linguistic theoretical framework.

In identifying the field of applied linguistics I believe the zoologist colleague's response to the celebrated British phonetician Daniel Jones is insightful: When asked how a zoologist would define a dog, Jones was told that a dog is a "four-footed mammal recognized as a dog by another dog" (cited by Strevens 1980: 18). It is, however, important to reiterate that the *dogness* forms a cline and each species has shared characteristics that distinguish one breed from another. That seems to be true of practitioners of applied linguistics too.

The applied linguists engaged in this "intellectual endeavor" must take Peter Strevens's (1980: 18) warning seriously and "redefine its bases from time to time." These attempts to define the bases of applied linguistics are not necessarily an indication of self-doubt but may indicate a continual unfolding of the field, defining issues of relevance and responsibility, reorganization of the theoretical apparatus, or, in some cases, just shedding theoretical baggage.

The Range of Leaks

My primary concern, then, is not about the bases of applied linguistics, but much larger than that. I propose to look at several dimensions of the field: the way applied linguistics is characterized by applied linguists, the way the field is perceived by other professionals, and the way applied linguists function as professionals. In doing so, I must hasten to add that to a large extent my own perception is conditioned by the perspective of what is termed the Third World or the developing world. In other words, my primary concern is how applied linguists have responded to the language-related problems of these parts of the world. One must pause here and ask some questions: What are the roles that linguists have traditionally played in Third World societies? One might ask, to use Bolinger's (1973) words, have linguists been essentially "social side-liners," and not social critics?

Applied linguists generally avoid questions of this type. But these are the types of questions other social scientists and humanistic scholars raise in their professional meetings: questions about the models we apply to describe and analyze the societies and speech communities we work in and/or on, questions about our professional responsibility toward these societies, questions about the ethical appropriateness of some of the practices we follow, questions about the training we provide to young scholars from the Third World, and so on.

It is a sad commentary that it is generally other professional groups (e.g., anthropologists and sociologists), both in the West and in developing countries, who have started asking such questions about our profession (e.g., see Hvalkof and Aaby 1981). Some have even begun to pass judgments on the whole profession, or on some segments of the profession. The questions are related to several roles that applied linguists perform as researchers, educators, consultants, policy makers, and messengers of various religions.

In discussing this aspect, my task has been made easier by two types of materials. First, the publication of several studies addressing the issues of professionalism in applied linguistics by applied linguists themselves (e.g., Paraksama 1990 and 1995; Pennycook 1994; Phillipson 1992; Skutnabb-Kangas 1984; Phillipson and Skutnabb-Kangas 1986; Tollefson 1991; Wolfson and Manes 1985). The issues these practitioners have raised are not merely of "social concern"; they go beyond that. They raise fundamental questions about the field and the implications of applied research. Second, and perhaps more important, are materials in the form of investigative reports provided by international agencies concerned with the "oppression of indigenous peoples in many countries"[1] and by agencies helping "aboriginal people to protect their rights."[2]

---

[1] See e.g., the International Work Group for Indigenous Affairs (IWGIA). Note in Hvalkof and Aaby (1981: 4).

[2] See e.g., the Survival International ("a non-political, non-denominational organization"). Note in Hvalkof and Aaby (1981: 5).

208   Leaking Paradigms

One would, of course, not take such materials seriously if these agencies did not have the same standing as, for example, Amnesty International and other human rights watch groups have in calling attention to issues of human rights violations.

The two types of issues – academic and social – may at first seem unrelated in discussing applied linguistics; but, in reality, they are closely related. The field of applied linguistics, we are rightly told, "makes abstract ideas and research findings accessible and relevant to the real world" (see also Bjarkman and Raskin 1986; and Lakoff 1975). Variables used to define applied linguistics are social concern and social relevance.[3] And Strevens (cited in Markee 1990: 317) articulates this position quite clearly when he warns us that "linguists are not exempt from being socially accountable from displaying a social conscience and therefore when possible they should use their knowledge and understanding in the service of humanity" (see also Hymes 1985).

This conceptualization of the field, including social accountability and relevance to the real world, naturally puts a heavy burden on the field and its practitioners. The evaluation of the field and the implications of applied research thus attract scrutiny from diverse groups of scholars, social activists, and targeted users of applied theory.

In sharing my concerns about the field and the uses of applied research, I am aware of the fact that what is of relevance for one group may be perceived as an imposition by another group, and what is "salvation" for one group may be interpreted as "proselytization" by another group. In doing so, one is disturbing the proverbial hornet's nest: "social concern" is not an innocent term; it is a double-edged sword, and there is more than one way of approaching and interpreting "social concerns" and "relevance."

What we see, then, is that applied linguistics has several types of "leaks" concerning the identity of the field, its theoretical foundations, and the motives of applied linguistic research as practiced by some linguists and professional organizations. All these concerns, of course, are not expressed by the same groups. What is a "leak" in the field for one beholder may be considered its strength by another. I am using the term *leak* in more than one sense, to refer to the perceived limitations of the paradigms of applied linguistics, to refer to the overwhelming ideological and methodological biases of the paradigms, and to raise questions concerning ethical issues and professionalism in applied linguistics research. The perceived leaks may, then, be characterized as:

---

[3] See e.g., views expressed in the Round Table in "Defining Our Field: Unity in Diversity," *Issues in Applied Linguistics.* December 1990, 1.2: 157–159. These views are also articulated in detail in Phillipson (1992).

a) Theoretical
b) Methodological
c) Pragmatic
d) Ethical

These leaks, as is evident, combine issues that do not focus purely on theory or methodology; they extend beyond these concerns into the realm of "relevance" and "social responsibility" toward "the real world," approaches to language-related problems of the people of the Third World, and attitudes toward the traditions and customs of the Third World. That there is this crossover from theory and methodology to the real world, to societal problems and their solutions, should be the strength of the field and the goal of the discipline. But, as Hymes (1985: vi) warns us, "It often seems in the academy that work which has the most to do with actual life is the least valued." Let me discuss these points in detail.

Theoretical Leak

The debate over outlining the peripheries of applied linguistics actually started in the 1960s in the United States and the United Kingdom. Once linguists made claims for the autonomous nature of their discipline, attempts were made to give a distinct identity to the field, and to articulate the main objectives of its practitioners.

What emerged from this prolonged – and often acrimonious – debate are two distinct conceptualizations of linguistic endeavor (Newmeyer 1986). One conceptualization emphasizes a divorce of the linguistic sciences from social context and concerns, while the second emphasizes the social realism of linguistics and its application in relevant language-related social concerns. One is characterized as "autonomous linguistics" and the second as "socially realistic linguistics." These two positions are discussed in e.g., Chomsky (1965), Newmeyer (1986), Firth (1930, 1957), Halliday (1973, 1975, 1978), Hymes (1974), Labov (1970), Lakoff (1972). B. Kachru (1981d), and de Beaugrande (1991). It is the second type of paradigm that relates linguistic form to function, and "speech" to the "speaker." The next logical step is to apply this knowledge to societal concerns and language-related problems.

And this takes us to the paradigms of applied linguistics. The response of the profession to social concerns has resulted in a number of different – often diametrically opposite – paradigms, particularly since the 1960s. We see this divergence in approaches on both sides of the Atlantic. The result of this division is split into what one might call the British track and the North American track.

210   Leaking Paradigms

The British track seems to emphasize a "multidisciplinary approach" in which linguistics, though essential, is not "the only discipline which contributes to" applied linguistics (Strevens, cited in Markee 1990: 316). On the other hand, in the United States, in spite of various types of disagreements, applied linguists have generally maintained their links with various linguistic paradigms starting with structural linguistics (cf. e.g., Charles Fries, Robert Lado).

In the literature, questions have been asked about whether applied linguistics is essentially autonomous or interdisciplinary. The autonomous character of applied linguistics may be seen in two ways. The first autonomous characterization may appear to some as rather extreme: that is, what applied linguists do is actually what general linguistics is all about. This view is in one respect close to Halliday's view that what is sociolinguistics in the United States is general linguistics in the United Kingdom. Sridhar (1990) has further discussed this position forcefully, not necessarily following Halliday's argument.

The second characterization of applied linguistics is that it is essentially applied theory: an extension of theoretical linguistics. And applied theory, in turn, contributes to theoretical linguistics by attestation, by extension of contexts of use, and by expansion of the range of data. In other words, application provides observational adequacy, relevance, and accountability. This characterization is clear in Widdowson's position (1979: 1–2). He conceives of applied linguistics as "a spectrum of inquiry which extends from theoretical studies of language to classroom."

We see evidence of such a relationship in Labov's study of the use of language in judicial contexts in three case studies: the U.S. Steel case, the "Thomfare" case, and the Prinzivalli case (Labov 1988). What Labov (1988: 160) shows is "the relations between theory and practice, theory and data, theory and facts." And he warns us that

within the academic framework facts are valued to the extent that they serve a theory, and only to that extent. Academic linguists are themselves engaged in the business of producing theories: theories are the major product and end-result of their activity. It seems to me that there is something backwards in this view, and we should seriously consider whether it might be reversed.

These theoretical underpinnings for applied theory have considerable advantages, as Firth (1957: xii) insisted: the theory must be "useful in renewal of connection with experience." Once the "renewal of connection" is lost, the leaks in applied linguistics begin to appear. The greater the theoretical leak, the more suspect a field becomes.

We see these leaks in the clusters of definitions of applied linguistics – more than a dozen – provided in, for example, the Kaplan volume (1980: 4–20). These form a cline in their claims of a relationship with linguistic theory. On the one hand, we see the field defined with a close relationship to the linguistic

The Range of Leaks 211

sciences (see e.g., Roger S. Kirsner, Roger H. Andersen, Tatiana Slama-Cazacu).[4] On the other hand, we have definitions using an elusive way to bypass theoretical issues, the issues of theoretical dependence of the applied language fields (Andersen et al. 1990).[5] Charles Ferguson, the guru of applied linguistics in North America, rightly cautions us that

> this dangerous business of pure versus applied, is not very meaningful. We should be talking of the application of the basic assumptions or the methods of the findings of linguistics in the solution of language problems, social or individual.

It is here that the theoretical leak begins: It seems to me that we are falling into three of traps by preferring hierarchical or "weak" definitions of the field to "strong" ones (Markee 1990: 315–323). First, in adopting the strong position, applied linguists will not be facing the criticism that one can do "applied linguistics" without drawing, even vaguely, on what is normally considered to be "linguistics" (Newmeyer 1983: 32). In the section "The Unrealistic Expectations of Many Applied Linguists" (1983: 132–135), Newmeyer's concern, however, is that "'applied linguistics' has come to be identified with almost any area of research or pedagogy involving language outside grammatical theory proper..." This was, however, the picture of applied linguistics in the 1980s, both in the United States and in the United Kingdom. That position has somewhat changed in recent years.

Second, such a position reduces the credibility gap that traditionally has developed between theory and its application in the United States and the United Kingdom. It is not that the so-called theoreticians deny that there are social issues related to language.

> It is just that the part of the mind or the faculty which knows these things is isolated from the part that knows what is called "theoretical linguistics." (Hymes 1985: v)

Third, the more we go toward a weak definition of the field, the more we contribute to "the generally low academic prestige of the discipline" (see Markee 1990 and Swales 1984;).

I am, therefore, making a distinction between applied linguistic research and interdisciplinary research: the former within the theoretical framework and training of the linguistic sciences per se, and the latter without such serious constraints. I believe that Ferguson (1957: 65) has a point when he says that

> much though we like our own conceptual framework and find it impressive in its own right, we can hardly tell, for example, a highly trained political scientist or sociologist studying political processes in language policy formation and implementation that he is

---

[4] See *Issues in Applied Linguistics* 1.2 (December 1990): 152–155. See also Kaplan (1980).
[5] See *Issues in Applied Linguistics* 1.2: 157–166.

212   Leaking Paradigms

not – in the same sense – engaging in the scientific study of language. Let us welcome other fields to the family of language sciences.

This distinction, then, would leave the door wide open for interdisciplinary research without creating a dichotomy between "strong vs. weak" applied linguistics, and thus expanding the credibility gap of our field of investigation.

Within these extremes, we also note that some paradigms of linguistics are not so emphatic about emphasizing the dichotomy between theory and its application. I am particularly thinking of the work of J. R. Firth and M. A. K. Halliday, and followers of their frameworks.

Methodological Leak

The methodological leaks in applied linguistics are essentially of three types. First, conceptualizations of speech communities in the Third World are often based on the generalizations of monolingual societies in that they consider societal monolingualism as a norm. The underlying methodology, then, determines how a speech community is defined and described.

One can ask, Does the model remain flexible enough to account for the characteristics of speech communities across cultures? Answers differ, as do interpretations. The questions are not merely of definitions; they also relate to societal realism, language use, and language interaction, and ultimately to conceptualization of the field itself. The implications of such underlying theoretical frameworks relate to description, explanation, generalization, and, above all, how multilingual and multicultural societies use languages. In several descriptions, including, some of those discussed in this volume, it has been shown that mutilingualism demands a different perspective for describing linguistic interaction at various levels beyond grammar and phonology. One sees it in discourse, repertoire, style, range, and literary creativity (see Ferguson 1982 [1992]; B. Kachru 1982d [1992d] and 1986a [1990]).

It is doubtful that the linguistic paradigms applied in investigating the linguistic behavior of multilingual societies actually do justice to them. The paradigm bias in applied research is apparent in various ways, for example:

(1) In preconceived notions of how a speech community functions,
(2) in field-work techniques,
(3) in descriptions, and
(4) in the analysis of bilinguals' creativity.

Second, there is indifference about the sociolinguistic contexts of the consumers of applied research, particularly in the Third World. A number of such examples are given in a provocative book by Phillipson (1992), which discusses various case studies in which several government agencies are involved. The cases he discusses are concerned, in particular, with what he

The Range of Leaks   213

labels "linguistic imperialism" with reference to English. Further evidence is given in various publications of Tollefson (see e.g., 1991). The same issues recur in what I have labeled "the Quirk concern" (B. Kachru 1991a).

The third point takes me to the question of method as the proverbial Procrustean bed: the view that all cultures, all speech communities, and all users of language must fit into one mold. This is particularly true of, for example, generalizations made about ESP.

Pragmatic Leak

What I consider the pragmatic leaks call to mind the following concerns: the first relates to "paradigms of inequality." In several recent studies the concern has been renewed that a variety of language-related issues cannot be studied and understood without reference to ideological, sociocultural, and political contexts. This applies to, for example, language teaching, language planning, and language in education as specifically articulated in e.g., Joseph and Taylor (1990), Fairclough (1989), Skutnabb-Kangas (1984ff.), and B. Kachru (1986a [1990]). This issue involves power and what has been termed "linguistic imperialism" or "cultural imperialism" (Phillipson 1992).

In this power imbalance, we generally notice a clear divide between the North and the South and the East and the West, in which the power to define and control has created a complex situation. The East African writer Ngugi aa Thiong'o (1991) describes this power of language succinctly:

The encounter between English and most so-called Third World languages did not occur under conditions of independence and equality. English, French, and Portuguese came to the Third World to announce the arrival of the Bible and the sword. They came clamouring for gold, black gold in chains, and gold that shines as sweat in factories and plantations. If it was the gun which made possible the mining of this gold and which effected the political captivity of their owners, it was language which held captive their cultures, their values, and hence their minds.

What particularly interests me in Ngugi's observation is his remark on language, "which held captive their cultures, their values, and hence their minds." Itseems to me that this "captivity" continues in various ways in the most active area of applied linguistics, that of teaching English as a second, foreign, or international language. It continues in the curriculum, it continues in applied research, and it reflects in the profession's attitude to the fast-expanding world of learners of English.

The second concern refers to "pragmatism" vs. "liberalism." It is evident that the paradigms of inequality are maintained and even justified by attacking pragmatic considerations as indicators of "liberalism." In applied linguistics, it is alleged that this liberalism shows up in "liberation linguistics"

214   Leaking Paradigms

(see e.g., Quirk 1988 and 1989). This question has been discussed in detail with reference to World Englishes (see Tickoo 1991). However, the issues raised here are not restricted to World Englishes but apply to several aspects of second language acquisition and teaching contexts.

The third concern is about "linguistic models" vs. "applied needs." In a provocative paper, Jernudd (1981: 43) raises questions concerning linguistics for the Third World and argues that the

adoption of linguistics at institutions of higher learning in its present internationally disciplinary form, and in its expression through the medium of English ... can be contrary to the public good in less developed countries (LDCs) and emerging speech communities.

Jernudd (1981) raises a host of questions that in the 1990s seemed to become much more important, since the dichotomy between the autonomous linguistics and socially realistic linguistics has implications for linguistic curriculum, teaching, hiring and training of future linguists, not only for the West, but also for the expanding educational system in the Third World. The questions are of the following types:

1) How relevant is the training imparted to students from Third World countries to the educational and societal needs of their countries?
2) In what sense is such training contributing toward the development of their local languages and the descriptions of these languages?

The fourth concern is that of "ethnocentrism" vs. "internationalism." Hockett (1983: 3) rightly tells us that "linguists and anthropologists do not automatically escape ethnocentrism. Like others, our first reaction to an alien practice may be rejection or even revulsion." In applied linguistics ethnocentrism is reflected in many ways: It is reflected in the way, for example, Africa, Asia, Latin America, and other parts of the Third World are viewed primarily as consumers of applied theory without seeking any theoretical or methodological initiative or contribution from scholars from those regions in solving their language-related problems.

Ethnocentrism is reflected in subfields within applied linguistics, for example, in approaches to paradigms developed for ESP (see Swales 1985; B. Kachru 1986c), and in research on communicative competence, especially with reference to teaching English. The main divide there is supposed to be between the sides of the Atlantic, as shown in Berns's review (1991) of Brumfit (1987). Berns points out that "in his introduction, Brumfit notes that 'the boundaries of the communicative movement are ill-defined, and there is no canonical text' (p. 5). Yet the effect of this volume is to create the impression of a canonical interpretation, one that is decidedly British" (105) What we have here is actually a "monolithic view" of a subfield.

Ethnocentricism is further reflected in the fact that Third World scholarship is considered peripheral in discussions of issues related to Asia and Africa. One gets the impression that the appropriateness and implementation of paradigms are a concern of the North, while the South is merely a consumer. The East–West distance in such scholarship continues to increase. I am, therefore, not surprised that African scholars in particular have been very articulate in expressing their resentment toward such ethnocentric scholarship. This resentment against ethnocentricism is clear, for instance, in Achebe's statement quoted earlier (1976: 11), that "I should like to see the word universal banned altogether from discussions of African literature until such time as people cease to use it as a synonym for the narrow, self-serving parochialism of Europe."

The final concern is about "partnership for profit." Once economic interests intervene, the pragmatic questions from the point of view of the consumer are the first to be sacrificed. Economic interests have consequences related to ideology and this is particularly true when we are told that "the worldwide market for EFL training is worth a massive 6.25 billion a year, according to a report from the Economic Intelligence Unit" (*EFL Gazette,* March 1989). One wonders, Does this interest in some way manifest itself in suggestions for language planning, in curriculum design, in teacher training, and so on?

These are understandably controversial questions, and they open a Pandora's box. But they do ask for answers from applied linguists, since their concerns extend beyond mere descriptions and analyses; they touch human societies. In the role of an applied linguist, then, one has to make judgments about those areas in which a language is used, and one has to make judgments about the power structure that controls the use of a language. In fact, Newmeyer (1986: 148) reminds us,

Indeed, in most sociolinguistic studies potential relevance for good is offset by potential relevance for evil, particularly given the "value-free" rhetorical style that characterizes much work in this area.

Ethical Leak

The ethical questions, to a large extent, are perhaps left to an individual practitioner of a discipline. However, as Bolinger (1973) has warned us, "truth" is a linguistic question, and ethical values do deserve professional attention. We have to be grateful that several practitioners in our field have started asking serious and provocative questions of ethical and social concern, questions that are upsetting the calm of the field.

I am sharing a concern here that gives an entirely different dimension to the question of ethics. The question is whether the profession of linguistics is

216   Leaking Paradigms

being used as a cloak to say, for example, "You give me your language, and I will save your soul!" In other words, how ethical is it to engage in religious or political proselytizing activities under the cover of applied linguistics? This is a question. This is a concern. And it asks for an answer.

This and related questions have never been debated by applied linguists. However, in Europe and in several Third World countries, this issue has been discussed with reference to two major linguistic organizations: the Summer Institute of Linguistics (SIL) and the Wycliff Bible Institute (WBI). The arms of these two organizations, as we shall see, have reached almost every part of the globe. It is claimed that "as of 1975, their own statistics showed a staff of 3,500 and more recent figures give over 4,250 people working in 900 plus languages and dialects in more than 30 countries." In 1983 it was claimed that "by 1990 plans call for entry into 800 new linguistic groups as well as for recruitment and training of 3000 additional staff members" (*Covert Action* [hereafter abbreviated *CA*] 1983: 42). The linguist C. F. Voegelin says that "the army [of SIL members] covers more territory than that occupied by the combined forces of all other linguists" (quoted in Newmeyer 1986: 60).

And now, having said this, one might pause and ask, What is wrong with recruiting or training linguists for spreading the word of the Lord? Answers differ, as do the interpretations of the motives of such groups. A collection of papers edited by Foren Hvalkof and Peter Aaby (1981) and published by the International Work Group for Indigenous Affairs (IWGIA), Denmark, and Survival International (SI), London, is alarming. We are told that IWGIA is a "politically independent, international organization concerned with the oppression of the indigenous peoples in many countries" (Hvalkof and Aaby, 1981: 4), and that the SI is a "non-political, non-denominational organization existing to help aboriginal peoples to protect their rights" (p. 5).

If the studies of these two groups are correct, the linguistic profession and our professional organizations cannot leave their charges, accusations, and allegations unanswered. The rejoinders to these allegations (e.g., Canfield 1983, which is a review of Hvalkof and Aaby 1981) leave much to be explained.[6]

The charges by the IWGIA and the SI are of several types. Not all of them are related to linguistic issues, but several are of concern to professional linguists, since they entail allegations of professional deception. Let me briefly mention some of these here.

---

[6] Canfield (1983) criticizes the book for disguising "accusations" as "anthropology." His main points are that "their [authors'] methods of argumentation are often unsound and the evidence they adduce for the assertions they make is often uncompelling" (57); also "the scholarly problem with the book, ethical problems aside, is that the editors and publishers call this 'anthropology'. Not so... Anthropology ought not to be used as a mask for yellow journalism or propaganda" (59).

The Range of Leaks 217

A. Dual Image The charge is that SIL/Wycliffe Bible Translators (WBT) maintains a dual image of "missionary for home/public consumption and scientific linguist for the government" (*CA*: 18: 42). What is meant is that the motives of the SIL/ WBT are not made clear. The Catholic Bishops of Lima have charged SIL with "making an active and tendentious campaign to convert the Indians of our Amazon to evangelical Protestantism [through] a vast proselytizing action hiding its true intentions behind a series of disguises" *(CA:* 18: 42).

The SIL literature claims that the goal of their work is to defeat Satan. How can Satan be defeated? By communicating the word of God to "heathen" and "ignorant" people. In this campaign against Satan, "all opponents of SIL/WBT are automatically branded as agents and working for Satan" *(CA:* 43).

Two anthropologists, Foren Hvalkof and Peter Aaby (1981: 173), claim that the fund-raising promotional literature of SIL/WBT "conveys the distinct impression that the Bibleless tribes are afflicted with witchcraft, superstitions, sickness, immorality, lack of self-respect, revenge killings and headhunting." In his very insightful and provocative book, Jacob L. Mey (1985) has devoted the section "A Tale of Two Tongues" (section 4.1: pp. 341–349), to a review of "three well-documented cases" (p.345) to illustrate efforts of removing from a political point of view "possible sources of instability by controlling the opposition as an effective way of perpetuating a Pax Americana in troubled areas of the world" (p. 345).

These cases are "The 'Project Camelot' in Chile," "Thailand Issue," and "The Role Played by Certain Members of the 'Summer Institute of Linguistics' in Keeping Underdeveloped Countries on the Path of Virtue" (345). What are Mey's arguments against the Summer Institute of Linguistics (SIL) and the Wycliffe Bible Translators (WBT)? He does not have "any serious criticism" of their linguistic achievements and the methods that they have developed (347) for the description and "grammaticalization" of "hundreds of indigenous languages, most of which had been totally unknown, or at best, incompletely or incompetently described until then" (347). Mey's concern is that

a number of people have lately questioned the legitimacy, in a broader, social context, of the missionaries' aims: *viz.* to describe languages in order to provide the illiterate natives with an alphabet and a grammar, so as to enable them to get acquainted with the Holy Scriptures in their own tongue. (347)

B. Ideological Ends for Altering the Translation of the Bible The charge is that the words of the Bible are altered to "fit their [SIL/WBT's] ideological thrust among indigenous people" *(CA:* 43). For example, in a leaflet entitled "Forjando una Manana Mejor" ('Forging a Better Tomorrow'), the first verse of the thirteenth chapter, the Book of Romans, is given as follows by the SIL (*CA*: 18: 43):

218   Leaking Paradigms

Obey your legal superiors, because God has given them command. There is no government on earth that God had not permitted to come to power.

The argument here is that this rendering crudely twists the passage found in both the English Revised Version of the Bible and its Spanish companion volume. The first sentence is adapted from "Let every soul be subject unto the higher powers," while the second is an outright distortion of "the powers that are ordained by God" (*CA*: 18: 43)

David Stoll, who in 1981 was preparing a book on the Summer Institute in Latin America with the assistance of the Louise M. Rabinowitz Foundation of New York, says that "Wycliffe has definite religious and political goals for other people. *It has used linguistic credentials* to mystify these objectives, exploiting the relativity of language to harness state power to the imposition of its, once again absolute, truth on native people" (Hvalkof and Aaby, 1981: 38; emphasis added).

Newmeyer (1986: 61) says concerning SIL:

Many feel that SIL's practice has been to "Americanize" as much as Christianize, thereby hastening the destruction of the indigenous culture in areas in which it operates.

>   *C. "Literacy Training" with "Narrow Objective"*   The charge is that the "so-called 'literacy' programs in a number of countries" (*CA:* 42) are for "public relations image" and "fund-raising" (p. 42). The goals for teaching literacy have a "very narrow objective," viz., "Teach people to read and write the contents of the Bible. Functional literacy when achieved, is a lower priority" (*CA:* 42).

I am primarily pointing out the roles performed by these groups as *helpful* linguists, applying their linguistic knowledge in other cultures. I do not believe that it is appropriate for my discussion to address the possibility of these organizations' "ends create the means" policies. It isnot a linguistic issue for me when it is alleged that "the SIL missionaries kidnapped a Peruvian Mayoruna boy (SIL later claimed the boy had 'run away'), and kept him in order that they would learn the Mayorna dialect" (*CA*: 44). Neither am I concerned with the charges that SIL/WBT "worked hand-in-hand with the local military . . . and, on a few documented occasions with U.S. military units and "advisors" (*CA:* 44), or that the objectives of such an alliance for "pacification" are to protect corporate interests, to gain communication for control of the indigenous people; and to implement "counter-insurgence efforts against an indigenous population" (*CA:* 44)

I will also not dwell on political motivations of such work or their business interests (see Hvalkof and Aaby 1981). The issues I am raising here are not opposed to proselytization per se or to taking the word of the Lord to the

Conclusion

"heathen." Perhaps that is a needed occupation and is, in any case, one of the oldest professions. The issues I am raising here concern professional ethics: the responsibilities of a profession, of an organization, that is explicitly aligned to a discipline.

This behavior, like the behavior of other organizations aligned to a variety of other religions and groups, raises a variety of important questions: Are there any issues of professional ethics involved here? How does one strike a balance between professional ethics and the roles one performs as a professional in society? And, perhaps more appropriate to us as members of professional organizations, how should responsible professional organizations react to such charges?

The Linguistic Society of America has concerned itself with social, political, and educational issues. The LSA has passed resolutions and allowed debate on several sociopolitically delicate topics. In 1972 the Linguistic Society of America "endorsed a widely publicized resolution of Anthony Kroch and William Labov that exposed the flimsy intellectual basis of [Arthur] Jensen's ideas" (Baugh 1988: 65). Jensen claimed that "black children are intellectually inferior to white children on genetic grounds" (Baugh 1988: 65, citing Kroch and Labov 1972). However, on the question of SIL/WBT, the Linguistic Society of America passed a resolution in its 1947 summer meeting that reads:

It is the sense of this group that the work being done by the Summer Institute, as exemplified also by the papers presented by its students at this meeting, should be strongly commended by our Society and welcomed as one of the most promising developments in applied linguistics in this country. (Eunice Pike 1981: 138)

But now, seven decades later, the questions being asked are not about "the most promising development in applied linguistics," but about the ethics of this applied linguistic work.

Conclusion

All language-related fields are interrelated to various degrees. It is, therefore, rewarding to ask ourselves from time to time: What are the underlying reasons for our perceptions of a speech community? What are the implications of our descriptive labels? And do some of us use our access to languages and cultures with motives which are open to question? The questions such self-examination raises are not just attitudinal, methodological, and theoretical; they are also ethical questions that the profession at large must address.

The concerns I have expressed are not mutually exclusive. In one way or another, these contribute to linguistic lameness: in some way all these relate to our profession – directly or indirectly. All are of vital importance to the Third

World, but they are not exclusively the problems of the Third World. There is an extensive body of studies on this topic from the developed countries. Baugh (1988: 72) gives a moving description of his experiences in the United States in his "Language and Race: Some Implications for Linguistic Science." He rightly cautions us that "a similar story could be told in many countries, where race and language correspond to social stratification." The concerns, therefore, are common, and the limitations, rewards, and exploitation of human language are shared.

Part V

World Englishes and the Classroom

13   Mythology in Teaching

Introduction

In this chapter I do not propose to enter into the uncertain domain of making a case for a particular "method," "approach," or teaching "strategy"; nor will I discuss issues related to curriculum, curriculum design, or English in language policies. I will instead present an overview of one major concern of English education in World Englishes, particularly in the contexts of Anglophone African and Asian countries. I believe that this concern cannot in a serious sense be separated from the classroom, from teacher training, and from the broader and fundamental issues related to the theme of "English education."

And this chapter has even a larger goal. It explores and addresses the national and international challenges and responses in the context of what is called English education. It is these challenges and responses that take us to provocative and insightful questions of English and ideology, English and politics, and a tantalizing question of English and economics. In turn, these concerns bring forth a string of vital and all-pervasive issues: What kind of power does English symbolize? What is the relationship between the English language and national and cultural identities? And, as educators, when we focus on English education, we are opening, as it were, the proverbial Pandora's box – there are layers and layers of daunting complexities. We must face questions related to attitudes, identities, and loyalties to a language that just five decades earlier in Anglophone Asia and Africa was our external masters' one long and powerful arm of control. And in a subtle way – a very subtle way indeed – that arm has reached practically every major region of the globe. And now, during the postcolonial era, this linguistic arm has a greater power and a firmer hold. This has confused and overwhelmed us.

It is indeed for this reason that our reactions to the language are mixed and varied. We have labeled English an "auntie tongue" (Sridhar 1989), a "Trojan horse" (Cooke 1988), the "other tongue" (B. Kachru 1992d), a "step-daughter" (Gupta 1993), a "step mother" and the "daughter tongue" (Loga M. Bhaskaran). We actually do not know where English fits into our complex linguistic kinship system. But that is not all. This language has evoked extreme reactions and

224   Mythology in Teaching

various levels of love and hate. Ngugi wa Thiong'o, the acclaimed African critic and creative writer, considers English "probably the most racist of all human languages" (Ngugi 1981: 14). But not so for the Indian philosopher and novelist Raja Rao, according to whom English is the most universal language; he equates its status with that of Sanskrit, using the term *universal* in a philosophical sense – as a language that elevates us all (Rao 1978).

It is therefore understandable that in postcolonial societies we, as individuals, as parents, as educators, and as policy makers, have to resolve – have to answer – a cluster of questions about English, about what English can do for us, and about the ideological content of the language. We cannot, and should not, deny the fact that the memories of the colonizers and the colonized last for an extended period, and leave their deep psychic effects, create attitudinal warping, and result in complex issues of identity and self-doubt. These issues and this type of "baggage of memories" are part of the challenges and they demand responses.

It is unfortunate that as the users of English, we have not yet effectively reacted to these challenges. And we have not as yet recontextualized and redefined the implications of the increasing global spread of English – the spread of a particular linguistic behavior to which we have contributed in the colonial era and continue to contribute in the postcolonial era in many fundamental ways with greater energy, with innovation, and with dynamism.

We have not, for example, addressed two questions relevant to the postcolonial functions of English. The first is about the types of shift needed in our attitudes and methods that are appropriate to new and changed contexts. And, second, we have not critically evaluated and examined the paradigms of language study, language analysis, language teaching, and teacher training and education. In other words, we seem to find it painful – psychologically and otherwise – to cut the umbilical cord that connected us in terms of the educational paradigms to the Inner Circle. We have allowed a variety of myths to continue about the global uses and users of English. We have refused to face the challenging issues and have very rarely provided responses suitable to our educational, cultural, and social contexts, as well as relevant to our needs and our uses of English. We have yet to respond to and reevaluate the prevalent myths about the English language. Instead we have nurtured and further cultivated such myths. This passive attitude has naturally sustained these myths in different reincarnations. These reincarnations may indicate change, but in reality, they essentially embody continuity, which strengthens the myth further.

Myths and Myth Makers

I used the term *myths* in the context of English education. Let me briefly mention what I mean by it in this context. And, who are the myth makers, and what are their motivations? We know that the intent and process of myth making are not innocent. The myths are ideologically, politically, and economically motivated, and they seem to gain a momentum, a power, and a life of their own. Educational myths have a subtle way of manifesting themselves in language policies and in language planning, and eventually, these myths become potent instruments of language control. In English education, a variety of myths have been cultivated over time. These have been refined and eventually sanctified as the basic tenets of the teaching of English in general, and of ELT programs in particular. We have accepted them and continue to use them as integral to English education and to our broader language policies.

Depth and Power of Myths

The myths about English are loaded linguistic weapons: their power is equal to the power World Englishes have acquired in the global context. The extent of this power is over the largest geographical space that a natural language has ever covered; its dominance has continued in increasing degrees over extended periods, and it has acquired unparalleled functional and societal depth. The uniqueness of the current spread of English, then, has a variety of unprecedented dimensions: geographical, in terms of its territorial spread; functional, in terms of its range of uses and the identities it has acquired and those it provides; and formal, in terms of its variation, and the types of innovations across cultures and languages (Kachru 1986a [1990].).

It is, therefore, not surprising that this unique linguistic resource is subject to a variety of "chains of control" that manifest themselves in a number of ways, for example:

- In prescriptions concerning *norms of language production,* e.g., standards;
- In prescriptions concerning *norms of language function,* e.g., genres of academic English, schema for communicative competence;
- In *norms for authentication and authority,* e.g., dichotomies such as native vs. nonnative, and
- In *norms for control of the canon,* and legitimization of the canon in literature and in language.

All these chains of control are often invisible and are reflected, in very subtle ways, in attitudes within curriculum design and in programs for training professionals for English education. These chains of control are again loaded weapons, and they – consciously or unconsciously – develop into paradigms of marginality, as discussed in Part III. These chains are used to authenticate our linguistic behaviors.

And returning to the myths, what actually happens is that initially a myth is just that: a myth. But slowly and skillfully a myth is used as a "magnifying

226   Mythology in Teaching

mirror," as Levi-Strauss puts it, in a different context (cited by Eribon 1991: 141). A myth can acquire power, actually an immense power, and a defining context. Thus myths usually become bases for hypothesis formation. Levi-Strauss talks of this in a very insightful way, though his context is not the English language. He says (cited by Eribon 1991: 141):

A myth offers us a grid that is definable only by its rules of construction. This grid makes it possible to decipher a meaning, not of the myth itself but of all the rest – images of the world, of society, of history, that hover on the threshold of consciousness, with the questions men ask about them. The matrix of intelligibility provided by the myth makes it possible to combine them all into a coherent whole.

Myths and Their Domains

The domains of myths are based on the underlying images of the language, of the society, of the history, and of the users of the language. These images, as it were, determine the intended uses of the chains of control. These chains are the instruments for creating what is believed, a "coherent whole" that has relevance for achieving the goals that the myth makers have planned for us. And these myths gain currency in the objectives determined in what we know professionally as "English education." There are additional vehicles too: professional journals and professional organizations. It is these – and other disseminating agencies – that help in establishing what Foucault has called the "regimes of truth" (Foucault 1980).

And the myths become most effective when they filter down into the classroom, in teacher training, in the curriculum, in resource and reference materials such as encyclopedias, dictionaries, manuals, handbooks, and guides, and, finally, when they acquire a status in language test construction and other instruments of evaluation. Their ultimate triumph occurs when they change our attitudes and define our identities.

And now, let me be specific and briefly mention some of these myths, just to illustrate my point about the mythology concerning English. I will list here what I consider six basic myths.

Myth 1: The Interlocutor Myth

The interlocutor myth is the heart of the problem in English education. The claim is made that the main reason for the diffusion of English is a compelling desire in the non-English-speaking world to interact with what are termed "native speakers of the language," i.e., native speakers of English. It is believed that the Outer and Expanding Circles hold the Inner Circle as the primary intended interlocutor. The reality is – and has been empirically validated to be – that an overwhelming majority of the users of English in the Outer Circle (e.g., Malaysia, Singapore, India, Sri Lanka, Nigeria) only minimally interact with the "native" speakers. A significant majority of English users in these countries use various localized varieties of English to interact with the Asians, the Africans, and the Europeans whose mother tongue is not English. These people from Asia and Africa and Europe use English for business transactions, for travel, for social interaction, and so on. The contexts of interaction do not necessarly involve speaking or interacting face to face. The same localized Englishes appear in written interactions, English newspapers, official communiqués, road signs, and advertising. These uses of English are uniquely African and Asian, and they belong to types of ESP and genres of English that do not always have currency in the Inner Circle.

These interactions show a wide range of formal variation, as has been documented in several studies (e.g., Cheshire 1991; B. Kachru 1992d[1982d]). The range in variation extends from educated localized varieties of English (e.g., Malaysian, Nigerian, Indian, or Singaporean) to a sub-ariety (e.g., Nigerian Pidgin, basilect, or Bazaar English). It may also be a mixed variety, often incorporating extensive lexical stock or grammatical features from one or more local languages (e.g., Chinese, Malay, Tamil, Yoruba, and Hausa).

Myth 2: The Cultural Identity Myth

The cultural identity myth has been discussed quite often. In recent years, it has been debated from the perspectives of African Americans, Chicanos, and other writers in World Englishes (see e.g. Gates 1992; B. Kachru 1994e). The myth implies that the English language and literature represent one canon, one culture, and one literary tradition – primarily the Judeo-Christian tradition, as represented in what some label as "Western culture." In other words, the underlying assumption in this myth is that English is essentially "monocultural."

This myth has two faces; its interpretation and effectiveness depend on which one wants to emphasize. In reality, the English language has now become unique in it cultural multifaces. One might study only one of the faces – e.g., the British or the Nigerian – or its diverse faces. The choice is that of the user of the medium. It has become one of the most powerful mediums, with diverse cultural and ideological messages and identities. It has become the Speaking Tree – the *waqwaq* tree (as discussed in Chapter 6) – with a trunk and strong branches, each with its own culture and ideologically distinct message (B. Kachru 1994e). That is how, for example, Gates Jr. (1992) sees it, that is how the Australian writer Ted Hughes (1993) sees it, and that is how Steiner (1975) sees it. But, unfortunately, that is not how most of the ESL profession sees it.

228 Mythology in Teaching

It is this diversity and pluralism that Thumboo (1976: ix) has in mind when he observes that "the language is remade, where necessary, by adjusting the interior landscape of words in order to explore and mediate the permutations of another culture and environment." What we have to recognize in English education is that World Englishes imply that in the varieties of English there is culture in texts and texts embody cultures. We do not have to go far to appreciate this concept. We see it, for example, in Malaysia and Singapore. We see it in the creativity and use of English in Lee Kok Liang, Basanti Karnikar, Shahnon Ahmad, Lloyd Fernando, Edwin Thumboo, Arthur Yap, Ramli Ibrahim, Latiff Mohidin, Catherine Lim, Kripal Singh, Philip Jayaratnam, and others.

The dozen names I purposely mentioned here represent a rainbow of ethnicities, of religions, of language backgrounds, and of conceptualizations of life and living in Islam, Christianity, Buddhism, and Hinduism, in short, a hybrid canon of its own. In one sense, these canons are unrelated to the original canon of the English language in the Inner Circle. They have their own growth and development, and their own contexts of creativity – unique mixes of languages and ideologies. However, they are part of the trunk: they represent distinct articulations of the Speaking Tree, as argued in Chapter 6.

The creativity has resulted in a type of literature in English in which, as Lim (1993: 224) insightfully observes, "the exhausted post-colonial obsession with adaptation of the master's tongue and master's culture is abandoned for a larger reach into an original racial part." The English language writers are, says Lim (1993: 234), "turning away from nationality to identity," and their expression is "a reflection of the serious realities which surround their authors."

It is for reflecting this sociolinguistic reality that the play *Caught in the Middle,* as *Asia Week* (May 24, 1987: 64) observes, goes "completely Malaysian." Here it is worth repeating Lloyd Fernando's comments in the article about his belief that Malaysian English creates realism in the play. And it does more than that, continues Fernando (64):

It exploits that [i.e., Malaysian English] with good humor. Malaysian English is now a dialect, recognized as such. In some situations, if you don't speak like that, you are regarded as a foreigner. By using it the playwright draws us into the magic circle.

This is a sensitive and delicate issue of identity. This makes English part of our linguistic behavior and that too on the terms of its cross-cultural users. The ELT profession has largely ignored this overwhelming reality of our times.

And now let us go beyond this region and add South Asia, West Africa, the Philippines, and the West Indies. What we see is a range of Nobel Laureates (Wole Soyinka, Derek Walcott), Booker Prize winners (e.g., Salman Rushdie), and Neustadt Prize winners (e.g., Raja Rao). But these canons, these traditions, have yet to be included in the discussion of the literary and

Myths and Their Domains

stylistic components of English education. The cultural identity myth of the Inner Circle continues to dominate.

Myth 3: The Exocentric Performance Myth

The two preceding myths have actually helped in sustaining and nourishing the myth that our linguistic performance in the Outer Circle must be consistent with exocentric (nonlocalized) models of English. A consequence of this myth is a rather futile ongoing debate about whose model of the language is appropriate. Whose linguistic performance is acceptable? The Received Pronunciation myth in Britain and the General American myth in the United States have a strong hold on us. In his several studies, Larry Smith and his coresearchers have shown that empirically these myths have very little validity for international intelligibility or international interaction (see e.g., Smith 1992).

Myth 4: The Native Speaker Idealization Myth

The preceding three myths have provided the bricks and mortar for firmly establishing the native speaker idealization myth. A native speaker is viewed – wrongly, I emphasize – as monolingual and monocultural. The genesis of this myth may be explained from many perspectives that cross disciplinary boundaries and do not involve purely academic issues, but those of ideology, the notion of "ownership" of the language, and indeed the notion of economic interests.

Myth 5: The Interlanguage Myth

If we accept the sociolinguistic reality of the earlier four myths, the interlanguage myth has its place secured. As discussed earlier, the interlanguage hypothesis in second language acquisition (SLA) research has often been generalized to include all the users of the institutionalized varieties of English in multilingual contexts. It is this myth that unleashed the counterproductive – and empirically suspect – fossilization and error analysis models (see e.g., Selinker 1993ff.). In recent years several studies have evaluated this myth from theoretical, applied, and pedagogical perspectives with specific reference to the institutionalized varieties of English (see e.g., Sridhar and Sridhar 1986 [1992]; Y. Kachru 1993a; B. Kachru 1994d).

Myth 6: The Cassandra Myth

The Cassandra myth seems to have been born with Paninian grammar (500 BC). In English education it is an age-old myth used against the myth breakers (or norm breakers). This myth works as the codifiers' weapon against those who

230   Mythology in Teaching

deviate from recognizing – and following – any of the myth makers' codes. It is always used against those who challenge and question the myths, or whose linguistic behavior is inconsistent with the myth makers' intended response from the language user.

The myth makers attribute a variety of motives to those who question the myths, as we see in the ongoing debate on this topic. The types of motives attributed are:

- A desire to break the norms prescribed by the Inner Circle;
- An underlying political and ideological agenda of "liberation linguistics" modeled on"liberation theology"; and
- A desire to acquire linguistic power and control.

It is claimed that these motives and their linguistic implications result in the decay and decline of the English language. But a more alarming prophecy for the Inner Circle is that these norm-breaking strategies reduce the power and control of the Inner Circle (see Part III).

Myths and the Profession

The mythology about English, built over an extended period, has deep and far-reaching implications. There are many questions to be answered: What relationship does this mythology have to the real world of English education? How relevant is this mythology to the sociolinguistic reality of World Englishes, to teacher training programs, and, of course, ultimately to the classroom? We have yet to answer these questions in a pragmatic sense.

The mythology is aggressively used in the paradigms of language acquisition, in methodology of teaching, in the tests that we administer to our students in the classrooms, in compilation of dictionaries, and in models and norms for creativity and linguistic innovations.[1] These research enterprises, theoretical and applied, are directly related to the tasks of teachers and teacher trainers. In other words, the paradigms provide the intellectual and practical tools of our trade. And these paradigms have a subtle way of penetrating the academic culture, the culture of teaching, and the discourse of teaching. And, as the paradigms gain acceptance, they gain currency within the system.

This point is clearly illustrated by the diffusion – and our acceptance over time – of a variety of teaching methods such as the direct method, the audiolingual method, the structural method, and now various incarnations of the communicative method. All these methods claim theoretical foundations, but we have never raised serious questions about their appropriateness to our

---

[1] For studies on this specific topic with regard to major languages of wider communication, including English, see Kachru and Kahane (1995).

contexts of education, our contexts of culture, and our educational systems. Why we did not – or do not – question these myths is that the mythology has conditioned us in such a way that we do not doubt the "regimes of truth." We do not analyze the structure that has developed our approaches to English education – the structure that is essentially based on the discourse and assumption of marginality.

Myths and the Discourse of Marginality

I have discussed in some detail, in Chapter 7, aspects of the discourse of marginality. I would like to make a distinction here between two types of such discourse. The first type is reflected in language teaching texts and pedagogical resource materials, and the second type in the theories and approaches that establish the academic foundations of English education.

The discourse of marginality used in the textbooks and other pedagogical resources has slow but lasting effects. During the past two decades analyses of a variety of studies have shown how this discourse is discreetly infused in textbooks. I am specifically thinking of studies of the following type: the grammars used, for example, in South Asia (Singh 1987), selected textbooks used in the United States (Y. Kachru 1994b), English textbooks used in Canada (Nicholls 1995), and English textbooks used in, for example, Asia (Baik 1994 and Baik and Shim 2002).

It is, however, the second type of discourse of marginality that has generally been ignored by the English language educators. This type of discourse is most prevalent in English language teaching, in second language acquisition research, and in applied linguistic research in general. The *depowering* discourse strategies that such paradigms use are to a large extent shared. These strategies are of various types. Let me summarize them here:

- The derationalizing strategy
- The normalizing strategy
- The negation strategy

The first strategy, the *derationalizing strategy,* is a very potent and disarming psychological weapon. To repeat a relevant point from Chapter 12, Selinker (1993), for example, uses this strategy especially in his defense of, for example, the "fossilization and simplicity" hypotheses. When the validity of these hypotheses is questioned in certain contexts, for example, in the specific contexts of the institutionalized varieties of English, Selinker adopts the derationalizing strategy He wonders "why colleagues appear *emotional* about this topic" (1993: 22, emphasis added). Note that the use of the potent term "emotional" completely marginalizes the argument, and introduces an external, nonacademic dimension. The contrast now is between rationality and

232   Mythology in Teaching

objectivity, on the one hand, and emotionalism, on the other. By using this skillful strategy, Selinker changes the emphasis from an academic argument to the psychological state of those who question the hypotheses.

The second strategy, the *normalizing strategy,* defines a context or a linguistic process – however different it may be – in a chosen way and then claims that "the settings and processes are similar" (Zuengler 1989: 93). This is one way of maintaining the universality of a hypothesis. This strategy is repeatedly used in discussions of transfer, input, and language identity – to give just three examples. It is the same strategy that is used for asserting the universality of specific teaching methods in diverse sociolinguistic contexts.

We now have considerable evidence that in the case of functions of World Englishes, these terms have to be used with great caution. Broad claims such as that all contexts in which English is used are identical, and that what applies to New York and Puerto Rico must apply to traditionally multilingual societies in Nigeria, Malaysia, Singapore, or India – and to Japan, Egypt, and Iran – have doubtful empirical validity. These generalizations are of minimal value to a language teacher and a teacher trainer. In fact, such a round-peg-in-a-square-hole approach is counterproductive.

The last strategy, the *negation strategy,* is essentially a strategy of nonrecognition. What it emphatically negates is the sociolinguistic and pedagogical differences between ESL and EFL, as is done by Quirk (see Quirk 1988, 1989). Instead, it emphasizes the dichotomy between *us* and *them,* native and nonnative, and Western and non-Western. One will not be wrong in claiming that for various historical reasons the foundation of English education is based on the *negation strategy.*

We do not have to go very far to seek answers to questions such as: What motivates these broad dichotomies? What types of sociolinguistic realties are negated? An experienced English educator in Malaysia, Singapore, India, and Nigeria would have no difficulty in detecting that the following types of realities are negated:

• The contexts of convergence in a multilingual society;
• the processes that lead to linguistic innovations (e.g., translation, mixing, calquing); and
• the pull of sociolinguistic contexts that result in new speech acts, speech functions, and other types of linguistic acculturation.

Myths and Myth Breakers

We professionals see that working in English education, then, encounters an overwhelming and powerful mythology. The myth breakers are presented to the profession as initiators of heresies and as violators of the sacred, and therefore having suspect motives. I shall present three examples to support this statement, which I have discussed earlier (B. Kachru 1991).

The first example relates to the attitude toward linguistic innovations by Asian and African writers in English. Bailey (1990: 86) views such linguistic innovations and creativity as a "managed ... revolutionary shift." However, note that the "revolutionary" literary innovations in James Joyce and e. e. cummings, to give just two examples, do not seem to evoke the same response. The second relates to the recognition of local innovations and variational distinctiveness, for example, in Singapore English, Indian English, and Nigerian English. Quirk (1989) detects in such recognition a manifestation of "liberation linguistics" perhaps not different from "liberation theology." The third view is that of Prabhu (1989: 16), who believes that the emphasis on variational distinctiveness is "a loud assertion or declaration of linguistic independence or secession," "a self-confinement of linguistic status."

In these three observations we note one underlying shared thread. In Bailey's perception the distinctiveness model of the varieties of English borders almost on linguistic anarchism; Quirk detects an underlying theological and sociopolitical notion of "liberation" extended to the study of World Englishes; and Prabhu characterizes the issues essentially as political assertion – and uses a loaded term, perhaps meaningless in this context – that of "secession," and equates it with "self-confinement of linguistic status."

It is evident that as English educators, as teachers and researchers, we must analyze these attitudes, reactions, and characterizations, for underlying them is a planned mythology for English education. This, then, takes me to the question, Why analyze the myths?

Why Analyze Myths?

I have presented here a cluster of selected myths – and there are many more such myths – that have attained important status in theoretical and applied research related to English education. It is these myths that provide a backdrop for the paradigms of marginality. The analysis of these myths and the resultant strategies of marginality are relevant to English education in Malaysia and Singapore, and other English-using Asian and African countries, for several reasons. One reason, of course, is ideological. The paradigms of underlying ideologies are based on specific conceptualizations about societies, about education, and about the intended end-product of the system. But more importantly, these myths contribute to maintaining economic power within certain ideological frameworks. That these hegemonic strategies are planned, cultivated, and promoted by very potent power structures is by now a well-documented argument (for references see e.g., Fairclough 1989; B. Kachru 1986d; Phillipson 1992; Tsuda 1994a and 1994b).

234   Mythology in Teaching

Other reasons are sociolinguistic, empirical, and pedagogical. That these generalizations apply to multilingual and culturally diverse contexts has yet to be proved (see e.g., Sridhar and Sridhar 1986 [1992]). And yet another reason is that these strategies establish a particular type of relationship between Anglophone Asian and African varieties and those who are in the Inner Circle – a relationship of imbalance. In the present relationship, a majority of the English-using speech community is primarily treated as consumers of methods, hypotheses, and models that have been conceptualized and formulated in sociolinguistic and educational contexts with doubtful validity in Asia and Africa. The attitude of the Inner Circle is one of patronage rather than one of partnership with the Outer Circle. And finally, taken together, it is these and other such myths that constitute a repertoire of the strategies of marginality.

These strategies of marginality may incorporate "designs" of various types. And it is significant to repeat here the warning of caution to English educators of Henry Widdowson (1994:389): "I think we need to be cautious about the designs we have on others peoples' worlds when we are busy designing our own."

How Are the Myths Perpetuated?

There are a variety of ways by which the Inner Circle, the creator of the "regimes of truth," perpetuates these psychological, ideological, and economic myths. The relationship of patronage, not always conscious, with the Outer Circle, is one way of perpetuating the myths.

The first powerful arm is that of the ELT graduate programs in the United States and Britain. In the United States alone there are about 150 such programs, varying from what may be termed academically sound – depending on one's perspective – to those that are of doubtful academic content. A majority of these programs are primarily dishing out, as one might characterize it, "TV dinners" for ESL professionals. A number of them award master's degrees. A small number of institutions – about twenty-five – award bachelor's degrees. However, increasingly, such programs are initiating interdisciplinary Ph.D. programs (e.g., Columbia, Georgetown, Hawaii, Illinois, Indiana, Pittsburgh, Texas at Austin, SUNY at Stony Brook, and UCLA). There are about thirty such Ph.D. programs.

A study by Vavrus (1991) explored whether "teacher trainees are receiving information about IVEs" [Institutionalized Varieties of English] (1991: 185). On the basis of a restricted survey, she found that "only UH and University of Illinois at Urbana-Champaign have elective courses that emphasize non-native varieties of English." (1991: 186).

The second arm is that of the professional journals. This is the most influential and effective academic arm, which provides direction for research and

Processes of Demythologization 235

Table 13.1. *Underrepresentation of Asia and Africa in professional journals*

Item	TESOL Quarterly	Applied Linguistics
1. Total articles published	118	106
2. Articles from Asia/Africa[2]	2	7
3. Total book reviews/notices	117	18
4. Reviews of books published in Asia/Africa	–	–
5. Review of books by Asian/African authors	1	–
6. Books reviewed on topics related to World Englishes/ nonnative Englishes/world literatures in English (Asian/African)	–	–

perpetuates it; it establishes the paradigms that eventually trickle down into the textbooks, into programs for teacher training, and into language evaluation. The periodicals also reflect the type of research conducted in the ESL academic programs, their agendas and direction.

In order to gain some idea of how the periodicals perpetuate the myths, I surveyed two leading professional journals, one British and one North American, for five years (1986–1990): *Applied Linguistics* and *TESOL Quarterly*. The results of my rather quick content analysis of the two journals are given in Table 13.1:

The third arm that contributes to this perpetuation is the books on ESP, genre analysis, academic English, and communicative competence (see e.g. Bhatia 1993; Swales 1990). This fast-proliferating industry of ideologically loaded textbooks considers the English-using world in Asia and Africa essentially as consumers of cultural, interactional, linguistic, and societal patterns of the Inner Circle. This takes us back to my myth number 2: the culture–identity myth.

Processes of Demythologization

It is appropriate to ask now, What are the processes, if any, for demythologization? The answer to this question is not easy. It is not easy because our dependence on this mythology has created immense self-doubt in our minds as users of English. We have in a way become accustomed to living a mythological lie about English education. Our critical evaluation of the

---

[2] The institutional identification of the contributor of a paper in Asia or Africa is not necessarily a guarantee that the paper was written by an Asian or African. It could be an expatriate serving in the region. Thus, it was difficult to identify clearly the national identity of the contributor.

236 Mythology in Teaching

theoretical and methodological tools of our trade is generally muted. There is a need to develop a vision about the ultimate goals of English education on a regional basis and across regions. We must recognize that English education is a vital part of our educational system, a vital tool of our regional and international interactions, and a major medium of our participation in international scholarship and research. I also believe that English is a significant resource for increasing our economic power as exporters of trained specialists – doctors, business experts, teachers, and so on across national boundaries – and as users of specialized knowledge and skills from other regions of the world. But we must also consider the price we are paying for this asset.

We need a shift in our research priorities. We have a paucity of longitudinal empirical research appropriate to our sociolinguistic contexts, to our diversity and identities, to our large multilingual and culturally diverse classrooms, and to our teacher training programs. We need to understand and emphasize, as Geertz (1983: 234) warns us in the context of anthropological research, that "the world is a various place." And it is "various" in many ways:

various between lawyers and anthropologists, various between Muslims and Hindus, various between little traditions and great, various between colonial thens and nationalist nows.

In English education, we have yet to incorporate this "variousness." But this concept is important for more specific reasons, for greater gains, as Geertz continues (1983: 234):

And much is to be gained, scientifically and otherwise, by confronting that grand actuality rather than wishing it away in a haze of forceless generalities and false comforts.

This is a challenge, and it needs a concerted response.

There seems to be an agreement on one point: that the complex contexts of our language interactions and our multilingual creativity in no way form part of our current conceptualization of English education. And in this negation of – or indifference to – the sociolinguistic and cultural realities is an ethnocentric idealized conceptualization of our societies, of teaching, and of the curriculum. One can think of a number of reasons for such intense suspicion of and indifference to multilingualism and other types of diversity. Among other reasons, the following have been articulated in the literature:

- Complexities of the multilingual societies in terms of their descriptions;
- Intricacies in writing the bilinguals' grammars;
- Emphasis on uniformity and homogeneity;
- Consideration of language "mixing" and "switching" as a linguistic "flaw";
- Consideration of diversity and variation as markers of chaos;

Conclusion 237

- Negative studies of bilingual education (particularly in the United States, United Kingdom, and Western Europe);
- Consideration of bilingual groups as marginal and problem generating;
- Consideration of bi-/multilingualism as retarding economic growth; and
- The romantics' attitudes toward bilingualism and the bilingual's creativity.

These positions are, of course, not generally accepted; and during the past two decades debate on these topics has become very vibrant and at the same time illuminating indeed.

I might add an aside here that relates to another prevalent myth in the United States and the United Kingdom that, I believe, underlies the preceding positions: the United States and United Kingdom are primarily monolingual societies. This is, again, a consciously nurtured myth, against which Hymes and others have forcefully argued (e.g., see Hymes 1981).

There is, however, no denying the fact that monolingualism has been a dominant underlying basis for theory formation, for educational planning, and for curriculum design. In ESL programs, this position is firmly used for training professionals in the field and for educating future teachers. Whenever multilingualism enters the picture, it is treated as an aberration and an inconvenient fact of life better ignored.

Conclusion

In English education across the circles – in the Outer Circle and the Expanding Circle – we have a great dilemma. We have an unresolved question: Are we the consumers soliciting patronage or are we partners in this very vital, fast-increasing global linguistic enterprise? And more importantly: Who has the "key" to our issues concerning English education?

The perceptions of our needs, our priorities, and our needed tools – theoretical, methodological, and educational – differ. They differ drastically. We have now to reexamine the myths we follow, the myths we believe in, and the myths we pass on to our students and colleagues. We must gravely and calmly analyze the relevance of such myths to our sociolinguistic contexts. And more specifically, we must reevaluate our past links with the English language, its teaching, research in this language, and our identification with the language. We must engage in self-examination and ask ourselves, Why is it that we have always shirked from taking bold local initiatives about presenting theoretical and pedagogical insights appropriate and relevant to English education and our creativity in English? Why is it that we have accepted primarily the role of receivers of patronage and not asserted our partnership?

Part VI

Research Areas and Resources

14　Research Resources

Introduction

This chapter includes research resources of two types: a brief historical survey of the conceptualization of World Englishes, and a selected guide to current resources for research and teaching including those from Anglophone Africa and Asia.

Conceptualization

The conceptualization of World Englishes actually began in the 1960s (see Kachru 1965), although organized actual engagement in discussions of the concept and its formal and functional implications started in 1978. It was during that year that two independently international conferences were organized with many conceptual similarities and a number of shared participants. The first was hosted by Larry E. Smith, April 1–15, at the East–West Center, Honolulu, Hawaii, United States; the second by me, June 30–July 2, in conjunction with the Linguistic Institute of the Linguistic Society of America, at the University of Illinois at Urbana-Champaign (UIUC), United States. Papers from these meetings were published in Smith (ed. 1981) and Kachru (ed. 1982d; 2nd edition, 1992d).

The Honolulu conference resulted in a signed statement and an agenda for the future that says that

as professionals, members of the Conference felt that the stimulus given to the question of English used as an international or auxiliary language has led to the emergence of sharp and important issues that are in urgent need of investigation and action. These issues are seen as summarized in the distinction between the uses of English for international (i.e. external) and intranational (i.e. internal) purposes. This distinction recognizes that, while the teaching of English should reflect in all cases the sociocultural contexts and the educational policies of the countries concerned, there is a need to distinguish between (a) those countries (e.g. Japan) whose requirements focus upon international comprehensibility and (b) those countries (e.g. India) which in addition must take account of English as it is used for their own intranational purposes. So far as we know, no organization exists that takes account of any language in the light of this

241

242   Research Resources

fundamental distinction... It is not for us to define or prescribe the policies to be adopted, but the papers and discussions at the Conference have identified a number of fundamental issues. These issues can be considered under four headings: (a) Basic Research; (b) Applied Research; (c) Documentation, Dissemination, and Liaison; and (d) Professional Support Activities. (Kachru and Quirk 1981:xiii)

The UIUC conference, on the other hand (Kachru, ed. 1982d: xiii–xiv),

broke the traditional pattern of such deliberations: no inconvenient question was swept under the rug. The professionals, both linguists and literary scholars, and native and non-native users of English, had frank and stimulating discussions. The English-using community in various continents was for the first time viewed in its totality. A number of cross-cultural perspectives were brought to bear upon our understanding of English in a global context, of language variation, of language acquisition, and of the bilinguals' – or a multilingual's – use of English.

The deliberations were insightful for the types of questions raised: the sociolinguistic and political contexts of the countries where English is used in the Anglophone world; the factors that determine the retention of English after the end of the colonial period; the sociolinguistic and linguistic profile of each variety, in terms of its range of functions and depth of societal penetration; and the linguistic and other processes of nativization and acculturation.

These conferences did more than request a shift in emphasis: they questioned the prevalent models and methods and sought a new direction consistent with the identities and functions of World Englishes.

In the past decades, special colloquia were organized as part of the annual International Teaching English to Speakers of Other Languages (TESOL) meetings, once with IATEFL in Belgium, and twice with the Georgetown University Round Table on Languages and Linguistics (1986 and 1987; see Lowenberg 1988). And on August 6–13, 1986, yet another conference was organized: "Language and Power: Cross-Cultural Dimensions of English in Media and Literature," at the East–West Center, Honolulu. This conference was more specific and its aim as stated in Kachru and Smith (eds., 1986: 117) was

(a) to explore the concept of the linguistic "power" of English with a cross-cultural perspective; and
(b) to provide data for the study of such "power" from various English-using countries in the domains of literature and the media (film and journalism).

A variety of theoretical and applied research areas were identified and discussed, with special reference to the Outer Circle and the Expanding Circle. These included:

(a) Preparation of in-depth empirical studies on the national uses of English;

Conceptualization   243

(b) Identification of the main characteristics of English for international communication at various linguistic levels (e.g., syntactic, phonological, morphological, lexical, stylistic, and discoursal);
(c) Descriptions of registers of English (e.g., films, newspapers, and advertising);
(d) Development of extensive sociolinguistic profiles of English in various regions;
(e) Comparison of contexts and methods of language teaching in diverse cultural and educational settings;
(f) Promotion of and research in literatures in English around the world ("World Literatures in English" and "Literatures in English") and the encouragement of their use in the study of literatures and literary criticism and in
  (i) the teaching of the English language,
  (ii) cross-cultural communication (e.g., commerce, business, diplomacy and journalism), and
  (iii) teacher preparation;
(g) Investigation into the possibility of implementing the recommendations of the Quirk Committee (Smith, ed., 1981: xvii–xvix) to establish resource centres which will serve as archives for linguistic data and as clearing houses for various areas of English studies;
(h) The study of local grammatical, linguistic and literary traditions, and the applications of these traditions to the analysis and description of World Englishes;
(i) The initiation and coordination of research in lexicographical studies of English.

At the 1988 International TESOL convention in Chicago, the Interim Committee that had organized the 1986 conference in Honolulu met and formed the International Committee for the Study of World Englishes (ICWE). One charge of the ICWE was to establish a network of interested scholars working on various aspects of World Englishes. On April 2–4, 1992, the ICWE met at the University of Illinois at Urbana as a cosponsor of the conference "World Englishes Today." At this meeting, a preliminary proposal for the International Association for World Englishes (IAWE) was discussed and the IAWE was formally launched. The second three-day international conference was held in Nagoya, Japan, in August 1994, followed by the third international conference, again at the East–West Center in Honolulu, Hawaii, December 19–21, 1996. The fourth international conference was held in Singapore, December 19–21, 1997.

The contexts, sociolinguistic and linguistic, within which English was discussed in these conferences were international and intranational. The term

244   Research Resources

World Englishes and its sociolinguistic and pragmatic justification were later. Why the use of *Englishes* (Kachru 1985b; Kachru and Smith 1988)? The term symbolizes the functional and formal variations; divergent sociolinguistic contexts, ranges, and varieties of English in creativity; and various types of acculturation in parts of the Western and non-Western worlds. This concept emphasizes "WE-ness," and not the dichotomy between us and them – the native and nonnative users. In this sense, then, English is a valuable linguistic tool used for various functions. The approaches to the study of World Englishes, therefore, have to be interdisciplinary and integrative; different methodologies must be used (literary, linguistic, and pedagogical) to capture and construct distinct identities of different Englishes, and to examine critically the implications of such identities in cross-cultural communication and creativity.

The term *World Englishes* is not intended to indicate any divisiveness in the English-using communities but to recognize the functions of the language in diverse pluralistic contexts. There are underlying theoretical, functional, pragmatic, and pedagogical considerations for this pluralization of the term. This term more succinctly characterizes the current global functions of English than do alternatives such as *English as an international language* (EIL), *English as a lingua franca* (ELF), or *English* as a *world language* (EWL). The term *international* is misleading in more than one sense: it signals an "international" English in terms of acceptance, proficiency, functions, norms, and creativity. That is far from the reality.

These issues are discussed and illustrated by various regional and variety-specific profiles in, for example, Bailey and Görlach (1982); Cheshire (1991); Crystal (1995); .B. Kachru (1982d [1992d], 1986 [1990]); and McArthur (1992). The term *lingua franca*, also frequently used to capture the global presence of English, was originally used by the Arabs and the Turks in reference to an intermediary contact language *(Vermittlungssprache)*, a trade jargon spoken in the maritime contacts in the Levant. Literally, it meant "language of the Franks," the term that the Arabs used to characterize vaguely their trade partners from the north of the Mediterraneam. It is from its practice as a trade language that the term *lingua franca* has developed the meaning of "language of commerce" and its more modern use as "common language" chosen for communication by people from different ethnolinguistic backgrounds. This functional or domain restriction certainly does not apply to current global uses of English.

Current Approaches

There is also another wider implication. Over four decades, we have seen that almost the total spectrum of applied linguistics research, the strengths and limitations of theoretical frameworks, and applications of such theories have

Current Approaches 245

been demonstrated with reference to varieties of English. It is, therefore, not surprising that the past five decades in applied linguistics have been dominated by English; it is the most common language in such fields as first and second language acquisition, stylistics, bilingual and monolingual lexicography, and theory of translation (Kachru 1990a: 5).

This survey highlights the current approaches to the study of theoretical and applied issues and controversies related to English in the Outer and Expanding Circles. The survey is divided into the following sections:

1. The spread and stratification of English
2. The characteristics of the stratification
3. Interactional contexts of World Englishes
4. The concept WORLD ENGLISHES
5. World Englishes in diaspora
6. Speech communities
7. Dynamics of English-using speech communities
8. Conceptual frameworks and World Englishes
9. Bilinguals' literary creativity and canonicity
10. Multicanons of literatures in World Englishes
11. Nativization and Englishization
12. Fallacies about users and uses
13. Monolingual paradigms and heteroglossic Englishes
14. The power and politics of English
15. Codification and authentication
16. The gatekeepers of the sacred cows
17. The faces of hegemony
18. The genres of atonement, guilt, burdens, and lies
19. Caliban's weapon
20. Teaching World Englishes

1. The Spread and Stratification of English

The unparalleled spread of English demands a fresh conceptualization in terms of its range of functions and the degree of its penetration in different non-Western societal contexts (Kachru 1986d: 129–131). The traditional dichotomy between native and nonnative is functionally uninsightful and linguistically questionable, particularly in discussions of the functions of English in multilingual societies (Kachru 1988b). The earlier distinction of English as a native (ENL), second (ESL), or foreign (EFL) language has been under attack for reasons other than sociolinguistic ones. Quirk now rejects this "terminological triad"; he says, "I doubt its validity and frequently fail to understand its meaning" (1988: 236; see also Kachru 1991: 5 and 1996d).

246   Research Resources

B. Kachru (1985b and later) represents the spread of English in terms of three concentric circles: the Inner Circle, the Outer Circle, and the Expanding Circle. These are defined with reference to the historical, sociolinguistic, and literary contexts. A major question here is, What is the number of users of English across the world? The answer to this question depends on what we mean by an "English-knowing" person. There is no one answer to this question; various educational and functional variables have been used. The estimates of the users of English range from a conservative figure of 700 to 800 million to a rather liberal figure of 2 billion people with some competence in English (see e.g., Fishman et al. 1977; Crystal 1985b; Zhao and Campbell 1995; Deneire and Goethals, eds., 1997).[1]

2. The Characteristics of the Stratification

The study of the spread and stratification of English in Anglophone Asian and Africa, within various theoretical frameworks, is essentially a post-1960 phenomenon. Such studies are the consequence of the theoretical and methodological insights gained by what are termed "socially realistic linguistics" approaches to language study, particularly those of the linguists J. R. Firth in the United Kingdom (Kachru 1981d) and William Labov in the United States. Lyons (1978: xvi) is right in showing parallels "between Labov's approach to linguistics and that of the 'British' school, which draws its inspiration from J. R. Firth." The result of "socially realistic" paradigms and the activism of their proponents was that linguistic pluralism and diversity were considered a part of multiculturalism and societal interaction. What started as a ripple resulted in a challenge to various traditionally held linguistic assumptions.

The exponents of stratification in the Outer Circle have been interpreted in two ways: as a lectal range (e.g., Platt 1977; Platt and Weber 1980) and as a cline in English bilingualism within multilingual contexts (Kachru 1983b and earlier; Pakir 1991a, 1991b; Bamgbose 1982). In terms of lectal range, Platt and Weber describe Singapore English in relation to three reference points on a continuum – acrolect, mesolect, and basilect – following Bickerton' s use of these terms in describing the creole continuum (Bickerton 1975).[2] This taxonomy of Singapore English is not accepted by all (see Tay 1986). The cline of

---

[1] Salikoko S. Mufwene: According to Wikipedia (which cites the 18th edition of *Ethnologue* 2015), visited on 28 August 2016, the number of English speakers world-wide is estimated at 942 million. No comment is provided about the level of fluency of nonnative speakers. The preamble to the table also says that, depending on the count, the total number can rise to as high as 2 billion.

[2] SSM: The terms are originally from William Stewart (1965): "Urban Negro speech: Sociolinguistic factors affecting English teaching." In: Shuy, R. (Ed.), *Social Dialects and Language Learning*. National Council of Teachers of English, Champaign, IL, pp. 10–18.

Current Approaches 247

bilingualism is related to the users and uses of English: one end of the cline represents what has been termed an educated variety (e.g. Indian English, Nigerian English), and at the other are the varieties termed, for example, Nigerian Pidgin (see, for discussion and references, Bamiro 1991), colloquial English in Malaysia and Singapore (see Pakir 1991a; Lowenberg 1991), bazaar English and butler English (see Kachru 1983b; Hosali and Aitchison 1986). These varieties are not restricted to the spoken mode, but are also used in new English literatures to characterize various types of interlocutors, social classes, and group identities, and to provide local color (see Kachru 1990a: 10–13).

3. Lnteractional Contexts of World Englishes

Another result of the application of socially realistic linguistics has been the shift of the focus onto the functions of English in various types of interactional contexts, in both the Inner and Outer Circles. The approaches and methodologies suggested by, for example, Halliday (1970, 1973, 1975, 1978), Hymes (1974), Saville-Troike (1982), and Labov (1972 a, 1972b) have been particularly insightful. They have been used to describe the communicative and discoursal strategies in nonnative varieties of English (e.g., Richards 1979; Magura 1984, 1985; Kachru 1986a; Valentine 1988, 1991).

A natural next step in this research was to extend these approaches to language pedagogy, as in Savignon and Berns (1984), Brumfit (ed., 1988; reviewed by Berns 1991), and Ramaiah (1985). The study and analysis of English in interactional contexts have resulted in studies such as the following:

(a) Discourse strategies (e.g., Smith, ed. 1987; Kachru 1982b)
(b) Speech acts (e.g., Kachru 1983: 128–144 for written texts; Kachru, ed. 1992d; Sridhar 1989: 99–116; Y. Kachru, ed. 1991c includes a bibliography and illustrative studies by D'Souza, Y. Kachru, Nelson, Tawake, and Valentine).
(c) Code mixing (e.g., Kamwangamalu 1989c; Bhatia and Ritchie (eds.) 1989).
(d) Genre analysis (e.g., V. Bhatia, ed. 1997)

4. The Concept World Englishes

One insightful interpretation of the concept WORLD ENGLISHES is given by McArthur (1993: 334). Referring to the journal *World Englishes* (1984), and specifically to its logo acronym WE, the author observes that the logo "serves to indicate that there is a club of equals here." In this interpretation the emphasis is "the democratization of attitudes to English everywhere on the globe." This conceptualization, adds McArthur, also dissolves the trinity of

248   Research Resources

ENL, ESL, EFL nations. However, McArthur' s interpretation, valid as it is, only relates to the question of language attitude, and not to other vital issues directly concerned with functions, identities, and creativity in Englishes in dynamic sociocultural and linguistic contexts in practically every English-using part of the world.

The linguistic, cultural, canonical, and literary implications of the spread of English outside the Inner Circle are discussed in e.g. Dissanayake (1985); Thumboo (1985b, 1992); McCrum et al. 1986 [1993]; Kachru (1987b, 1988b, 1992e, and later); Görlach (1991a); Greenbaum (ed. 1985); and Greenbaum and Nelson (eds. 1996).

5. World Englishes in Diaspora

There are two major diasporas associated with English, if we exclude the close-to-home expansion toward Wales in 1535, when it was united with English-speaking England. The first was English expansion in Scotland in 1603, when the Scottish monarchies ceased to existas distinct identities. The major expansion out of the British Isles, however, was to North America, Australia, New Zealand, and Canada. These diasporas involved gradual and planned movements of English-speaking populations. The speech community was spreading its wings on the two remote continents, and in doing so it was also altering the linguistic behavior of the natives of those territories.

It is the second diaspora that planted the language in today's Anglophone Asia and Africa. This diaspora included the following major features:

- It initially involved limited – very limited – numbers of English speakers. But, as time passed, various strategies of educational planning, proselytization, and trading in the language were used to increase bilingualism in English;
- It placed English into contact with genetically and culturally unrelated languages in far-flung parts of the world; and
- It created a new ecology for the teaching of English in terms of linguistic inputs, norms, identities, and methodology.

The Concentric Circle model is intended to capture such historical, educational, and functional distinctiveness (see e.g., B. Kachru 1982d [1992d]; Smith, ed. 1981, and later; McCrum et al. 1986 [1993]; Crystal 1995; and McArthur 1992).

In defining the *nativeness* of Englishes, yet another distinction is useful: *genetic* nativeness as opposed to *functional* nativeness. One refers to the historical relationship and the other to the nativeness of a language in terms of its functional domains and range, as well as its depth in social penetration and resultant acculturation. A profile of the functional nativeness of English in the English-using communities must include the following:

1. The sociolinguistic status of a variety in its transplanted context;
2. The range of functional domains in which English is used;
3. The creative processes used to articulate local identities;
4. The linguistic exponents of acculturation and nativization;
5. The types of crossover contributing to the African and Asian canons of creativity; and
6. The attitude-specifying labels used for the variety.

The second diaspora thus provides a body and substance to the concept WORLD ENGLISHES. The issues this diaspora raises are in several ways unique to English among the languages of wider communication (see e.g., B. Kachru 1988b, 1988a, 1996a; see also Algeo 1996 for his comment on the use of the term "diaspora" and Mufwene 2001 for the "ecology of language" particularly, pp. 21–24).

6. Speech Communities

In recent years a variety of typologies and models have been used to characterize the English-using communities (e.g., Crystal 1995; Görlach 1991a; B. Kachru 1985b; and McArthur 1992). One such proposal is the Concentric Circle model, which is more than a mere heuristic metaphor for schematizing the spread of English (e.g., B. Kachru 1985b, 1992e, 1994d; and B. Kachru and Nelson 1996). There are underlying historical, political, sociolinguistic, and literary contexts that motivate this schematization.

The following points regarding the contexts in which the institutionalized varieties of English are used are worthy of note:

1. There is recognition of English in overall language policy of the nation (e.g., India, Nigeria, Singapore);
2. There is an extended tradition of contact literatures in English that are often recognized as part of the national literatures;
3. There is deep social penetration of the language, which has resulted in several varieties (e.g., Singlish, basilect);
4. There are distinct linguistic exponents of the processes of Englishization at various levels of the language and in literatures that had contact with English (B. Kachru 1994e, 1995b);
5. There is an extended range of functions of English in diverse sociolinguistic contexts that has resulted in localized registers and genres in Asian, African, and other varieties of Englishes;

250   Research Resources

6. There are Englishized varieties of local languages – and some of these varieties have even acquired distinct names; and
7. There is acculturation of the English language for articulating local social, cultural, and religious identities and as an access language for such identities (see Y. Kachru 1991c and later).

7. Dynamics of English-Using Speech Communities

What is the numerical global and regional demographic distribution of the English-using speech communities? A precise answer is difficult. The English-using speech communities are continuously growing, evolving, and changing. English certainly is one major language in which global bilingualism/multilingualism is rapidly increasing – it is the preferred targeted second or umpteenth language. The numbers of users and uses of English estimated in the 1960s, 1970s, and 1980s became repeatedly outdated within a decade or so. The demographic profile of the Outer and Expanding Circles is overwhelming and constantly changing.

The estimates of English-knowing South Asians in the 1960s and the 1970s do not represent the figures of the 1990s – the increase is sharp and, for some, it is alarming (see e.g., Kachru 1996d and Phillipson 1992). And in the 1990s the presence of English in Asia was simply mind-boggling, as it was in other regions of the world. The hunger for learning the language – with whatever degree of competence – is simply insatiable.

- The estimated English-using bilingual population in Asia is rapidly increasing. That is more than or the same as the total population of the United States, the United Kingdom, and Canada (see e.g., Kachru 1997c);
- India, in the Outer Circle, with more than 335 million English-using people, comprises the largest number of bilinguals in English;
- China, in the Expanding Circle, has more than 200 million users of English, at a conservative estimate (Zhao and Campbell 1995);
- There is extensive creativity in English in Asia in a wide variety of literary genres (see e.g., B. Kachru 1994e; Thumboo 1992); and
- The initiatives in planning, administration, acquisition, and spread of English in Asia are primarily in the hands of the Asians. This is also true of English-using Africa.

8. Conceptual Frameworks and World Englishes

The theoretical, methodological, and ideological questions related to World Englishes have now transcended the concerns of pedagogy, which was virtually the main concern before the 1960s. And now a number of the sacred cows of theoretical and applied linguistics are under attack as a consequence of two major developments: the insights gained by sociolinguistic descriptions, analyses, and methodology, as well as the research initiatives and ideas provided by scholars from the Outer Circle.

What constitutes the sacredness of these sacred cows and how these attained that status have been discussed earlier. The acquisitional questions relate to the relevance of concepts such as INTERFERENCE, INTERLANGUAGE, ERROR, and FOSSILIZATION (Kachru 1990a, 1990d, 1996b; Lowenberg 1984, 1986a, 1986b; Sridhar and Sridhar 1986 [1992]; and S. Sridhar 1994). The sociolinguistic questions relate to, for example, the *pluricentricity* of English, its ideological connotations, the new ideologies represented by Englishes in the Outer Circle, and the expansion of literary and cultural canons of English. (For discussions and references see e.g., Kachru 1988b: 210–211, 1990a: 13–14; Mazrui 1973; Ngugi 1986, 1991; Pennycook 1994; Phillipson and Skutnabb-Kangas 1986). The pedagogical issues relate to models for teaching, methods of teaching, and curriculum design relevant for various methods (Berns 1991; Phillipson 1992; see also relevant papers in Kachru, ed. 1982d [1992d]). The theoretical issues surrounding World Englishes concern three vital concepts: the SPEECH COMMUNITY, the NATIVE SPEAKER, and the IDEAL SPEAKER–HEARER of English (Kachru 1988b: 213–218).

The conceptualization of a speech community varies from Bloomfield's vague definition to Le Page's and Gumperz's complex definitions (see Hudson 1980: 25–30). When we attempt to characterize the English users in multilingual societies, the task becomes even more complex. The sociolinguistic reality of the uses and users of English across cultures is captured by the term *speech fellowship* originally suggested by Firth and discussed in earlier chapters (Kachru 1988b: 224). Related to SPEECH COMMUNITY is the concept NATIVE SPEAKER used as a lighthouse by both linguists and language teachers. Worth repeating here are the following two remarks by Ferguson (1982):

The whole mystique of native speaker and mother tongue should probably be quietly dropped from the linguists' set of professional myths about the language.
[a] universal explanatory principle or a general theory of language should account for all linguistic behavior. Variation in structure as between Ll and L2 seems just as interesting a subject as dialect or register variation in a complete monolingual community.

These two statements by Ferguson and others have yet to be systematically applied to our understanding and description of World Englishes (see Christophersen 1988; Kachru 1986a, 1996 and later; Paikeday 1985; and Pride 1981).

The prescriptive concerns are directly related to the diversification of English. And diversification, like Hydra, is multiheaded and raises many issues. It is argued that diversification is "symbolic of subtle sociolinguistic messages."

252   Research Resources

The intended message may be to use diversity as an exponent of *distance,* as a marker of creativity potential, or as an expression of the Caliban *syndrome* (Kachru 1988b: 218 and 1997b).

The most debated question in diversification concerns the models, norms, and standards for English in the Outer Circle. This question has been discussed in detail in several studies, with appropriate references (see e.g. Kachru ed. 1982d, [1992d] originally presented in 1979; see also Kachru 1983c, 1986a, 1992e; Bedard and Maurais 1983; Tickoo, ed. 1991). During the past decades, the concerns related to models have been revisited, and the two approaches to the controversy are presented in Quirk (1988, 1989), Kachru (1988b, 1990a, 1991, 1992e), Kandiah (1995), and Parakrama (1995). For more extensive discussion and additional references see the papers in Tickoo (ed. 1991; including Honey 1991). The main motivations for codification seem to be a) attitudinal, based on markers of power and elitism, and class and caste; b) social standing and ethnicity; c) social acceptance; and d) integration, with preference for the melting-pot hypothesis.

In terms of diversification, traditionally there have been three types of English-using speech fellowships: *norm-providing*, *norm-developing*, and *norm-dependent.* The norm-providing varieties are used in the Inner Circle. Among these varieties, American and British Englishes (to use cover terms) are considered more appropriate than the varieties used in Australia and New Zealand. The situation, however, is dynamic. Until recently, the British variety (Received Pronunciation) was attitudinally – and pedagogically – a preferred pronunciation model, but that situation is now gradually changing in favor of the American model (Kachru, 1981a: 21–43). We see now increasing interest in what may be termed *variational pluralism* – that is, exposure to several varieties of English.

The norm-developing speech fellowships refer to the users of English in the Outer Circle. The users of such varieties do not have identical attitudes about an endocentric (locally defined) norm – far from it. Among the users of these varieties, there is ambivalence between linguistic norm and linguistic performance, but generally the localized norm has a well-established linguistic, literary, and cultural identity (e.g., Singapore English, Nigerian English, Indian English; about which see Kachru 1982d [1992d], 1993, 1994e, 1995b; Cheshire, ed. 1991). The norm-dependent varieties are used in the Expanding Circle (e.g., in Korea, Iran, Saudi Arabia). The norms are essentially external (American or British).

A string of questions concerning norms, codification, and attitudes continue to be raised in the literature (see e.g., Finegan 1980; Greenbaum, ed. 1985; Baxter 1980; Kachru 1976; Newbrook 1986; Nihalani 1991; Prator 1968).

There are two other questions related to descriptive and prescriptive concerns about English in the Outer Circle: What determines the difference between an *error* (or mistake) and an innovation? And what are the variables

Current Approaches   253

of intelligibility for World Englishes across languages and cultures? The first question has been addressed in Kachru (1982d [1992d]) with relevant references (see also Y. Kachru, ed. 1991c). The second question has a long history of discussion, mainly in the pedagogical literature. The most insightful work on this topic was done by Larry Smith, who approached this question within the framework of English as an *international* and *intranational* language (EIIL). An extensive partially annotated bibliography of more than 163 items, divided into five sections, is in Smith and Nelson (1985). It covers general, sociolinguistic and language-specific, syntactic, phonological, and reading studies until 1985. The question of intelligibility is viewed in a wide context, making a distinction between a) *intelligibility*, relating toword/utterance recognition; b) *comprehensibility*, dealing with word/utterance meaning (locutionary force); and c) *interpretability*, concerned with meaning behind word/utterance (illocutionary force). Smith and Nelson also suggest "some of the issues" that should be on the agenda of researchers on this topic (pp. 335–336). These include the following:

1. How does the English proficiency of the speaker correlate with the intelligibility, comprehensibility, and interpretability of his/her speech?
2. How does the English proficiency of the listener correlate with his/her ability to comprehend, interpret, and find intelligible what he/she hears?
3. How does topic difficulty for the speaker correlate with the intelligibility, comprehensibility, and interpretability of his/her speech?
4. How does topic difficulty for the listener correlate with his/her ability to comprehend, interpret, and find intelligible what he/she hears?
5. How does the communicative setting (quiet living room vs. noisy bar, for example) affect intelligibility, comprehensibility, and interpretability?
6. What are the effects of familiarity, either with the individual speaker or with the variety of the language spoken, on intelligibility, comprehensibility, and interpretability?

They further suggest:

7. Future research should investigate the correlation of speaker and listener effort to communicative success.
8. More research is needed on the effects of listener and speaker attitudes toward different varieties of spoken English on the intelligibility, comprehensibility, and interpretability of those varieties.
9. Intelligibility, comprehensibility, and interpretability studies should be undertaken with nonnative speakers from different countries.
10. Studies should be undertaken to determine how intelligible, comprehensible, and interpretable native speakers are to nonnative speakers as well as other native speakers of different national varieties of English.

254   Research Resources

9. Bilinguals' Literary Creativity and Canonicity

The term *bilinguals' creativity* is used for "those creative linguistic processes which are the result of competence in two or more languages" (Kachru 1986b). This concept is not used for acquisitional inadequacies in a language, but refers to

first, the designing of a text which uses linguistic resources from two or more-related or unrelated-languages; second, the use of verbal strategies in which subtle linguistic adjustments are made for subtle psychological, sociological, and attitudinal reasons. (Kachru 1986b)

A paradigm example of the bilinguals' creativity is the development of contact literatures in World Englishes (Kachru 1986b, 1992e, 1994e, 1995b, 1996d, 1996b, 1996c; King 1974, 1980).

The contact literatures in English are the result of the contact of English with other languages in multilingual and multicultural contexts in e.g. Africa and Asia. As time passes, the contact varieties acquire stable characteristics in their pronunciation, syntax, vocabulary, and discoursal and stylistic strategies. The long-term contact manifests itself in nativization and acculturation. Nativization refers to the process that creates a localized linguistic identity of a variety (e.g., Indian English, Scottish English; see Pandharipande 1987). On the other hand, acculturation gives English distinct local cultural identities. It is in this sense that claims have been made that World Englishes have acquired multicultural identities and pluricentricity (Kachru 1986a, 1991; Steiner 1975; Thumboo 1992; Lim 1993). One important, and as yet not fully recognized, result of this contact is that the literary and cultural canons related to the English language in the Outer Circle acquire distinct characteristics: literary, cultural, and ideological (see Sections 10 and 19).

The contact literatures in English are thus both nativized and acculturated, and these show convergence of two or more, often unrelated, linguistic and literary traditions. A long tradition of such writing is found in South Asia, West Africa, the Philippines, and Southeast Asia. These literatures have by now gained national and international recognition, as is evident, for example, by the award of the Nobel Prize in literature to the Nigerian English writer Wole Soyinka in 1986 and to Derek Alton Walcott in 1992, by the Neustadt Award to the Indian English writer Raja Rao in 1988, and by the award of the Booker Prize to, for example, Salman Rushdie in 1995, Chinua Achebe in 1987, Michael Ondaatje in 1992, and Ben Okri in 1991.

In literary studies, the bilingual's creativity in English demands recognition of at least three facts: that the institutionalized nonnative varieties have an

Current Approaches 255

educated variety and a cline of subvarieties; that writers in contact literatures in English engage in "lectal mixing"; and that in such writing there are style shifts that are related to the underlying sociolinguistic and cultural contexts. The results of such style shifts, appropriate to non-Western cultural contexts, are new discourse strategies, use of distinctly different speech acts, and development of new registers in English. (For references, illustrations, and discussion, see Kachru 1982a, 1983b, 1987b, 1996d, 1997e; Y. Kachru, ed. 1991c; Sridhar 1992; see also relevant sections in Bailey and Görlach 1982; Kachru 1985b; and Platt et al. 1984).

In pedagogical studies the impact of bilingualism in the classroom is currently under study both in the United Kingdom and in the United States, but very little empirical research has been done in the non-Western countries. (A useful annotated bibliography on this topic is Devaki et al. 1990, which lists 855 items; see also Strevens 1982.)

There is now awareness, though muted, of the fact that traditional (and some contemporary) approaches to the teaching of English developed in the Western contexts cannot be accepted without question for the non-Western contexts (see e.g., B. Kachru 1996b; Y. Kachru 1985a; and Tickoo 1988). The main reasons for questioning these approaches, as articulated in Kachru (1986b: 24–25), are the following:

a. The data for analysis are restricted to classroom assignments, etc., on the basis of which broad variety-specific generalizations are made;
b. The sociolinguistic context and its implications for creativity are not taken into consideration; and
c. A majority of approaches ignore *nativization* and *acculturation* in the institutionalized varieties.

For further discussion, see Y. Kachru (1985c, 1987); B. Kachru (1982b); Pride (ed. 1982); Lowenberg (1984); and S. Sridhar (1992, 1994).

With reference to literary creativity in English, Thumboo (1992) raises some insightful questions and argues:

This challenge confronts every bi- or multilingual writer. His bilingualism is one of three broad types – proficient, powerful, or limited – his position in this cline is not static, because quite often one language gains dominance. A bilingual person has at least two language universes, and each language works with its own linguistic circuits. How the two associate depends on whether the languages as neighbors inhabit the same space and time and can bend to serve creative purposes.

It is now recognized that such creativity, both literary and of other types, has opened up research avenues with wide implications for language acquisition, language function, and language identity. The following issues come to mind.

256   Research Resources

The first is the much-debated question of *language deficiency* vs. *difference.* These two aspects were traditionally studied within the paradigm of *error* analysis (e.g., Richards, ed. 1979). Since the 1960s, analyses have been provided that introduce the concepts of INNOVATION and CREATIVITY as bearing on the differences (Kachru, 1965, 1983b and later). The second issue is the recognition of innovations used for stylistic effect as "foregrounding." I am particularly thinking of what are termed *new English literatures* (see e.g., King 1974, 1980). Referring to such writing, Carter and Nash (1990:20) observe that there is continually a need to point out that there are

> many literatures in the world which are written in English but which are produced a long way from England. There is English literature written in the United States, Australia and South Africa; and less obviously, there is English literature written in countries in which English is an institutionalized second language, e.g. India, Singapore, Nigeria, Kenya, or the Philippines, and where it is produced by writers for whom English is not a mother tongue. (see also Steiner 1975: 4)

The third issue is the recognition of various text types, code-mixed or non-code-mixed, which are intentionally meant for bilingual readers who share the writers' linguistic repertoire and cultural and literary canon. The writers of such texts do not seem to make concessions to the native speaker of the language. This is evident in written media, literary genres, and localized culturally dependent registers (e.g., matrimonial advertisements, invitations, obituaries; see e.g. Dubey 1991; Kachru, ed. 1982d: ch. 20 and earlier; Nwoye 1992). The fourth issue is recognizing the functional appropriateness of localized sublanguages and registers. For example, it is argued that there is a need for a paradigm shift in the claims of ESP research and methodology (see e.g. Kachru 1988a, presented in 1985; Swales 1985). The fifth is providing contrastive typologies of linguistic and cultural conventions. It is the differences in these conventions that result in the pragmatic failure or success of various language types (see Candlin 1987; B. Kachru 1986b; Sridhar, 1989; Y. Kachru, ed. 1991c and earlier; Valentine 1988, 1991). The sixth issue is describing the formal and functional characteristics of bilinguals' language mixing and switching (see case studies and references in Bhatia and Ritchie 1989; Bhatt 1996; and particularly Kamwangamalu 1989c for earlier research).

10. Multicanons of Literatures in World Englishes

Interlocutors in World Englishes have a variety of linguistic, cultural, and social backgrounds; the situation is that a speaker of a Bantu language may interact with a speaker of Japanese, a Taiwanese, an Indian, and so on. There are some historical analogues of this situation, though the degree of the spread and uses of English is unparalleled. The analogues that come to mind are Latin in medieval Europe (see Kahane and Kahane 1979, 1986) and Sanskrit in traditional South Asia. This extensive use of English over a long period has resulted in multicanons of English (Kachru 1991, 1994b, and later).

This development of multicanons is particularly vital when English is being used as a tool to present distinct canons unrelated to the traditional canonical associations of English. This, of course, is not always done consciously. It is part of the acculturation of English in "un-English" sociocultural and linguistic contexts. This has happened to the English language in the United States and Australia, too, but the situation is somewhat different in these two countries. They share with "mother English" a Judeo-Christian tradition, a literary past, and a general cultural heritage. This is not the case for English in Africa, in South Asia, in Southeast Asia, and in the Philippines (see Kachru 1992e; for an overview of such literatures, see King 1974; see also Chishimba 1984; Magura 1984).

11. Nativization and Englishization

The two processes of nativization and Englishization have developed, as it were, two faces of English, one showing what the contact has formally done to various varieties of English, and the other showing what impact the English language and literature have had on other languages of the world. Englishization is not restricted to phonology, grammar, and lexis; it has had a deep impact on discourse, registers, styles, and literary genres. One can see this process active in three major spheres associated with the spread of English: 1) the traditional region of cultural and literary contact in which mostly cognate languages of English are used (e.g., in Western and parts of Eastern Europe); 2) the English-using regions of the world in the Outer Circle of English, which are noncontiguous with England geographically and genetically unrelated or not closely related (e.g., parts of Africa and Asia); and 3) the Expanding Circle, which includes, in various degrees of use of English, the rest of the world, such as Japan, China, and Latin America.

The vocabularies of the languages of the world have been most receptive to borrowing from English. It is claimed, for example, that 81 percent of the borrowed vocabulary of Japanese is of English origin. There are three ways in which such lexical borrowings manifest themselves: in loan words, loan shifts (calques), and hybridization, in which English and another language are combined (see e.g., Kachru 1994b; Bhatia and Ritchie, eds. 1989; Viereck and Bald, eds. 1986).

The literary impact of this influence is equally important. English provides a model for developing literary genres, has contributed thematic innovations, and has introduced new ideological paradigms, which in turn have resulted in new literary movements. The result is that classical stylistic traditions have changed, and innovations have become institutionalized (Kachru 1990b and 1994e).

258   Research Resources

12. Fallacies about Users and Uses

A variety of fallacies dominate the profession and professional societies involved in the teaching of English. Consider, for example, the following myths: that English is learned essentially for its international currency. It is generally overlooked that actually English is primarily used as an important vehicle for intranational communication across diverse linguistic, ethnic, and religious groups. It is likewise often held that English is learned exclusively or primarily to interact with people of the Inner Circle, who represent Judeo-Christian traditions. This is only partially true. English is also used as an important tool for imparting local cultural traditions and cultural values (Kachru 1983b, 1990a, 1990b; 1992e and later). It has also been claimed that the goal of learning and teaching English is to adopt a native model. Attitudinally this may be partially true of "norm-dependent" countries, but this assumption cannot be generalized. A number of scholars have held the view that a majority of Outer Circle English-using countries use *interlanguages* (e.g., Selinker 1972b). The validity of this hypothesis has been questioned in several studies (Sridhar and Sridhar 1986; S. Sridhar 1994; Y. Kachru 1993a). It is also believed that native speakers as teachers, consultants, advisers, and evaluators have an important input in the teaching of English, in policy formation, and in organizing the channels for the spread of English. That actually is not true of the real ELT contexts in most of the world. Finally, it is argued that recognition of the sociolinguistic and pragmatic realities of World Englishes reveals underlying philosophical and political positions. In Quirk's (1989) view, such a position has its roots in "liberation theology." If recent history has given us a "liberation theology," why not also a "liberation linguistics"? Quirk asks. And then he adds:

The trouble, as the Kingman Committee sees it [in reference to the report of the committee presided over by Sir John Kingman], is that such an educational fashion went too far, grossly undervaluing the baby of standard English while overvaluing the undoubtedly important bathwater of regional, social and ethnic varieties: giving the impression that any kind of English was as good as any other, and that in denying this, nothing less was at stake than "personal liberty" itself. (For a detailed discussion of this fallacy, see Kachru 1988b, 1991,1995c.)

13. Monolingual Paradigms and Heteroglossic Englishes

The earlier conceptualizations prevalent in the ELT profession divide the English-using speech communities into ENL/ESL and EFL. It has been argued that this tripartite division is sociolinguistically, pragmatically, and functionally flawed (see Kandiah 1993, 1995; Parakrama 1990, 1995; B. Kachru 1982d [1992d] and later; Sridhar and Sridhar 1986 [1992]; Lowenberg 1992; Nelson

Current Approaches 259

1992 and later). An extreme version of earlier conceptualization is found in Prator (1968), and in recent years, in Quirk (1985, 1988, 1989). (See B. Kachru 1991 and Parakrama 1995, particularly pp. 16–28, for discussions of Prator 1968.) The issue is not just one of emotion and identity but of historical, sociolinguistic, and linguistic realities. Tickoo (1991) includes some important papers articulating various voices on this topic.

14. The Power and Politics of English

An urge to derive maximum economic benefits from the English language has also resulted in a competition between the United States and United Kingdom. The economic stakes are immense, as is obvious from the following statement: "The worldwide market for EFL training is worth a massive £6.25 billion according to a new report from the Economic Intelligence Unit" *(EFL Gazette* March 1989; see also Romaine 1992).

The very existence of their power thus provides the Inner Circle incentives for devising ways to maintain attitudinal and formal control; it is both a psychological and a sociopolitical process. Linguistic control is yet another such strategy, exercised in three ways: by the use of various channels of codification and by controlling these channels; by the attitude toward linguistic innovations (in the Outer Circle); and by suggesting dichotomies that are sociolinguistically and pragmatically unrealistic. These dichotomies divide users of English into *us* vs. *them* (see Kachru 1986d: 132–133; McArthur 1986). The following studies discuss aspects of this question, either specifically with reference to English, or in relation to language in general: Baik (1995), Knappert (1968), Kramarae et al. (1984), McArthur (1986), Ngugi (1986, 1991), Mazrui (1967, 1973), O'Barr (1976), O'Barr and O'Barr (1976), Phillipson and Skutnab-Kangas (1986), Pennycook (1994), Phillipson (1992), Ram (1983, 1991), Read (1974), Singh (1987), Tollefson (1991), Tromel-Plotz (1981), and Kachru (1986d: 133–134, 1996d).

15. Codification and Authentication

The evidence for challenging earlier presuppositions about the codification and authentication of English has drawn scrutiny. In spite of these challenges and institutionalized linguistic identifies of World Englishes, there continues to be a paucity of reference materials and resources for all varieties. There is lack of materials in lexicographical resources, grammatical descriptions, and guides to genres and styles. In the resource materials, the term *international* is generally not used in the sense in which we understand it: it is used to include just North America, Britain, and Australia. An example of such a restricted – and ethnocentric – use of the term is in the *International Dictionary of English*

260   Research Resources

(1995), released with great fanfare to provide an illustration of the internationalization of the language. (In this case the concept INTERNATIONAL refers to "America, Britain, and Australia,") The scarcity of materials is not due to a lack of debate on the relevance and application of traditional standards, criteria, and views on linguistic prescriptivism and codification. The debate has become rather intense during the past two decades or so. The representative positions are discussed in, for example, Tickoo (ed. 1991; see particularly section III, "English in the World: Issues and Attitudes").

The localized (e.g., Indian, Nigerian, Singaporian) and regional (e.g., West African, South Asian, Southeast Asian) uses of Englishes have motivated a three-way variety-specific distinction, i.e., innovation, deviation, and mistake (error). An innovation entails a contextual and formal explanation, as do for example innovations in transplanted American, Australian, and Canadian Englishes. The range of such innovations is not restricted to lexical items. It includes various variety-specific speech acts, genres, and registers (see e.g., Y. Kachru, ed. 1991c and later). A *deviation* has a comparative and a contrastive implication – it is generally explained with reference to another variety of English. In the case of the Outer Circle varieties, the point of reference is generally the Inner Circle (see e.g., B. Kachru 1996a for additional references). A mistake (or an error) is acquisitional deficiency in phonology, grammar, pragmatics, and so on. It is important to point out that in a long tradition of debates on these issues the preceding distinctions have not been made in the case of the Outer Circle. And such creativity in the case of the United States, Canada, Australia, or even Scotland has traditionally not been viewed with much understanding by the gatekeepers of English in the United Kingdom. Home (1995 [1991]: x) expresses this concern about attitudes toward Australian English.

There was a time when the idea of "Australian English" could seem a contradiction in terms. How could there be an Australian English when Australia itself was English? Any straying from standard usage as ordained in the United Kingdom was not Australian English. It was *bad* English.

The preceding distinctions are particularly crucial for understanding literary creativity in, and acculturation of, different varieties of World Englishes. This aspect of World Englishes has been discussed under the broad topics of "the Empire talks back" and "The Empire writes back" (see e.g., Ashcroft et al. 1989; B. Kachru 1982d [1992d], especially pp. 301–326, and 1993; Lim 1993).

16. The Gatekeepers of Sacred Cows

The gatekeepers of the canon and other linguistic sacred cows have a variety of motives, agendas, and national interests. There are essentially three major groups of gatekeepers: the protectors of canon; the ELT enterprise (Susan Butler terms it "ELT Empire"; see Butler 1996); professional networks of various types. The gatekeepers, however, have not been able to prevent the development and acceptance of what Gates Jr. (1992) has so aptly termed "loose canons." The term *canon*, of course, is very elusive.

In the role of gatekeepers the most influential group is the ELT enterprise itself. Phillipson (1992) and Pennycook (1994) provide powerful critiques of one of the most influential arms of this profession, the British Council. In recent years, the council has presented its mandate, as outlined in its charter, in a more forthright manner. Roger Bowers, assistant director-general of the British Council, for example, says, "The promotion of the English language is absolutely central as one of the 'Charter obligations' of the British Council" (1995: 88). And he continues:

We want to maintain the position of the English language as a world language so that it can serve on the widest possible stage as the vehicle for *our national values and heritage.*(emphasis added)

To this statement Bowers adds, "along with those of other English-speaking nations" (1995: 88). He further observes:

Now this begins to sound like linguistic imperialism, and if Braj Kachru were here, he would strongly object (as he has in the past) to putting national before supranational interests and to placing commerce before philosophy.

We see that the arm of the "ESL empire" has been long and mighty and has reached into various areas, including lexicography. In the context of Southeast Asian Englishes, an Australian lexicographer, Susan Butler (1997; see also Butler 1996), observes:

Some words from this region [Southeast Asia] do turn up in existing dictionaries but it seems to me that these items had currency in colonial days – British or American – and were recorded from a colonial interest and point of view. As the empire faded, the lexicography ceased. *The new colonialism of the region emanates from the ESL empire, which has an unjustified fear that its strength would be undermined if there was to be any recognition of the rights to existence and claims to authority of the transported variety of English.* (emphasis added)

There is yet another group of gatekeepers: the networks of various types of professionals who control the publication of books, journals, and so on (see e.g., Brown 1995; B. Kachru 1995c; Vavrus 1991).

17. The Faces of Hegemony

The hegemonic roles of English in various English-using speech communities have multiple faces and, indeed, are analyzed within a variety

262   Research Resources

of theoretical, ideological, and economic frameworks. The reactions range from extreme love to hate, and ecstasy to agony (see a summary and references in B. Kachru 1996d).

The first face is that of the "linguistic imperialism" associated with the three major countries, the United Kingdom, the United States, and Australia. In the past, this role for Australia was restricted to the Australian continent, particularly with what was done in a planned way to the aboriginal languages and cultures, but now Australia views its role within the regional context – that of Southeast Asia – with an eye on South Asia. (For references see the symposium "Linguistic Imperialism" in *World Englishes* 12.3: 335–373.) The second face of this hegemony is ideological – that of the Westernization of other cultures. This refers to the cultural, ideological, and Judeo-Christian constructs of the language and the implication of such constructs for non-Western cultures and societies (see e.g., Das Gupta 1993; Pennycook 1994). The third face of this hegemony is the country- or region-specific debate on the continued role of English in the postimperialist period in a country – for example, the Philippines, India, or Malaysia. (For further discussion see B. Kachru 1996d; Tickoo 1991.) The other aspects of the hegemonic roles of English that are often discussed are elitism; inculcation of alienation toward one's own culture, society, and language; and so on (see e.g., Das Gupta 1993; Parakrama 1995; Tripathi 1992; Tsuda 1994a, 1994b).

18. The Genres of Atonement, Guilt, Burdens, and Lies

The postcolonial or the postimperial period of English has now given us a variety of conceptualizations of colonialism and its linguistic arms: psychological, ideological, and political. This body of writing has resulted in scholarly self-reflexivity regarding various language attitudes. Such self-reflexivity has considered the various intellectualizations regarding language imposition in the colonial context and the lingering effects of this imposition on the psyche of individuals and societies. This reassessment of past linguistic colonialism has developed into at least three distinct genres:

- *Genre of "atonement,"* which is believed to be one way for the present generation of the perpetrators of the original "linguistic sins" to search for the colonizer within themselves;
- *Genre of "burden":* In several recent studies there are suggestions that there is a duty to undo the constructs of a "new orientalism" in the discipline of English literary studies (see e.g., Spivak 1993, with specific reference to "the Indian teachers of English");
- *Genre of "lies,"* which presents yet another introspection of the colonized's mind – another side of the attitude toward the English studies. This is the

opposite side of what has been characterized as "Caliban's linguistic weapon" – the functions of English that are integrative and liberating (see e.g., Rajan 1992).

In multiple ways English has performed – and continues to perform – a variety of integrative roles: cultural, literary, and political. Caliban could take only so much abuse, so much linguistic kicking. The empire not only "talked" back but also wrote back. The result is a vibrant idiom, discourse, and narrative of localized and national political discourses at one level of society in Asia and Africa. It is true that English became elitist and a marker of a specific type of *Otherness*. The linguistic elitism of English, however, was not much different from that of Sanskrit, of Persian, and of the H(igh) varieties of a majority of the local languages. It is through such "talking back" with localized innovations and national discourses of emancipation that "the enslaving medium" turned into "an insurgent weapon" (Soyinka 1993: 88). The "guilt," "burden," and "lies" hypotheses are thus only part of a very complex story that need not overshadow the use of English as an initiator of sociocultural and political introspection and rejuvenation. The English language was used as a vehicle to open up the past and to access the Western views of the colonized people, their histories, cultures, and regions.

The past is full of linguistic, cultural, and religious convergences and types of hybridity. The blends are such that one has to reflect hard to analyze each linguistic and cultural layer to determine what is colonial, *less* colonial, and *noncolonial*. This actually is the sociolinguistic reality of a majority of English-using communities. Therefore, one has a difficult task in analyzing various layers – linguistic, cultural, and educational. One has to separate the colonial from the nativized constructs, which have become part of the pluralistic traditions. What we see in this debate, then, is that some "lies" are convenient to live with, while other "lies" are convenient to talk about – some are politically correct to ignore and others are politically correct to articulate. A "lie" for one member of an English-using community is viewed differently by another English user. India's Raja Rao believes that there is "an honesty in choosing English, an honesty in terms of history" (cited in Jussawalla and Dasenbrock 1992). However, we may contrast this view with that of Ngugi, who considers English as the most racist of languages (1981: 14).

At one level the attitude of, for example, India's Raja Rao and Nigeria's Wole Soyinka has created an identity with the language. Once English acquires a new identity – African, Asian, Australian – it is actually like establishing an autonomy that liberates the language both in its *madhyama* "medium," and in its *mantra*, "the message." In saying this, I am not looking for good in colonialism – far from it. I am making a distinction between *madhyama* and *mantra* as discussed in B. Kachru (1997f).

264   Research Resources

19. Caliban's Weapon

The most potent metaphor for turning the colonial language into Caliban's linguistic weapon is used by West Africa's Nobel laureate in English Wole Soyinka (1993: 88), who observes:

Black people twisted the linguistic blade in the hands of the traditional cultural castrator and carved new concepts onto the flesh of white supremacy. The customary linguistic usage was rejected outright and a new, raw, urgent and revolutionary syntax was given to this medium which had become the greatest single repository of racist concepts.

Soyinka's observation is consistent with broader reality about postimperial English: that the Empire writes back in the tongue that was a colonial linguistic arm (see e.g., Ashcroft et al. 1989; Jussawalla and Dasenbrock 1992; B. Kachru 1990b, 1993, 1997f).

20. Teaching World Englishes

In planning a course on World Englishes, one is generally confronted with three questions, two of which relate to the conceptualization of the topic, and the third to resources for teaching such a course (see e.g., Brown 1995; Brown and Peterson 1997). The two content-related questions are, Why teach World Englishes? And, two, how does one motivate a paradigm shift both attitudinally and methodologically in the classroom? The third question concerns the resources available for teaching such a course. These will, of course, vary according to the linguistic, cultural, and academic situations, and with respect to the experience of the instructor and goals of the students.

Why Teach World Englishes?   The literary face of World Englishes opens up a mine of topics in textual, stylistic, and thematic terms (see e.g., Brumfit & Carter 1986; Kachru 1986e; Kachru ed., 1982d [1992d]; Thumboo 1992; see references in Bailey and Görlach 1982).

The pedagogical issues have been addressed in Strevens (1980, 1988), Tickoo (1991), and Berns (1991); for the Western perspective on the history of English language teaching see Howatt (1984), and for a critique of the Western approaches to English language teaching see Tollefson (1991), Phillipson (1992) and Pennycook (1994).

What Motivates the Paradigm Shift?   The issue concerning the need for paradigm shift raises questions related to the sociolinguistic profiles in each English-using region: the underlying dynamic forces characteristic of the spread of English and its retention in the postcolonial period; the typologies of nativization and Englishization; the sociological and educational contexts in which English is taught and the implications of such contexts on methods of teaching and curriculum development; the types of personnel staffing and administering the ESL/EFL programs; the attitudes of planners, teachers, and learners toward exonormative varieties and the localized educational varieties and subvarieties; the role writers and the media play in the Outer Circle in diffusing local ideologies through English; the role English plays in "modernization" and "Westernization" in non-Western regions; the role, if any, that the Inner Circle plays in the ongoing spread of English and its codification; and the ways in which the nonnative literatures in English (e.g., Asian, African) can be used as a resource for cross-cultural awareness and for understanding linguistic creativity and innovations.

The aim is to make professionals and advanced students aware of the following aspects, among others:

1. SOCIOLINGUISTIC PROFILE: An overview of World Englishes in their world context, with in-depth focus on selected major varieties and their users and uses. It is useful to make a distinction between the practice of English in a monolingual society as opposed to a complex multilingual society (e.g., Ferguson 1966).

2. VARIETY EXPOSURE: A discussion of repertoires within major native and nonnative varieties of English; varieties within a variety, their uses and users; specific texts related to different interactional contexts; mixing and switching and their implications; as well as features they share or do not share at various linguistic levels.

3. ATTITUDINAL NEUTRALITY: One might focus on one specific variety and demonstrate the formal and functional reasons for the distinctiveness of the variety. It is desirable to show why attitudinal neutrality is essential to capture e.g. the Africanness (Bokamba 1982), the Indianness (Kachru 1965, 1983b), of specific varieties.

4. RANGE OF USES: The functional and pragmatic appropriateness of the lectal range of English in private and public discourse and the reasons for the use of pidgins and basilectal (or colloquial) varieties in such contexts, and the significance of variety shifting for various types of identities. The range of uses may be related to the concept CLINE with reference to a) the participants in a speech event, b) intelligibility within the speech fellowship(s), and c) the roles in which English is used (see Kachru 1983b: 236–237).

5. CONTRASTIVE PRAGMATICS: The rationale for the use of distinct discoursal and stylistic innovations, and their appropriateness to the local cultural conventions (e.g., linguistic strategies used for persuasion, phatic communion, apologies, condolences, or obituaries).

266   Research Resources

6. MULTIDIMENSIONALITY OF FUNCTIONS: The linguistic implications of the functional ranges of English in the media, literary creativity, administration, government, and the legal system.
7. EXPANSION OF THE CANONS: The literary, linguistic, and cultural implications of multiple Western and non-Western canons of English.
8. CROSS-CULTURAL INTELLIGIBILITY: The implications of the diffusion and multilinguistic and literary identities of English regarding international and intranational intelligibility.

What Are the Resources for Teaching?   In the 1970s, this question would have been difficult to answer. One would have had to depend primarily on papers from journals and selected notes. However, as Görlach (1991a: 11) rightly observes, "The books published in 1982–84 make up a particularly impressive list: it is no exaggeration to say that the following ten books more or less suffice to teach a full academic course on the topic." Görlach's ten books are Bailey and Görlach (1982), Kachru (ed. 1982d, 1983b, 1986a [1990]), Platt et al. (1984), Pride (1981), Todd (1984), Trudgill and Hannah (1982; 2nd edition 1985), Trudgill (1986), and Wells (3 vols., 1982). This is an impressive list indeed. I would add to this list Cheshire (1991), Crystal (1995), McArthur (ed. 1992), McCrum et al. (1986), and Smith (1981, 1987). McCrum et al. (1986) also provides the advantage of an accompanying series of documentaries that students of any level would find very instructive. Three other books useful for focusing on specific theoretical and pedagogical topics are Lowenberg (ed. 1988), Quirk and Widdowson (1985), and Tickoo (1991). Of a small number of books published before the 1980s, one stands out: Fishman et al. (1977). The following is a list of other types.

Bibliographies: Viereck, Schneider, and Görlach (1984) provide a general bibliography, up to the early 1980s (reviewed in Kachru 1986f). A supplement to the bibliography, published in 1992 (*English World-Wide* 13.1: 1–50), includes 794 entries and covers the period 1984–1991. There are several bibliographies specifically for various regions, e.g., Aggarwal (1982) for South Asia. See also references in Kandiah (1991), Kachru (1983b, 1981d), and Schmied (ed. 1990).

The following studies provide valuable bibliographical references for *specific areas*: **Southeast Asia**: Bloom (1986), Foley (1988), Noss (1983), Tay (1991); **Ireland**: Harris (1991); **Canada**: Chambers (1991); **New Zealand**: Bell and Holmes (1991); **Australia**: Guy (1991); **East Africa**: Abdulaziz (1991); **Southern Africa**: Chishimba (1991); **West Africa**: Bokamba (1991); **the Caribbean**: Winford (1991); **the Pacific**: Romaine (1991). Another bibliographical source for an overview and relevant references is Burchfield (ed.) (1994). *Issue-oriented studies*: a) **Models**: Kachru (1985b,

Current Approaches   267

1986c, 1986a, 1992d; ed. 1982d, 1996d, 1996a), Strevens (1982), Tickoo (1991); b) **Intelligibility**: extensive and partially annotated bibliography in Smith and Nelson (1985) and Smith (1981); c) **Sociolinguistic issues**: Tickoo (1991), Kachru (1986a, 1988b, 1990a), K. Sridhar (1986), and Cheshire (1991); d) **Testing**: Lowenberg (1992).

Literatures in English: King (1974, 1980); Taiwo (1976); Kachru (1986a); Thumboo (1992). For South Asia, see Singh et al. (1981).

In the 1990s, a variety of initiatives were undertaken to make available resources for researchers and educators in understanding the global spread of English and its various implications. The following items are illustrative:

1. *Companions and Encyclopedias*: Burchfield (ed. 1994), and earlier volumes of the Cambridge History of the English Language, e.g., Blake (ed. 1992) and Hogg (ed. 1992); Cheshire (ed. 1991); McArthur (1992); Mccrum et al. (1986 [1993]); and Crystal (1995).

2. *Journals*: In the 1990s, the global spread of English drew attention from the news media, popular books, and scholarly research. In different ways – with various emphases – one finds topics related to World Englishes discussed in the media. A major focus of some journals and magazines is on World Englishes. These include *English World-Wide: A Journal of Varieties of English* (1980–, John Benjamins, Amsterdam and Philadelphia); *World Englishes: Journal of English as an International and Intranational Language* (1985–, Basil Blackwell, then Oxford); *English Today* (1985–, Cambridge University Press); *World Literature Written in English* (1961–, University of Guelph, Guelph, Ontario, Canada).

3. *Organizations*: One organization that specifically focuses on various dimensions of World Englishes is the International Association for World Englishes (IAWE). It is slowly spreading its wings and considers all users of English – Asian, African, European – as active and equal partners in its deliberations and concerns. IAWE conferences have been held in various places around the world, including Honolulu, Hawaii; Urbana, Illinois; Portland, Oregon (USA); Nagoya, Japan; Tokyo, Japan; Singapore; Regensburg, Germany; Hong Kong; Vancouver, Canada; Cebu, the Philippines; Melbourne, Australia; New Delhi, India; and Istanbul, Turkey.

4. *Corpora and Dictionaries*: There are two other major initiatives that contribute to the body of resources. First is the Survey of English Usage, initiated by Sir Randolph Quirk. In 1988, Quirk's successor, Sidney Greenbaum, extended its scope and proposed the International Corpus of English (ICE). The extension of the corpus and inclusion of countries from Asia and Africa – major regions from the Outer Circle – are, as Greenbaum rightly says, "a splendid example of international cooperation in research" (Greenbaum 1991: 7; see also Greenbaum and Nelson 1996). This proposal

268   Research Resources

received enthusiastic support; and now scholars from the following countries are participating in the project: Australia, Belgium, Canada, Denmark, Germany, Hong Kong, India, Jamaica, Kenya, the Netherlands, New Zealand, Nigeria, Northern Ireland, the Philippines, Singapore, Sweden, Tanzania, the United Kingdom, the United States, Wales, the Democratic Republic of Congo, Zambia, and Zimbabwe.

The second initiative is that of the Macquarie Library Pty Ltd., Australia. Their "Australia's own!" *Macquarie Dictionary* (1991 [1981]) has already provided an identity to Australian English. This additional project of Macquarie's is to produce the *Macquarie Concise Dictionary: World English in an Asian Context*. It will represent, says the announcement, "the authentic voice of the language as it is used throughout Asian countries." This collaborative venture combines the lexicographic expertise of the Macquarie Dictionary researchers and the academic research of Asian scholars (see Butler 1996).

In Conclusion   The overview in this chapter is indeed selective in terms of both what it covers and which references are included. I am conscious of the fact that this survey presents just the tip of the multidimensional iceberg of what are now World Englishes, varied functions, and a plurality of users. It will be complemented by other scholars as World Englishes as a research area thrives.

Select Bibliography

Abdulaziz, M. M. H. (1991) East Africa (Tanzania and Kenya). In Cheshire (ed.) (1991), pp. 391–401.

Abercrombie, David (1951) R. P. and Local Accent. *The Listener* (September 6, 1951). [Reprinted in D. Abercrombie (1964) *Studies in Phonetics and Linguistics*, London: Oxford University Press.]

Achebe, Chinua (1960) *Things Fall Apart*. London: Heinemann Achebe.
(1965) English and the African Writer. *Transition* 4.18: 27–30. Also in Mazrui 1975.
(1966) The English language and the African writer. *Insight* 20 (Oct.–Dec.).
(1976) *Morning Yet in Creation Day*. Garden City, NY: Doubleday.
(1992) Chinua Achebe. In Jussawalla and Dasenbrock (1992), pp. 63–81.

Aggarwal, N. K. (1982) *English in South Asia: A Bibliographical Survey of Resources*. Gurgaon and Delhi: Indian Documentation Service.

Agnihotri, R. and Khanna, A. (eds.) (1994) *Second Language Acquisition: Sociocultural and Linguistic Aspects of English in India*. New Delhi: Sage.

Alatis, James E. and G. R. Tucker (eds.) (1979) *Language in Public Life*. Georgetown Round Table on Languages and Linguistics. Washington, DC: Georgetown University Press.

Alfonso, Anthony (1966) *Japanese Language Patterns*. Tokyo: Sophia University Press.

Algeo, J. (1996) Review of *South Asian English: Structure, Use, and Users*. Edited by R. J. Baumgardner. Urbana: University of Illinois Press, 1996. *World Englishes* 15.3, 408–409.

Alladina, Safder and Edwards, Viv (1991) *Multilingualism in the British Isles* (2 vols.). London: Longman.

Altieri, Charles (1990) *Canons and Consequences: Reflections on the Ethical Force of Imaginative Ideals*. Evanston, IL: Northwestern University Press.

Ashcroft, Bill, Helen Tiffin, and Gareth Griffiths (1989) *The Empire Writes Back: Theory and Practice Inpost-Colonial Literatures*. London and New York: Routledge.

Asrani, U. A. (1964) *What Shall We Do about English?* Ahmedabad: Navajivan.

Awooner, Kofi (1973) *Ride Me, Memory*. New York: Greenfield Review Press.

Ayyar, Indira (1993) Language Crossover in the Syntax of Spoken Indian English. Unpublished Ph.D. dissertation submitted to the State University of New York at Stony Brook.

270   Select Bibliography

Baik, Martin (1994) Syntactic features of Englishization in Korean. *World Englishes* 13: 155–66.

(1995) *Language, Ideology, and Power: English Textbooks of Two Koreas*. Seoul: Thaehaksa.

Baik, Martin Jonghak and Rosa Jinyoung Shim (2002) Teaching World Englishes via the Internet. *World Englishes* 21: 427–30.

Bailey, Richard W. (1982) The English language in Canada. In Bailey and Görlach (1982), pp. 134–176.

(1987) Resistance to the spread of English. Paper presented at Georgetown University Round Table, March 1987 (manuscript).

(1990) English at its twilight. In C. Ricks and L. Michaels eds. *The State of the Language*. Berkeley: University of California Press, pp. 83–94.

(1992) *Images of English*. Cambridge: Cambridge University Press.

(1996) Attitudes toward English: The future of English in South Asia. In Baumgardner (ed.) (1996), pp. 40–52.

Bailey, Richard W. and Manfred Görlach (eds.) (1982) *English as a World Language*. Ann Arbor: University of Michigan Press.

Bakhtin, Mikhail (1981) *The Dialogic Imagination*. Austin: University of Texas Press.

Bamgbose, Ayo (1982) Standard Nigerian English: Issues of identification. In B. Kachru (1982d), pp. 99–111.

Bamgbose, Ayo, Ayo Banjo, and T. Thomas (eds.) (1995) *New Englishes: A West African perspective*. Ibadan: Mosuro.

Bamiro, E. (1991) Nigerian Englishes in Nigerian English literature. *World Englishes* 10.1: 7–17.

Barnes, Sir Edward (1932) *The History of Royal College (Colombo)* (earlier called Colombo Academy) Colombo: H. W. Cave.

Baron, Dennis (1982) *Grammar and Good Taste: Reforming the American Language*. New Haven, CT: Yale University Press.

Bassnett, Susan and Andre Lefevere (eds.) (1990) *Translation, History and Culture*. London and New York: Pinter.

Baugh, John (1988) Language and race: Some implications for linguistic science. In F. Newmeyer (ed.) *Linguistics: The Cambridge Survey*. Cambridge: Cambridge University Press, Vol. 4, pp. 64–74.

Baumgardner, Robert J. (1993) *The English Language in Pakistan*. Karachi: Oxford University Press.

(1995) Pakistani English: Acceptability and the norm. *World Englishes* 14.2: 261–271.

(ed.) (1996) *South Asian English: Structure, Use, and Users*. Urbana: University of Illinois Press.

Bautista, Maria L. S. (1990) Tagalog-English code-switching revisited. *Philippine Journal of Linguistics* 21.2: 15–29.

(1991) Code-switching studies in the Philippines. *International Journal of the Sociology of Language* 88: 19–32.

(ed.) (1996) *Readings in Philippine Sociolinguistics*, 2nd ed. Manila: De La Salle University Press.

Select Bibliography

(ed.) (1997) *English is an Asian Language: The Philippine Context.* Sydney: Macquarie Library.

Baxter, J. (1980) How should I speak English? American-ly, Japanese-ly, or internationally? *JALT Journal* 2: 31–61. Also in Brown (ed.) (1991), pp. 53–71.

Bedard, E. and J. Maurais, (eds.) (1983) *La norme linguistique.* Quebec: Direction Generale des Publications Governementales du Ministere des Communications.

Beebe, James and Maria Beebe (1981) The Filipinos: A special case. In Ferguson and Heath (1981), pp. 322–338.

Bell, A. and Janet Holmes (1991) New Zealand. In Cheshire (ed.) (1991), pp. 153–168.

Bell, Roger (1976) *Sociolinguistics: Goals, Approaches, and Problems.* London: Botsford.

Bennett, William J. (1992) *The De-Valuing of America: The Fight for Our Culture and Our Children.* New York: Summit Books.

Berns, Margie (1985) *Functional Approaches and Communicative Competence: English Language Teaching in Non-Native Contexts.* Ph. D. dissertation, University of Illinois at Urbana-Champaign.

(1990) *Contexts of Competence: Social and Cultural Considerations in Communicative Language Teaching.* New York: Plenum.

(1991) Review of "Communicative Language Teaching," special issue *Annual Review of Applied Linguistics* (1987), volume 8. *World Englishes* 10.1: 102–106.

Bernstein, Basil (1964) Elaborated and restricted codes: Their social origins and some consequences. *American Anthropologist* 66: 55–69.

Bernstein, Richard (1994) *Dictatorship of Virtue: Multiculturalism, and the Battle for American Future.* New York: A. A. Knopf.

Bhabha, Homi K. (1994) *The Location of Culture.* London and New York: Routledge.

Bhatia, Kailashchandra (1967) *A Linguistic Study of English Borrowings in Hindi* (in Hindi). Allahabad: Hindustani Academy.

Bhatia, Tej K. (1992) Discourse functions and pragmatics of mixing: Advertising across cultures. *World Englishes* 11.2/3: 195–215.

Bhatia, Tej K. and William Ritchie (guest eds.) (1989) Code-mixing: English across Languages. Special Issue of *World Englishes* 8.3.

Bhatia, Vijay K. (1983) Simplification vs. easification: The case of legal texts. *Applied Linguistics* 4.1.

(1993) *Analysing Genre: Language Use in Professional Settings.* London and New York: Longman.

(guest ed.) (1997) *Genre Analysis World Englishes*, 16.3.

Bhatt, Rakesh. (2001) World Englishes. *Annual Review of Anthropological Linguistics* 537–550.

(guest ed.) (1996) Symposium on constraints on code-switching. *World Englishes* 15.3.

Bickerton, Derek. (1973) The nature of a creole continuum. *Language* 49: 640–669.

(1975) *Dynamic of a Creole System.* Cambridge: Cambridge University Press.

Bjarkman, Peter C. and Victor Raskin (eds.) (1986) *The Real-World Linguist: Linguistic Applications in the 1980s.* Norwood, NJ: Ablex Publishing.

272   Select Bibliography

Blake, N. (ed.) (1992) *The Cambridge History of the English Language*. Vol. 2. *1066–1476*. Cambridge: Cambridge University Press.

Bloom, Allan (1987) *The Closing of the American Mind: How Higher Education Has Failed Democracy and Impoverished the Souls of Today's Students*. New York: Simon & Schuster.

Bloom, David (1986) The English language in Singapore. In Basant K. Kapur (ed.) *Singapore Studies: Critical Surveys of the Humanities and Social Sciences*. Singapore: Singapore University Press, pp. 337–458.

Bloomfield, Leonard (1933) *Language*. New York: Holt, Rinehart & Winston.

Bokamba, Eyamba G. (1982 [1992]) The Africanization of English. In B. Kachru (ed.) (1982d [1992d]), pp. 125–147.

(1991) West Africa. In Cheshire (ed.) (1991), pp. 493–508.

Bolinger, Dwight L. (1973) Truth Is a linguistic question. *Language* 49.3: 539–550

(1980) *Language: The Loaded Weapon*. London: Longman.

Bosmajian, Haig (1974) *The Language of Oppression*. Washington, DC: Public Affairs Press.

Bourhis, Richard Y. (ed.) (1984) *Conflict and Language Planning in Quebec*. Multilingual Matters, 5. Avon, UK: Multilingual Matters, pp. xvi–304.

Bowers, R. (1995) You can never plan the future by the past: Where do we go with English? In Ayo Bamgbose, Ayo Banjo and Andrew Thomas (eds.) *New Englishes: A West-African Perspective*. Ibadan: Mosuro, pp. 87–112.

Brass, Paul R. (1974) *Language, Religion and Politics in North India*. London: Cambridge University Press.

Bright, W. (ed.) (1966) *Sociolinguistics*. The Hague: Mouton.

Brown, Adam (ed.) (1991) *Teaching English Pronunciation: A Book of Readings*. London: Routledge.

Brown, Kimberley (1995) World Englishes: To teach or not to teach? *World Englishes* 14: 233–245.

Brown, Kimberley and Jay Peterson (1997) Exploring conceptual frameworks: Framing world Englishes paradigm. In Smith and Forman (1997).

Brown, Roger and A. Gilman (1960) The pronouns of power and solidarity. In T. A. Sebeok (ed.) *Style in Language*. Cambridge, MA: MIT Press, pp. 253–276.

Brumfit, Christopher J. (ed.) (1982) *English for International Communication*. Oxford: Pergamon Institute of English.

Brumfit, Christopher. (1987) Applied linguistics and communicative language teaching. *Annual Review of Applied Linguistics*. 8: 3–13.

(1988) Applied linguistics and communicative language teaching, *Annual Review of Applied Linguistic 1987* 8: 3–13.

Brumfit, Christopher J. and R. A. Carter (eds.) (1986) *Literature and Language Teaching*. Oxford: Oxford University Press.

Burchfield, Robert (ed.) (1994) The Cambridge History of the English Language. *Vol. 5*. English in Britain and Overseas: Origins and Development. Cambridge: Cambridge University Press.

Burling, Robbins (1982) *Sounding Right*. Rowley, MA: Newbury House.

Butler, Susan (1996) World Englishes in an Asian context: The Macquarie dictionary project. *World Englishes* 15.3: 347–357.

Select Bibliography 273

(1997) Selecting South-East Asian words for an Australian dictionary: How to choose in an English not your own. In Edgar W. Schneider (ed.) *Englishes around the World: Studies in Honour of Manfred Görlach*. Amsterdam: John Benjamins, pp. 273–286.

Canale, Michael and Merrill Swain (1980) Theoretical bases of communicative approaches to second language teaching and testing. *Applied Linguistics* 1: 1–47.

Candlin, Christopher (1982) English as an international language: Intelligibility, interpretability. In C. J. Brumfit (ed.) *Notes on a theme: English for international communication*. Oxford: Pergamon Press, pp. 95

(1987) Beyond description to explanation in cross-cultural discourse. In Smith (ed.), 22–35.

Canfield, Robert. (1983) Accusation and "anthropology." *Reviews in Anthropology* 10: 55–61.

(1986) Acquisition in "Anthropology." In *Review of Anthropology* (winter 1986): pp. 55–61.

Carter, R. (1987) *Vocabulary: Applied linguistic perspectives*. London: Allen Unwin.

Carter, R. and W. Nash (1990) *Seeing Through Language*. London: Basil Blackwell.

Chamberlain, D. and R. J. Baumgardner (eds.) (1988) *ESP in the Classroom: Practice and Evaluation* (ELT Documents 128). London: Macmillan.

Chambers, J. K. (1991) Canada. In Cheshire (ed.) (1991), pp. 89–107.

Chaudenson, Robert (2001) *Creolization of Language and Culture*. London: Routledge.

Cheshire, Jenny (1991) The UK and the USA. In Cheshire (ed.) (1991), pp. 13–34.

(ed.) (1991) *English around the World: Sociolinguistic Perspectives*. Cambridge: Cambridge University Press.

Chishimba, Maurice M. (1985) *African Varieties of English: Text in Context*. Ph.D. dissertation, University of Illinois, Urbana.

(1991) Southern Africa. In Cheshire (ed.) (1991), pp. 435–445.

Chomsky, Noam (1965) *Aspects of the Theory of Syntax*. Cambridge, MA: MIT Press.

(1986) *Knowledge of Language: Its Nature, Origin, and Use*. New York: Praeger.

Christophersen, Paul (1988) Native speakers and world English. *English Today* 4.3: 15–18.

(1990) Comments. *English Today* 6.3: 61–63.

Clyne, Michael (1982) *Multilingual Australia: Resources, Needs, Policies*. Melbourne: River Seine.

ed. (1992) *Pluricentric Languages: Differing Norms in Different Nations*. Berlin: Mouton de Gruyter.

Coffey, Bernard (1984) ESP – English for specific purposes. in *Language Teaching Abstracts* 17.1.

Conner-Linton, Jeffrey and Caroline Adger (guest eds.) (1993) Ethical issues for applying linguistics. Special issue of *Issues in Applied Linguistics* 4.2.

Cooke, D.(1988) Ties that constrict: English as a Trojan Horse. In *Awareness: Proceedings of the 1987 Ontario Conference*. Toronto: TESL Ontario, pp. 56–62.

Cooper, Robert L. (ed.) (1982) *Language Spread: Studies in Diffusion and Language Change*. Bloomington, IN: Indiana University Press.

274 Select Bibliography

(1985) Fantasti! Israeli attitudes towards English. In Greenbaum (1985), pp. 233–241.

Coppieters, Rene (1987) Competence differences between native and near-native speakers. *Language* 63: 544–573.

Coulmas, Florian (ed.) (1988) *With Forked Tongues: What Are National Languages Good for?* Ann Arbor, MI: Karoma.

Craig, Hardin (1950) *A History of English Literature*. New York: Oxford University Press.

Crew, W. (ed.) (1977) *The English Language in Singapore*. Singapore: Eastern University Press.

Crystal, David (1985a) Comment (on Quirk 1985). In Quirk and Widdowson (1985), pp. 9–10.

(1985b) How many millions? The statistics of English today. *English Today* 1: 7–9.

(1992) *An Encyclopedic Dictionary of Language and Languages*. Oxford: Blackwell.

(1995) *The Cambridge Encyclopedia of the English Language*. Cambridge: Cambridge University Press.

(1997) *English as a Global Language*. Cambridge: Cambridge University Press.

Das, S. K. (1989) The common reader and translation of poetry. International Journal of Translation *(January)* 1.1: 33–40.

Das Gupta, J. (1970) *Language Conflict and National Development: Group Politics and National Language Policy in India*. Bombay: Oxford University Press.

Daiches, David. (1960) *A Critical History of English Literature*. New York: Ronald Press.

Dasgupta, Probal (1993) *The Otherness of English: India's Auntie Tongue Syndrome*. Delhi: Sage.

Davidson, Fred (1993a) Testing English across Cultures: Summary and Comments. *World Englishes* 12.1: 113–125.

(guest ed.) (1993b) Symposium on testing English across cultures. *World Englishes* 12.1: 85–126.

Davies, Allan (1989) Is international English interlanguage? *TESOL Quarterly* 23: 457–467.

(1991) *The Native Speaker in Applied Linguistics*. Edinburgh: Edinburgh University Press.

Day, Lal Behari (1913 [1874]) *Bengal Peasant Life*, 2nd ed. London: Macmillan.

Day, Richard R. (1981) ESL: A factor in linguistic genocide? In Janet Cameron Fisher, Mark A. Clarke and Jacquelyn Schachter (eds.) *On TESOL '80: Building Bridges: Research and Practice in Teaching English as a Second Language*. Washington, DC: TESOL, pp. 73–78.

(1985) The ultimate inequality: linguistic genocide. In Wolfson and Manes (1985), pp. 163–181.

Dayananda, J. T. (1986) Plain English in the United States. *English Today* 5: 13–16.

De Beaugrande, Robert (1991) *Linguistic Theory: The Discourse of Fundamental Works*. London/New York: Longman.

Select Bibliography   275

DeCamp, David (1971) Toward a generative analysis of a post-creole speech continuum. In Dell Hymes (ed.) *Pidginization and Creolization of Languages*, Cambridge: Cambridge University Press, pp. 349–70

De Kadt, Elizabeth (1993) Language, power, and emancipation in South Africa. *World Englishes* 12.2: 157–168.

Dendrinos, Becky (1992) *The EFL Textbook and Ideology*. Athens: N. C. Grivas.

Deneire, Marc (1993) Democratizing English as an international language. *World Englishes* 12.2: 169–178.

Deneire, Marc and M. Goethals (guest eds.) (1997) *English in Europe*. Special issue of *World Englishe*, 16.1.

Denison, Norman (1968) Sauris: A trilingual community in diatypic perspective. *Man* 3: 578–592.

(1977) Language death or language suicide? *International Journal of the Sociology of Language* 12: 13–22.

Desai, Anita (1996) A coat of many colors. In Baumgardner (1996), pp. 221–230.

Desai, Maghanbai P. (1964) *The Problem of English*. Ahmedabad: Navajivan Publishing House.

Desani, G. V. (1951) *All About H Hatterr*. New York: Farrar, Straus & Young [Reprinted 1972, New York: Lancer Books].

Devaki, L., K. Ramasamy, and A. Srivastava (1990) *An Annotated Bibliography on Bilingualism, Bilingual Education and Medium of Instruction*. Mysore: *Central Institute of Indian Languages*.

Di Pietro, Robert J. (1982) *Linguistics and the Professions*. Norwood, NJ: Ablex.

Dissanayake, Wimal (1985) Towards a decolonized English: South Asian creativity in fiction. *World Englishes* 4.2: 233–242.

(1989) Introduction: Literary history, narrative, and culture: Perplexities of meaning. In Wimal Dissanayake and Steven Bradbury (eds.) *Literary History, Narrative and Culture: Selected Conference Papers*. Honolulu: University of Hawaii Press.

Dissanayake, Wimal and Mimi Nichter (1987) Native sensibility and literary discourse. In L. Smith (1987), pp. 114–122.

Dittmar, Norbert (1976) *A Critical Survey of Sociolinguistics: Theory and Applications*. New York: St. Martin's Press.

Dixon, Robert M. W. (1980) *The Languages of Australia*. Cambridge: Cambridge University Press.

Dressler, Wolfgang and Ruth Wodak-Leodolter (1977) Language death. *International Journal of the Sociology of Language* 12: 5–11.

D'Souza, Dinesh (1991) *Illiberal Education: The Politics of Race and Sex on Campus*. New York: Free Press.

D'souza, Jean (1987) *South Asia as a Sociolinguistic Area*. Ph.D. dissertation, University of Illinois, Urbana.

(1988) Interactional strategies in South Asian languages: Their implications for teaching English internationally. *World Englishes* 7.2: 159–171.

(1991) Speech acts in Indian English fiction. *World Englishes* 10.3: 307–316.,

Dubey, V. (1991) The lexical style of Indian English newspapers. *World Englishes* 10.1: 19–32.

276   Select Bibliography

Dubois, Betty Lou (1982) The construction of noun phrases in biomedical journal articles. *Pragmatics and LSP.*

Eagleson, Robert D. (1982) English in Australia and New Zealand. In Bailey and Görlach (1982), pp. 415–438.

Eble, Connie E. (1976) Etiquette books as linguistic authority. In Reich (1976).

Edelman, Murray (1964) *The Symbolic Uses of Politics.* Urbana: University of Illinois Press.

Eliot, T. S. (1919 [1951]) Tradition and the individual talent. In *Selected Essays.* London: Faber and Faber.

(1920 [1960]) Euripides and Professor Murray. In *The Sacred Wood.* London: Methuen, pp. 91–97.

Emeneau, Murray B. (1956) India as a linguistic area. *Language* 32: 3–16.

Eribon, Didier (1991) *Conversations with Claude Strauss.* Translated by Paula Louisa (Chicago: University of Chicago Press).

Eribon, Didier (1991) *Michel Foucault.* (Cambridge, MA: Harvard University Press).

Erlich, Victor (1965) *Russian Formalism: History, doctrine.* The Hague: Mouton.

Escure, Geneviève. (1981) Decreolization in a creole continuum: Belize. In Arnold Highfield and Albert Valdman (eds.) *Historicity and variation in creole studies,* Ann Arbor, MI: Karoma, pp. 27–39.

Fairclough, Norman (1989) *Language and Power.* New York: Longman.

Ferguson, Charles A. (1966) National sociolinguistic profile formulas. In Bright (ed.) (1966), pp. 309–315.

(1975) Applications of Linguistics. In Robert Austerlitz (ed.), *The Scope of American Linguistics* (papers of the First Golden Anniversary Symposium of the Linguistic Society of America). Lisse: Peter De Ridder Press.

(1976) The Ethiopian linguistic area. In Lionel Bender et al. (eds.) *Language in Ethiopia.* London: Oxford University Press, pp. 63–76.

(1978) Multilingualism as object of linguistic description. In Linguistics in the seventies: Directions and prospects Edited by Brad. B. Kachru. Special issue of *Studies in the Linguistic Sciences* 8.2: 97–105,

(1982 [1992]) Foreword. In B. Kachru (1982d [1992d]), pp. xiii–xvii.

(1996) *Sociolinguistic Perspectives: Papers on Language in Society 1954–1994.* Edited by T. Huebner. New York/Oxford: Oxford University Press.

Ferguson, Charles A. and Shirley B. Heath (1981) *Language in the USA.* Cambridge and New York: Cambridge University Press.

Fernandez-Armesto, Felipe (1995) *Millennium: A History of the Last Thousand Years.* New York: Scribner.

Fernando, Chitra (1977) English and Sinhala bilingualism in Sri Lanka. *Language in Society* 6: 341–360.

Fettes, Mark (1991) Europe's Babylon: Towards a single European language? *History of European Ideas* 13: 201–213.

Fiedler, Leslie A. and Houston A. Baker, Jr. (eds.) (1981) *English Literature: Opening up the Canon.* Baltimore: John Hopkins University Press.

Finegan, Edward (1980) *Attitudes toward English Usage: The History of a War of Words.* New York: Teachers College Press.

Select Bibliography 277

Firth, John R. (1930 [1966]) *Speech*. London: Benn's Sixpenny Library [Reprinted, London: Oxford University Press].

(1957) *Papers in Linguistics*. London: Oxford University Press.

(1959) The treatment of language in general linguistics. In F. R. Palmer (ed.) *Selected Papers of J. R. Firth* (1968). Bloomington: Indiana University Press.

Fishman, Joshua A. (1968) Sociolinguistic perspectives on the study of bilingualism. *Linguistics* 39: 21–49.

(1971) *Advances in the Sociology of Language*. The Hague: Mouton. Fishman, Joshua A. (1998–1999) The new linguistic order. *Foreign Policy* 113: 26–40.

Fishman, Joshua A., Andrew W. Conrad, and Alma Rubal-Lopez (eds.) (1996) *Post-imperial English: Status Change in Former British and American Colonies, 1940–1990*. Berlin and New York: Mouton de Gruyter.

Fishman Joshua A., Robert L. Cooper, and Andrew W. Conrad (1977)*The* Spread of English: The Sociology of English as an Additional Language. Rowley, MA: Newbury House.

Fishman, Joshua A., Charles A. Ferguson, and Jyotirindra Das Gupta (eds.) (1968) *Language Problems of Developing Nations*. New York: John Wiley.

Foley, Joseph (ed.) (1988) *New Englishes: The Case of Singapore*. Singapore: Singapore University Press.

(1995) English in Mauritius. *World Englishes* 14.2: 205–222.

Forster, Leonard (1970) *The Poet's Tongues: Multilingualism in Literature* (The de Carle Lectures at the University of Otago 1968). Cambridge: Cambridge University Press (in association with University of Otago Press).

Foucault, Michel (1980) *Power-Knowledge: Selected Interviews and Other Writings, 1972–1977*. Edited by Colin Gordon. Translated by Colin Gordon et al. New York: Pantheon.

Freudenthal, Hans (1960) *Lincos: Design of a Language for Cosmic Intercourse*. Amsterdam: North-Holland.

Friedrich, Paul (1962) Language and politics in India. *Daedalus* 91: 543–559.

Garcia, 0. and R. Ortheguy (eds.) (1989) *English across Cultures, Cultures across English*. New York: Mouton de Gruyter.

Gates, Jr., Henry Louis (1992) *Loose Canons: Notes on the Culture Wars*. New York: Oxford University Press.

(1993) The wearing of America. *The New Yorker* (April 15): 112–117.

Geertz, Clifford (1983) *Local Knowledge*. New York: Basic Books.

Geis, Michael L. (1982) *The Language of Television Advertising*. New York: Academic Press.

Gill, Saran K. et al. (eds.) (1995) *INTELEC '94: International English Language Education Conference: National and International Challenges and Responses*. Bang Malaysia: Pusat Bahasa Universiti Kebangsaan Malaysia.

Gokak, V. K. (1970) *The Golden Treasury of Indo-Anglican Poetry*. New Delhi: Sahitya Academi.

Gonzalez, Andrew (1987) Poetic imperialism or indigenous creativity? Philippines literature in English. In L. Smith (1987), pp. 141–156

278   Select Bibliography

Görlach, Manfred (1991a). *Englishes: Studies in Varieties of English. 1984–1988.* Amsterdam and Philadelphia: John Benjamin.

(1991b). Lexicographical problems of new Englishes. In Görlach 1991a), 36–68.

Graddol, David (1997) *The Future of English? A Guide to Forecasting the Popularity of the English Language in the 21st Century.* London: British Council.

Grant, Charles (1831–1832) Observations on the state of society among the Asiatic subjects of Great Britain, particularly with respect to morals, and the means of improving it. In *General Appendix to Parliamentary Papers 1831–1832.* London, pp. 60–66.

Greenbaum, Sidney (ed.) (1985) *The English Language Today.* Oxford: Pergamon Press.

(1990) Standard English and the international corpus of English. *World Englishes* 9.1: 79–83.

(1991) ICE: The international corpus of English. *English Today* 28.7.4: 3–7.

Greenbaum, Sidney and Cecil Nelson (guest eds.) (1996) Studies on international corpus of English. Special issue of *World Englishes* 15.1.

Gupta, Anthea F. (1993) *The Step-Tongue: Children's English in Singapore.* Clevedon, UK: Multilingual Matters.

Gupta, R. and K. Kapoor (eds.) (1991) *English in India: Issues and Problems.* Delhi: Academic Foundation.

Guy, G. (1991) Australia. In Cheshire (ed.) (1991), pp. 213–226.

Halliday, Michael A. K. (1970) Language structure and language function. In Lyons, J. (ed.), *New Horizons in Linguistics.* Harmondsworth, UK: Penguin. 140–165.

(1973) *Explorations in the Functions of Language.* London: Edward Arnold.

(1975) *Learning How to Mean: Explorations in the Development of Language.* London: Edward Arnold.

(1978) *Language as a Social Semiotic: The Social Interpretation of Language and Meaning.* Baltimore: University Park Press.

Hardgrave, Robert L., Jr. (ed.) (1998) *Word as Mantra. The Art of Raja Rao.* New Delhi: Katha.

Harris, J. (1991) Ireland. In Cheshire (ed.) (1991), pp. 37–50.

Hartford, Beverly, Albert Valdman, and Charles R. Foster. (eds.) *Issues in International Bilingual Education: The Role of the Vernacular.* New York: Plenum.

Hashmi, A. (1989) Prolegomena to the study of Pakistani English and Pakistani literature in English. Paper presented at the International Conference on English in South Asia, Islamabad, 4–9 January 1989.

Haugen, Einar (1950) Problems of bilingualism. *Lingua* 2.3: 271–290.

(1985) The language of imperialism: Unity or pluralism? In Wolfson and Manes (1985: 3–17).

Hock, Hans Henrich (1986) *Principles of Historical Linguistics.* Berlin: Mouton de Gruyter.

Hockett, Charles (1958) *A Course in Modern Linguistics.* New York: Macmillan.

Hogg, R. (ed.) (1992) The Cambridge History of the English Language. *Vol. 1.* The Beginnings to 1066. Cambridge: Cambridge University Press.

Home, D. (1995) Foreword: Making English Australian. *The Macquarie Dictionary,* 2nd ed. Sydney, Australia: The Macquarie Library.

Select Bibliography 279

Honey, J. (1991) The concept 'standard English' in first and second language contexts. In Tickoo (ed.) (1991), pp. 23–32.

Hosali, P. and Jean Aitchison (1986) Butler English: A minimal pidgin? *Journal of Pidgin and Creole Linguistics* 1.1: 51–79.

Howatt, A. P. R. (1984) *A History of English Language Teaching*. Oxford: Oxford University Press.

Hudson, R. A. (1980) *Sociolinguistics*. Cambridge: Cambridge University Press.

Hughes, Robert (1993) *Culture of Complaint: The Fraying of America*. New York and Oxford: Oxford University Press.

Huntington, Samuel P. (1996a) *The Clash of Civilizations and the Remaking of World Order*. New York: Simon & Schuster.

(1996b) The West unique: Not universal. *Foreign Affairs* (Nov.-Dec.) 75.6: 28–46.

Hvalkof, Foren and Peter Aaby (1981) "Is God American: An Anthropological Perspective on the Missionary Work of the Summer Institute of Linguistics." (Denmark: International Work Group for Indigenous Affairs [IWGIA]).

Hymes, Dell (1974) *Foundations in Sociolinguistics: An Ethnographic Approach*. Philadelphia: University of Pennsylvania Press.

(1981) Foreward. In Charles A. Ferguson and Shirley Brice Heath (eds.) *Language in the USA*. Cambridge: Cambridge University Press, pp. v–ix.

(1992) The Concept of Communicative Competence Revisited. In Pütz, Martin (ed.) *Thirty Years of Linguistic Evolution: Studies in Honour of Rene Dirven on the Occasion of His Sixtieth Birthday*. Amsterdam: John Benjamins, pp. 31–57

Hymes, Dell, Vera P. John, and Cazden. eds. (1985 [1972]) *Functions of Language in the Classroom*. (Prospect Heights, IL: Waveland Press).

Ituen, Stephen A. U. (1980) *Special Needs and Expectations for the Teaching of International Languages: A Case Study of French in Nigeria and English in Ivory Coast*. Ph.D. dissertation, University of Toronto.

Iyengar, K. R. Srinivasa (1962 [1985]) *Indian Writing in English*. New Delhi: Sterling.

Jernudd, Bjorn H. (1981) Planning language treatment: Linguistics for the third world. *Language in Society* 10: 43–52.

John, K. K. (n.d.) *The Only Solution to India's Language Problem*. Madras: Published by the author.

Joseph, John E. and Talbot J. Taylor (eds.) (1990) *Ideologies of Language*. London/ New York: Routledge.

Jussawalla, Feroza and Reed Way Dasenbrock (eds.) (1992) *Interviews with Writers of the Post- colonial World*. Jackson: University Press of Mississippi.

Kachru, Braj B. (1965) The *Indianness* in Indian English. *Word* 21: 391–410.

(1976) Models of English for the third world: White man's linguistic burden or language pragmatics? *TESOL Quarterly* 10: 221–239.

(1977) The new Englishes and old models. *English Language Forum* (July) 15.3: 29–35.

(1979) The Englishization of Hindi: Language rivalry and language change. In Irmengard Rauch and Gerald F. Carr (eds.) *Linguistic Method: Essays in Honor of Herbert Penzl*. The Hague: Mouton, pp. 199–211.

280 Select Bibliography

(1980) The new Englishes and old dictionaries: directions in lexicographical research on non-native varieties of English. In L. Zgusta (ed.) (1980), pp. 71–104.

(1981a) American English and other Englishes. In Ferguson and Heath (1981), pp. 21–43; also in Kachru 1986a (*Alchemy*) (1990), pp. 127–146.)

(1981b) *Kashmiri Literature*. Wiesbaden: Otto Harrassowitz.

(1981c) The pragmatics of non-native varieties in English. In L. Smith (1981), pp. 15–39.

(1981d) Socially realistic linguistics: The Firthian tradition. *International Journal of the Sociology of Language* 31: 65–89.

(1982a) The bilinguals' linguistic repertoire. In Hartford, Valdman, and Foster (1982), pp. 25–52.

(1982b) Meaning in deviation: toward understanding non-native English texts. In B. Kachru (1982d), pp. 325–350.

(1982c) Models for non-native Englishes. In B. Kachru (1982d), pp. 31–57.

(ed.) (1982d) *The Other Tongue: English across Cultures*, 1st ed. Urbana: University of Illinois Press.

(1983a) The bilinguals' creativity: Discoursal and stylistic strategies in contact literatures in English. *Studies in the Linguistic Sciences* 13.2: 37–55. Also in Kachru (1986a), pp. 159–173.

(1983b) *The Indianization of English: The English Language in India*. New Delhi: Oxford University Press.

(1983c). Normes regionales de l'anglais. In Bedard and Maurais (eds.) (1983), pp. 707–730.

(1984a) The alchemy of English: social and functional power of non-native varieties. In Kramarae et al. (1984), pp. 176–193.

(1984b) Regional norms for English. In Savignon and Berns (1984), pp. 55–78.

(1985a) ESP and non-native varieties of English: Toward a shift in paradigm. Paper presented at the International Conference on English for Specific Purposes, Sri Lanka, 1–5 April 1985.

(1985b) Standards, codification, and sociolinguistic realism: the English language in the Outer Circle. In Quirk and Widdowson (1985), pp. 11–30.

(1985c) Institutionalized second language varieties. In Greenbaum (ed.) (1985), pp. 211–226. Revised version in Kachru (1986a), pp. 19–32.

(1986a) *The Alchemy of English: The Spread, Functions and Models of Non- native Englishes*. Oxford: Pergamon Press [Reprinted by Urbana IL: University of Illinois Press, 1990].

(1986b) The bilingual's creativity and contact literatures. In Kachru (1986a), pp. 159–173. (also in *Annual Review of Applied Linguistics* (1985) New York: Cambridge University Press, pp. 20–33.

(1986c) ESP and non-native varieties of English: Toward a shift in paradigm. *Studies in the Linguistics Sciences* 16.1: 13–34

(1986d) The power and politics of English. *World Englishes* 5.2–3: 121–140.

(1986e). Non-native literatures in English as a resource for language teaching. In Brumfit and Carter (eds.) (1986), pp. 140–149.

Select Bibliography

(1986f) Review of *A bibliography of writings on varieties of English* by W. Viereck et. al. *English World-Wide* 6.2: 132–135.

(1987a) The bilingual's creativity: Discoursal and stylisitic strategies in contact literature. In L. E. Smith (1987), pp. 125–140.

(1987b) The past and prejudice: Toward de-mythologizing the English canon. In Ross Steele and Terry Threadgold (eds.) *Language Topics: Papers in Honor of M A. K. Halliday*. Amsterdam: John Benjamins.

(1988a) ESP and non-native varieties of English: Toward a shift in paradigm. In D. Chamberlain and R. J. Baumgardner (eds.) *ESP* in the Classroom: Practice and Evaluation. London: Macmillan, pp. 9–28.

(1988b) The spread of English and sacred linguistic cows. In Peter H. Lowenberg (ed.), *Language Spread and Language Policy: Issues, Implications and Case Studies*. Georgetown University Round Table on Language and Linguistics, 1987. Washington, DC: Georgetown University Press, pp. 207–228.

(1988c) Toward expanding the English canon: Raja Rao's Credo for Creativity. *World Literatures Today* (October) IV.4: pp. 3–8.

(1989a) Indian English. Unpublished seminar. July.

(1989b) World Englishes and applied linguistics. *Studies in the Linguistic Sciences* 19.1: 127–152.

(1990a) World Englishes and applied linguistics. In M. A. K. Halliday, John Gibbons and Howard Nicholas (eds.) *Learning, Keeping and Using Language.*. Amsterdam and Philadephia: John Benjamins, Vol II; *World Englishes* 9.1: 3–20

(1990b) Cultural contact and literary creativity in a multilingual society. In J. Toyama and N. Ochner (eds.) *Literary Relations East and West*. Honolulu: University of Hawaii Press, pp. 194–203.

(1991) Liberation linguistics and the Quirk concern. *English Today* 7.1: 3–13. Also in Tickoo 1991.

(1992a) Cultural contact and literary creativity in a multilingual society. In Edward C. Dimock Jr., Braj B. Kachru, and Bh. Krishnamurti (eds.) *Dimensions of Sociolinguistics in South Asia: Papers in Memory of Gerald Kelley*. New Delhi: Oxford & IBH, pp. 149–159.

(1992b) Meaning in deviation: Toward understanding non-native English texts. In B. Kachru (1992d), pp. 301–326.

(1992c) Models for non-native Englishes. In B. Kachru (1992d), pp. 48–74.

(ed.) (1992d) *The Other Tongue: English across Cultures*, 2nd ed. Urbana: University of Illinois Press.

(1992e) The second diaspora of English. In Machan and Scott (1992), pp. 230–252.

(1993) The Empire Talks Back: Review of *Interviews with Writers of the Post-Colonial World*, edited by F. Jussawalla and R. W. Dasenbrock. *World Englishes* 13.3: 393–400.

(1994a) English in South Asia. In Burchfield (1994), pp. 497–553.

(1994b) Englishization and contact linguistics. *World Englishes* 13.2: 135–154.

(1994c) Speech community. In *The Encyclopedia of Language and Linguistics*. Oxford: Pergamon Press and Aberdeen University Press, pp. 4176–4178.

282   Select Bibliography

(1994d) World Englishes: Approaches, issues and resources. In H. Douglas Brown and Susan T. Gonzo (eds.) *Readings on Second Language Acquisition.*. New York: Prencice-Hall. (an earlier version in *Language Teaching: The International Abstracting Journal of Language Teachers and Applied Linguistics.* January 1992. Cambridge: Cambridge University Press, pp. 1–14.

(1994e) The speaking tree: A medium of plural canons. In James Alatis (ed.), *Educational linguistics, cross-cultural communication, and global independence* (Georgetown Round Table on Language and Linguistics, 1994). Washington, DC: Georgetown University Press, pp. 6–22..

(1995b) Transcultural creativity in world Englishes and literary canons. In Barbara Seidlhofer and Guy Cook (eds.) *Principle and Practice in Applied Linguistics: In Honour of Henry Widdowson.* Oxford: Oxford University Press, pp. 271–287.

(1995c) Teaching world Englishes without myths. In S. K. Gill et al. (eds.), *INTELEC '94: International English Language Education Conference, National and International Challenges and Responses.* Bangi, Malaysia: Pusat Bahasa Universiti Kebangsaan, pp. 1–19.

(1996a) English as lingua franca. In H. Goehl, P. H. Nelde, I. Stary, and W. Wolck (eds.) *Contact Linguistics: An International Handbook of Contemporary Research.* Berlin and New York: Walter de Gruyter, pp. 906–913.

(1996b) The paradigms of marginality. *World Englishes* 15.3: 241–255.

(1996c) South Asian English: Toward an identity in diaspora. In Baumgardner (1996), pp. 9–28.

(1996d) World Englishes: Agony and ecstasy. *Journal of Aesthetic Education* 30.2: 135–155.

(1997a) Past imperfect: The other side of English in Asia. In Smith and Forman (1997), pp. 68–89.

(1997b) World Englishes 2000: Resources for research and teaching. In Smith and Forman (1997), pp. 209–251.

(1997c) World Englishes and English-using communities. *Annual Review of Applied Linguistics* 17.

(1997e) English as an Asian language. In Bautista (1997).

(1997f) Caliban's creative chaos 75th anniversary Jubilee lecture, College of Liberal Arts and Sciences, University of Illinois, May 1, 1997

(1998a) World Englishes 2000: Resources for research and teaching. In Larry E. Smith and Michael L. Forman (eds.) (1997), pp. 209–251.

(1998b) English as an Asian language. *Links & Letters* 5. pp. 89–198.

(1998c) Raja Rao: Madhyama and mantra. In Hardgrave, Jr. (ed.) (1998), pp. 60–87.

Kachru, Braj B. and Henry Kahane (eds.) (1995) *Cultures, Ideologies, and the Dictionary: Studies in Honor of Ladislav Zgusta.* Tübingen: Max Niemeyer.

Kachru, Braj B. and Cecil Nelson, (1996) World Englishes. In S. L. McKay and N. H. Hornberger (eds.) *Sociolinguistics in Language Teaching.* Cambridge: Cambridge University Press, pp. 71–102.

Select Bibliography 283

Kachru, Braj B. and Randolph Quirk (1981) Introduction. In Larry E. Smith (ed.) (1981), pp. xiii–xx.

Kachru, Braj B. and Larry E. Smith (eds.) (1986) *The power of English: Cross-cultural dimensions of literature and media. Special issue of* World Englishes 5: 2–3.

(1988) World Englishes: An integrative and cross-cultural journal of WE-ness. In *Robert Maxwell and Pergamon Press: 40 Year's Service to Science, Technology and Education.* Oxford: Pergamon Press, pp. 674–78.

Kachru, Yamuna (1983) Cross-cultural texts and interpretation. *Studies in the Linguistic Sciences* 13.2: 57–72.

(1985a) Discourse analysis, non-native Englishes and second language acquisition research. *World Englishes* 4.2: 223–232.

(1985b) Discourse strategies, pragmatics and ESL: Where are we going? *RELC Journal* 16.2: 1–30.

(1985c) Applied linguistics and foreign language teaching: A non Western perspective. *ERIC Document* ED 256175.

(1987) Cross-cultural texts, discourse strategies and discourse interpretation. In L. Smith (1987), pp. 87–100.

(1989) Modernization of Indian languages: English in unplanned corpus planning. Paper presented at the 1989 Mid-America Linguistics Conference, University of North Iowa. October 6–7.

(1991a) Culture, style and discourse: Expanding noetics of English. *South Asian Language Review* 1.2: 11–25.

(1991b) Speech acts in World Englishes: Toward a framework for research. *World Englishes* 10.3: 299–306.

(ed.) (1991c) Symposium on speech acts in world Englishes. *World Englishes* 10.3: 295–340.

(1993a) Review of *Rediscovering Interlanguage. World Englishes* 12.2. 265–268.

(1993b) Social meaning and creativity in Indian English speech acts. In James E. Alatis (ed.) *Language, Communication, and Social Meaning* (Georgetown Round Table on Languages and Linguistics 1992). Washington, DC: Georgetown University Press, pp. 378–387.

(1994a) Monolingual bias in second language acquisition research. *TESOL Quarterly* 28.4: 795–800.

(1994b) World Englishes and ESL textbooks: Issues of cultural awareness. Paper presented at the annual meeting of American Association of Applied Linguistics, Baltimore, MD, March 7.

(1995a) Contrastive rhetoric and world Englishes. *English Today* 11.1: 21–31.

(1995b) Cultural meaning and rhetorical styles: Toward a framework for contrastive rhetoric. In Barbara Seidlhofer and Guy Cook (eds.) *Principles and Practice in Applied Linguistics: Studies in Honor of H. G. Widdowson.* London: Oxford University Press.

(1996) Culture, variation, and languages of wider communication: The paradigm gap. In James Alatis et al. (eds.) *Linguistics, Language Acquisition, and Language Variation: Current Trends and Future Prospects* (Georgetown Round Table on

284 Select Bibliography

Languages and Linguistics 1996). Washington, DC: Georgetown University Press. 178–195.

(1997) Culture and argumentative writing in world Englishes. In L. Smith and L. Forman (eds.) (1997).

Kachru, Yamuna and Tej K. Bhatia (1978) The emerging "dialect" conflict in Hindi: A case of glottopolitics. In Aspects of sociolinguistics in South Asia. Special issue of *International Journal of the Sociology of Language* 16. Edited by Braj B. Kachru and S. N. Sridhar.

Kahane, Henry and Renee Kahane (1979) Decline and survival of western prestige languages. *Language* 55: 183–198.

(1986) A typology of the prestige language. *Language* 62.3: 495–508.

Kamwangamalu, Nkonko (1989a) Code-Mixing across Languages: Structure, Function, and Constraints. Ph.D. dissertation, University of Illinois, Urbana.

(1989b) Code-mixing and modernization. *World Englishes* 8.3: 321–332.

(1989c). A selected bibliography of studies on code-mixing and code- switching (1970–1988). *World Englishes* 8.3: 433–440.

Kandiah, Thiru (1971) New Ceylon English (Review article). *New Ceylon Writing* 90–94.

(1981) Lankan English schizoglossia. *English World-Wide: A Journal of Varieties of English* 2.1: 63–81.

(1991) South Asia. In Cheshire (ed.) (1991), pp. 271–287.

(1993) New varieties of English: The creation of the paradigm and Its radicalization. Sections V.2–V, *Navasilu* 11 and 12: 153–163.

(1995) Foreword: Centering the periphery of English: Towards participatory communities of discourse. In *De-Hegemonizing language standards*. by A. Parakrama. London: MacMillan 1995, pp. xv–xxxvii.

Kaplan, Robert (1980) *On the Scope of Applied Linguistics*. Rowley, MA: Newbury House.

(ed.) (1982) *Annual Review of Applied Linguistics 1981*. Rowley, MA: Newbury House.

Kaul, Jai Lal (1945) *Kashmiri Lyrics*. Srinagar: Rinemisary.

Kennedy, Graeme (1985) Comment. In Quirk and Widdowson (1985), pp. 7–8.

Kermode, Frank (1979) Institutional control of interpretation. *Salmagundi* 43: 72–86.

King, Bruce A. (ed.) (1974) *Literatures of the World in English*. London: Routledge and Kegan Paul.

(1980) *The New English Literatures: Cultural Nationalism in the Changing World*. New York: St. Martin Press.

Kramarae, Cheris, Muriel Schulz, and William M. O'Barr (eds.) (1984) *Language and Power*. Berverly Hills, CA: Sage.

Krishnamurti, Bh. (1978) Language planning and development: The case of Telugu. *Contributions to Asian Studies* 2: 37–56.

Krishnamurti, Bh. and Aditi Mukherjee (eds.) (1984) *Modernization of Indian Language in News Media*. Osmania University Publications in Linguistics, 2. Hyderabad, India: Department of Linguistics, Osmania University.

Kristeva, Julia (1969) *Semiotike*. Paris: Sevil.

Select Bibliography 285

Kroch, Anthony and William Labov. (1972) Linguistic Society of America: Resolution in response to Arthur Jensens (1969). *Linguistic Society of America Bulletin* (March).

Kujore, Obafemi (1985) *English Usage: Some Notable Nigerian Variations*. Ibadan: Evans Brothers.

Kunnan, Antony J. (1990) Applied Linguistics: Autonomous and interdisciplinary. *Issues in Applied Linguistics* 1.2: 142–148

Labov, William (1970) The study oflanguage in its social context. *Studium Generale* 23: 30–87.

   (1972a) *Language in the Inner City: Studies in the Black English Vernacular*. Philadelphia: University of Pennsylvania Press.

   (1972b) *Sociolinguistic Patterns*. Philadelphia: University of Philadelphia Press.

   (1988) Judicial testing of linguistic theory. In D. Tannen (ed.) *Linguistics in Context: Connecting Observation and Understanding*. Norwood, NJ: Ablex, pp. 159–182.

Lakoff, Robin (1972) Language in context. *Language* 48: 907–927.

   (1975) Linguistic theory and the real world. *Language Learning* 25.2: 309–338.

Lal, P. (1969) *Modern Indian Poetry in English: An Anthology and a Credo*. Calcutta: Writer's Workshop.

Langeland, Agnes Scott (1996) Rushdie's language: An analysis of how Salman Rushdie destabilizes the Western bias in English. *English Today* 12.1: 16–22.

Lannoy, Richard (1971) *The Speaking Tree: A Study of Indian Culture and Society*. New York: Oxford University Press.

Leech, Geoffrey N. (1966) *English in Advertising*. London: Longman.

Lefevere, Andre (1990) Translation: Its geneology in the West. In Susan Bassnett and Andre Lefevere (eds.),*Translation: History and Culture*. London and New York: Pinter.

Lehiste, Ilse (1988) *Lectures on Language Contact*. Cambridge, MA: MIT Press.

Leibowitz, Arnold H. (1969) English Literacy: Legal Sanction for Discrimination. *Notre Dame Lawyer Press* 5.7: 7–67.

Leibowitz, Arnold H. (1976) Language and the law: The exercise of political power through official designation oflanguage. In O'Barr and O'Barr (1976), pp. 449–466.

Le Page, Robert. 1968. Problems of descriptions of multilingual communities. *Transactions of the Philological Society* 67: 189–212.

   (1978) *Projection, Focussing, Diffusion: Or, Steps towards a Sociolinguistic Theory of Language, Illustrated from the Sociolinguistic Survey of Multilingual Communities. Stages I. Cayo District, Belize (Formerly British Honduras) and II. St. Lucia*. (St. Augustine, Trinidad: Society for Caribbean Linguistics).

Levine, Lawrence W. (1996) *The Opening of the American Mind: Canons, Culture, and History*. Boston: Beacon Press.

Lim, Shirley (1993) Gods who fail: Ancestral religions in the new literatures in English from Malaysia/ Singapore. In L. C. Y. Ong and I. K. Ong (eds.) *S. E. Asia Writes Back!*. London: Skoob Books, Vol. 1, pp. 224–237.

286   Select Bibliography

Lowenberg, Peter H. (1984) *English in the Malay Archipelago: Nativization and Its Function in a Sociolinguistic Area*. Ph.D. dissertation, University of Illinois, Urbana.

(1986a) Sociolinguistic context and second-language acquisition; acculturation and creativity in Malaysian English. *World Englishes* 5.l: 71–83.

(1986b). Non-native varieties of English: Nativization, norms, and implications. *Studies in Second Language Acquisition* 8.1: 1–18.

(ed.) (1988) *Language Spread and Language Policy: Issues, Implications, and Case Studies*. GURT 1987. Georgetown University Round Table on Languages and Linguistics: Baltimore, MD (GURT) and Washington DC: Georgetown University Press.

(1991) Variation in Malaysian English: The pragmatics of language in contact. In Cheshire (ed.) (1991), pp. 364–75.

(1992) Testing English as a world language: Issues in assessing non-native proficiency. In B. Kachru (1992d), pp. 108–121.

Lowenberg, Peter H. and S. N. Sridhar (eds.) (1986) World Englishes and Second Language Acquisition Research. Special issue of *World Englishes* 5.l.

Lyons, J. (1978) Foreword. In the British edition of Labov, 1972b. Oxford: Blackwell, pp. xi–xxiii.

Machan, Tim William and Charles T. Scott (eds.) (1992) *English in Its Social Context: Essays in Historical Sociolinguistics*. New York and Oxford: Oxford University Press.

Magura, Benjamin J. (1984) *Style and Meaning in Southern African English: a Sociolinguistic Study*. Ph.D. dissertation, University of Illinois, Urbana.

(1985) Southern African Black English. *World Englishes* 4.2: 251–256.

Maher, Cherissie and Martin Cuffs (1986) Plain English in the United Kingdom. *English Today* 5: 10–12.

Markee, Numa (1990) Applied Linguistics: What's That? in *System* 18.3: 315–323.

Masavisut, N., M. Sukwiwat, and A. Wongmontha (1986) The power of the English language in Thai media, *World Englishes* 5: 197–207.

Masica, Colin P. (1976) *Defining a Linguistic Area: South Asia*. Chicago: University of Chicago Press.

Mathews, M. M. (1931) *The Beginnings of American English: Essays and Comments*. Chicago: University of Chicago Press.

Mazrui, Ali (1967) Language and politics in East Africa. *Africa Report* 12.6: 59–62.

(1973) *The Political Sociology of the English Language: An African Perspective*. The Hague: Mouton.

(1975) *The Political Sociology of the English Language: An African Perspective*. The Hague: Mouton.

McArthur, Tom (1986) The power of words: Pressure, prejudice and politics in our vocabularies and dictionaries. *World Englishes* 5.2–3: 209–219.

(1987) The English languages? *English Today* (July).

Select Bibliography   287

(ed.) (1992) *The Oxford Companion to the English Language*. Oxford: Oxford University Press.

(1993) The English Language or the English Languages? In W. F. Bolton and David Crystal (eds.) *Penguin History of Literature*. Vol. 10. *The English Language*. London: Penguin Books. 323–41.

(1994) Organized Babel: English as a global lingua franca. In James E. Alatis (ed.) Educational Linguistics, Crosscultural Communication, and Global Interdependence, *Georgetown University Round Table on Languages and Linguistics, 1994*. Washington, DC: Georgetown University Press, pp. 233–242

McCormack, William C., and Stephen A. Wurm (eds.) *Language and Society: Anthropological Issues*. The Hague: Mouton.

McCrum, Robert, William Cran, and Robert MacNeil (1986) *The Story of English*. New York: Viking.

McDonald, Marguerite G. (1988) Fossilization and an emerging social dialect. *Lenguas Modernas* 15: 115–124.

McDougal, S. Myres, H. D. Lasswell, and Lung-chu Chen (1976) Freedom from discrimination in choice of language and international human rights. *Southern Illinois University Law Journal* 1: 151–174.

Mencken, H. L. (1919) *The American Language*. New York: Alfred A. Knopf.

Mey, Jacob L. (1985) *Whose Language? A Study in Linguistics Pragmatics*. Amsterdam and Philadelphia: John Benjamins.

Michaels, Leonard and Christopher Ricks (eds.) (1988 [1990]) *The State of the Language*. Berkeley: Univeristy of California Press.

Mufwene, Salikoko S. (1994) New Englishes and criteria for naming them. *World Englishes* 13.1: 21–31.

(guest ed.) (1997) Symposium on English-to-pidgin continua. *Englishes* 16.2.

(2000) Some sociohistorical inferences about the development of African-American English. In Shana Poplack (ed.) *The English History of African American English*. Oxford: Blackwell, pp. 233–263.

(2001) *The Ecology of Language Evolution*. Cambridge: Cambridge University Press.

(2005) *Créoles, écologie sociale, évolution linguistique*. Paris: L'Harmattan.

(2008) *Language Evolution: Contact, Competition and Change*. London: Continuum Press.

(2009) The indigenization of English in North America. In Thomas Hoffmann and Lucia Siebers (eds.) *World Englishes: Problems, Properties, Prospects. Selected Papers from the 13th IAWE Conference*. Amsterdam: Benjamins, pp. 353–368.

(2014) The English origins of African American Vernacular English: What Edgar Schneider has taught us. In Sarah Buschfeld, Magnus Huber, Thomas Hoffmann, and Alexander Kautzsch (eds). *The Evolution of Englishes: Empirical and Theoretical Perspectives on World Englishes*, Amsterdam: John Benjamins, pp. 350–365.

(2015a) The emergence of African American English: Monogenetic or polygenetic? Under how much substrate influence? In Sonja Lanehart (ed.) *The Oxford*

288   Select Bibliography

Handbook of African American Language, Oxford: Oxford University Press, pp. 57–84.

(2015b) Colonization, indigenization, and the differential evolution of English: Some ecological perspectives. *World Englishes* 34: 6–21. (Special issue in memory of Yamuna Kachru, ed. by Larry E. Smith.)

Mukattash, L. (1986) Persistence of fossilization. *IRAL* 24: 187–203.

Mukherjee, Meenakshi (1971) *The Twice-Born Fiction: Themes and Techniques of the Indian Novel in English*. Delhi and London: Heinemann.

Murray, Gilbert (1910) *Medea*. London: George Allen and Unwin.

Nadkami, M. V. (1995) *Bilingualism and syntactic change in Konlwni. Language* 51.3: 672–683.

Naipaul, Vidiadhar S. (1977) *India: A Wounded Civilization*. New York: Vintage.

Narasimhaiah, C. D. (nd.) Indian writing in English: A reply to Dom Moraes. In C. N. Narashimhaiah and C. N. Srinath (eds.) *Indian Literature in English: Contemporary Assessments*. Bangalore: Wiley Eastern (P) (A Dhvanyaloka Publication).

(ed.) (1976) *Commonwealth Literature: a Handbook of Select Reading Lists*. Madras: Oxford University Press.

(ed.) (1978) *Awakened Conscience: Studies in Commonwealth Literature*. Delhi: Sterling.

(1986) The cross-cultural dimensions of English in religion, politics and literature. *World Englishes* 5: 221–230.

(1991) *N for Nobody: Autobiography of an English Teacher*. Delhi: B. R. Publishing Corporation

Narayan, R. K. (1961) *The Man-eater of Malgudi*. New York: Viking.

Nelson, Cecil (1982) Intelligibility and non-native varieties of English. In Braj B. Kachru (1982d), pp. 58–73.

(1984) Intelligibility: The Case of Non-Native Varieties of English. Unpublished Ph. D. dissertation. University of Illinois at Urbana.

(1985 [1992]) My language, your culture: Whose communicative competence? *World Englishes* 4.2: 243–250. Also in B. Kachru (1992d), pp. 327–339.

(1988a) *Why NEs are not LIPOAs ('Interlanguage')*. Paper presented at the Annual TESOL Convention, Chicago.

(1988b) The pragmatic dimension of creativity in the other tongue. *World Englishes* 7.2: 173–181.

(1995) Intelligibility and world Englishes in the classroom. *World Englishes* 14.2: 273–279.

Nesfield, J. C. (1895) English Grammar Series. *Book IV.* Idiom, Grammar and Synthesis for High Schools. Calcutta: Macmillan.

Newbrook, M. (1986) Received Pronunciation in Singapore: A Sacred cow. *Commentary* (National University of Singapore) 7: 20–27. Also in Brown (ed.) (1991).

Newman, Edwin (1974 and 1976) *Edwin Newman on Language: Strictly Speaking and a Civil Tongue*. New York: Warner Books, Inc. [Paperback edition, 1980].

Select Bibliography

Newmeyer, Frederick J. (1983) *Grammatical Theory: Its Limits and Its Possibilities.* Chicago: University of Chicago Press.

Newmeyer, Frederick (1986) *The Politics of Linguistics.* Chicago: The University of Chicago Press.

Ngugi wa Thiong'o (1981) *Writers in Politics.* London: Heinemann.

(1986) *Decolonising the Mind: The Politics of Language in African Literature.* London: James Currey; Portsmouth, NH: Heinemann.

(1991) English: A language for the world? *The Yale Journal of Criticism* 4.2: 283–93.

(1992) *Writers in Politics.* London and Exeter, NH: Heinemann.

Nicholls, Jane (1995) Cultural pluralism and the multicultural curriculum: Ethical issues and English language textbooks in Canada. In Tickoo (ed.) (1995), pp. 112–121.

Nichols, Patricia C. (1984) Networks and hierarchies: language and social stratification. In Kramarae et al. (1984), pp. 23–42.

Nihalani, P. (1991) Co-articulation and social acceptability: Pragmatic implication for world Englishes. *World Englishes* 10.3.

Noss, R. B. (ed.) (1983) *Varieties of English in Southeast Asia.* Singapore: SEAMEO Regional Language Centre.

Nwoye, O. G. (1992) Obituary announcements as communicative events in Nigerian English. *World Englishes* 11.1.

O'Barr, William M. (1976) The study of language and politics. In O'Barr and O'Barr (1976), pp. 1–27.

O'Barr, William M. and Jean F. O'Barr (eds.) (1976) *Language and Politics.* The Hague: Mouton.

Okara, Gabriel (1963) African speech, English words. *Transition* 10 (September): 15–16.

(1964) *The Voice.* London: Heinemann.

Omar, Asmah Haji (1996) Imperial English in Malaysia. In Fishman, Conrad and Rubal-Lopez, (eds.) (1996), pp. 513–533.

Orwell, Sonia and Ian Angus (1968) *The Collected Essays, Journalism and Letters of George Orwell.* London: Secker & Warburg.

Owolabi, Kola (ed.). (1995) *Language in Nigeria: Essays in Honour of Ayo Bamgbose* Ibadan: Group Publishers.

Paikeday, Thomas M. (1985) *The Native Speaker Is Dead!* Toronto: Paikeday Publishing.

Pakir, Anne (1988) Education and Invisible Language Planning: The Case of English in Singapore. Paper presented at the 1988 Regional Seminar on Language Planning in Multilingual Settings: The Role of English. National University of Singapore, Singapore, September 6–8.

(1991a) The status of English and the question of "standard" in Singapore: sociolinguistic perspective. In Tickoo (ed.) (1991), pp. 109–30.

(1991b) The range and depth of English-knowing bilinguals in Singapore *World Englishes* 10.2: 167–79.

ed. (1992) *Words in a Cultural Context.* [Proceedings of the lexicography workshop, September 9–11, 1991]. Singapore: University of Singapore Press.

290   Select Bibliography

Palmer, F. R. (ed.) (1968) *Selected Papers of J. R. Firth*. Bloomington, IN: Indiana University Press.

Pandharipande, Rajeshwari (1987) On nativization of English. *World Englishes* 6.2: 149–5

Pandit, Prabodh. B. (1972) *India as a Sociolinguistic Area*. Poona: Poona University Press.

Panikkar, K. M. (1953 [1961]) *Asia and Western Dominance, A Survey of the Vasco Da Gama Epoch on Asian History, 1498–1945*. London: George Allen & Unwin.

Parakrama, A. (1990) *Language and Rebellion: Discoursive Unities and the Possibilities of Protest*. London: Katha.

(1995) *De-Hegemonizing Language Standards*. London: MacMillan.

Paranjape, Makrand (1993) *Indian Poetry in English*. Madras: Macmillan.

Parthasarathy, R. (1987) Tradition and creativity: Stylistic innovations in Raja Rao. In L. Smith (1987), pp. 157–165.

Pattanayak, D. P. (1985) Diversity in communication and languages: Predicament of a multilingual national state: India, a case study. In Wolfson and Manes (1985), pp. 399–407

Pennycook, Alastair (1994) *The Cultural Politics of English as an International Language*. London: Longman.

Phillipson, Robert (1992) *Linguistic Imperialism*. Oxford: Oxford University Press.

Phillipson, Robert and Tove Skutnabb-Kangas (1986) *Linguicism Rules in Education*. Part 1. Roskilde, Denmark: Roskilde University Center, Institute VI.

Platt, John H. (1977) The sub-varieties of Singapore English: their sociolectal and functional status. In Crewe (ed.) (1977), pp. 83–95.

Platt, John and K. Singh (1985) The use of localized English in Singapore poetry. *English World-Wide* 5.1: 43–54.

Platt, John H. and Heidi Weber (1980) *English in Singapore and Malaysia: Status, Features, Functions*. Kuala Lumpur: Oxford University Press.

Platt, John, Heidi Weber, and M. L. Ho (1984) *The New Englishes*. London: Routledge and Kegan Paul.

Prabhu, N. S. (1989) *The Mathetic Function of English As a World Language. Paper presented at the International Conference on English in South Asia*, Islamabad, Pakistan.

Prator, Clifford (1968) The British heresy in TESL. In Fishman, Ferguson, and Das Gupta. (1968), pp. 459–476.

Pride, John B. (1979) A transitional view of speech functions and code-switching. In McCormack and Wurm (1979).

(1981) Native competence and the bilingual/multilingual speaker. *English World-Wide* 2.2: 141–53.

(ed.) (1982) *New Englishes*. Rowley, MA: Newbury House.

Pütz, Martin (ed.) (1995) *Discrimination through Language in Africa? Perspectives on the Namibian Experience*. Berlin and New York: Mouton de Gruyter.

Select Bibliography 291

Quirk, Randolph (1985) The English language in a global context. In R. Quirk and H. G. Widdowson (eds.) *English in the World: Teaching and Learning the Language and Literatures*. Cambridge: Cambridge University Press, pp. 1–6.

(1986) *Words at work: Lectures on textual structure*. Kent Ridge, Singapore: Singapore University Press, National University of Singapore.

(1988) The question of standards in the international use of English. In Lowenberg (1988), pp. 229–241.

(1989) Language varieties and standard language. *JALT Journal* 11.1: 14–25.

Quirk, Randolph, Sidney Greenbaum, Geoffrey Leech, and Jan Svartvik. (1972) *A Grammar of Contemporary English*. New York: Seminar.

(1985) *A Comprehensive Grammar of the English Language*. London: Longman.

Quirk, Randolph and Henry Widdowson (eds.) (1985) *English in the World. Teaching and Learning the Language and Literatures*. London, Cambridge and New York: Cambridge University Press.

Rajan, R. ed. (1992) *The lie of the land: English literary Studies in India*. Delhi: Oxford University Press.

Ram, T. (1983) *Trading in Language: The Story of English in India*. Delhi: GDK.

(1991) English in imperial expansion. In Gupta, R. S. and Kapoor, K. (eds.) *English in India: Issues and problems* Delhi: Academic Foundation, pp. 28–57.

Ramaiah, L. S. and N. S. Prabhu (1985) *Communicative language teaching: A bibliographical survey of resources*. Gurgaon: Indian Documentation Service.

Ramanujan, A. K. (ed.) (1991) *Folktales from India: A Selection of Oral Tales.from Twenty-two languages*. New York: Pantheon Books.

Rank, Hugh (ed.) (1974) *Language and Public Policy*. Urbana, IL: National Council of Teachers of English.

Rao, Raja (1960) *The Serpent and the Rope*. London: Murray.

(1938 [1963]) *Kanthapura*. London: Allen and Unwin (earlier edition published in 1937).

(1978) The caste of English. In Narasimhaiah (1978), pp. 420–422.

(1988) *The Chessmaster and His Moves*. New Delhi: Vision Books.

Read, Allen Walker (1974) What is 'linguistic imperialism'? *Geolinguistics* 1: 5–10.

Redish, Janice R. (1985) The plain English movement. In Greenbaum (1985), pp. 125–138.

Reich, Peter A. (ed.) (1976) *The Second LACUS Forum*. Columbia, SC: Hornbeam Press.

Richards, Jack. (1979) Rhetorical and communicative styles in the new varieties of English. *Language Learning*. 29.1: 1–25.

(ed.) (1979b). *Error analysis: Perspectives on second language analysis*. London: Longman.

Richards, Jack, John Platt, and Heidi Webber (1985) *Longman dictionary of applied linguistics*. Harlow, UK: Longman.

Rickford, John R. (1987) *Dimensions of a Creole Continuum: History, Texts, and Linguistic Analysis of Guyanese Creole*. Stanford, CA: Stanford University Press.

292   Select Bibliography

Ricks, Christopher and Leonard Michaels (eds.) (1990) *The State of the Language*. Berkeley: University of California Press.

Robinett, Betty Wallace and Jacquelyn Schachter (eds.) (1983) *Second Language Learning: Contrastive Analysis, Error Analysis, and Related Aspects*. Ann Arbor: University of Michigan Press.

Romaine, Suzanne. (1991) The Pacific. In Cheshire (ed.) (1991), pp. 619–36.

(1992) English: From village to global village. In Machan and Scott (1992), pp. 253–260.

Rubin, Joan (1976) Language and politics from a sociolinguistic point of view. In O'Barr and O'Barr (1976), pp. 389–404.

Rushdie, Salman (1989) *The Satanic Verses*. London and New York: Viking.

(1991) Commonwealth literature does not exist. In *Imaginary Homelands. Essays and Criticism*. New York: Viking, pp. 61–70.

(1993) *Midnight's Children*. Delhi: Rupa.

Safire, William (1980) *On Language*. New York: Times Books.

Said, Edward W. (1993) *Culture and Imperialism*. New York: Alfred A. Knopf.

Salisbury, Richard F. (1976) Language and politics of an elite group. The Tolai of New Britain. In O'Barr and O'Barr (1976), pp. 367–385.

Samarin, William, J. (ed.) (1976) *Language in Religious Practice*. Rowley, MA: Newbury House.

Sankoff, Gillian (1976) Political power and linguistic inequality in Papua New Guinea. In O'Barr and O'Barr (1976), pp. 283–310.

Sareen, S. K. (1989) The factor of intertextuality in translation. *International Journal of Translation* (New Delhi) 1.1: 41–48.

Sato, Charlene (1985) Linguistic inequality in Hawaii: The post-creole dilemma. In Wolfson and Manes (1985), pp. 255–272.

Savignon, Sandra. (1983) *Communicative Competence: Theory and Classroom Practice*. Reading, MA: Addison-Wesley.

(1987) Communicative Language Teaching. *Theory into Practice* 26.4: 235–242

Savignon, Sandra and Margie Berns (eds.) (1984) *Initiatives in Communicative Language Teaching: A Book of Readings*. Reading, MA: Addison-Wesley.

Saville-Troike, Muriel. (1982) *The Ethnography of Communication: An Introduction*. London: Basil Blackwell.

Schachter, Jacquelyn (1990) On the issue of completeness in second language acquisition. *Second Language Research* 6: 93–124.

Schmied, Josef (ed.) (1990) *Linguistics in the Service of Africa, with Particular Reference to Research on English and African Languages*. Bayreuth: University of Bayreuth.

Selinker, Larry (1972) Interlanguage. *International Review of Applied Linguistics in Language Teaching* 10: 209–31.

(1972b) Interlanguages. In B. W. Robinett and J. Schachter (eds.) *Second Language Learning, Error Analysis, and Related Aspects*. Ann Arbor: University of Michigan Press, pp. 173–96.

(1992) *Rediscovering Interlanguage*. London: Longman.

(1993) Fossilization as simplification. In Makhan L. Tickoo (eds.) *Simplification: Theory and Application*. Singapore: SEAMEO Regional Language Centre.

Select Bibliography

Seth, Vikram (1993) *A Suitable Boy.* New York: Harper Collins.

Shah, Amritlal B. (1968) *The Great Debate: Language Controversy and University Education.* Bombay: Lalvani.

Sharp, Henry (ed.) (1920) *Selections from Educational Records.* Calcutta: Bureau of Education, Government of India.

Shastri, S. V. (1985) Toward a description of Indian English: A standard corpus in machine- readable form. *English World-Wide* 6.2: 275–278.

Shibles, W. (1995) Received pronounciation and Real phonetic. *World Englishes* 14.31: 357–376.

Shills, Edward (1988) Citizen of the world: Nirad C. Chaudhuri. *The American Scholar.* (Autumn): 549–573.

Sidhu, Charan Dass (1972) *Indian education; a primer for reformers.* (Delhi, National Publishing House).

Singh, A., Verma, R., and Joshi, I. (eds.) (1981) *Indian Literature in English 1927–1979: A Guide to Information Sources.* Detroit: Gale Research.

Singh, Frances B. (1987) Power and politics in the content of grammar books: The example of India. *World Englishes* 6.3: 253–261.

Singh, Rajendra, J. Lele, and G. Martohardjono (1988) Communication in a multilingual society: Some missed opportunities. *Language in Society* 17: 43–60.

Skutnab-Kangas, Tove (1984) *Bilingualism or Not: The Education of Minorities.* Clevedon: Multilingual Matters.

Smith, Anne-Marie (1986) *Papua New Guinea English.* Ph.D. dissertation, University of Papua New Guinea.

Smith, Larry E. (ed.) (1981) *English for Cross-Cultural Communication.* London: Macmillan.

(ed.) (1983) *Readings in English as an International Language.* London: Pergamon.

(ed.) (1987) *Discourse across Cultures: Strategies in World Englishes.* New York: Prentice Hall.

(1992) Spread of English and issues of intelligibility. In B. Kachru (1992d), pp. 75–90.

Smith, Larry E. and Michael L. Forman (eds.) (1997) *World Englishes 2000.* Literary Studies East and West. Honolulu: University of Hawaii Press, Vol. 14.

Smith, Larry E. and Cecil L. Nelson (1985) International intelligibility of English: Directions and resources. *World Englishes* 4.3: 333–42.

Smith, Larry and Sridhar, S. N. (guest eds.) (1992) The Extended Family: English in Global Bilingualism. Special issue of *World Englishes.* 11: 2–3.

Smitherman, Geneva (1984) Black language as power. In Kramarae et al. (1984), pp. 101–115.

Soyinka, Wole ([1988] 1993) Language as boundary. In *Art, Dialogue and Outrage: Essays on Literature and Culture.* New York: Pantheon Books, pp. 82–94.

Spivak, G. (1993) The burden of English. In C. A. Breckenridge and P. Vader Veer (eds.) *Orientalism and the Post Colonial Predicament. Perspectives on South Asia.* Philadelphia: University of Pennsylvania Press, pp. 134157.

Sridhar, Kamal K. (1986) Sociolinguistic theory and non-native varieties of English. *Lingua* 68.1: 39–58.

294   Select Bibliography

(1989) *English in Indian Bilingualism*. Delhi: Manohar.

Sridhar, Kamal K., and S. N. Sridhar (1986[1992]) Bridging the paradigm gap: Second language acquisition theory and indigenized varieties of English. *World Englishes* 5.1: 3–14; also in B. Kachru (1992d), pp. 91–107.

Sridhar, S. N. (1988) Language variation, attitudes, and rivalry: the spread of Hindi in India. In P. Lowenberg (1988).

(1990) What are applied linguistics? *Studies in the Linguistic Sciences* 20.2: 165–176. Also in *International Journal of Applied Linguistics* (1993) 3.1: 3–16.

(1992) The ecology of bilingual competence: Language interaction in indigenized varieties of English. *World Englishes* 11.2/3: 141–50.

(1994) A reality check for SLA theories. *TESOL Quarterly* 28.4.

(1996) Toward a syntax of South Asian English: Defining the lectal range. In Robert J. Baumgardner (ed.) *South Asian English: Structure, Use and Users*. Urbana: University of Illinois Press, pp. 55–69.

Steele, Ross, and Terry Threadgold (eds.) (1987) *Language Topics: Papers in Honor of M A. K. Halliday*. Amsterdam: John Benjamins.

Steiner, George (1975) *Why English? Presidential address delivered in 1975*. London: The English Association.

Stewart, William (1965) Urban Negro speech: Sociolinguistic factors affecting English teaching. In Roger Shuy (ed.). *Social Dialects and Language Learning*, Champaign, IL: The National Council of Teachers of English, pp. 10–18.

Street, Brian V. (1984) *Literacy in Theory and Practice*. Cambridge: Cambridge University Press.

Strevens, Peter (1977) *New Orientations in the Teaching of English*. London: Oxford University Press.

(1980) *Teaching English as an International Language*. Oxford: Pergamon.

(1982) World English and the world's English – or, whose language is it anyway? *Journal of the Royal Society of Arts* (June 1982): 418–428.

(1988) Language learning and language teaching: toward an integrated model. In Tarmen (ed.) (1988), pp. 299–312.

Stubbs, Michael (1986) *Educational Linguistics*. Oxford: Basil Blackwell.

Svartvik, J. ed. (1992) Directions in Corpus Linguistics. Proceedings of Nobel Symposium, 82.

Swales, John (1984) A review of ESP in the Arab world 1977–1983 – trends, developments, and retrenchments. In Swales, John and Mustapha, H. (eds.), *English for Specific Purposes in the Arab World*, 1984. Birmingham: Languages Studies Unit, University of Aston, pp. 9–21.

(1985) ESP – the heart of the matter or the end of the affair? In Quirk and Widdowson (1985), pp. 212–23)

(1990) *Genre Analysis: English in Academic and Research Settings*. Cambridge: Cambridge University Press.

Taiwo, 0. (1976) *Culture and the Nigerian Novel*. New York: St. Martin's Press.

Tambiah, S. J. (1967) The politics of language in India and Ceylon. *Modern Asian Studies* 1: 215–240.

Select Bibliography 295

Tannen, Deborah (ed.), (1988) *Linguistics in Context: Connecting Observation and Understanding Norwood*, Norwood, NJ: Ablex.

Tawake, Sandra (guest ed.) (1995) Symposium on World Englishes in the classroom. *World Englishes* 14.2.

Tay, M. W. J. (1986) Lects and institutionalized varieties of English: The case of Singapore. *Issues and Developments in English and Applied Linguistics* 1: 93–107.

(1991) Southeast Asia and Hong Kong. In Cheshire (ed.) (1991), pp. 319–332.

Tharoor, Shashi (1989) *The Great Indian Novel*. New Delhi: Penguin.

Thumboo, Edwin (1970) Malaysian poetry: Two examples of sensibility and style. In K. L. Goodwin (ed.), *National Identity* (Papers delivered at the Commonwealth Literature Conference, University of Queensland, Brishbane, August 9–15, 1968). London and Melbourne: Heinemann.

(1985a) English literature in a global context. In Quirk and Widdowson (1985), pp. 52–60.

(1985b) Twin perspectives and multi-ecosystems: Tradition for a commonwealth writer. *World Englishes* 4.2: 213–221.

(1988) The literary dimensions of the spread of English: Creativity in the second tongue. In Lowenberg (ed.) (1988). Revised version in Kachru (ed.) (1992), *The Other Tongue*.

(1992) The literary dimension of the spread of English. In B. Kachru (1992d), pp. 255–282.

Tickoo, Makhan L. (1988) In search of appropriateness in EF(S)L teaching meterials. *RELC Journal* (December) 19.2.

(ed.) (1991) *Languages and Standards: Issues, Attitudes, Case Studies*. [Anthology Series 26]. Singapore: SEAMEO Regional Language Centre.

(ed.) (1995) *Language and culture in multilingual societies: Viewpoints and visions*. [Anthropology Series 36]. Singapore: S&AMEO Regional Language Centre.

Tikku, G. L. (1971) *Persian Poetry in Kashmir 1339–1846: An Introduction*. Berkeley: University of California Press.

Tipping, Llewelyn (1933) *Matriculation English Grammar of Modern English Usage*. London, Macmillan.

Todd, L. (1984) *Modem Englishes: Pidgins and Creoles*. Oxford: Blackwell.

Tollefson, J. W. (1991) *Planning Language, Planning Inequality: Language Policy in the Community*. London: Longman.

(ed.) (1995) *Power and Inequality in Language Education*. Cambridge: Cambridge University Press.

Tripathi, P. (1992) The chosen tongue. *English Today* (October 3–11) 32.8.

Tromel-Plotz, Senta (1981) Languages of oppression: Review article. *Journal of Pragmatics* 5: 67–80.

Trudgill, Peter (1976–77) Creolization in reverse: reduction and simplification in the Albanian dialects of Greece. *Transactions of the Philological Society* pp. 32–50.

296　Select Bibliography

(ed.) (1984a) *Language in the British Isles*. (Cambridge and New York: Cambridge University Press).

(ed.) (1984b) *Applied Sociolinguistics*. (Orlando, FL: Academic Press).

(1986) *Dialects in Contact*. Oxford: Blackwell.

Trndgill, Peter and Hannah, J. (1982) *International English: A Guide to Varieties of Standard English*. London: Arnold.

Tsuda, Yukio (1994a) *The Hegemony of English in International Communication*. Paper presented at the annual convention of International Communication Association. Sydney, Australia.

(1994b) The diffusion of English: Its impact on culture and communication. *Keio Communication Review* 16: 49–61.

Valentine, Tamara (1988) Developing discourse types in non-native English: Strategies of gender in Hindi and Indian English. *World Englishes* 7.2: 143–158.

(1991) Getting the message across: Discourse markers in Indian English. *World Englishes* 10.3.

Vavrus, F. (1991) When paradigms clash: The role of institutionalized varieties in language teacher education. *World Englishes* 10.2: 181–195.

Viereck, Wolfgang and Wolf-Dietrich Bald (1986) *English in Contact with Other Languages*. Budapest: Akademiai Kiad6.

Viereck, Wolfgang, Edgar W. Schneider, and Manfred Görlach (1984) *A Bibliography of Writings on Varieties of English. 1965–1983*. Amsterdam: Benjamins.

Walker A. G. H. (1984) Applied sociology of language: Vernacular language and education. In Peter Trudgill's *Applied Sociolinguistics*. New York: Academic Press, pp. 159–202.

Ward, Ida C. (1929) *The Phonetics of English*. Cambridge: Heffer.

Wells, J. (1982) *Accents of English* (3 vols.). Cambridge: Cambridge University Press.

Widdowson, Henry (1971) The teaching of rhetoric to students of science and technology. *CILT Reports and Papers* 7: 31–41.

(1979) Pidgin and babu. In Henry Widdowson (ed.) *Explorations in Applied Linguistics*. Oxford: Oxford University Press.

(1983) *Learning Purpose and Language Use*. Oxford: Oxford University Press.

(1994) The Ownership of English. *TESOL Quarterly* 26.2: 337–389.

Wijesinha, Rajiva (ed.) (1988) *An Anthology of Contemporary Sri Lankan Poetry in English*. Colombo: The British Council and English Association of Sri Lanka.

Williams, Frederick (1970) *Language and Poverty*. Chicago: Markham.

Williams, Jessica (1987) Non-native varieties of English: A special case of language acquisition. *English World-Wide* 8: 161–199.

(1989) Language acquisition, language contact and nativized varieties of English. *RELC Journal* (June 1989) 20.1: 39–67.

Winford, Donald. (1988) The creole continuum and the notion of the community as locus of language. *International Journal of Social Language* 71: 91–105.

(1991) The Caribbean. In Cheshire (ed.) (1991), pp. 565–584.

Select Bibliography 297

Wolfson, Nessa and Joan Manes (eds.) (1985) *Language of Inequality*. The Hague: Mouton.

Wren, P. C. and H. Martin (1954) *High School English Grammar and Composition*, rev. ed. New Delhi: S. Chand.

Yule, Henry and A. C. Burnell (1886) *Hobson-Jobson: A Glossary of Colloquial Anglo-Indian Words and Phrases and of Kindred Terms, Etymological, Historical, Geographical, and Discursive*. London: J. Murry.

Yunick, Stanley (1997) Genre, registers and sociolinguistics. *World Englishes* 16.3: 321–336.

Zabus, Chantal (1995) Relexification. In Ashcraft, Griffiths, and Tiffin (1995), pp. 314–318.

Zell, Hans M. and Helene Silver (eds.) (1971) *A Reader's Guide to African Literature*. New York: Africana Publishing Corporation, pp. 20–59.

Zentella, Ana Celia (1981) Language variety among Puerto Ricans. In Ferguson and Heath (1981), pp. 218–238.

Zgusta, Ladislav ed. (1980) *Theory and Method in Lexicography: Western and Non-Western Perspectives*. Columbia, SC: Hornbeam Press

Zhao, Y. and Campbell, K. (1995) English in China. *World Englishes* 14.3: 377–390.

Zimmer, Heinrich R. (1972) *Myths and symbols in Indian art and civilization*. Princeton, NJ: Princeton University Press,

Zuengler, Jane (1989) Identity and interlanguage development and use. *Applied Linguistics* 10: 80–96.

Author Index

Aaby, Peter, 207, 216–218
Achebe, Chinua, 13–16, 31, 33–34, 54, 58, 60, 75, 97, 112, 114, 142, 160–161, 196, 215, 254
Alatis, James E., 85, 109, 166
Algeo, J., 249
Angus, Ian, 86–87

Bailey, Richard W., 24, 28, 41, 49, 51–53, 57–58, 62, 99, 110, 152, 174–176, 178–179, 190, 233, 244, 255, 264, 266
Bald, Wolf-Dietrich, 5, 257
Bamgbose, Ayo, 68, 136, 173, 246
Baron, Dennis, 72, 74, 77
Baugh, John, 219–220
Bautista, Maria L. S., 46, 54
Bell, A., 192, 266
Berns, Margie, 12, 48, 136, 156, 199, 214, 247, 251, 264
Bhabha, Homi K., 130
Bhatia, Tej K., 39–40, 90, 247, 256–257
Bhatia, Vijay K., 235, 247
Bhatt, Rakesh, 116, 256
Bickerton, Derek, x, 246
Bokamba, Eyamba G., 5, 28, 265–266
Bolinger, Dwight L., 85–86, 103, 187–188, 191, 203, 207, 215
Brumfit, Christopher, 19, 102, 214, 247, 264
Butler, Susan, 11, 46, 54, 261, 268

Chaudenson, Robert, x
Cheshire, Jenny, 5, 28, 46, 227, 244, 266–267
Chishimba, Maurice M., 33, 68, 74, 95, 155, 160, 257, 266
Chomsky, Noam, 11, 70, 157, 169–170, 209
Clyne, Michael, 3, 168
Crystal, David, 7, 12, 23, 45, 64, 96, 115–116, 121, 127, 141, 149, 157–158, 177, 185, 192, 244, 246, 248–249, 266–267

Das Gupta, J., 86, 262
Dasenbrock, Reed Way, 13, 15, 263–264

Davies, Allan, 11, 169
Day, Richard R., 58, 81, 99, 103, 116, 145
DeCamp, David, x
Desai, Anita, 14–15, 58, 112, 116–117
Desani, G. V, 31, 111, 131
Di Pietro, Robert J., 85
Dittmar, Norbert, 90–91
D'Souza, Dinesh, 48, 113
D'souza, Jean, 29, 116, 159, 247

Edelman, Murray, 85, 90–91

Fairclough, Norman, 9, 213, 233
Ferguson, Charles A., 11, 29, 78, 158–159, 171, 187, 211–212, 251, 265
Fernandez-Armesto, Felipe, 51, 61
Finegan, Edward, 74, 87, 252
Firth, John R., 70, 91–92, 136, 146, 202, 209–210, 212, 246, 251
Fishman, Joshua A., 26, 46, 54, 61, 85, 90, 96, 152, 201, 246, 266
Foley, Joseph, 28, 266
Forster, Leonard, 63, 115, 127–128
Foucault, Michel, 17–18, 92–93, 102–104, 168, 226

Gates, Jr., Henry Louis, 47–48, 61, 113, 118, 227, 261
Geertz, Clifford, 65, 236
Görlach, Manfred, 28, 57, 99, 152, 190, 244, 248–249, 255, 264, 266
Graddol, David, 54
Greenbaum, Sidney, 87, 137, 186, 248, 252, 267–268
Gupta, Anthea F., 86, 90, 223, 262

Halliday, Michael A. K., 16, 91–92, 119, 136, 153, 157, 176, 187, 202, 209–210, 212, 247
Harris, J, 266
Haugen, Einar, 64, 99, 181
Hock, Hans Henrich, 141, 159, 201, 214
Hockett, Charles, 214

Author Index

Holmes, Janet, 266
Honey, J., 110, 252
Hudson, R. A., 11, 156, 251
Huntington, Samuel P., 49–52
Hvalkof, Foren, 207, 216–218
Hymes, Dell, 9, 92, 119, 168, 202, 208–209, 211, 237, 247

Iyengar, K. R. Srinivasa, 36–37

Jernudd, Bjorn H., 214
Jussawalla, Feroza, 13, 15, 263–264

Kachru, Braj B., ix-xv, 3, 7, 9, 11, 15, 19–21, 25–26, 28–29, 32–33, 39–40, 42, 45–48, 51–52, 56–57, 59, 62–63, 65, 68, 71–72, 74–75, 77, 79, 83, 89, 91–92, 99, 105, 110–112, 114, 119, 122, 124–125, 132, 135–136, 138–140, 142, 144, 146, 148, 152–157, 160, 162, 164, 166–167, 169, 172–173, 177, 179, 186–187, 190–192, 194, 199, 201, 209, 212–214, 223, 225, 227, 229–230, 233, 241–242, 244–267
Kachru, Yamuna, 15, 43, 74, 90, 111–112, 124, 132, 135, 144, 160, 166, 170, 173, 178, 229, 231, 247, 250, 253, 255–256, 258, 260
Kahane, Henry, 21–22, 29, 99, 230, 257
Kahane, Renee, 21, 29, 257
Kamwangamalu, Nkonko, 39, 247, 256
Kandiah, Thiru, 36, 252, 258, 266
Kaplan, Robert, 90, 206, 210–211
Kennedy, Graeme, 140–141, 177
Kermode, Frank, 47, 113
Kramarae, Cheris, 86–87, 90, 259
Krishnamurti, Bh., 92
Kroch, Anthony, 219

Labov, William, 90, 92, 99, 136, 187–188, 202, 209–210, 219, 246–247
Lakoff, Robin, 188, 199, 208–209
Lannoy, Richard, 45, 109
Lefevere, Andre, 63, 117–118, 129, 131
Leibowitz, Arnold H., 85, 91, 99
Le Page, Robert, 156, 251
Lim, Shirley, 16, 34, 144, 195, 217, 228, 254, 260
Lowenberg, Peter H., 12, 68, 74, 148, 153–155, 166, 170, 172, 179, 187, 191, 242, 247, 251, 255, 258, 266–267
Lyons, J., 197–198, 246

Magura, Benjamin J., 74, 155, 247, 257
Manes, Joan, 87, 207
Markee, Numa, 208, 210–211

Mazrui, Ali, 13, 85, 94–95, 154, 251, 259
McArthur, Tom, 5, 11, 32, 99, 110, 166, 177, 187, 244, 247–249, 259, 266–267
McCrum, Robert, 26, 248, 266
McDougal, S. Myres, 91, 101
Mencken, H. L., 24, 119
Mey, Jacob L., 217
Mufwene, Salikoko S., x, xii-xv, 26, 246, 249
Mukherjee, Aditi, 92
Murray, Gilbert, 129

Naipaul, Vidiadhar S., 112
Narasimhaiah, C. D., 51, 80, 94, 144
Narayan, R. K., 16, 30, 58, 75, 112, 116, 149
Nelson, Cecil, 3, 12, 16, 35, 43, 60, 72, 123, 166, 169, 247–249, 253, 258, 267–268
Newmeyer, Frederick J., 209, 211, 216, 218
Ngugi, wa Thiong'o, 12–13, 36, 58, 60, 114, 120, 142, 148, 161, 213, 224, 251, 259, 263
Nichols, Patricia C., 91, 100

O'Barr, William M., 85, 90–91, 259
Okara, Gabriel, 31, 60, 75, 112
Orwell, George, 86–87
Orwell, Sonia, 86–87
Owolabi, Kola, 173

Paikeday, Thomas M., 9, 11, 28, 64, 115, 148, 157–158, 192, 251
Pakir, Anne, 54, 109, 135, 144, 246–247
Pandharipande, Rajeshwari, 254
Pandit, Prabodh. B., 89, 126
Parakrama, A., 252, 258–259, 262
Paranjape, Makrand, 127–128
Pennycook, Alastair, 179, 207, 251, 259, 261–262, 264
Phillipson, Robert, 9, 12, 19, 99, 101, 114, 135–136, 156, 179, 207–208, 212–213, 233, 250–251, 259, 261, 264
Platt, John H., 28, 68, 152, 190, 246, 255, 266
Prabhu, N. S., 176–179, 199, 233
Prator, Clifford, 140–141, 157, 172, 177, 189, 252, 259
Pride, John B., 91, 157, 186, 190, 251, 255, 266
Putz, Martin, 46

Author Index

Quirk, Randolph, 12, 18–19, 28, 32, 42, 68, 71, 87, 95, 110, 135–141, 143, 145–149, 151–153, 155, 157, 159–161, 163–164, 175–179, 187, 189–191, 201–202, 213–214, 232–233, 242–243, 245, 252, 258–259, 266–267

Ramaiah, L. S., 199, 247
Ramanujan, A. K., 128, 180
Rao, Raja, 14–16, 30–31, 33–34, 37, 58–59, 75, 111–112, 114, 116–117, 128–129, 142, 148, 160, 224, 228, 254, 263
Richards, Jack, 191, 247, 256
Rickford, John R., x
Robinett, Betty Wallace, 191
Romaine, Suzanne, 55, 259, 266
Rushdie, Salman, 14–15, 20, 46–47, 57, 75, 118–119, 130, 148, 254

Safire, William, 72
Said, Edward W., 113
Samarin, William, J., 85
Sankoff, Gillian, 85
Sato, Charlene, 99
Savignon, Sandra, 198, 247
Saville-Troike, Muriel, 247
Schachter, Jacquelyn, 170, 191
Schneider, Edgar W., 266
Selinker, Larry, 147, 170, 179, 191–192, 229, 231–232, 258
Seth, Vikram, 16, 22, 125
Shills, Edward, 64, 115–116, 121, 127
Skutnabb-Kangas, Tove, 99, 101, 135–136, 156, 207, 213
Smith, Anne-Marie, 94
Smith, Larry E., 3, 12, 15, 21, 32, 51, 72, 100, 111–112, 123, 125, 128, 130, 136, 152, 157, 160, 164, 186–187, 191, 194, 229, 241–244, 247–248, 253, 266–267
Smitherman, Geneva, 100
Soyinka, Wole, 16, 58–60, 112, 130, 160, 228, 254, 263–264

Sridhar, Kamal K., 132, 148, 154, 156, 170, 172, 179, 191, 229, 234, 251, 258, 267
Sridhar, S. N., 20, 132, 135, 148, 154, 170–172, 210, 223, 229, 234, 247, 251, 255–256, 258
Steiner, George, 4, 43, 64, 96, 154, 227, 254, 256
Stewart, William, 246
Street, Brian V., 197–198
Strevens, Peter, 7, 23, 74, 136, 157, 206, 208, 210, 255, 264, 267
Stubbs, Michael, 118, 168
Swales, John, 211, 214, 235, 256

Tay, M. W. J., 213, 246, 266
Tharoor, Shashi, 16, 112, 125
Thumboo, Edwin, 16, 30–31, 34, 54, 56, 75, 100, 111, 124, 136, 157, 194, 228, 248, 250, 254–255, 264, 267
Tickoo, Makhan L., 57, 83, 110, 175, 214, 252, 255, 259–260, 262, 264, 266–267
Tikku, G. L., 122
Todd, L., 266
Tollefson, J. W., 207, 213, 259, 264
Tromel-Plotz, Senta, 18, 85–86, 99, 149, 179, 259
Trudgill, Peter, 168, 171, 188, 266
Tsuda, Yukio, 233, 262

Valentine, Tamara, 247, 256
Vavrus, F., 234, 261
Viereck, Wolfgang, 5, 257, 266

Weber, Heidi, 28, 246
Wells, J., 266
Widdowson, Henry, 32, 110, 135, 187, 210, 234, 266
Wijesinha, Rajiva, 36, 144
Winford, Donald, x, 266
Wolfson, Nessa, 87

Subject Index

acculturation, 4–5, 21, 28–29, 60, 62, 72, 76, 83, 96, 112, 115, 142, 146, 148, 152, 175, 232, 242, 244, 249–250, 254–255, 257, 260
acrolect, 11, 40–41, 73, 90, 167, 172, 246
African American Vernacular English (AAVE), 136
Africanization, 5, 28, 57, 60
Afro-Saxons, 95, 154
alchemy of English, 22, 75, 105
American English, 32, 42, 51, 81, 90, 102, 119, 136, 159
Anglocentricity, 12, 19
anticolonialism, 12, 155
applied linguistics, 85, 185–190, 199, 201, 203, 206–214, 216, 219, 244–245, 251
attitudinal Codification, 147
Australian English, 32, 260, 268

basilect, x–xi, 11, 38, 40, 73, 90, 97, 119, 144, 151, 167, 172, 227, 246, 249, 265
bazaar, 68, 73, 97, 119, 131, 141, 151, 247
British Commonwealth, xiii–xv, 14–15, 118
British Council, xiv, 54, 66, 81, 118, 261
British Empire, xiv, 25–26
British English, 40, 125, 252
brown sahibs, 154

Caliban, 47–48, 55, 57–58, 61–62, 148, 161, 245, 252, 263–264
Caliban syndrome, 161, 252
camel-in-the-tent strategy, 98
Canada, 4, 6, 8, 24, 32, 52, 70, 88, 231, 248, 250, 260, 266–268
canon, 5, 15–20, 23, 30–32, 34, 46–48, 54–57, 59–63, 65, 109–115, 117, 119–121, 123–124, 126, 129, 131–132, 143, 154, 161–162, 166, 173, 178, 214, 225, 227–228, 245, 248–249, 251, 254, 256–257, 260–261, 266
canonical English, 15, 17, 34
Cassandra, 21, 48–49, 87, 165, 229

Cassandra myth, 229
cline, 18, 49–50, 73, 123, 125, 140, 174, 192, 204, 206, 210, 230, 246–247, 255, 265
"close-the-ranks" strategy, 98
Coca-colonization, 50
code of control, 95
codification, 84
colonial auxiliaries, xiii
communicative competence, xii, 12, 16, 21, 82, 101, 162, 188, 198, 204, 214, 225, 235
"completeness" issue, 170
comprehensibility, 123–124, 204, 241, 253
concentric circles, xi, xiii, 5, 25, 67, 69, 111, 166, 186, 246, 248–249
contextualizational approach, 189
conflict model, 17, 91–92
correlative model, 90, 92
creole, ix–xi, 246
cultural bomb, 13, 142, 148, 161
cultural crossover, 113, 123, 131
cultural identity myth, 227, 229
cultural imperialism, 213
cultural separateness, 145
culture wars, 45, 62, 111

deficit approach, 146, 188
deficit linguistics, 136, 140, 150
democratization of attitudes, 247
demythologization, 15, 17, 34
depth, 4, 9, 25, 29, 53, 68, 76, 78, 85, 88, 95–98, 101, 109, 119, 151, 204, 225, 242, 249, 265
deviation, 9, 35, 83, 146, 188–189, 204, 260
derationalizing strategy, 231
deviational approach, 189
diaspora, xiv, 4, 24, 26, 28–29, 31–33, 35–36, 39–44, 158, 167–168, 245, 248–249
diversification, ix, 3, 26, 28–29, 31, 33, 148, 151–153, 155, 157, 160–164, 251–252
domain model, 90
dormancy, 97

301

302   Subject Index

ecstasy, 3, 5, 17, 22, 45, 262
educational codification, 147
endocentric model, 190
endocentric norm, 140, 164
EIL, 244, see *English as an international language*
ELF, 244, see *English as a lingua franca*
England, ix, xii, xiii–xiv, 4, 32, 42, 74, 94, 98, 147, 198, 248, 256–257
English as an international Language (EIL), xii, 244
English as a lingua franca (ELF), xii, 76, 244
English as a world language (EWL), xii, 83, 164, 176, 244
English-in-twilight hypothesis, 175
Englishization, xv, 39, 72, 74, 123, 159, 166, 245, 249, 257, 265
ethnocentricism, 129, 200, 214–215
exocentric model, 20
exocentric performance myth, 229
Expanding Circle, x, xii–xv, 5, 18, 20, 53, 67–69, 72, 82, 96, 104, 140, 147, 187, 190, 199, 226, 242, 250, 252, 257
exploitation colonies, xiii–xiv, 67
Extended Circle, 67, 163
ELT Empire, 54, 183, 261
EWL, 244, see *English as a world language*

fellowship, xii, xiv–xv, 5, 33, 35, 48, 70–71, 78–80, 82, 84, 87, 100, 123, 137, 148, 162, 187, 191, 194, 201, 251–252, 265
fossilization, 11, 83, 154, 169–170, 179, 191–192, 200, 202, 229, 231, 251
functional model, 91–92
functional polymodel, 189
functional range fallacy, 168

global access, 46

hegemony, 8, 164, 245, 262
heritage, 113, 142, 161, 257, 261
heteroglossic Englishes, 245
Hybrid English, 51
hybridity, 59, 62–63, 263
Hydra, 45, 153, 251

ideal speaker, 11, 70, 148, 156–157, 251
India, xiii–xiv, 4–8, 10, 14–16, 19–22, 25, 27–28, 30–31, 33–38, 43, 45, 51–53, 58–59, 68–70, 74–75, 79, 82, 86, 88–89, 92, 97–98, 101, 104, 109, 111–112, 114–116, 120–121, 123–128, 131, 135–136, 142–147, 149–151, 154–155, 158–160, 162, 168, 173, 175, 180, 192–194, 199, 217, 224, 227, 232–234, 241,

247, 249–250, 252, 254, 256, 260, 262–263, 265, 267–268
Indianization, 5, 28
indigenization, ix–xv, 57
indigenized Englishes, x–xii, xv, 51, 68
Industrial Revolution, 26
inequality, 12, 99, 213
information control strategy, 98
ingroupness, 145
Inner Circle, ix–xv, 6, 8, 29, 45, 47, 50, 52–53, 67–69, 71–74, 76, 80, 86–87, 90, 95, 99–102, 105, 109, 111, 148, 156–157, 159–160, 168, 172–175, 178, 186–187, 190, 193, 195–196, 199–200, 204, 224, 226–230, 234–235, 246, 248, 252, 258–260, 265
innovation, 18, 21, 51, 57, 59, 63, 67, 72–78, 87, 89, 99, 111, 113, 119, 126, 130, 138, 146–148, 152–153, 159, 167, 175, 179, 192, 204, 224–225, 230, 232–233, 252, 256–257, 259–260, 263, 265
intelligibility, 3, 12, 15–16, 35, 43, 72, 78–79, 81, 123, 128, 130, 162–163, 226, 229, 253, 265–266
interactional approach, 146, 189
intercultural crossover, 123
interference, 10–12, 29, 35, 71, 153–154, 192, 201–202, 251
interlanguage, 11, 20, 147, 154–155, 169–170, 179, 191–192, 200, 229, 251, 258
interlanguage myth, 229
interlocutor expectancy, 159–160
interlocutor fallacy, 168
interlocutor myth, 226
international English, 48, 109
international intelligibility, 72, 163, 229
internationalism, 214
internationalization, 66–67, 162–164
interpretability, 16, 123–124, 204, 253
intrinsic power, 88
invisible policies, 54
Ireland, 5, 24, 28, 201, 266, 268

Kenya, 6, 12, 16, 19, 26, 57–58, 70, 79, 82, 114–115, 194, 256, 268
killer, 12, 101, 120
knowledge paradigm, 174, 176

language imperialism, 95
language planning, 10, 103, 144–145, 175, 213, 215, 225
leaking, 19, 191
leak, 19, 191, 208–213
liberation linguistics, 18–19, 118, 136–137, 140, 174–175, 179, 213, 230, 233, 258

Subject Index

lingua franca, x–xv, 48, 68, 76, 114, 244
linguicide, 86, 101, 104
linguistic bomb, 148
linguistic elitism strategy, 98
linguistic emancipation, 140
linguistic hierarchy, 88
linguistic imperialism, 213, 261–262; see also *language imperialism*
linguistic paranoia, 102
linguistic power, 17, 85, 87, 92–93, 103, 230
link language, 26, 96, 104

madhyama, 55, 58, 109
mahabharata, 30, 112
mantra, 46, 55–56, 58, 60, 65, 109, 181, 263
marginality, 178–181, 225, 231, 233–234
marketability strategy, 99
mathetic function, 176–177
meaning potential, 16, 153, 173
mesolect, x-xi, 11, 40, 73, 246
methodology fallacy, 168
Minute on Indian Education, 154
mission civilisatrice, 94
mixing, 18, 39, 41, 56, 80, 89, 91, 143, 161, 169–170, 172–173, 194–195, 204, 232, 236, 247, 255–256, 265
modernization, 13, 50, 69, 92, 95, 104
mother English, 32, 257
mother tongue, 11, 54, 64, 116, 121–122, 127–128, 143, 158–159, 174, 227, 251, 256
multiculturalism, 111, 113, 118–119, 246

native Englishes, x, xii, 28, 79, 83, 175, 235
native speaker, 4, 7–9, 11, 15, 20, 29–30, 33, 42–43, 64, 71, 73–74, 84, 105, 127, 146–148, 151, 156–160, 164, 167–168, 170, 177, 193–196, 226, 229, 246, 251, 253, 256, 258
native speaker idealization myth, 229
nativization, xv, 5, 21, 28, 66, 69, 75, 96, 152, 164, 172–173, 175, 178, 204, 242, 249, 254–255, 257, 265
nativist monomodel, 189
negation strategy, 231–232
New Englishes, 43
New Zealand, 4, 6, 24, 28, 32, 71, 75, 79, 97, 102, 159, 190, 248, 252, 266, 268
Nigeria, 5–6, 13, 15–16, 19–21, 27, 29, 31, 33–35, 53, 56–58, 62, 67, 70, 75, 79, 82, 89, 97, 104, 111, 114–115, 119, 125, 128, 147, 151, 162, 172–173, 175, 190, 193–194, 227, 232, 247, 249, 252, 254, 256, 260, 263, 268
nonnative Englishes, xi–xii, 83, 175, 235

norm, 3, 5, 9, 11, 15, 18, 20, 30–32, 40, 42, 48–49, 51, 58, 60, 64–66, 70–74, 76–78, 80–83, 88, 111–115, 120–121, 128, 136–137, 140, 144–145, 159–160, 164, 168, 170, 172, 174, 176, 179, 192, 201, 204, 211–212, 225, 229–232, 244, 248, 252, 258, 265
norm-providing, 5, 42, 252
norm-developing, 5, 82, 252
norm-breakers, 72, 229
norm-dependent, 5, 252, 258
norm-makers, 72
normalization strategy, 179

Orientalist vs. Occidentalist debate, 10
Outer Circle, ix–xv, 5–6, 10–11, 16, 18–21, 31–32, 35, 40, 53, 67–69, 71, 73–75, 80, 82, 89–90, 95–101, 103–105, 111, 114, 140, 143–144, 146, 153, 155, 157–159, 161–163, 168, 173–175, 178, 180, 185–191, 193–194, 196–202, 204, 227, 229, 234, 237, 242, 246–247, 250–252, 257–260, 265, 267
oppression, 91–93, 207, 216
Orientalism, 262
other tongue, the / "other" tongue, 11, 22, 54, 64, 116, 121–122, 127–128, 143, 158–159, 174, 223, 227, 251, 256

panregional communication, 12, 36
paradigm lag, 169, 178
paradigm myopia, 173, 178
paradigm misconnection, 173
paradigm trap, 200
paradigm shift, 9, 19, 119, 138, 148, 256, 264
periphery, peripheries, 18, 47, 55–56, 64, 119, 159, 209
periphery shift, 159
pidgin, 68, 172, 265
plain English, 103
pluricentricity, 4–5, 25, 42–43, 46–47, 49, 96, 105, 136, 154–155, 174, 204, 251
power, 3, 5, 12, 17–19, 21–22, 25–26, 30–31, 60–62, 72, 77, 85–105, 110–111, 113–114, 119–120, 129, 140–142, 144–146, 148–149, 154–155, 160, 164, 167, 178–180, 186–187, 190, 199, 213, 215, 218, 223, 225–227, 230–234, 236, 242, 245, 252, 255, 259, 261
power of English, 5, 12, 17, 19, 86, 88, 95, 98–99, 103–105, 178, 187
pragmatic success, 20, 22, 93, 95, 141, 193–196, 198
pressure group, 99, 143, 145
psychological Codification, 77, 147

304   Subject Index

Raj, 4, 9, 14, 16, 25, 30–31, 33–34, 37, 58, 75, 98, 111–112, 116–117, 128–129, 136, 142, 145, 148, 160, 224, 228, 254, 263
ramayana, 30–31
range, 4, 9, 12, 15, 18, 22, 25, 40, 49, 52–53, 55, 63, 68, 73, 76, 80, 83, 85, 88, 91, 93, 95–98, 101, 115, 119–120, 126, 128, 136, 151, 153, 160, 164, 167–168, 172–178, 187, 194, 200, 204, 210, 212, 225, 227–228, 242, 244–246, 249, 260, 262, 265–266
regimes of truth, 168, 226, 231, 234

sacred cow, 10, 62, 148, 152–153, 156–157, 164, 245, 250–251, 260
Sanskrit, 7, 10, 14, 16–17, 29–31, 34, 37, 59–60, 68, 76–77, 93, 111–112, 116, 122–123, 127–129, 140, 146–147, 158–159, 177, 186, 224, 257, 263
secularization, 155
Scotland, 24, 32, 201, 248, 260
settlement colonization, xiii
social concern, 187, 203, 207–209, 215
social critic, 188, 207
social issue, 187, 211
social sideliner, 203
sociolinguistic ostrich, 179
South Africa, 4–5, 27, 75, 81, 158, 256
Speaking Tree, 45, 65, 109–110, 112, 114, 116, 118, 120, 227–228
speech community, 8, 11, 17, 28, 33, 48, 52, 62, 67, 70–71, 78–79, 86–87, 91, 93, 109, 114, 145, 148, 156–157, 168–169, 171, 212, 219, 234, 248, 251

speech fellowship, 5, 33, 48, 70–71, 78–79, 82, 84, 87, 100, 123, 137, 148, 162, 187, 191, 194, 201, 252, 265
stratification of English, 245–246
Switching, 18, 37, 39, 91, 143, 161, 169, 172–173, 194–195, 236, 256, 265

target language issue, 172
transcreation, 20, 59, 116, 121, 127–129
transcultural creativity, 116, 121, 123, 127–128, 130–131
transculturational process, 121
translation, 5, 8, 26, 117, 121–122, 124–129, 131–132, 186, 232, 245

United States, 4, 7–8, 19, 24–25, 42–43, 46, 48, 52, 62–63, 74–75, 77–78, 81, 86, 88, 90, 94, 102, 114, 118, 140, 147, 149–150, 168, 174–175, 180, 188, 191, 197, 201, 209–211, 220, 229, 231, 234, 237, 241, 246, 255–257, 259–260, 262, 268
"us/them" distinction, 158

variational approach, 189
variety tolerance, 163
vehicular load, 95
verbal-repertoire model, 91
visible language, 54, 144–145

war of cultures, 62–63
Westernization, 13, 94, 104, 155, 262
White Man, 94
white supremacy, 60, 264
world language, 25, 50, 52, 55, 66, 83, 164, 176, 178, 244, 261

Lightning Source UK Ltd.
Milton Keynes UK
UKOW05n0604090317

296239UK00014B/348/P